Cambridge Guide to Psychodynamic Psychotherapy

A unique and accessible guide to contemporary psychodynamic psychotherapy and its applications.

An author line-up of experienced educators guides the reader through the breadth of psychodynamic concepts in a digestible and engaging way. The key applications of psychodynamic psychotherapy to a range of presentations are explored, including anxiety, depression, problematic narcissism as well as the dynamics of 'borderline' states. Specific chapters cover the dynamics of anger and aggression, and working with people experiencing homelessness. The guide will be a valuable resource for novice and experienced therapists, presenting a clear, comprehensive review of contemporary psychodynamic theory and clinical practice.

Highly relevant for general clinicians, third-sector staff and therapists alike, the chapters also examine staff-client dynamics and the development of psychologically informed services underpinned by reflective practice.

Part of the Cambridge Guides to the Psychological Therapies series, offering all the latest scientifically rigorous and practical information on key, evidence-based psychological interventions for clinicians.

Adam Polnay is a Consultant Medical Psychotherapist and Psychoanalytic Psychotherapist at the State Hospital, Carstairs, and leads the Edinburgh Psychotherapy Department. He is also affiliated with Edinburgh University and leads the psychodynamic training for psychiatrists in South-East Scotland.

Rhiannon Pugh is a Consultant Medical Psychotherapist and Psychoanalytic Psychotherapist based in Edinburgh and was Associate Postgraduate Dean in the Scotland Deanery from 2007 until 2022.

Victoria Barker is a Consultant Medical Psychotherapist and Psychoanalytic Psychotherapist who leads the City & Hackney Specialist Psychotherapy Service within the East London NHS Foundation Trust.

David Bell is a Consultant Psychiatrist, formerly at the Adult Department at the Tavistock and Portman NHS Foundation Trust where he was Director of

Postgraduate Training and led a specialist service (the Fitzjohn's Unit) for people with enduring and complex problems. He is a past president of the British Psychoanalytical Society.

Allan Beveridge is a retired psychiatrist who continues on the staff of the British Journal of Psychiatry as Psychiatry and Pictures Editor and Co-Book Review Editor. He is also History and Humanities Editor of the Journal of the Royal College of Physicians of Edinburgh.

Adam Burley is a Consultant Clinical Psychologist and professional lead for the Rivers Centre, a specialist trauma service in NHS Lothian. He also facilitates reflective practice groups for a range of third sector and other organisations.

Allyson Lumsden is an Adult Psychotherapist and Group Analyst within the NHS and third sector. Allyson is also a trainer for therapists studying with the Institute of Group Analysis.

C. Susan Mizen is a Consultant Medical Psychotherapist and an Honorary Consultant Psychiatrist in the Devon Partnership NHS Trust. She is also chair of the Talking Therapies Task Force.

Lauren Wilson is a Consultant Medical Psychotherapist specialising in psychodynamic psychotherapy working within the Edinburgh Psychotherapy Department of the Royal Edinburgh Hospital.

Cambridge Guides to the Psychological Therapies

Series Editor

Patricia Graham
Consultant Clinical Psychologist Director of Psychological Services, NHS Lanarkshire, UK

The go-to resource for up-to-date, scientifically rigorous, and practical information on key, evidence-based psychological interventions.

This series of clinical handbooks provides clear and concise guides to understanding and delivering therapy, and offers clinicians a handy reference for matching a specific therapy to a particular patient. Each book follows a consistent style, with chapters on theory, technique, indications and efficacy, so that healthcare professionals can move seamlessly between different volumes to learn about various therapies in a consistent, familiar and trusted format. The books also provide guidance on relevant adaptations for each therapy, such as for children, adolescents and older people, as well as different methods of delivery, such as group interventions and digital therapy.

Books available in the series

Cambridge Guide to Cognitive Behavioural Therapy (CBT)
Jessica Davies, Kenneth Laidlaw and Paul Salkovskis

Cambridge Guide to Cognitive Behavioral Analysis System of Psychotherapy (CBASP)
Massimo Tarsia, Todd Favorite and James McCullough Jr.

Cambridge Guide to Dialectical Behaviour Therapy (DBT)
Jim Lyng, Christine Dunkley, Janet Feigenbaum, Amy Gaglia and Michaela Swales

Cambridge Guide to Interpersonal Therapy (IPT)
Laura Dietz, Fiona Duffy and Patricia Graham

Cambridge Guide to Mentalization Based Therapy (MBT)
Anthony Bateman, Peter Fonagy, Chloe Campbell, Patrick Luyten and Martin Debbané

Cambridge Guide to Psychodynamic Psychotherapy
Adam Polnay, Rhiannon Pugh, Victoria Barker, David Bell, Allan Beveridge, Adam Burley, Allyson Lumsden, C. Susan Mizen and Lauren Wilson

Cambridge Guide to Schema Therapy
Robert N. Brockman, Susan Simpson, Christopher Hayes, Remco van der Wijngaart and Matthew Smout

"This excellent book does exactly what it says it will; to be a guide to what psychodynamic psychotherapy is, how to do it well and for whom it works best. For too long, psychodynamic psychotherapy has been plagued by what we now might call 'deep fakes'; first, the idea that psychological therapists who think this way hold strange and esoteric sets of beliefs about how the mind works, and second, that there is no evidence that treatments based on this paradigm might be helpful. Both these deep fake ideas have been conclusively proved wrong; this helpful book makes clear why this is. The book includes a range of chapters covering different themes and clinical topics in psychiatry; the writing is clear and the approach practical. I have no doubt that the future of psychiatry needs to be psychodynamic, and this book shows why psychodynamic thinking applied to psychiatry not only makes it more interesting, it makes us as psychiatrists more human and more effective."

Dr Gwen Adshead
Consultant Forensic Psychiatrist and Psychotherapist
Broadmoor Hospital, Berkshire

"I thoroughly enjoyed reading this book and found it accessible and informative. The various authors conveyed the principles, practices, research, theories, and history of psychoanalysis in a way that was engaging and easy to understand, even for those such as myself, from outside the field. For clinicians (specialists and generalists alike) understanding the unconscious processes taking place in the consulting room can be invaluable in delivering effective care to our patients, and this book was able to provide insights into this important area."

Dame Clare Gerada
President, Royal College of General Practitioners (RCGP)
PRCGP FRCPsych FRCP (Hons)

"Unlike psychoanalytic authors whose writing is oriented mainly toward colleagues with extensive analytic training, these contributors intend their chapters to reach audiences that may be new to a psychoanalytic frame of reference, or sceptical of it, or confused by it. Somehow, they have also made the book interesting and clinically relevant to experienced psychoanalytic readers ... I know from experience that it is not easy to produce a multi-authored compendium whose final product embodies an overall continuity and integration, and so I am impressed that the authors of this volume have managed that feat. I urge readers of all mental health disciplines, professional involvements, and theoretical orientations to spend time with this worthy and important book. I think you will find it as fascinating and clinically helpful as I did."

Nancy McWilliams
Distinguished Retired Professor
Rutgers Graduate School of Applied & Professional Psychology

Cambridge Guide to Psychodynamic Psychotherapy

Adam Polnay
The State Hospital (Carstairs) and Royal Edinburgh Hospital

Rhiannon Pugh
DocHealth, London

Victoria Barker
East London NHS Foundation Trust

David Bell
British Psychoanalytic Society

Allan Beveridge
Royal College of Psychiatrists

Adam Burley
NHS Lothian

Allyson Lumsden
NHS Greater Glasgow and Clyde

C. Susan Mizen
Devon Partnership NHS Trust

Lauren Wilson
Royal Edinburgh Hospital

CAMBRIDGE
UNIVERSITY PRESS

CAMBRIDGE
UNIVERSITY PRESS

Shaftesbury Road, Cambridge CB2 8EA, United Kingdom

One Liberty Plaza, 20th Floor, New York, NY 10006, USA

477 Williamstown Road, Port Melbourne, VIC 3207, Australia

314–321, 3rd Floor, Plot 3, Splendor Forum, Jasola District Centre, New Delhi – 110025, India

103 Penang Road, #05–06/07, Visioncrest Commercial, Singapore 238467

Cambridge University Press is part of Cambridge University Press & Assessment, a department of the University of Cambridge.

We share the University's mission to contribute to society through the pursuit of education, learning and research at the highest international levels of excellence.

www.cambridge.org
Information on this title: www.cambridge.org/9781009108508

DOI: 10.1017/9781009104425

First published 2023

A catalogue record for this publication is available from the British Library.

A Cataloging-in-Publication data record for this book is available from the Library of Congress

ISBN 978-1-009-10850-8 Paperback

'. . .these brief imperfect meetings have a tale to tell,'

Emily Dickinson, 1851 (page 57)

Contents

Foreword xi
Nancy McWilliams
Preface xv
Adam Polnay and Rhiannon Pugh
A Note from the Series Editor xviii
Acknowledgements xix

Part 1: An Overview of the Model

1 **An Historical Overview of Psychodynamic Psychotherapy** 1
Allan Beveridge

2 **The Supporting Theory of Psychodynamic Psychotherapy** 18
Adam Polnay and Rhiannon Pugh

3 **A Brief Description of the Empirical Basis of Psychodynamic Psychotherapy** 51
Victoria Barker and Adam Polnay

4 **An Outline of Psychodynamic Psychotherapy** 65
Rhiannon Pugh and Adam Polnay

Part 2: The Model of Psychodynamic Psychotherapy into Practice

5 **Framing a Psychodynamic Space** 79
Adam Polnay

6 **The Goals of Psychodynamic Psychotherapy** 89
Rhiannon Pugh

7 **Psychodynamic Psychotherapy Technique** 98
Rhiannon Pugh and Adam Polnay

8 **The Overall Structure of Psychodynamic Therapy** 128
Adam Polnay

9 **Psychological Assessment and Formulation in Psychodynamic Psychotherapy** 151
Victoria Barker

10 **Some Reflections on the Supervisory Process** 162
David Bell

Part 3: Application for Mental Health Presentations

Applications of Psychodynamic Psychotherapy with Accompanying Case Study Description for Each Presentation

11 **Psychodynamic Approaches to Anxiety** 171
Lauren Wilson

12 **The Psychodynamics of Depressing/Depressed States** 184
Adam Polnay

13 **Dynamics of Borderline States of Mind** 200
Victoria Barker

14 **Narcissistic Difficulties, a Trans-Diagnostic Presentation Requiring a System-Wide Approach** 211
C. Susan Mizen

Part 4: Application of Psychodynamic Psychotherapy in Different Populations and in Different Settings

Beyond 1:1 Therapy: Working Psychodynamically with Clinicians, Teams, and Organisations

Adam Burley and Adam Polnay

15 **Applications of Psychodynamic Theory and Principles outside of Specialist Psychotherapy Settings** 231

16 **An Introduction to the Dynamics of Anger, Aggression and Violence** 244

17 **Psychologically Informed Organisations and Services** 258

18 **Psychodynamic Reflective Practice Groups** 269

19 **Psychodynamic Consultation to Clinical Teams** 278

Other Forms and Settings of Psychotherapeutic Work

20 **A Psychodynamic Approach to Working with People Experiencing Multiple Exclusion Homelessness** 291
Adam Burley

21 **Psychodynamic Psychotherapy Online and by Phone** 300
Lauren Wilson

22 **Group Analysis and its Applications** 310
Allyson Lumsden

Glossary of Terms 322
Adam Polnay
Index 325

Foreword

Nancy McWilliams, PhD, Distinguished Retired Professor
Rutgers Graduate School of Applied & Professional Psychology

It is my pleasure to make some introductory comments for the *Cambridge Guide to Psychodynamic Psychotherapy*, whose contributors have produced a clear, comprehensive review of contemporary psychodynamic theory and practice. Readers who have come to expect impenetrable jargon and unsubstantiated opinion from authors in the psychodynamic tradition will be happily surprised: the contributions to this volume are readable, even-handed, evidence-based, and highly relevant to clinical work and general professional experience.

Unlike psychoanalytic authors whose writing is oriented mainly toward colleagues with extensive analytic training, these contributors intend their chapters to reach audiences that may be new to a psychoanalytic frame of reference, or sceptical of it, or confused by it. Somehow, they have also made the book interesting and clinically relevant to experienced psychoanalytic readers. They address clinicians, supervisors, administrators, and other professionals who work with patients of heterogeneous backgrounds, across the socioeconomic spectrum, in short- and long-term therapies, and in both inpatient and outpatient settings. With this diverse audience in mind, they have covered the relevant conceptual territory of current psychodynamic thinking and demonstrated its beneficial applications across a broad range of professional practice.

Their accomplishment is best appreciated in the context of the long history of psychoanalytic ideas in Western intellectually oriented subcultures. In the era when psychoanalysis was 'the latest thing', it was common to regard Freud's new 'science of the mind' with undiluted enthusiasm and with anticipation of a revolution in mental health and social well-being. In many departments of psychiatry, doctors who had graduated from a psychoanalytic training programme found themselves on a fast track to personal status and institutional power. Middle-class people teased each other about their 'Freudian slips', opined about their own and others' 'complexes', and headed in large numbers to an analyst's couch. Psychotherapy training programmes taught psychoanalytic concepts as the core of their curricula. As might be expected of any social movement that became embraced so uncritically (Marxism comes to mind as a comparable phenomenon), psychoanalysis eventually disillusioned those who had expected miracles.

Currently, the psychodynamic perspective finds itself subject to distortions that may be as extreme as those it evoked in its early days, but this time in the direction of devaluation rather than idealisation. For example, it has become commonplace to regard psychoanalytically based treatments as outdated, empirically unsupported, contaminated by the personal failings of Sigmund Freud and inapplicable to contemporary clinical challenges. In the United States, some of my colleagues who have been treating patients psychodynamically have been characterised as practising 'unethically'. Such allegations reflect common misunderstandings, such as beliefs that there is no basis in scientific evidence for psychoanalytic approaches, or that psychodynamic treatments must go on for years before achieving significant changes, or that scientists have demonstrated the superiority of competing ways of understanding and treating mental suffering.

While it is true that over the long history of the psychoanalytic movement, analysts have been guilty of some major misunderstandings and mistakes, it is not true that the movement Freud set in motion is fatally flawed or irrelevant to current clinical practice. In fact, over decades of efforts to understand and ameliorate psychological problems, the psychoanalytic community has accumulated a vast amount of clinically derived wisdom and empirically derived knowledge that has corrected many of its earlier errors. A scholarly tour of the contemporary psychodynamic landscape that is neither idealising nor devaluing, a central achievement of the *Cambridge Guide*, is thus long overdue.

In this volume, the authors engage with the psychodynamic tradition without being polemical or dismissive of other perspectives. They are notably free of the insularity and arrogance that characterised some psychoanalysts in the movement's heyday, attitudes that have had a destructive effect on the reputation of psychoanalysis as a field and on the readiness of professionals to consult psychodynamic ideas for their relevance to understanding mental processes and solving personal and interpersonal problems. Instead of talking down to their readers, they have communicated what is of most practical value to working professionals, who inevitably face challenging and often bewildering encounters with human psychological distress.

To many of us who are committed to passing on the clinically useful elements of psychoanalytic thinking, it can be irritating that when readily appreciated psychoanalytic concepts get traction in the public mind, they come to be regarded as 'common sense', whereas analytic ideas that are either wrong or overgeneralised are derided as 'nonsense' and are erroneously seen as evidence of the intellectual bankruptcy of the whole psychoanalytic enterprise. The former category of 'common sense' includes, among many other psychoanalytic concepts, terms such as Freud's notion of 'defences' or Adler's 'inferiority complex' or Erikson's 'identity crisis' or Bowlby's 'attachment' or Winnicott's 'good-enough mother'. The area of 'nonsense' includes, for example, Freud's assumptions that all women suffer elementally from penis envy, or that the nineteenth-century Viennese, middle-class version of an Oedipal phase is universal, or that all men have unconscious homosexual longings. While this process of social redefinition goes on, practitioners of non-psychoanalytic orientations rediscover ideas that have been central to psychoanalysis, call them by new names (e.g. 'unconscious' becomes 'implicit', 'repression' becomes 'cognitive avoidance', 'object representation' becomes 'core schema') and hail them as unprecedented discoveries.

Practising therapists tend to be integrative, to be grateful for any concept that makes our difficult job easier, irrespective of the affiliation of the theorist supplying the formulation. One way of looking at what has sometimes been called 'unconscious plagiarism' is as a reflection of the fact that we are all trying to understand and help the same suffering human animal. It would be strange indeed if clinicians of differing theoretical orientations did not run into similar clinical challenges and devise similar ways of engaging with them, expressed in whatever language permeated each therapist's training background. Yet this phenomenon also suggests that in the field of mental health, we keep reinventing the proverbial wheel rather than contributing to the progress of clinical science. The *Cambridge Guide* may have a critical role to play in correcting misimpressions, clarifying what psychodynamic ideas have to offer, and moving all of us forward toward an appreciation of what elements of clinical practice are worth keeping irrespective of what they are called by adherents of particular philosophies of treatment.

This book begins with an historical overview of psychoanalytic theories and of the main empirical foundations of the psychodynamic orientation. It moves then to clinical practice, focusing on framing the treatment, formulating goals, and employing particular interventions, ending with commentary on the overall structure of psychoanalytic treatment and supervision. In the third section, applications to specific problems of anxiety, depression, borderline conditions, and problematic narcissism are explored. The last section moves the reader outside the clinical office and into applications to organisations and clinical teams, with a special focus on problems of anger, aggression, and violence. Finally, the authors address therapy relevant to homeless individuals, treatment via phone or computer, and group analysis. While the first sections of the book constitute essential reading for anyone seeking to understand mainstream clinical applications of psychoanalytic theories, the later sections would be highly useful for professionals in roles other than direct clinical service. All this material is accessibly written, presented in the context of the empirical evidence that supports it, and illustrated by vignettes that bring relevant concepts to life.

I know from experience that it is not easy to produce a multi-authored compendium whose final product embodies an overall continuity and integration, and so I am impressed that the authors of this volume have managed that feat. I urge readers of all mental health disciplines, professional involvements, and theoretical orientations to spend time with this worthy and important book. I think you will find it as fascinating and clinically helpful as I did.

Preface

One of our principal aims for this book is to provide a readable and welcoming guide to psychodynamic psychotherapy. We have found the psychodynamic approach offers a helpful 'guide to life' both for ourselves and also for a considerable number of people we work with. So, we are enthusiastic about sharing our understanding of this approach and are grateful for this opportunity. To help with the writing process, we found it grounding to remember that this book is intended as a 'guide' as opposed to being an exhaustive account. Our associations took us to a travel guidebook that helps people to find their way about a place, pointing out areas of interest to the visitor. We hope this book serves a similar purpose for the reader, both for new travellers to the area of psychodynamic psychotherapy and those looking for further explorations having been here before.

The psychodynamic field is broad. There is more than one 'school', with overlaps as well as differences. Our clinical approach is to draw on, and at times integrate, approaches from the various slants on psychodynamic therapy, focusing on aspects that we have found particularly useful in clinical practice. A recurrent theme of this book is that the therapist adapts their approach to each patient, while retaining the core principles of psychodynamic theory and practice.

A psychodynamic understanding of human relations and functioning is intertwined with social circumstances (including poverty, inequality, and other adversities) as well as the biological and medical. This book assumes that a practitioner working in a psychodynamic way will already have a background in a relevant profession that provides this overview. This brings a safety and grounding to therapeutic work that the practitioner can draw on, and a wider perspective about important social or medical issues that may need to be considered either before therapy or in parallel with it.

Part 1 of this book offers an overview of the psychodynamic approach, providing the underpinnings to concepts and clinical practice that follow in later parts. Chapter 1 is an historical vantage point on the development of psychodynamic psychotherapy, written by Allan Beveridge, an historian of psychiatry and a psychiatrist. Beveridge critiques an idealised portrayal of the development of psychodynamic theory: a struggle of the misunderstood hero (Sigmund Freud) against his unseeing detractors. Instead, Beveridge offers a more nuanced and integrated account, situating psychodynamic therapy amongst wider influences and describing practitioners' mistakes and wrong turns as well as insights and helpful clinical discoveries. To see ourselves as others may see us does not always make for comfortable reading, but then again, as we describe later in the book, no process of deep learning or therapeutic change is without some discomfort for the individual. No discipline that wants to progress stays still. While we find much of the work of early psychodynamic theorists to be of great value, it is also the case that psychodynamic psychotherapy has evolved with subsequent clinicians refining or more radically building on early work. These developments in psychodynamic theory and a contemporary perspective are discussed in Chapter 2. Chapter 3 outlines the empirical basis of psychodynamic psychotherapy and Chapter 4 an overview of the model. Chapter 4 pulls together key aspects of history, theory, research and clinical practice, and as such, if a reader wishes to read a single chapter to tap into the psychodynamic approach, this chapter may be a suitable choice.

Part 2 brings the psychodynamic model more squarely into practice. We start by describing how to frame a psychodynamic space (Chapter 5), before discussing the goals of psychodynamic therapy (Chapter 6). Chapter 7 covers psychodynamic technique and Chapter 8 the overall structure of therapy. Chapter 8 expands on important processes of change which have been mentioned in Part 1, including working with the formulation, using the therapy relationship and mourning. Chapters 7 and 8 could be read as a pair. Chapter 9 concentrates on the initial encounter between patient and therapist and the practice of psychodynamic consultation. David Bell concludes Part 2 with some reflections on the supervisory process and its importance for how knowledge and practice may be transmitted from one generation of practitioners to the next, for better or for worse (Chapter 10). Bell stimulates awareness of the potential in psychodynamic work for 'thought-provoking ideas (discoveries)' but also how, without reflection, these may be 'degraded into ritualised practices'.

In Part 3 we apply a psychodynamic approach to a number of common presentations, illustrated by case study descriptions. We examine a psychodynamic approach to anxiety (Chapter 11), depressing/depressed states (Chapter 12) and borderline states (Chapter 13). Chapter 14 by Susan Mizen moves more into the inpatient setting. Mizen uses the lens of narcissistic difficulties to examine encounters where staff and patients get stuck in entrenched positions with seemingly no way out and suggests a practical and relational approach to working in this area. A common thread in Part 3 is how a psychodynamic approach considers underlying meanings and dynamics that sit behind various 'symptoms', locating feelings as part of a lively and active internal world.

Part 4 applies psychodynamic psychotherapy to different populations and settings and is divided into two main sections. The first section in Part 4 is a group of chapters titled, 'Beyond 1:1 Therapy – Working Psychodynamically with Clinicians, Teams and Organisations'. This applies psychodynamic ideas to working in settings where relationships are central to their operation (such as all healthcare, secure facilities, as well as education, social work and other caring services). This section was borne out of requests by non-psychotherapist staff for digestible written material in this area; this section is also suitable for psychotherapists working with staff teams. Chapter 15 is an introduction to applied psychodynamic work. Drawing on the work of Hinshelwood and others, its central thesis is the importance of noticing and thinking about our responses to working with patients and service users as part of the everyday process of caring, and that this requires work due to the 'invisibility' of relationships. Chapter 16 examines the dynamics of anger, aggression, and violence. Chapter 17 outlines the principles of a 'psychologically informed' service – that is, how practically to organise and structure a service to offer good care, and access to it, for those service users with more complicated relationships with care. A psychologically informed approach is underpinned by spaces for reflective practice for staff – this forms the subject of Chapter 18. Chapter 19 draws on many of the themes discussed in Chapters 15–18, describing a process of psychodynamic consultation for clinical teams.

The second section of Part 4 looks at other forms and settings of psychodynamic work. Chapter 20 sets out a psychodynamic approach to working with people experiencing multiple exclusion homelessness. Chapter 21 addresses working psychodynamically online and by phone – a topic that came urgently to our attention due to Covid-19. Chapter 22 provides an introduction to group analysis and its applications.

Regarding case material, the authors confirm that these are either works of fiction or General Medical Council guidelines on confidentiality have been followed. A note on pronouns. Usually, we use 'they' when referring to people. However, a psychodynamic approach is often interested in the detail of interpersonal interactions, and in some instances using 'they' for both the patient and the therapist would be ambiguous as to who is being referred to. Therefore, at times, for clarity, we use different pronouns for patient and therapist, most commonly 'he' for patient and 'she' for therapist.

A Note from the Series Editor

I remember when I first met Sarah Marsh, Editor at Cambridge University Press – it seems like a lifetime ago now. We met at a café in central Edinburgh in June 2017 to discuss an idea that she had to create a series of books focussed on evidenced based psychological therapies. The idea was simple – the books would be attractive to a trainee and simultaneously to an expert clinician. We wanted to enable readers to conceptualise a psychological difficulty using different theoretical models of understanding, but not become overwhelmed by the volume of information. We saw the need for a series of books that could be easily read and yet would examine complex concepts in a manageable way.

So, when Sarah asked me if I would become the Series Editor, I couldn't say no. What we could never have predicted back then, when making early plans for the series, was that we would soon face a global pandemic. There were days when we didn't even know whether we could leave our house or if our children could go to school – the world effectively stopped. Yet through all the chaos, uncertainty and fear, I saw the determination and successes of those around me shine through. I was in awe of the resilience of my own son, Patrick, who lived his adolescence in 'lock-down'. I watch him now and the young man he has become – he walks tall with a quiet confidence. I am so proud as he and his friends laugh together and now enjoy what most of us had previously taken for granted: their freedom at university. In a similar way, I watched the many authors of these books, most of whom are busy and tired clinicians, continue to dedicate their precious time to this venture – an incredible achievement through a most challenging time. They each welcomed me into their academic, clinical and theoretical worlds, from all over the globe. They have all been an honour to work with. I would personally like to thank every contributor and author of this series for their hard work, determination and humour even in the darkest of days. Despite all of the unknowns and the chaos, they kept going and achieved something wonderful.

I would like to thank Sarah, and Kim Ingram at Cambridge, for giving me the opportunity to be Series Editor. I have loved every minute of it; it has been a longer journey than we anticipated but an amazing one and for that I am incredibly grateful. Sarah and Kim are my friends now – we have literally lived through a global pandemic together. It has been my absolute pleasure to work together and in collaboration with Cambridge University Press.

Patricia Graham, Series Editor
Consultant Clinical Psychologist, NHS Lanarkshire, UK

Acknowledgements

We are very grateful to all the patients and staff that we have learned from along the way. We thank all the clinicians who critically read parts of this book and whose constructive feedback has been invaluable: Carine Minne, Aileen Ogilvie-Riley, Allan Beveridge, Angela Drinnan, Emma Lewington, Katy Lewis, Katharine Logan, Flora Michalopoulou, Siobhan Murphy, Jane Naismith, Jon Patrick, and John Shemilt. Thanks to Robert Bangham for his patience in working with us in crafting the illustrations. We are grateful to Kim Ingram and Sarah Marsh at Cambridge University Press, and to Patricia Graham for encouraging us with this book and for her helpful direction. This book was commissioned by Dr Patricia Graham (series editor) and Cambridge University Press. Adam Polnay and Rhiannon Pugh edited the volume and would like to thank all the co-authors.

A. P. and R. P. are grateful for each other's support and encouragement throughout the writing process.

A. P.: I would like to thank Jon Patrick and all my past and present supervisors for their influence on many chapters. I am grateful to The State Hospital (Carstairs), NHS Lothian and the University of Edinburgh for their support. Most of all, to my family, thank you all for your support throughout this project in many ways, and for your tolerance of the time this has entailed.

R. P.: I would like to thank all my supervisors past and present, and my family.

Part 1: An Overview of the Model

Chapter 1

An Historical Overview of Psychodynamic Psychotherapy

Table of Contents

Introduction 1
The Beginnings of Modern Psychotherapy 2
Sigmund Freud 3
Clinical Practice 5
Freud's Legacy 5
The First World War and Shell Shock 7
Early Twentieth Century Developments 8
Anna Freud 9
Melanie Klein and Object Relations Theory 9
The Scottish Contribution: Ian Suttie and Ronald Fairbairn 10
The 'Middle Group': Michael Balint, John Bowlby, and Donald Winnicott 11
Michael Balint 11
John Bowlby 11
Donald Winnicott 12
The Turn to the Child 13
Psychosis 13
Concluding Remarks 14

Introduction

In accounts of the evolution of psychiatry, historians have offered opposing opinions as to the role played by psychotherapy. In *A History of Medical Psychology*, Gregory Zilboorg portrays psychiatry as emerging from a dark and brutal past of physical and coercive treatment to a new, enlightened era, ushered in by Freudian-inspired therapies.[1] By contrast, in *From the Era of the Asylum to Prozac*, Edward Shorter maintains that Freudian psychoanalysis represented a calamitous wrong turn from the path being forged by biological psychiatry.[2] He claims that, whereas psychoanalysis offered no real help, or even made patients worse, advances in the biological sciences have led to a greater understanding of psychiatric illness and to effective treatment. A third narrative is provided by Fulford et al who see the history of psychiatry as recurrently veering between biological and psychological explanations of mental illness.[3] For many clinicians, the task has been to reconcile these seemingly polarised approaches. For example, Jeremy Holmes has emphasised that biological research has made an important contribution to the theory and practice of psychotherapy.[4] Indeed, Freud in his *Project for a Scientific Psychology* expressed the hope that science would ultimately uncover the biological underpinning of psychoanalysis.

If one concentrates on the history of psychological therapies in psychiatry and, in particular, on psychodynamic psychotherapy, when and where does one begin? Does it all begin with psychoanalysis and Freud in *fin de siècle* Vienna? Or with hypnotism and Jean-Martin Charcot in nineteenth-century France? Or, in the late eighteenth century with 'moral treatment' and Pinel in Paris, and William Tuke in York? Or, with the demonstration of animal magnetism by Franz Anton Mesmer in Munich in 1775? Or, as Henri Ellenberger has suggested in his magisterial *The Discovery of the Unconscious*, can we trace the roots of psychotherapy all the way back to ancient and classical civilisations with their religious and magical rituals?[5] Historians have observed that such claims for its ancient lineage are a means of lending authority to present-day psychotherapy: it is the distillation of age-old wisdom, such an historical reading implies.[6] In a survey of the modern era, the psychologist Frank Tallis maintains that Freud and subsequent psychotherapists have built up a substantial, but often neglected, body of knowledge about the workings of the mind that not only alleviates human misery but can serve as a guide to how we conduct our lives.[7] Some scholars have claimed that most of the insights into the human condition proffered by psychotherapists can be found in the work of great writers and thinkers such as Shakespeare, Pascal, Schopenhauer, Nietzsche, and Dostoyevksy.[8] Freud, who was deeply read and aware of such arguments, would have countered that psychoanalysts had provided a 'scientific' explanation for the intuitions of the artists, a contention that has been by no means universally accepted.

This chapter will first consider the origins of psychodynamic psychotherapy and then the work of Freud, before looking at subsequent developments. These include the growing acceptance of Freudian thought in Britain following the phenomenon of shell shock in the First World War; the founding of the Tavistock Clinic; the formulation of object relations theory; and the turn to a child-centred perspective by John Bowlby and Donald Winnicott in response to the experiences of children who were evacuated during the Second World War. The history of psychodynamic psychotherapy is extensive, and one cannot cover everything in a short chapter. We will not have space to cover important developments in the USA, South America, Germany, or the Paris school. The role of US-based psychoanalysts Heinz Kohut and Heinz Hartmann are mentioned in Chapter 4; the influence of contemporary US clinicians and educators is apparent throughout this book, in particular the work of Glen Gabbard and Nancy McWilliams.

The Beginnings of Modern Psychotherapy

The birth of modern psychotherapy can be traced back to the eighteenth century and two separate developments: the introduction of 'moral treatment' into the asylum and the development of mesmerism.[9] 'Moral treatment', probably better understood as psychological treatment, was a reaction against the coercive asylum treatment of chains and physical punishment. Instead, the patient was to be treated with respect and kindness and to be encouraged to gain self-control of their unruly urges. So-called moral treatment was introduced into France by Philippe Pinel at the Bicetre and Salpetriere Hospitals in Paris, and into Britain by William Tuke at the York Retreat. These developments were famously deconstructed by Michel Foucault in his book, *Madness and Civilisation*, in which he depicted moral treatment as merely replacing the external chains with internal, 'mental chains': the inmate became his or her own prison guard, monitoring themselves for disturbed thoughts or intentions.[10] Whether one accepts Foucault's interpretation or not, the era did represent a major shift from physical to psychological conceptions of how the mentally ill should be treated. Towards the end of the eighteenth century, the German doctor Franz Anton Mesmer developed animal magnetism or 'mesmerism', an early version of hypnotism, which relied on powerful suggestion and the force of the doctor's personality. The phenomenon of mesmerism seemed to suggest that the mind contained elements that were outwith conscious control. Mesmerism and its creator fell into disrepute, but the use of hypnotism was revived in the second half of the nineteenth century at the Salpetriere Hospital by the eminent neurologist Jean-Martin Charcot who used it to treat patients suffering from hysteria. Charcot held that ideas could lodge in the mind where they could be transformed into bodily symptoms. The young Sigmund Freud attended Charcot's demonstrations and was greatly influenced by his exposure to the ideas of the 'Napoleon of the neuroses', as the French physician was dubbed.

The term 'psycho-therapeutics' was coined in 1872 by the English doctor Daniel Hack Tuke, a great grandson of William Tuke, in his work *Illustrations of the Influence of the Mind upon the Body in Health and Disease, designed to elucidate the Action of the Imagination.*[11] The term was taken up in 1886 by the French clinician Hippolyte Bernheim in his discussions of hypnotism. By the end of the nineteenth century the term was ubiquitous and was widely adopted by writers and artists.

According to Ellenberger, chronologically speaking the French doctor Pierre Janet, whose professional life spanned from 1885 to 1935, was the first to found a new system of dynamic psychiatry aimed at replacing those of the nineteenth century, and because of this his work is also a link between the previous dynamic psychotherapy, as exemplified by Charcot, and the newer systems of Freud and others.[12] Paul Brown maintains that modern dynamic psychiatry began in 1892 at the Salpetriere when Janet 'made the revolutionary proposal that in hysteria, it was the *idea* representing the organ or its function which was lost to consciousness'.[13] His work was also one of the main sources for Freud, Adler, and Jung. Although Freud initially acknowledged his debt to Janet in formulating his theories about hysteria, 30 years later he denied that psychoanalysis was based on that research.

Sigmund Freud

Freud continues to divide opinion, as George Makari neatly highlights:

> Sigmund Freud was a genius. Sigmund Freud was a fraud. Sigmund Freud was really a man of letters, or perhaps a philosopher, or a crypto-biologist. Sigmund Freud discovered psychoanalysis by delving deep into his own dreams and penetrating the mysteries of his patients. Sigmund Freud stole most of his good ideas from others and invented the rest out of his own odd imagination. Freud was the maker of a new science of the mind that dominated the West for much of the twentieth century. Freud was an unscientific conjurer who created a mass delusion.[14]

Sigmund Freud was born in Freiburg, Austria–Hungary in 1856 and studied medicine in Vienna.[15,16]After attending Charcot's demonstrations in Paris, Freud published, along with his colleague Josef Breuer, *Studies on Hysteria* in 1895. The authors maintained that 'hysterics' suffered from painful, unpleasant traumatic memories, which were unconsciously repressed. These repressed memories were converted into the physical symptoms of hysteria.

Building on these early clinical experiences with 'hysterical' patients, Freud developed a method of therapy that, in 1896, he was to call 'psychoanalysis'. Hypnosis, as recommended by Charcot, was abandoned, and, instead, the patient was asked to say whatever came into their head or to 'free associate'. By doing so, they would reveal clues about their neurosis, which were held to lie hidden and 'repressed' in their unconscious. In 1899, Freud published *The Interpretation of Dreams* in which he claimed that dreams represented the unconscious fulfilment of wishes, which were often disturbing and sexual in nature. As a result, they had to be disguised. Freud called such disguises the 'manifest content' of the dream. This material was then 'interpreted' or translated by the psychoanalyst into the 'latent content': what the dream 'really' meant. In *The Interpretation of Dreams,* Freud also sketched a model of mind as comprising the unconscious, pre-conscious and conscious systems. Pre-conscious material and processes were closer to the surface and could be rendered conscious more easily than unconscious processes. Freud called this the 'topographical model', the analogy being to a schematic map (i.e. topography) of the mind. In *The Psychopathology of Everyday Life*, Freud extended his method of interpretation to human behaviour generally. He claimed that supposedly accidental phenomena, such as slips of the tongue and forgetting words, were actually meaningful and that they revealed the speaker's unconscious wishes and desires.

In *The Interpretation of Dreams*, Freud examined Oedipus whose story was related in *Oedipus Rex*, the Greek tragedy by Sophocles. Freud maintained that Oedipus acted out a wish that was universal in childhood: the son falls in love with his mother and wants rid of his father. Freud would later call this phenomenon the 'Oedipus complex'. In his 1905 work *Three Essays on the Theory of Sexuality*, Freud outlined the stages of psycho-sexual development: the infant progressed from an initial 'oral' stage through an 'anal' to a 'phallic' stage. This process was completed by around the age of five. The child then developed the 'Oedipus complex', which, if male, led him to desire his mother and hate his father whom he feared would castrate him; if the child was female, she would desire her father and conclude that she had *already* been castrated. At about the age of six, the Oedipus complex was eventually repressed and the child's sex drive disappeared, only to remerge at puberty. If the infant failed to negotiate these stages and became arrested or 'fixated' at a particular stage, then neurotic symptoms would arise in later life. (Please see Chapter 2, Box 6, for a contemporary clinical perspective on 'oedipal' dynamics and the transition of moving from a dyadic relationship to navigating three-person relationships.) Neurosis in adulthood represented a return or 'regression' to this early fixated level. In 1923, Freud proposed a new tripartite model of mind, which encompassed the ego, the id, and the superego. The id represented the primitive, unconscious basis of the psyche and was dominated by basic urges. The ego was the guide to reality and acted as an inhibiting agency. The superego represented parental authority, which had been internalised.

Increasingly in his later years, Freud commented on the wider society and the human condition. In 1920, he published *Beyond the Pleasure Principle* in which he argued that human beings had a tendency to be drawn towards the 'pleasure principle', but that the 'reality principle' served to delay pleasure if there were risks involved. In *The Future of an Illusion* of 1928, he attacked religion as a 'universal obsessional neurosis'. In his 1930 book *Civilization and Its Discontents*, Freud observed that there was an irreconcilable tension between the individual who sought instinctual freedom and society, which sought conformity and the repression of desire. As a result, individuals were doomed to feel discontent. In 1938, Freud was forced to flee Nazi Europe with his wife and daughter, Anna.[17] They sought refuge in London, where Freud died in 1939.

Clinical Practice

Freud held that the most suitable case for analysis was a young adult of good intelligence, reasonably educated, well-motivated, and of reliable character. Patients with psychosis or an organic brain condition were unsuitable. Freud saw patients six times a week. He would sit behind the patient who lay on a couch. He advised that the analyst should only make occasional comments and that the physician should be 'opaque' to the patient. The analyst must not permit pity for his suffering patients to overwhelm him. He must not offer reassurance as this would keep the neurosis in place.[18] Gay has observed that although Freud outlined a rather austere therapeutic technique, in practice he didn't always follow his own prescriptions.[19] He could be chatty, give advice, and even befriend some of his patients. Elsewhere in his writings, he emphasised the emotional receptiveness of the analyst towards the patient. He wrote that the analyst 'must turn his own unconscious like a receptive organ towards the transmitting unconscious of the patient. He must adjust himself to the patient as a telephone receiver is adjusted to the transmitting microphone.'[20]

Freud encountered a phenomenon in analysis which he called 'transference'. This was the process by which the patient displaced on to their analyst feelings and ideas, which derived from previous significant figures in his or her life, and then related to the analyst as if they *were* the significant figure.[21] Initially transference was seen as a problem preventing recovery. However, by 1912 Freud had come to see it as an essential part of the therapeutic process.

Anthony Clare examined Freud's published case histories and was struck by how few there were.[22] He found that there were only six extended accounts by Freud of patients undergoing psychoanalysis: the Schreber case; Little Hans; Dora; the Rat Man; the Wolf Man; and an unnamed female patient. Two were not treated first-hand by Freud. In the case of Schreber, Freud based his analysis on the patient's memoirs, and in the case of Little Hans, he spoke to the father but not the little boy. Clare judged that the Wolf Man was no better and that the Rat Man was Freud's only therapeutic success, although details of his follow-up were sparse, making a definitive judgment difficult. Against Clare's rather bleak judgment, other commentators have praised Freud's clinical abilities. For example, in his biography, Gay gives a very thorough account of Freud's clinical style and judges that it was humane, thoughtful, and, at times, daring.[23] And, although he only published six full case histories, Freud saw very many patients throughout his professional life, most of whom he did not write up for publication, though his papers do contain many shorter clinical excerpts.

Freud's Legacy

Freud's legacy remains contested. Ellenberger feels that Freud's originality resides in four innovations: firstly, his model of the dream where he distinguishes between its manifest and latent content; secondly, his observation that the manifest content is a distortion of the latent content; thirdly, his technique of free association as a method of analysing the dream; and lastly, his practice of systematic dream interpretation as a tool of psychotherapy.[24]

There is, however, a vast literature, much of it critical, of the founder of psychoanalysis.[25,26,27,28] Critics have objected to what they see as the psychic determinism of Freudian theory, which manifests itself in several ways: firstly, it rests on an out-of-date mechanistic model of the mind, based on the closed, deterministic world-view of nineteenth-century physics; secondly, it lacks an ethical dimension – if the behaviour of human beings is entirely the result of mental mechanisms, then they are not free to make ethical choices; and thirdly, it neglects the interpersonal and social context. Such limitations were to be addressed by later psychotherapists. For example, Rycroft and others have argued that psychoanalysis is better understood as a hermeneutic activity, rather than as part of the natural sciences.

Rycroft writes:

> Although psychoanalysis is usually presented as a causal theory which explains psychological phenomena as the consequences of prior events, a number of analysts . . . argued that it . . . is really a theory of meaning, and that Freud's crucial observation that hysterical symptoms were psychogenic was really the discovery that they have meaning, i.e. that they could be interpreted as gestures and communications. Advocates of this view argue that theories of causality are only applicable to the world of inanimate objects and that Freud's attempt to apply deterministic principles derived from the physical sciences to human behaviour fails to take account of the fact that man is a living agent capable of making decisions and choices and of being creative.[29]
>
> (See also Clinical Example 1: Everything may mean something, in Chapter 7.)

An important early criticism was advanced by Ellenberger. Although admiring of Freud, he described what he called the 'Freudian Legend', and outlined two of its cardinal features:

> The first is the theme of the solitary hero struggling against a host of enemies, suffering 'the slings and arrows of outrageous fortune' but triumphing in the end. The legend considerably exaggerates the extent and role of anti-Semitism, the hostility of the academic world, and of alleged Victorian prejudices. The second feature . . . is the blotting out of the greatest part of the scientific and cultural context in which psychoanalysis developed, hence the theme of the absolute originality of the achievements, in which the hero is credited with the achievements of his predecessors, associates, disciples, rivals and contemporaries.[30]

Ellenberger warns against accepting at face value the traditional account of the emergence of psychoanalysis, an account largely promulgated by Freud and loyally recounted by his some of his early followers. As Paul Roazen has suggested, Freud had very little ability to tolerate criticism from his followers or deviance from his theories. Fellow analysts who developed their own ideas were dismissed as 'heretics'.[31] This was the fate of, amongst others, Carl Jung, Alfred Adler, and also, to some extent, Sandor Ferenczi. Though it should be noted that initially and for several years, Freud had a good relationship with these men, particularly Ferenczi and Jung, the latter of whom he saw as the 'Crown Prince', entrusted to continue Freud's work after he was gone.

J. A. C. Brown notes that after the defections of Adler and Jung:

> . . . orthodox Freudians began to show the peculiar intolerance to criticism . . . and, as in certain religious and political bodies but in sharp contrast to what is usually regarded as scientific procedure, those within the group were expected not to criticize its fundamental beliefs and those without were informed that they had no authority to do so.[32]

Roazen comments: 'Whether he liked to admit it or not, Freud had become the head of a sect ... If one sees psychoanalysis as partly a religious phenomenon, then it is not surprising if the followers were united in their worship of Freud and of the unconscious.'[33]

Jung, like many others, objected to Freud's emphasis on the sexual drive being the sole determinant of human behaviour, arguing that other factors, such as the spiritual, were also important. He also objected to Freud's notion that the first five years of life determined future development. For Jung, all stages in life were important, a journey which he saw as a process of 'individuation'. Adler, likewise, objected to the Freudian emphasis on sexuality and posited the concept of the inferiority complex, whereby individuals strive to counter their feelings of physical and mental inadequacy. Ferenczi criticised the idea that the analyst should be remote and unresponsive, arguing that they should interact with the patient. He developed what he called 'active therapy' and 'mutual analysis', which involved bestowing affection on patients and introducing an element of mutuality into the relationship. According to Brown, Ferenczi was the first to recognise the importance of the interpersonal aspect of analysis.[34] However, some of Ferenczi's experiments went too far and served to confuse the boundary between patient and therapist in a way that was unhelpful to both. Ferenczi should be given credit, though, for his early recognition that children who had been sexually abused suffered particular psychological damage. In the 1940s, he described how the abused child might dissociate when overwhelmed by their traumatic experience. The child had to deal with their guilty feelings and confusion about their part in the abuse: were they to blame, or was it the adult perpetrator?

Later analysts, such as Eric Fromm and Karen Horney, maintained that it was important to consider the role that society played in an individual's difficulties and that it was not just a matter of the internal workings of the mind.[35,36] Freudian theory has also attracted criticism from feminists (see Chapter 2, Box 6).

At the beginning of this section, we quoted Makari who acknowledged that the founder of psychoanalysis continues to divide opinion. However, in the conclusion to his book *Revolution in the Mind*, he judged:

> Psychoanalysis emerged from the rubble of postwar Europe as the leading modern theory of the mind. Its model of unconscious passions, its notion of defence and inner conflict, and its method of unravelling self-deception, encroached upon traditional sources of self-understanding like religion. In the U.S., psychoanalysis made its way into the courts, schools and hospitals, and informed literature, cinema, television, journalism, theatre, and art. Its ideas spread into popular discourse as adages, clichés, and jokes.[37]

Indeed, many contemporary psychotherapists hold that Freud made formative contributions to therapeutic practice, which include the concepts of transference, inner conflict, repression, and the superego, all of which remain useful today in the understanding of mental life.

The First World War and Shell Shock

The First World War and, in particular, the phenomenon of shell shock was to have a great impact on the standing of psychotherapy in Britain.[38] The term shell shock was coined by the experimental psychologist Dr Charles Myers in 1915 to describe the mental disintegration that afflicted many soldiers fighting on the Front. Conventional psychiatric approaches, built on notions that mental disorder was the result of brain disease and hereditary degeneration, proved to be ineffective and misguided. For a start, the condition seemed to disproportionately affect the officer class, most of whom had shown no previous signs of degeneration. Secondly, physical methods of treatment were of little benefit. In contrast, psychotherapeutic approaches proved to be more fruitful. Three clinicians were prominent in pushing psychotherapeutic approaches: William McDougall, William Brown, and, most famously, W. H. Rivers, whose article in *The Lancet* in 1917, 'Freud's Psychology of the Unconscious', was very influential and helped bring about the acceptance of Freud's ideas in medical circles. Although these clinicians were influenced by Freud, they did not agree with his central tenet that sexual factors played a crucial role in the cause of neurosis. Instead, they maintained that the soldier experienced a conflict between doing his duty and trying to stay alive. For many it was an impossible choice, which eventually led to mental disturbance, or more specifically shell shock. There was a widespread feeling amongst British doctors after the First World War that shell shock had effectively 'disproved' Freud's theory of the primacy of sexual factors in the aetiology of neurosis.

During the war, Rivers was based at Craiglockhart Hospital in Edinburgh, and he used a modified form of Freudian psychotherapy. His clinical work, which included treating the poet Siegfried Sassoon, has subsequently achieved wider public attention due to the novels of Pat Barker and the accompanying film. Ben Shephard[39] argues that Rivers's views had a considerable impact on British medicine, while Malcolm Pines[40] has judged: 'it was Rivers who, probably more than anyone else, made psychoanalytical thinking acceptable to a wide circle of influential persons – psychiatrists, psychologists, and anthropologists'.

Before 1914 there were only a small number of doctors using psychological methods to treat nervous disorders and most of these were based in private practice in and around London.[41] The situation was a little different in Scotland, and, for example, Isobel Hutton, the first woman psychiatrist at the Royal Edinburgh Asylum, described how the asylum chief Dr George Robertson welcomed Freudian ideas, which helped to contribute to the relatively positive attitude to psychoanalysis in Scottish psychiatry at the time.[42] However, the vast majority of British neurologists and asylum doctors took no practical interest in psychotherapy. By the end of the war this situation had changed dramatically. There was a great increase in the number of doctors practising and being trained in psychotherapy. Drs Maurice Craig and Henry Head established the Cassel Hospital in London, whose remit was to provide psychotherapy for the civilian population. The Tavistock Clinic was also founded during this period and it too provided psychotherapy for the public. The concept of mental disorder expanded, and it came to be seen as something that could afflict anyone, not just those of 'tainted stock'. From the early 1920s a proliferation of books on psychotherapy were published. These changes had been brought about by the war-time experience of shell shock.

Early Twentieth Century Developments

The Tavistock Clinic was established in 1920 as one of the first outpatient clinics in Britain to provide systematic psychodynamic psychotherapy for patients who could not afford private fees.[43] Its founding medical director was Hugh Crichton-Miller who had worked with shell shock victims in the First World War. He wished to bring Freudian theory to the civilian population and, in particular, to those suffering from neuroses and personality disorder. He brought an eclectic approach to the clinic, which embraced other therapies, but in the years following the Second World War, orthodox psychoanalysis came to dominate the institution. The period from 1930 to 1960 saw an upsurge of interest in psychoanalysis in

Britain, greatly stimulated by the many refugees fleeing Nazi Europe and settling in Britain. As we have seen, this included Freud and his daughter Anna in 1938, but also Hannah Segal and Michael Balint. During this period, there emerged the Tavistock Institute of Human Relations, which became responsible for teaching and research.

Anna Freud

In 1936, Anna Freud published *The Ego and the Mechanism of Defence*, which developed her father's concept of the ego and the role of defence mechanisms. Her work was favourably received in America by the so-called ego psychologists such as Heinz Hartmann. Anna Freud, along with Melanie Klein, was a pioneer in establishing psychoanalytic psychotherapy for children. Unfortunately, they strongly disagreed with each other's theoretical position and clinical approach. As Likierman has observed, the technique of child analysis developed through disputes and conflicts, leading finally to an open confrontation, described as the 'controversial discussions'.[44] These took place between 1941 and 1945 in London, to where both women had emigrated. No consensus could be reached. Anna defended her father's position against Klein's view that the Oedipus complex occurred earlier than Freud had speculated. Unlike Klein, Anna thought that children were not capable of developing transferences the way adults could. She emphasised the importance of forming a supportive bond with a child in analysis. Since children were still under the influence of their parents, she argued, the internal structure of their mind had not yet fully formed and was not capable of developing a transference relation with a therapist.[45] Anna Freud emphasised the importance of the environment in a child's development, an environment which in the first instance mainly involved the mother whom the analyst must not displace but rather work alongside.[46]

Melanie Klein and Object Relations Theory

Melanie Klein was responsible for an approach to psychoanalysis that came to be known as object relations theory.[47,48] Object relations theory aimed to replace Freud's drive theory with a radically different model which emphasised the primacy of relations with others. It was concerned with exploring the relationship between real people in the external world and the internal images of them that individuals formed. It sought to examine how these two entities, external and internal 'objects', interacted.

Klein was an Austrian analyst who moved to London in the 1920s at the invitation of Ernest Jones, a British colleague of Freud and his first major biographer.[49] Klein depicted the mental life of the child and adult as being an intricate web of phantasied relations between the self and others, both in the external world and in the internal world of internal 'objects'. She maintained that aspects of the internal world, such as feelings or images, could be 'projected' externally, while aspects of the outer world could be 'introjected' into the inner world. Klein worked with children as well as adults, and her technique with children involved using play and art materials (Figure 1.1).

Klein held that the crucial period in life was infancy when the baby experienced an intolerable conflict between love and hate. The baby tried to resolve this conflict by projecting the aggressive part of him or herself on to the outer world. The infant perceived 'objects' as partial: they were split into the all-good, as represented by the nourishing 'good breast', or the all-bad as represented by the unsatisfying 'bad breast'. At a later period, the infant was said to develop a more balanced relation to the mother and see her as a whole

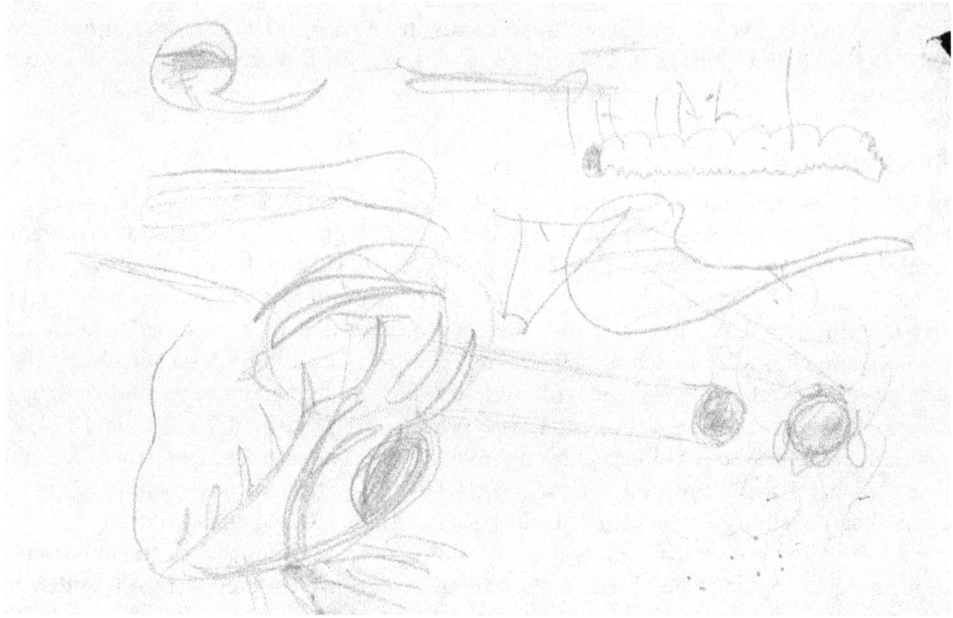

Figure 1.1 Drawing by 'Richard', one of Klein's patients, in 1941. Klein described this work with 'Richard' in detail in 'Narrative of a Child Analysis' in 1961.[50] Klein viewed child's spontaneous play as the equivalent of free association in the adult. Her work, along with other early child psychotherapists, influenced the subsequent development of the discipline of play therapy.[51] Reproduced with kind permission of The Melanie Klein Trust.

person made up of good and bad qualities. However, the infant also felt guilt, remorse, and depression at the realisation that they had entertained violent emotions about the mother. This led to what Klein termed the 'paranoid position' and the 'depressive position', with the former defending the child against the 'depressed' feelings (i.e. more mixed and realistic feelings) of the latter. As Lisa Appignanesi has observed, Klein's complex theory gradually permeated wider society and led to the impossible implication for the mother that she was both utterly passive and infinitely responsible for her child.[52]

The Scottish Contribution: Ian Suttie and Ronald Fairbairn

Some of the early criticism of Klein and of Freud came from Scotland. The Glasgow psychiatrist Ian Suttie, author of *The Origins of Love and Hate*, objected to the Kleinian picture of the infant as paranoid and aggressive.[53] Instead, Suttie held that the infant had an innately benign and sociable relationship with others, and that negative qualities only emerged if normal development had been impaired by a troubled upbringing. Suttie quoted with approval Ferenczi's contention that it was the therapist's 'love' that cured the patient. In *Freud and the Post-Freudians*, Brown contrasted Suttie's *The Origins of Love and Hate*, which he maintained offered a democratic and matriarchal perspective, based on love, with what he saw as Freud's authoritarian and patriarchal perspective, based on the sexual drive.[54]

The Edinburgh analyst Ronald Fairbairn objected that Freud's theory was mechanistic, atomistic, and was expressed in depersonalised language.[55] His own theory shifted from

Freud's drive model to a relational one. Where Freud had suggested that the infant was born into the world unrelated to others and became related only secondarily as they provided him or her with pleasure, Fairbairn held that infants were orientated towards others from the start. Subsequent emotional and mental difficulties were seen not as deriving from conflicts over pleasure-seeking impulses, but disturbances in relations with others. Fairburn also criticised Melanie Klein, in particular her notion that all the action took place within the child's head, and argued, instead, for the importance of seeing the child's parents as real people, rather than objects of fantasy.

Towards the end of his career, Fairbairn became critical of the standard analytic method. He maintained that 'The relationship existing between the patient and analyst is more important than the details of technique.'[56] Gomez[57] has judged that Fairbairn's work had a far-reaching effect on how psychotherapy was practised. Analysts began to accept that patients needed a genuine relationship with their therapist rather than just merely being given interpretations. Suttie and Fairbairn have been seen by Gavin Miller[58] as providing a particularly Scottish perspective on psychoanalysis characterised by a philosophy of questioning from first principles the foundations of Freudian theory, and by an emphasis on kinship and community, rather than on the isolated and self-seeking ego of classical analysis. In later years, Dr Jock Sutherland, who had been the Medical Director of the Tavistock Clinic from 1947 to 1968, returned to his native Edinburgh, where in 1972 he was instrumental in the formation of the Scottish Institute for Human Relations, considered the Scottish counterpart to the Tavistock.

The 'Middle Group': Michael Balint, John Bowlby, and Donald Winnicott

In the post-war period, there emerged a permanent split in the training programme at the Tavistock: one group followed Melanie Klein, and another, Anna Freud.[59] Those who were appalled by the dogmatisms of the Kleinians and Freudians joined the so-called Middle Group, which included Michael Balint, Jock Sutherland, John Bowlby, Donald Winnicott, Charles Rycroft, and Marion Milner.

Michael Balint

Michael Balint was an Hungarian psychoanalyst who had been analysed by Ferenczi. He is remembered for creating the 'Balint groups'.[60] Balint realised that from a practical point of view, the high cost and time-consuming nature of psychoanalysis militated against it making a major impact on the general population. Instead, he proposed that frontline workers in the mental health field should be trained in psychodynamic thinking. He set up groups where clinicians would meet regularly with a psychoanalytically trained facilitator to discuss case material brought by participants. Such groups proved very successful, and versions of them still run today (see Chapter 18).

John Bowlby

John Bowlby, along with Donald Winnicott, played a major role in shaping the post-war establishment's consensus on parenting.[61] Bowlby was one of the few clinicians to play an influential part, both within British psychoanalysis and in the setting up of the NHS after the war. Bowlby had been sent away early to boarding school by his rather cold, upper-class family, and was acutely sensitive to the importance of separation for young children.[62] After the Second World War, he undertook groundbreaking investigations into the lives of children who had been evacuated or displaced during the conflict. In his *Forty-Four Thieves: Their Characters and Home Life*, Bowlby argued that prolonged separation of small children from their homes and their mothers led in many cases to the development of a criminal character. In the 1951 WHO Report, *Maternal Care and Mental Health*, Bowlby concluded that it was essential for their mental health that an infant or young child experienced a warm, intimate, and continuous relationship with their mother or her permanent substitute. If not, the child would subsequently show signs of deprivation, manifest by depression or an excessive need for love or revenge. He emphasised the importance of the quality of this *real* relationship rather than the infant's fantasies about it. As Appignanesi has commented, Bowlby's work consolidated the theory that mothers needed to stay as close to their infants as possible, while fathers went out to work to provide money for the home.[63]

Drawing on research in ethology as well as psychoanalysis, Bowlby fully developed his theory of 'attachment' in his influential trilogy: *Attachment* (1969), *Separation* (1973), and *Loss, Grief and Mourning* (1980). He argued that the mother or 'attachment figure' should acknowledge the infant's needs for comfort and protection, while also respecting their need for autonomy. If this 'secure attachment' was successfully achieved, then the child would develop an internal model of the self as valued and reliable. If it was unsuccessful, the result was an 'insecure attachment' and the creation of an unworthy and incompetent self. Bowlby saw therapy as a 'reparative', emotional process, and maintained that it was not just about attaining intellectual insights. However, the understanding of attachment has evolved since Bowlby outlined his initial theories and there is now a recognition that insecure attachment is common and does not inevitably lead to major emotional problems, although it does influence how an individual develops psychologically (see Chapter 2).

Donald Winnicott

Donald Winnicott was a paediatrician by training and, like Bowlby, had studied the effects on young children of being evacuated from their homes during the Second World War.[64,65] Appignanesi sees him as a romantic who believed that an infant who enjoyed a relationship with a 'good-enough mother' would develop an authentic and creative self.[66] Winnicott constructed a theory to explain how the self emerged out of its relations with others. He held that a lack of contact with others or, alternatively, an immersion in the world of others, presented dangers. He focused on the conditions that enabled the child to see his or herself as separate from others. The mother provided a crucial role in helping the self of the infant to emerge. If maternal provision was inadequate, the infant self might fragment. The infant would become overwhelmed by the demands of others and would lose touch with their own spontaneous needs. This would result in a split between the 'true self' and the 'false self'. The 'true self' would hide away, while the 'false self', which was moulded by maternal expectations, would deal with the outside world. The 'false self' served to protect the integrity of the 'true self'. In adult life, if this strategy failed, the self could fragment into several parts and psychosis could develop. Winnicott's work was to influence the radical Scottish psychiatrist R. D. Laing when he came to depict the inner world of psychosis.[67]

Winnicott believed that Klein had described the infant in isolation from the actual reciprocal primary relationship in which he or she developed. He noted that Freud and Klein had emphasised the role of disillusionment in human development, during which growing up was portrayed as a process of mourning, but, in contrast, he contended, development was better viewed as a creative process of collaboration between mother and child. Adam Phillips has judged that one of Winnicott's major contributions to therapy 'was to have evolved a genuinely collaborative model of psychoanalytic treatment in which the analyst creates a setting that also makes possible the patient's self-interpretations'.[68] The therapist's role was not to be overly interpretative, but to provide a congenial milieu in which the patient would make a journey of self-discovery.

The Turn to the Child

Commentators have noted how the focus in psychoanalytic thinking shifted from the sex instinct to the mother and child relationship. Just as the experience of shell shock in the First World War had been influential in the development and acceptance of psychoanalytic theory, the problems of evacuated children in Britain during the Second World War changed psychoanalytic thinking about childhood.[69]

As Appignanesi observes:

> Mothers displaced castrating fathers as the crucial authority dominating both childhood and the inner life: it was on the base of that earliest and fundamental relationship, not the paternal one, that all future relations, of love and power, of attachment and dependence, would be placed.[70]

Phillips pointed out that this new conception of child development had social consequences, especially for women:

> Just as women were being encouraged to stay at home again after their crucial work during the war, coercive and convincing theories about the importance for children of continuous mothering, of the potential dangers of separation, began to be published which could easily be used to persuade them to stay there.[71]

Another consequence of the Second World War was the development of both group psychotherapy and the 'therapeutic community'. In the 1940s at the Northfield Military Hospital near Birmingham, two clinicians, John Rickman and Wilfred Bion, set up what was known as the 'first Northfield experiment'.[72,73] This was taken over by Michael Foulkes for a second experiment, this time comprising group psychotherapy. The lessons learnt informed the future use of group psychotherapy with civilian populations in the post-war period. Also working at the Northfield Hospital was Tom Main, who coined the term 'therapeutic community'. Main introduced a more democratic structure to the hospital which involved patients in decision-making and which sought 'resocialisation of the neurotic individual.'[74] In civilian life, he continued this work at the Cassel Hospital, as did Maxwell Jones at the Henderson Hospital. In Europe, Victor Frankl, who had survived the Nazi concentration camps, returned to Vienna where he introduced his existential-inspired 'Logotherapy', founded on his belief that human beings were primarily concerned with finding a meaning to their life.[75]

Psychosis

Although Freud generally did not think that people with psychotic illnesses could be treated with psychoanalysis, he observed that 'so many things that in the neuroses have to be laboriously fetched up from the depths are found in the psychoses upon the surface, visible to every eye'.[76]

The attempt to use psychotherapy to treat patients with psychosis was practised much more in America than Britain. An exception was R. D. Laing, who had trained at the Tavistock in the late 1950s. Holmes credits Laing with introducing British readers to therapists such Harry Stack Sullivan, Harold Searles, and Fromm-Reichmann and their psychoanalytic models of psychosis. Holmes writes:

> Laing's long-term influence should not be underestimated . . . He validated the inner world and experience of the severely mentally ill, seeing psychotic phenomena as covert communications, often about traumatic or painful experiences, rather than meaningless manifestations of a dysfunctional brain. He emphasised the family context of psychosis.[77]

Concluding Remarks

This brief history has shown how social and cultural factors have influenced both the theory and practice of psychodynamic psychotherapy. We have seen how the two world wars had a significant impact on the development of psychotherapy. We have also seen how Freud's original theories were challenged and, it could be argued, this has led to improvements in how psychotherapy is conducted and thought about. The therapist is more active and responsive to the patient. Courses of treatments are shorter. Patriarchal assumptions have been exposed, and, in theorising about psychotherapy, more attention is paid to the role of the mother and her interaction with her child.

Some commentators, though, have seen the emergence of psychotherapy in modern times and the apparent extension of its concepts to all aspects of everyday life as a cause for concern. The sociologist Frank Furedi has used the term 'therapy culture' to decry what he sees as people's loss of the ability to be stoical and accepting in the face of the inevitable hardships of life.[78] Instead, people increasingly see themselves as passive victims in need of therapy. While there is undoubtedly some truth in Furedi's contention, he has been criticised for minimising human suffering and advocating an old-fashioned stiff-upper-lip approach to mental pain.

At the beginning of this chapter, we observed that there has often been a conflict between psychotherapeutic and biological approaches to the treatment of mental illness but that many clinicians wished to see a rapprochement between the two sides. This would seem to be vital. No matter what advances are made in biological psychiatry, the patient remains a unique individual with a unique set of experiences and personal history. Contemporary neuroscience has a tendency to see human beings as malfunctioning mechanisms. Psychodynamic psychotherapy, with its stress on attending in great detail to the individual's life story, is especially placed to ensure that the patient as a person does not disappear.

References

1. G. Zilboorg. *A History of Medical Psychology.* New York, W. W. Norton, 1941.
2. E. Shorter. *A History of the Asylum. From the Era of the Asylum to the Age of Prozac.* New York, Oxford University Press, 1997.
3. K.W.M. Fulford, T. Thornton and G. Graham. *Oxford Textbook of Philosophy and Psychiatry.* Oxford, Oxford University Press, 2006.
4. J. Holmes. Psychodynamic psychotherapy – rise, decline, revival. In Bloch S., Green S.A., Holmes J., eds. *Psychiatry: Past, Present, and Prospect.* Oxford, Oxford University Press, 2014; 383–400.

5. H.F. Ellenberger. *The Discovery of the Unconscious. The History and Evolution of Dynamic Psychiatry*. New York, Basic Books, 1970.
6. S. Marks. Psychotherapy in historical perspective. *Hist Human Sci* 2017; **30 (2)**: 3–16.
7. F. Tallis. *The Act of Living. What the Great Psychologists Can Teach Us About Surviving Discontent in an Age of Anxiety*. London, Little Brown, 2021.
8. R. Webster. *Why Freud Was Wrong. Sin, Science and Psychoanalysis*. London, Fontana, 1996.
9. T. Burns, E. Burns-Lundgren. *Psychotherapy. A Very Short Introduction*. Oxford, Oxford University Press, 2015.
10. M. Foucault. *Madness and Civilization. A History of Insanity in the Age of Reason*. (trans: Howard R). Tavistock Publications, London, 1967.
11. S. Shamdasani. 'Psychotherapy': the invention of a word. *Hist Human Sci*. 2005; **18 (1)**: 1–22.
12. H.F. Ellenberger. *The Discovery of the Unconscious. The History and Evolution of Dynamic Psychiatry*. New York, Basic Books, 1970.
13. P. Brown, P. Janet, 1859–1947. In Freeman H., ed. *A Century of Psychiatry*. London, Mosby, 1999; 99–103.
14. G. Makari. *Revolution in the Mind. The Creation of Psychoanalysis*. London, Duckworth, 2008.
15. P. Gay. *Freud. A Life for Our Time*. Cambridge, Dent, 1988.
16. J. Whitebrook. *Freud. An Intellectual Biography*. Cambridge, Cambridge University Press, 2017.
17. M. Edmundson. *The Death of Sigmund Freud. Fascism, Psychoanalysis and the Rise of Fundamentalism*. London, Bloomsbury, 2007.
18. P. Gay. *Freud. A Life for Our Time*. Cambridge, Dent, 1988.
19. P. Gay. *Freud. A Life for Our Time*. Cambridge, Dent, 1988.
20. S. Freud. Recommendations to Physicians Practising Psycho-Analysis. In Strachey, J. (Ed. & Trans.) *The Standard Edition of the Complete Psychological Works of Sigmund Freud* Volume XII (1911–1913). London: Hogarth Press; 1958. p. 114.
21. C. Rycroft. *A Critical Dictionary of Psychoanalysis*. Harmondsworth, Penguin Books, 1972.
22. A. Clare. Freud's cases: the clinical basis of psychoanalysis. In: Bynum, W.F., Porter, R., Shepherd, M., eds. *The Anatomy of Madness. Volume 1*. London, Tavistock, 1985; 271–288.
23. P. Gay. *Freud. A Life for Our Time*. Cambridge, Dent, 1988.
24. H.F. Ellenberger. *The Discovery of the Unconscious. The History and Evolution of Dynamic Psychiatry*. New York, Basic Books, 1970.
25. S. Fisher, R. Greenberg. *The Scientific Credibility of Freud's Theories and Therapies*. Columbia, Columbia University Press, 1985.
26. E. Gellner. *The Psychoanalytic Movement. The Cunning of Unreason*. London, Fontana, 1992.
27. E.R. Torrey. *Freudian Fraud. The Malignant Effect of Freud's Theory on American Culture and Thought*. New York, Harper Collins, 1992.
28. F.C. Crews, ed. *Unauthorized Freud. Doubters Confront a Legend*. New York, Viking Books, 1998.
29. C. Rycroft. *A Critical Dictionary of Psychoanalysis*. Harmondsworth, Penguin Books, 1972.
30. H.F. Ellenberger. *The Discovery of the Unconscious. The History and Evolution of Dynamic Psychiatry*. New York, Basic Books, 1970.
31. P. Roazen. *Freud and His Followers*. London, Allen Lane, 1976.
32. J.A.C. Brown. *Freud and the Post-Freudians*. Harmondsworth, Penguin, 1964.
33. P. Roazen. *Freud and His Followers*. London, Allen Lane, 1976.

34. J.A.C. Brown. *Freud and the Post-Freudians.* Harmondsworth, Penguin, 1964.
35. J.A.C. Brown. *Freud and the Post-Freudians.* Harmondsworth, Penguin, 1964.
36. A. Bateman, J. Holmes. *Introduction to Psychoanalysis. Contemporary Theory and Practice.* London, Routledge, 1995.
37. G. Makari. *Revolution in the Mind. The Creation of Psychoanalysis.* London, Duckworth, 2008.
38. M. Stone. Shellshock and the psychologists. In Bynum, W.F., Porter, R., Shepherd, M., eds. *The Anatomy of Madness. Volume 2.* London, Tavistock, 1985; 242–271.
39. B. Shephard. *A War of Nerves. Soldiers and Psychiatrists 1914–1994.* London, Jonathan Cape, 2000.
40. M. Pines. The development of the psychodynamic movement. In Berrios G. E., Freeman H., eds. *150 Years of British Psychiatry 1841–1991.* London, Gaskell, 1991; 206–231.
41. M. Stone. Shellshock and the psychologists. In Bynum, W.F., Porter, R., Shepherd, M., eds. *The Anatomy of Madness. Volume 2.* London, Tavistock, 1985; 242–271.
42. M. Pines. The development of the psychodynamic movement. In Berrios G. E., Freeman H., eds. *150 Years of British Psychiatry 1841–1991.* London, Gaskell, 1991; 206–231.
43. H.V. Dicks. *Fifty Years of the Tavistock Clinic.* London, Routledge & Keegan, 1970.
44. M. Likerman, Anna Freud and Melanie Klein. In Freeman H., ed. *A Century of Psychiatry.* London, Mosby, 1999; 106–111.
45. F.R. Rodman. *Winnicott. Life and Work.* Cambridge, MA, Perseus, 2003.
46. L. Appignanesi. *Mad, Bad and Sad. A History of Women and the Mind Doctors from 1800 to the Present.* London, Virago Press, 2008.
47. J.R. Greenberg and S.A. Mitchell. *Object Relations in Psychoanalytic Theory.* Massachusetts, Cambridge, Harvard University Press, 1983.
48. L. Gomez. *An Introduction to Object Relations in Psychoanalytic Theory.* London, Free Association Press, 1997.
49. B. Maddox. *Freud's Wizard. The Enigma of Ernest Jones.* London, John Murray, 2006.
50. M. Klein. *Narrative of a Child Analysis.* New York, Basic Books, 1961.
51. D.C. Ray. History, rationale, and purpose of play. In *Advanced Play Therapy.* London, Routledge; 2011; 1–16.
52. L. Appignanesi. *Mad, Bad and Sad. A History of Women and the Mind Doctors from 1800 to the Present.* London, Virago Press, 2008.
53. I. Suttie. *The Origins of Love and Hate.* London, Routledge, 2014 (originally published in 1935).
54. J.A.C. Brown. *Freud and the Post-Freudians.* Harmondsworth, Penguin, 1964.
55. D. Tantam. Fairbairn. In Freeman, H, Berrios, G.E., eds. *150 Years of British Psychiatry. Volume II. The Aftermath.* London, Athlone, 1996; 549–64.
56. R. Fairbairn. Freud: the psychoanalytic method and mental health. *Br J Ment Psych.* **30**, 53–62.
57. L. Gomez. *An Introduction to Object Relations in Psychoanalytic Theory.* London, Free Association Press, 1997.
58. G. Miller. Scottish psychoanalysis. A rational religion. *J Hist Behav Sci.* 2004.**44** (1), 38–58.
59. D. Burston. *The Wing of Madness.* Cambridge, MA, Harvard University Press, 1996.
60. J. Holmes. Psychodynamic psychotherapy – rise, decline, revival. In Bloch S., Green S.A., Holmes J., eds. *Psychiatry: Past, Present, and Prospect.* Oxford, Oxford University Press, 2014; 383–400.
61. L. Appignanesi. *Mad, Bad and Sad. A History of Women and the Mind Doctors from 1800 to the Present.* London, Virago Press, 2008.
62. J. Holmes. Psychodynamic psychotherapy – rise, decline, revival. In Bloch S., Green S.A., Holmes J., eds. *Psychiatry: Past, Present, and*

Prospect. Oxford, Oxford University Press, 2014; 383–400.

63. J. Holmes. Psychodynamic psychotherapy – rise, decline, revival. In Bloch S., Green S.A., Holmes J., eds. *Psychiatry: Past, Present, and Prospect*. Oxford, Oxford University Press, 2014; 383–400.
64. F.R. Rodman. *Winnicott. Life and Work*. Cambridge MA, Perseus, 2003.
65. A. Phillips. *Winnicott*. London, Fontana, 1988.
66. L. Appignanesi. *Mad, Bad and Sad. A History of Women and the Mind Doctors from 1800 to the Present*. London, Virago Press, 2008.
67. A. Beveridge. *Portrait of the Artist as a Young Man. The Early Writings and Work of R. D. Laing, 1927–1960*. Oxford, Oxford University Press, 2011.
68. A. Phillips. *Winnicott*. London, Fontana, 1988.
69. A. Phillips. *Winnicott*. London, Fontana, 1988.
70. L. Appignanesi. *Mad, Bad and Sad. A History of Women and the Mind Doctors from 1800 to the Present*. London, Virago Press, 2008.
71. A. Phillips. *Winnicott*. London, Fontana, 1988.
72. B. Shephard. *A War of Nerves. Soldiers and Psychiatrists 1914–1994*. London, Jonathan Cape, 2000.
73. M. Pines. Group psychotherapy. In Freeman H., ed. *A Century of Psychiatry*. London, Mosby, 1999; 141–5.
74. D. Millard. Therapeutic communities. In Freeman H., ed. *A Century of Psychiatry*. London, Mosby, 1999; 155–9.
75. V. Frankl. *Man's Search for Meaning. An Introduction to Logotherapy* (4th ed.). Boston, Beacon Press, 1992.
76. S. Freud. *An Autobiographical Study* (trans. J. Strachey). New York, W. W. Norton & Co., 1952.
77. J. Holmes. Psychodynamic psychotherapy – rise, decline, revival. In Bloch S., Green S. A., Holmes J., eds. *Psychiatry: Past, Present, and Prospect*. Oxford, Oxford University Press, 2014; 383–400.
78. F. Furedi. *Therapy Culture. Cultivating Vulnerability in an Uncertain Age*. London, Routledge, 2003.

Chapter 2

The Supporting Theory of Psychodynamic Psychotherapy

Table of Contents

Introduction 18
The Importance of Early Development 19
Development of the Internal Relational World – Object Relations 21
Accommodating to the World As We Find It 25
The Dynamics of Insoluble and Overwhelming Problems 26
Core Psychodynamic Theory 26
Internal Conflict 27
Defence Mechanisms 27
Resistance 29
Theoretical Approach to Working with Defences and Resistance 30
Movement between Defensive 'Splitting' and a More Integrated Position 31
Key Transitions in Life 32
Relational Dynamics 32
Projection 33
Projective Identification 34
Containment 37
Who Is in the Therapy Room? The Dynamics of the Transference 39
Countertransference 41
The Narcissistic Constellation 44
Developmental Theories 45
Narcissistic Object Relations 46
An Outline of Psychodynamic Approaches to Change – Theory 47
Concluding Remarks 47

Introduction

At its heart, psychodynamic theory is interested in the underlying dynamics of humans and their relationships. Psychoanalytic theory covers a wide breadth of matters, and, as discussed in Chapter 4, there are various 'schools' with much overlap, but also differences. As such, this theory chapter can in no way be exhaustive, but is intended as an accessible introduction to this rich area. We draw on, and at times integrate, various aspects of psychodynamic therapy, focusing on aspects of theory that we have found particularly useful in clinical practice.

Adverse social circumstances including poverty, inequality, and social injustice are hugely influential on human relationships and are linked with adverse interpersonal experiences in childhood. This dimension is crucial for an understanding of human development, as is awareness of the correlation between childhood experiences of neglect, abuse, and family difficulties on a person's subsequent physical and mental health.[1] These aspects are expanded on in Chapter 15. Beyond the scope of this chapter is an understanding about war, displacement, and refugees in terms of the impacts on human development and implications for therapeutic work (see e.g. R. K. Papadopoulos's 'Refugees, trauma and adversity-activated development'[2]).

Throughout this chapter we will expand on some key aspects of early psychoanalytic theory, including the work of Freud, which has already been touched on in Chapter 1. Later psychodynamic theorists have often used Freud's psychoanalytic ideas as their starting point and many of his concepts remain in common use in contemporary psychodynamic psychotherapy, although the way they are used has often changed.

This chapter will commence with a clinical vignette which will be used to illustrate some of the theoretical concepts throughout the chapter.

Clinical Example 1 Andrew

Andrew, a 45-year-old dentist, came to therapy with a long history of depression for which he had been admitted to hospital on several occasions. Initially he seemed motivated and keen to attend, but quite quickly became convinced that the therapist disliked him and began to write numerous letters demanding reassuring responses and suggesting that he be discharged as he was obviously a hopeless case. Eventually the therapist began to dread seeing the patient and started to hope that he would drop out of therapy.

Both patient and therapist were initially happy to work together, so how can we understand what happened here? We will explore this as the chapter progresses.

The Importance of Early Development

In our life as an infant, we are totally dependent on others. How expression of our basic needs is met – and the 'fit' between the nature and intensity of our needs and the capacities of the family environment – is important in the development of our sense of self and others. This is a basic place to start, but much else of what follows relates to this.

As the psychoanalyst and neuropsychologist Solms explains: 'The human infant is not a blank slate; like all other species, we are born with innate needs. These needs [. . .] are felt and expressed as emotions.'[3] Object relations and attachment theory (see later) emphasise a central human need to **seek and be in contact with caregivers**. Developing a safe-enough, trusting relationship with one or more caring figures provides a secure base, which brings the capacity for learning, exploration, play, and the expression and meeting of other needs (see Box 2.1 for other innate needs). Separation from key caregivers is felt as panic, and loss of them as despair.[3]

Whilst we have innate needs in common with each other, the personal expression and character of these vary according to an individual's temperament. Furthermore, the nature of the interactions between the infant and those around him influences how the infant expresses and relates to his needs and feelings.

Box 2.1 Innate emotional needs

- To **seek and be in contact with** people who look after us (as described above)

Other needs include (after Solms[3]):

- To **explore** and interact with the world and people in it, as our bodily and emotional survival depends on this. This is a 'foraging or seeking or "wanting" instinct', which is felt as interest and curiosity.
- To '**care** for and nurture others, especially our offspring'.
- Other needs include to **escape dangerous situations** (felt as fear), and a need to try and **remove frustrating** things that get 'between us and satisfaction of our needs' (felt as rage). There is a need for **sexual partners** (felt as lust), the timing of which is a complex discussion beyond the scope of this chapter, but suffice to say that this matures during adolescence.

The need for play

- Psychodynamic theory regards playing as being vital, not just for cognitive and motor development, but for its importance in developing creativity and 'transitional spaces'. The latter refers to the use of play and objects as a transition from the early intimate feeding and nurturing relationship with a parent to something more separate. Play gives, as Suttie describes, 'that reassuring contact with his fellows which he has lost when mother's nurtural services are no longer offered or required'.[4]

From an infant observation and neuroscience perspective, in the daily life of an infant they experience many 'highly arousing, affect-laden and short interpersonal events that expose the infant to high levels of cognitive and social information'.[5] This refers to the ordinary processes of family life, which mostly function in good-enough ways. For example, a baby has a need to be close to someone and therefore cries. This is noticed by the parent or carer who moves closer, perhaps holding the infant. Through these early interactions and how they feel, the infant learns, gradually, something about their own inner and outer worlds.

Gwen Adshead, psychiatrist and psychotherapist, describes the importance of communication and understanding of feelings in human relationships: 'An individual who experiences a strong emotion is able to transmit that experience to others (and *vice versa*).'[5] In accounting for this observation, Adshead draws on the neuroscience of the operation of mirror neurons[6] which 'fire when another's emotional experience is witnessed'.[5] Adshead continues:

> 'The closer the emotional tie, the more pronounced the experience: we do feel the pain of others, especially those with whom we are in close relationships.[7] Caregivers of infants, both human and non-human, regulate the stress responses of those infants through attachment relationships.'

Through repeated cycles of interactions in which the child experiences the caregiver as recognising their mental states, the infant develops the capacity to reflect on their own feelings, and also reflect on the mental states of others.[8] This is referred to as 'reflective functioning' or 'mentalizing'. The more someone develops these reflective abilities in their early years, the easier they are likely to find navigating relationships as they grow up. This modern conception has its roots in earlier psychodynamic theory, particularly the work of Bion (see Box 2.2). Finding containment for feelings through these kinds of interactions with a trusted other continues in various forms throughout adult life – including in the therapeutic relationship (see section on Containment later in this chapter).

Box 2.2 Bion and containment

W. R. Bion's conception of emotional containment and of container/contained has been influential on subsequent understandings of how we manage our feelings and get to know ourselves.

Bion captures the infant's world as not wholly blissful, but as sometimes confusing, strange, and with intense feelings. In 'A theory of thinking' (1962) Bion uses the example of an infantile fear of dying or disintegrating to illustrate a process of containment. He writes how 'normal' development follows if the relationship between infant and mother 'permits the infant to project a feeling, say, that it is dying into the mother and to reintroject it after its sojourn [in the mother] has made it tolerable to the infant psyche'.[9] In this case the mother is the 'container' and the infant's anxieties are 'contained'. Conversely, if these projections are repeatedly not accepted, the infant might reintroject 'not a fear of dying made tolerable, but a nameless dread'.

The process of an infant developing their reflective abilities has many influences, including neurodevelopmental factors, wider social circumstances, and the parent's capacity to reflect on their own and others' feelings. This latter dimension is, in turn, influenced by the parent's experiences of being parented. Hence the concept arises of intergenerational patterns of mental health, ranging from being good-enough to cycles of distress and deprivation and everything in between. Fonagy and Allison,[10] drawing on attachment research,[11] explain that when family circumstances are such that the child has 'not benefitted from the opportunity to be understood and thought about in [a good-enough] way by a sensitive caregiver' then the child's development of the capacity to notice and reflect on their own feelings and those of others may be compromised. At the more extreme end, when a child's feelings are repeatedly met with indifference, attack, or neglect (e.g. if their fear is ignored), this can have important adverse effects on the child's emotional development – both in terms of the kinds of templates the child forms of relationships, and also the psychological defences that develop to manage uncontained feelings.

As Winnicott explains, with regard to parent-infant attunement, the parent or carer does not need to get every interaction 'right'; this is neither possible or desirable.[12] In fact, attempting 'perfect' care may be a dynamic more likely to communicate that distress and discomfort cannot be tolerated. With family life, as in therapy, mistakes happen and people get things 'wrong'. These situations potentially offer opportunities for coming to terms with external realities and the ordinary limitations and disappointments of life; as well as providing experiences of repairing relationships after ruptures. Furthermore, Winnicott posits that the disappointment when the other 'gets it wrong' can help the individual with developing a sense of being their own person who is separate from the other[12] – a gradual realisation that *I'm going to have to do something about this myself then, you can't do it all for me.*

Development of the Internal Relational World – Object Relations

Influenced by repeated encounters with caring figures (external 'objects') in our early months and years, we develop – through learning – mental representations of these interpersonal interactions.[13] We develop mental representations of what others and the outside world are felt to be like ('object-representations') in relation to self-representations, which are oriented towards, and influenced by, these representations of others (see Box 2.3).

Box 2.3 Development of object relations theory

'The shadow of the object falls on the ego.' Mourning and Melancholia, Freud[15]

Contained in this 1917 paper are the beginnings of the idea of internal objects. Freud describes how an aspect of the ego can become identified with an external other. The ego is a term for the part of experience felt as 'I'.[16] Later, in his structural model, Freud suggested that as the child grows up, the 'superego' is formed by an aspect of the ego which has adopted parental values (a process referred to as 'internalisation'). The superego influences and is influenced by other aspects of the mind. For example, someone may be described as having a 'harsh' superego if their superego is never satisfied and makes harsh criticisms towards the ego, leaving the ego feeling criticised and inadequate.

Fairbairn (who was introduced in Chapter 1) builds on earlier theorists. He postulates that there are dynamic aspects of the person's mind, which function semi-independently whilst also influencing each other. Similar to aspects of Bowlby's attachment theory approach, Fairbairn describes how, growing up, we develop an internal model of the relationship with our key external 'objects' (i.e. caregivers). Continuing these theoretical ideas, Ogden (1983) postulates that an internal object relationship comprises a pair of 'dynamically unconscious suborganizations of the ego, one identified with the self and the other with the object in the original early object relationship. These aspects of ego stand in a particular relationship to one another, the nature of which is determined by the infant's subjective experience of the early relationship.'[17] Chapter 4 discusses this topic further from a contemporary neuroscience perspective.

Language

The term 'object' links to the language of grammar where in a sentence there is a subject and an object, as in the phrase: 'the object of somebody's affection' (or attention, hate, fear, etc.). The psychodynamic use of the term 'object' derives from early Freudian drive theory as referring to the object of a drive – usually a person or a part of a person. The term has persisted and evolved within the field. Although the word 'object' might initially evoke a notion of a static thing, in psychodynamic therapy the words 'object' and 'object relations' refer to lively dynamics of our inner and interpersonal life.

As Adshead explains, as the infant grows, it is experiences of the *relationship with caregivers*, rather than the memory of any particular caregiver, that influences the natures of our inner object relations.[5] These inner object relations are the underpinnings of fundamental aspects of our lives: how we relate to ourselves and others; how we regulate and respond to our affects and needs and those of others. From a neuroscience perspective, self- and object-representations 'are not "things" stored in memory, but connections among mental units (ideas, memories, sensations, affects, etc.) that "fire together"'.[14]

There is a consensus across psychodynamic schools of thought that our internal world (and our defences and difficulties ensuing from this) is not shaped purely by external experiences. Inner objects are not exact replicas of real caregivers, but how we inwardly experience these relationships and events using our own specific defences. In other words, we interpret the external world in our own highly individualised ways.[18] Some psychoanalytic writers, for example Melanie Klein, emphasise the important role of the infant's constitutional ways of experiencing, interpreting, and relating to the external world, and how these factors may influence how others response to the infant.[19] As Cierpka explains:

'children do not only identify with the caregiver and familial relations and functions, they also influence and change them from the beginning of their lives'.[20] What this means is that, depending on circumstances, the child can contribute to the very relationship patterns they identify with.

Internal object relationships 'are repeated again and again throughout life' (see Clinical Example 2).[13] Object relationships provide a template for subsequent relationships – predicting what others will be like and what position the self will be cast in by others. The roles can be reversed as when an individual, at times, takes up the position of the object-representation and casts others in the role of the self-representation (see Figure 8.2 in Chapter 8). Object relationships also influence the main ways that a person relates to themself. The question of why one would identify with a 'bad' object is discussed further in Chapter 12.

Clinical Example 2 Ben: to illustrate the link between internal and external worlds

Ben was a man in his fifties with a paranoid presentation. He had an internal world dominated by a suspicious, persecutory object in relation to a representation of self as afraid and scrutinised. He had experienced his father as a violent man, and his mother as unable to protect him. In the present day, Ben experienced his neighbours according to the template of his inner persecutory object and felt they were unaccountably hostile towards him – accordingly, he automatically treated them with suspicion, aggression, and put security cameras up. His neighbours felt threatened by him and acted on these feeling by treating the patient in unfriendly and sometimes frankly hostile ways. Ben himself did not recognise this account of his interpersonal behaviour – he experienced himself and his actions as wholly benign and that the neighbours were unaccountably treating him in a terrible way. When Ben moved house because of the 'bad neighbours', the problem soon recurred.

These internal relational dynamics – sometimes referred to as the internal 'drama' – can take myriad forms, including abandoning, rejecting, absent, intrusive, passive, demanding, as well as, of course, many benign forms. If the infant has had 'good-enough' experiences, internal object relationships are likely to be benign, able to be influenced by external reality, and flexible – this is sometimes referred to as a 'good object'. This leads to good mental health, the ability to trust others and make use of caring relationships, and reality testing. However, due to a difficult early environment or constitutional factors or both, this internal world can operate with harsh, critical, internal object relationships which can be persecutory and more rigidly held. What seem like troubling or destructive ways of being in relationships as an adult, can be understood in terms of the context and subjective experiences where they were learnt.

Clinical Example

Clinically, when we talk about object relations, what does this look like? Picking up the example of the dentist Andrew in Clinical Example 1, over time in therapy, it transpired that, time and again, his relationships were dominated by a dynamic between:

- a criticising and rejecting object-representation, associated with feeling of dislike and irritation towards himself and others.
- a rejected, useless, and unlikable self-representation, associated with a feeling of low mood.

This is depicted in Figure 2.1.

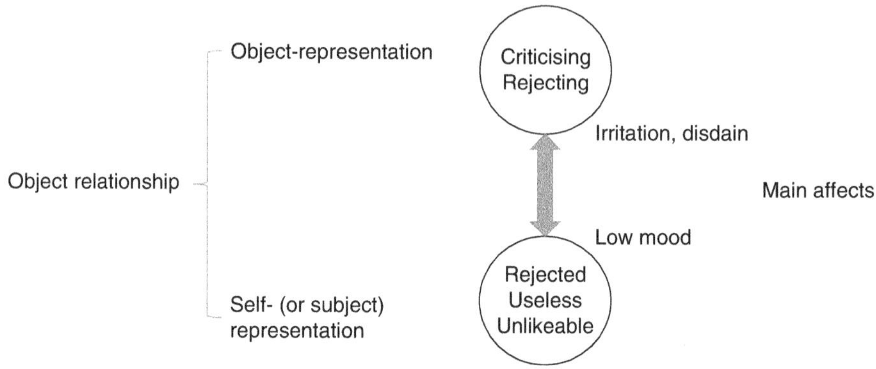

Figure 2.1 Schematic illustration of a key object relationship in operation for Andrew from Clinical Example 1.

Box 2.4 Most of mental functioning operates unconsciously

Thinking about an adult who comes for psychotherapy, significant ways that they interact with themselves and with others are often so automatic as to seem unremarkable or unnoticeable to the patient.

The reason behind this is that most of our inner life, our intentions, and how we relate to our self and others happens automatically, without us being consciously aware. Solms explains that: 'Consciousness ("working memory") is an extremely limited resource, so there is enormous pressure to consolidate and automatise learned solutions to life's problems … only 5% of our goal-directed actions are conscious'.[3] Early interpersonal learning is 'procedural'; as with riding a bike, procedural learning operates unconsciously. (See Chapter 4 for more detail about memory systems.)

These relational patterns may be observed and become clearer through how the patient relates to the therapist (the 'transference' – see later in this chapter).

Note that these dynamics operate largely unconsciously (see Box 2.4). Andrew did not come to therapy saying 'I tend to treat myself in a rejecting way, leaving a part of me feeling useless'. Instead, he was aware of feeling low and suicidal. A patient's presenting feelings are a signal that something is happening in his internal world; feelings may also signal that one or more innate emotional needs are not being met. That is, Andrew's low mood may also signal that his need for nurturing contact with others was not being met. Furthermore, Andrew was not initially aware that the criticism he experienced repeatedly from others (including the therapist) had anything to do with how he perceived or treated others. Instead he told story after story about hostile bosses, and invited discharge from the therapist as he must be a 'hopeless case'.

A patient's feelings and repeated patterns of interpersonal dynamics can give indications as to the underlying internal object relationship. The therapist's observations of these dynamics – and the patient having the space to listen in to himself – provide a way in for the patient to becoming better acquainted with his inner world and his relationships with external others. The steady therapeutic relationship offers a relationship where underlying patterns 'can be thought about and understood in a way that frees people to change'.[21] The theory of this is expanded later in this chapter (and Chapter 4), and the practice in Chapters 7 and 8.

To summarise, under the influence of early childhood relational experiences, transgenerational patterns of relating, social circumstances, and constitutional factors (and the interaction between all these), the individual develops an inner world with internal objects, which operate mostly unconsciously and in relation to each other.

Accommodating to the World As We Find It

No human's development is smooth and without predicaments, difficult periods, or crises. How we negotiate the predicaments we face is strongly influenced by the kinds of relationships we have. Are we generally able to express our needs and feelings and, if so, how are these received and responded to? The infant learns how to manage the inevitable mismatches between his innate needs and the realities of the outside world to make the best out of situations he is faced with (see Box 2.5). Later in life, we continue to learn about how to be in relationships, but the early period is particularly formative for brain development, heightened by the infant's vulnerability and dependence on others.

We develop patterns of responses to manage competing pressures from the external world, our internal objects, and our needs. These responses include learning how to compromise and how to meet these needs symbolically (classically, this is referred to as 'ego functioning'). We learn interpersonal ways of being and acting to get the best out of the world as we experience it, and develop psychological defences to avoid overwhelming emotional pain and distress.[3] In summary, in our early years, we learn templates of 'how to be with the other' that remain and influence us throughout our adult lives.

Box 2.5 Bowlby and attachment theory

Bowlby, working as an analyst during the Second World War, noticed the effects of evacuation on children as they were separated from their caregivers. Using these observations and also the behaviours of very young animals around their caregivers, he developed his attachment theory. This theory was different from the drive theories of Freud in that Bowlby considered that the human infant was primarily relationship seeking – not just for reduction of unpleasant feelings, but because proximity to the caregiver made the infant feel safe and secure. Bowlby theorised that attachment seeking had a basis in evolution and biology in that proximity to a more experienced adult kept the infant safe from environmental dangers.

Bowlby described secure attachment, which was associated with good-enough and responsive caregiving by the adult, and insecure attachment – further divided into disorganised, avoidant, and ambivalent. These attachment styles can be directly observed in children and adults.[22] Attachment style is relatively stable across a person's lifespan, though it is not fixed.[23] Securely attached children seek out care when distressed and can make use of relationships to feel understood and to regulate their feelings. Children with a more avoidant pattern tend to avoid caring figures when distressed and may themselves disconnect from their feelings and indeed appear undisturbed on the surface; however, distressing feelings are likely to intensify as they remain unprocessed and may suddenly and unexpectedly surface before retreating again. Individuals with highly ambivalent attachment 'may seek and then reject help. They are likely to be fearful of asking for help, and this fear can cause increasing arousal and ultimately hostility towards those they are approaching for help'.[5] These patterns can be understood as the infant adapting to get the best out of the relationships he finds himself in.

The Dynamics of Insoluble and Overwhelming Problems

We learn unconscious interpersonal adaptations ('solutions') to problems, even if they do not seemingly work very well. When we are overwhelmed with an insoluble problem and cannot work out how to reconcile core emotional needs with the situation we find ourselves in, the automatic (unconscious) interpersonal 'solutions' we learn will necessarily be inadequate. There are many kinds of attempted solutions. This might involve, for example, learning to retreat from relationships and be as invisible as possible. Other adaptations might include: learning to please others to keep others' affection; using aggression to feel powerful and distanced from vulnerable feelings; or using other defences to provide relief from intense or unacceptable feelings experiences (see later in this chapter).

Although the best adaptation at the time, these 'solutions' may cause difficulties later in life if these ways of being persist and continue to influence us even as external circumstances change. Solms explains the subtle but important point that our inadequate but least-bad 'solutions' to insoluble difficulties *are treated by us as if they do work well.*[3] Hence an adult patient may hold on tightly to a habitual way of operating in the world learnt as a child or infant, even though they may intellectually understand that it currently does not work well and is responsible for present-day distress (see Clinical Example 3). This lack of awareness about relational patterns and difficulty in modifying these is related to a number of factors, including: our 'lack of conscious access to implicit procedures' and associations; our unconscious avoidance of the painful process of getting to know personal patterns that developed in relation to insoluble problems;[14] and fear about doing something different with unknown results.

Clinical Example 3 Anna: holding on to old 'solutions'

Anna, a psychiatric nurse, undertook one-year of weekly therapy. She missed a few early sessions as she felt compelled to take on additional shifts at work, although inwardly she felt completely overwhelmed by her workload. She realised, after some months of therapy, that her way of never showing her needs was driving her into a depression. At work, she felt overwhelmed with the stress and pressure of the job, but she kept this hidden from others, not letting her manager know – hence she kept on being given more work. It transpired that she had learnt this interpersonal 'solution' as a child in the context of being the oldest child in what was experienced as a fragile home environment (her father was frequently admitted to hospital and Anna assumed a caring role). Anna recalled feeling afraid and overwhelmed during her primary school years, with a sense there was no one to depend on. It seemed that it gradually became habitual not to turn to others.

Through repression of her unmet needs, she carried this solution into adulthood as if it did work well. Despite an intellectual understanding of the situation, for many months into the therapy, the notion of any departure from this familiar and unquestioned way of being was unthinkable.

Core Psychodynamic Theory

We now move on from the topic of early development to look at elements of 'classic' psychodynamic theory. This section moves us closer to the dynamics encountered in therapy sessions.

Internal Conflict

The notion of internal dynamic conflict is particularly associated with Freud's topographical model (1900) and structural model (1923).[24] For Freud, the inner world does not run smoothly with 'one mind'. At the heart of Freud's model is a portrayal of how different aspects of the internal world and external reality influence each other and may be in conflict. The essence of this conception continues into modern psychodynamic practice, although schools of thought have subsequently developed the specifics.

There are many kinds of conflict that might emerge. These include conflicts between wanting care versus refusing help; needing to control others versus wanting to submit; or feeling guilty versus blaming others.[20] There may also be a conflict between core emotional needs. A therapist working with an object relations approach would approach unconscious conflict as arising from the dynamics of underlying object relationships and associated defences. In particular, there may be 'conflicts between certain units of self- and object representations'.[25] For example, a person with a controlling/submitting conflict may internally have both sides of this dynamic – an object-representation characterised by the need for control with a linked self-representation characterised by a pattern of submitting. In one mode of operating, a fight for authority and control may dominate the relational scene, with associated fear of being controlled by others and anger if faced with the prospect of being told what to do. In a more passive mode, the self-representation is more to the fore with the person anxious to submit to others and be led, rather than asserting their ideas and risking 'breaking the rules'.[20]

Patients often seek therapy because of their instability or unease with internal conflict, which may manifest as anxiety or another symptom. This idea is discussed further in Chapter 7 (the section on 'Working Through') and Chapter 11 (the section 'Anxiety as a Signal of Internal Conflict'). A premise of psychodynamic therapy is that it is helpful to become more aware of our inner conflicts as this allows us to understand better the meaning of these, which is the starting point for change.

Defence Mechanisms

This section on psychodynamic defences complements and overlaps with the section earlier on 'Accommodations to the World As We Find It'. These related concepts are perhaps best understood as slightly different approaches to the same issue – that of finding psychological safety and survival. Both sections outline the benefits as well as the limitations and side effects of protective mechanisms.

In Freud's affect-trauma model (1885–1897), defences were thought of as being necessary to defend against painful affects coming into consciousness. This concept evolved with the development of the structural theory (1923) (see Box 2.6).

Defences were considered to be mechanisms to minimise inner tension and conflict when the gulf between different aspects of the inner world and external reality was too large to be accommodated without some form of distortion or manoeuvre. A contemporary perspective builds on Freud's 1923 conception, bringing it into the relational realm: defences are still viewed as being about avoiding painful affects, minimising conflict, and regulating distress, but are also to do with accommodating to difficulties in relationships. Defences are psychological configurations (or 'strategies') that operate to help preserve 'a sense of self-esteem in the face of shame and narcissistic vulnerability, ensuring a sense of safety when one feels dangerously threatened by abandonment or other perils, and

Box 2.6 Freud's structural model

The structural theory (1923)[24] is a useful prototype for understanding how there may be conflict between different aspects of the mind. The structural theory describes the tripartite model which is familiar to many and which consists of the 'id', 'ego', and 'superego'.

In this model the 'id' is to do with instinctive 'drives' and the impulse to seek pleasure and avoid pain – this corresponds to a modern conception of innate needs. The ego is to do with thought and action (mostly conscious) and usually operates with rational, reality-based thinking. The ego is in contact with the external world via the senses. According to Freud, the superego is formed by the child's introjection of the parents' values and ways of living and is thought to be the vehicle of conscience. A large part of the superego operates unconsciously.

The ego mediates between the id, superego, and the external world – hence the concept of dynamic conflict: 'The poor ego [...] serves three severe masters and does what it can to bring their claims and demands into harmony with one another...' .[26] When this is not possible, mechanisms of defence come more into operation.

insulating oneself from external dangers ... '.[13] Research using observer ratings has demonstrated that defences are brought into play when an individual is under increased stress.[27,28] However, in some individuals, defences are employed 'as if the danger is always present', inadvertently increasing a person's vulnerability and distress.[29]

Defences may be internally directed, regulating impulses and affects as an aspect of self-regulation, and/or interpersonally directed 'involving others in psychosocial arrangements or collusions for regulating mental balance'.[30] Defences can be thought about as being on a spectrum from 'archaic' to 'neurotic' through to 'mature'. As with most aspects of mental life, defences are thought to operate mostly unconsciously, though as we move into mature defence mechanisms, we have increasing awareness of their operation. As McWilliams writes: 'virtually any psychological process can be used defensively'.[31] Indeed, the topic of psychodynamic defences is a large one, and a detailed account of the various defence mechanisms is beyond the scope of this chapter (see e.g. Vaillant[32] for more information). For clinical practice, rather than learning by rote about many different defences and fitting these to the patient, it may be more attuned to the patient to try get to know their personal ways of trying to maintain equilibrium and avoid distress. Certainly in terms of speaking with patients, Lemma's supervisory advice is helpful: 'It is far more useful clinically to describe in plain language what the patient is trying to do and why they need to do it than to use the shorthand of labels.'[33] Having set this context, we now outline a number of illustrative defences.

Archaic defences (sometimes referred to as 'primitive' defences) refer to defences first used in early development. They may persist into later life as ways of managing marked inner disturbance, particularly when someone lacks the capacity to make use of caring relationships to feel emotionally contained, or when such supports are not available. Examples of archaic defences include splitting, projection, and projective identification – these three important mechanisms are described in more detail in subsequent sections of this chapter (and also in Chapters 13 and 14). Denial is another archaic defence, referring to the distortion of external reality to reduce overwhelming distress – for example, in the aftermath of the death of a relative, a person may not consciously be in contact with the reality that a loved one has died. As a further example, when we hurt or harm another person, we may be in denial about our destructive impact on others to ward off difficult feelings of guilt and the painful realisation that we have hurt someone else. Dissociation can be considered an archaic defence, occurring as a reaction to trauma and serving to protect a person in the moment from unbearably painful or horrific experiences. As McWilliams explains, a drawback of this defence is 'its tendency to [subsequently] operate automatically under conditions in which one's survival is not realistically at risk, and when more discriminating adaptations to threat would extract far less from one's overall functioning'.[31]

Moving on to 'neurotic' defences, a key defence is repression. As illustrated in the case of Anna from earlier (Clinical Example 3), repression refers to the pushing out of awareness of distressing, painful, or conflictual internal experiences (but not to the extent of distorting external reality – that moves into denial). As therapy progressed, Anna became more aware of her needs for others and how and why she avoided expressing her vulnerability in relationships – however, this growing awareness caused her marked anxiety and so, for a period, she continued to repress her inner feelings and her need for others. Repression may be successful for a while – potentially someone's whole life – but the underlying affect or need does not go away. In fact, it may be more likely to intensify by virtue of it being neglected, and at some point it may return either in the original form or in a displaced manner, a phenomenon referred to as 'the return of the repressed'. A patient may suffer but, to paraphrase Tynan, not know that he is 'keeping a secret' from himself.[34] Another neurotic defence is 'reaction formation' – this is the adopting of an opposite position to what one feels or wants, as the original position feels unacceptable or overwhelming. For example, caring for someone else when one actually wishes to be cared for, or showing excessive kindness towards someone whom one dislikes. 'Displacement' refers to the redirection of feelings or intentions away from the original intended recipient on to someone or something else because the original direction was anxiety-provoking in some way. A classic example of this phenomenon is taking our anger out on our loved ones when we come home from work, when the real target of our anger is something or someone at work.

Examples of 'mature' defences include sublimation (the channelling of difficult feelings or wishes into a productive endeavour as a way of managing the feelings), humour, and intellectualisation (assuming an abstract, intellectual approach to protect oneself from difficult emotions).

Vaillant found that the use of mature defences is associated with higher adaptive functioning and that more archaic defence mechanisms are more likely to be associated with difficulties in functioning.[27] Different clinical presentations are associated with particular types of defence usage. For example, splitting, projection, and projective identification are common in someone operating at a borderline developmental level of psychological organisation (see Chapter 13). Through the therapeutic encounter, a patient may become more aware of when their defences come into operation, and what their functions are. Some research suggests that psychodynamic psychotherapy can modify the pattern of defences used from archaic to more mature.[35]

Resistance

Freud's original use of the term resistance was used to describe those dynamics in the patient which specifically oppose the progress of therapy. In 1936, Anna Freud emphasised the extent to which the resistances could provide information about the patient's mental functioning. Thus resistance became an object of analytic study in itself – rather than being something that only gets in the way of therapeutic progress.

Some examples of resistance include: ending therapy prematurely; coming late or missing sessions altogether; silences during sessions or alternatively speaking a lot but with little affect; automatically dismissing all the therapist's interventions as useless or wrong.[36] An alternative but more unobtrusive form of resistance would be to agree with everything the therapist says but not changing anything outwith the sessions. This is not a comprehensive list however as resistances are subtle and individualised because people coming to therapy will all have had their own difficulties with different ways of dealing with them.[37]

There is a close link between resistance and defences. Resistance refers to when, during therapy, existing defences are activated and old ways of being (the adaptations described earlier) are held onto tightly to defend the status quo, particularly when the prospect of change may be on the horizon.

Theoretical Approach to Working with Defences and Resistance

Not all defences are pathological and they are present for a reason. It is only when they are used rigidly or in an overgeneralised manner that they can cause problems. It is therefore important for psychotherapists to respect defences and not to interpret them over enthusiastically or too quickly.

From a theoretical perspective, the task is not to try and 'break through' defences or overcome resistance by force like smashing through a dam. It is likely that many therapists might privately recognise that, from time to time, we have found ourselves trying to prise a patient away from their defences, perhaps due to our feelings of frustration when working long-term with someone who has a rigid defensive structure (Therapist: *'But can't you see how keeping going with this is making you feel worse?'* Patient: *'But you don't understand . . . '*). Such an approach tends to make the person grip on tighter to their defences and increases their resistance to change.

Instead, as Schafer describes, the aim is to repeatedly come alongside the patient to understand as fully as possible the function of the defences and the resistance, and then empathise with this.[38] This approach does not mean colluding with the patient's defences or denying their potential destructive impact on the patient or others – indeed the defences can and should be spoken about explicitly. Continuing the dam metaphor, the task is to take an interest in why the dam needed to be built, why do its contents need to be held back? Clinically this might translate into questions such as: *What does taking the drugs do for you? What would it feel like to change? What would you lose? What is making you stop yourself crying?* Only once the patient understands the function of their defences and feels understood by the therapist, then, very slowly, they may find it possible to contemplate a journey towards change and the anxieties this brings. Chapter 7 on technique expands further on how to apply this theory in practice.

To let go of something that has kept someone going for so long is not easy. Often, letting go of defences requires a sort of mourning process – this might entail facing and coming to terms with regret for the years lost caught up in defensive ways of being; letting go of the hope for an ideal solution; or mourning the loss of the security derived from a certain way of being, even if that way of being is inadequate for present-day circumstances (see Chapter 8 for further on mourning).

Movement between Defensive 'Splitting' and a More Integrated Position

Melanie Klein postulated that the early infant cannot make sense of the world in an integrated and realistic way. Coupled with a lack of object permanence (i.e. the ability to grasp that something still exists even when it is not physically present), relationships are not experienced as having shades of grey. Instead, according to Klein, others and the self may be experienced in extreme polarisations of either all good (associated with loving feelings) or all bad (associated with fear, anger, and hatred). This division into good and bad is called splitting, and the state of mind where splitting occurs is referred to as the 'paranoid-schizoid position'. 'Paranoid' refers to the persecutory 'bad object' and 'schizoid' to the splitting up of whole, realistic relational experiences into polarised 'good' and 'bad' parts. One might see something of this in how a baby's blissful state of peace in himself and security in others can collapse quickly to one of anger and upset at the other who appears to have 'gone bad'; this switch occurring when the mismatch between the baby's needs and what he experiences grows beyond a certain point.

Developmentally, from around the middle of the first year onwards, the infant can begin to move from the split position into a more integrated position where others are experienced as having both 'good' and 'bad' parts, and correspondingly the infant experiences new and more mixed feelings.[39] The infant requires a sufficient experience of security in their world to move into this more integrated position (referred to classically as the 'depressive' position) as it entails the loss of the ideal relationship. The integrated position is more complicated and realistic, with less certainty, and comes with feelings of concern for others and the infant's own impact on them.

To summarise, the 'depressive' position refers to a state of mind capable of integrating various dimensions of experience (it does not refer to a state of depression). The 'paranoid-schizoid' position refers to a state of mind characterised by polarised extremes of perception and experience.

If the infant does not feel secure enough – due to a combination of the infant's environmental experiences and biological vulnerabilities – the paranoid-schizoid position may not be easily left due to the fact it preserves the child's sense of the ideal object relationship. For example, if faced with experiences of abusive or neglectful relationships with caregivers, it may be more bearable for a child to hold on to a sense of relationships at home as being ideal, with all the 'bad' located (projected) elsewhere (e.g. teachers, health or social work professionals). This position protects the child from recognising a position which may be overwhelming: that the people the child depends on for survival are also a source of threat and pain. In some circumstances, paranoid-schizoid functioning may persist as the default state into adulthood even if the external world changes. If a person functions predominantly in the paranoid-schizoid position as an adult, they may fail to see the destructive aspects of others who are initially idealised, leading potentially to falling into relationships that repeat early abusive experiences. Equally, a person may not register the good aspects of others who are experienced as 'all bad' persecuting or abandoning figures – as with Ben in Clinical Example 2. Frequently, experiences of good and bad alternate. Additionally, the person may struggle to derive benefit from caring professionals, with 'no person fully coming up to expectations'.[40]

The post-Kleinian psychoanalyst John Steiner considers that a 'normal developmental' aspect of splitting persists throughout life: all people – not just those with borderline difficulties – move between the paranoid-schizoid and the depressive position, sometimes on a moment-by-moment basis.[41] This can shed some light on our tendency as individuals (and also in groups, organisations, and as countries) to move away from regarding ourselves, other people, and ideas as having many characteristics and as inhabiting 'grey areas'; and to move towards more polarised extremes of perception.[29] Increased stress and anxieties make us more likely to retreat into the paranoid-schizoid position; more inner security permits movement back into the integrated position where 'depressive' realities can be faced and losses mourned. This concept may be useful clinically within a session in tracking how someone (or a group or organisation) is functioning at a basic developmental level and in guiding what kind of responses may be therapeutic. It is one kind of 'analytic listening' (see Chapter 7).

Key Transitions in Life

Whilst tuning into paranoid-schizoid or depressive functioning is one way of understanding and listening to a patient, the therapist can also listen for other developmental transitions. Human emotional and relational development is a complex and interesting business. There are various schemes for characterising the phases or tasks of development such as those by Erikson or Mahler – but the essence is that at different stages in our lives we are more likely to be faced with certain kinds of developmental challenges, tasks, or transitions. More important perhaps than learning all of these by rote, is to recognise the importance of taking an interest in the whole trajectory of someone's life.

In the earliest months, the vulnerable and dependent infant may be faced with 'archaic' and intense anxieties, dependent on the other for emotional and physical containment to help navigate these. A toddler has to negotiate a transition from a 'two-person world' into three-person dynamics – that is, recognising and coming to terms with the reality that there are others who share the attention of their main caring figure (see Box 2.7 on contemporary perspective on the Oedipal situation). There are currents of separation and reunion, such as are encountered at starting nursery or school, and the development of one's own sense of being an individual. Development continues through adolescence with the challenges this brings and the potential for confusion. Moving into adulthood there is the development of sexual maturity to be navigated, and later on the phases of mid and later life which carry the potential for crises to do with a sense of despair, loss of personal potency, or passing time.

With some patients, a useful lens for understanding can be observing when and in what transition, developmental issues may have become 'stuck'. Some patients present with very early developmental difficulties; others are preoccupied with jealousy and being left out. For some adults the adolescent confusions are as alive as they ever were, whilst others have functioned well until transitions such as the birth of their child or the prospect of retirement brought breakdown or the fear of it. Tuning into these undercurrents in someone's presentation may help the therapist to pick up what may be central predicaments and dynamics for the patient; the therapist may then direct the patient's interest and attention to these in the service of understanding what is happening in the present.

Relational Dynamics

We now turn our focus even more on to relational dynamics, with an emphasis on how this aspect of theory supports the practice of psychodynamic psychotherapy. The concepts we will present on relational dynamics come alongside the previous section on 'Core Theory',

Box 2.7 Moving from a dyadic relationship to navigating three-person relationships – a contemporary perspective on Oedipal dynamics

The historical concept of the Oedipus complex was mentioned in the opening chapter. Whilst there are a variety of schools of thought, much modern-day psychotherapy and feminist thought is critical towards Freud's conception of the Oedipus complex, not least for its lack of understanding about girls' development and the notion of castration fears and phantasies. Even one of his most sympathetic biographers Peter Gay concedes: 'Freud seemed to have adopted the position that the little girl is a failed boy, the grown woman a kind of castrated man.'[42]

However, there is relevance to modern-day psychotherapy in Freud's attempt to grasp the dynamics of a key transition – the movement from a 'two-person world' into three-person dynamics. A modern perspective is about the developmental task the infant (regardless of their sex or gender) faces as they grow up in recognising and coming to terms with the reality that there are others (e.g. another parent, siblings) who share the attention of their main caring figure. With three (or more) people there is the need for sharing, for waiting, and the potential to feel left out, excluded, and jealous. Suttie (1935), an early critic of Freud's Oedipus complex, framed the developmental task as noting the infant's initial dependency on the other and that 'the surrender of the sheltered role entails emotional stresses' (p. 239).[4] This role may not be surrendered easily, and in this phase the child may experience and display rage towards the father or indeed anyone else experienced as taking away the mother's love. This can provide a useful lens for understanding the episodic upset of children as they grow up and grapple with the reality that they are not the centre of their mother's world, but one of several loves.

It can take time, but it is considered that most of us are able to navigate through this transition reasonably well, although dealing with feelings of jealousy and exclusion can remain a lifelong work in progress. The parent(s) in a young family have the potential to provide a model for the child about how these difficult feelings can be borne and managed.

The child's ability to work through these issues may be disrupted if one of the parents, say, the child's father, himself has significant issues with feeling left out or excluded. This might lead the father to excessively compete for the mother's attention, and hence not provide a container for the child's feelings of exclusion and rage. This is especially so if a parent acts aggressively in connection to feeling excluded, or alternatively retreats and excludes himself from the family.[43]

and there are many links between the present section and what has come earlier in this chapter. For example, projection has already been mentioned in the context of defences and in the paranoid-schizoid position. Therapeutic 'containment' links conceptually to early infant-parent communication discussed earlier in the section on 'Early Development'; and 'transference' was introduced earlier when discussing how a person's object relations can become observable in the therapy relationship (Box 2.3).

Projection

Projection is where impulses, feelings, or desires that are intense, unacceptable, or particularly distressing to the individual are unconsciously attributed to another person. In other words, what is inside is experienced as coming from the outside. Experiences arising from the self- or object-representation, or both, may be projected. Projection is a phenomenon that all of us can unconsciously employ to varying degrees, particularly at times of increased intensity of feelings or disturbance. More intense and prolonged projection is associated with borderline states. One way of understanding Anna from Clinical Example 3 is that she projects her own vulnerability and needs onto others: *Other are needy, I am not.* This gives her a more acceptable experience of a caring relationship, albeit one where her own needs are not properly attended to.

The term 'projection' can sound obscure, and a helpful analogy is that of an image projector used to transfer (i.e. project) images from film on to a surface. The psychological process of projection is in some ways similar, in that we project a picture onto others (the surface), derived from our own internal world (the film). To extend the analogy further, the projector bulb may be projecting dimly, meaning the surface remains not so different from how it looked originally, with some ambiguity remaining. Or the image may be intensely projected, completely colouring and changing the appearance of the surface projected onto. So it is with psychological projection, that our inner experiences may be projected to greater or lesser degrees onto others.

The person who is the object of an individual's projections may not be random. Particularly in a group situation, an individual may be more likely to project onto someone who appears – even if superficially – a good 'fit' for whatever is being projected. For example, in an opening session of a therapy group, an insecure group member kept on referring to the younger and quieter of the two therapists as looking frightened.

A projection may be partial in that the individual retains some connection to the experience being projected – as when someone is having a bad day and feels irritated and angry, whilst also experiencing others as short-tempered and brittle (when they may actually not be). When employed for more defensive purposes, a projection may be 'clean' with the originator retaining little or no conscious connection with the state being projected. It all resides in the other – as in when someone who harbours underlying guilt about something consciously feels utterly blameless and is convinced everyone else is at fault.

Grosz explains the function and consequences of projection: 'In the short term, this gives us some relief – "I'm not bad, you are." But in denying and projecting a part of ourselves into another, we come to regard these [. . .] aspects as outside of our control'.[44] Furthermore, when projection is employed extensively by an individual (or a group), their ability to reality test is reduced, and the world may appear to be populated by the very things that are felt to be dangerous or unacceptable.

Some experiences that are projected seem counter-intuitive. In therapy, a person might project their 'good' attributes, such as their own abilities, onto the therapist – endowing the therapist with all the resources, whilst the patient assumes a reverent but passive role themselves. It may transpire, for example, that it feels frightening for the person to risk using their abilities, given past experiences of being ignored or rejected when they applied themself. This projecting out of one's inner resources in this way is depleting for the protector, who is cut off from their inner resources and they may have a feeling of 'emptiness'.

Projective Identification

Projection is closely linked with projective identification. When a person more intensely or forcefully projects an inner experience onto another, the other person may pick up on the projections in their own feelings and responses. This phenomenon is known as projective identification – that is, the recipient identifies with what is being projected onto them, or rather *into* them. In ordinary language, it gets 'under the skin'. Like with projection, projective identification is also ubiquitous, especially with more 'mature' forms (see below).

When projection alone is happening, the person being projected onto may be surprised at what is being attributed to them. A person may say to their clinician: 'you dislike me'. When the clinician actually quite likes them, this is projection (without projective identification). This contrasts with a situation when an individual has (unconsciously) interacted with their clinician in such a way that has evoked a feeling of dislike in the clinician towards the patient. This can be seen to have happened in the example of Andrew from Clinical Example 1, when the therapist begins to dread seeing him and has a desire to discharge him.

The infant's communication of his inner feelings and states in early infant-parent dynamics was discussed at the start of this chapter – this mode of communication continues throughout the lifespan. Infants do not have words to communicate feelings but certainly communicate feelings through non-verbal means (tone of voice, style of interactions, body movements and posture, facial expression). A similar process occurs in adults in projective identification, with an addition being the use of more complex language and a wider repertoire of accompanying actions.

Projective identification in therapy can be thought of as being a two-step process. As Gabbard describes:

'1. A self or object representation (often accompanied by an affect state) is projectively disavowed by unconsciously placing it into someone else.
2. The projector exerts interpersonal pressure that nudges the other person to experience or unconsciously identity with that which has been projected.'[13]

In the explanations that follow, it is helpful to hold in mind that projective identification is a process that takes places unconsciously – that is, the feelings and 'aims' involved are not necessarily in our conscious awareness, though it is possible that matters may become more conscious through the course of therapy. Bion describes a mature form of projective identification as being a way of communicating an aspect of our experience that we feel, at some level, we can't manage, in the hope that the other will help us manage it. The aim being 'to introduce into the object a state of mind, as a means of communicating with it about this mental state'.[45] An example is someone in an anxious state in a therapy session who appeals to the therapist to 'do something to help' – in this way the anxious state is communicated to the therapist who themselves palpably start to feel anxious. A response is sought from the other person, the hope being for containment and understanding about the state that is projected (see the next section on 'Containment'). A contemporary perspective is that projective identification is not only about communicating difficult feelings – as with the infant, in adults too, warm and loving feelings may be communicated to the other.[46]

One way to think about projective identification is to consider working in an outpatient clinic. Throughout the clinic you will not feel exactly the same, you may feel sad, anxious, hopeless, protective, and so on depending on who you are with. The evocation of these feelings is not random or mysterious but considered to be stimulated by the patient's use of projective identification and is brought about subliminally by the patient's tone of voice, body language, and topics chosen for discussion. To summarise, if a therapist pays close attention to how they are feeling during a session and notes a feeling that may be foreign to them, this could be projective identification at work.

Bion describes a more defensive and archaic form of projective identification where an internal experience is so unwelcome to a person that they cannot tolerate contact with it. At the far end of this spectrum, with increasing inner disturbance, an experience is projected out forcefully, for immediate relief, to evacuate the feelings. This 'last resort' kind of defence is associated with varying degrees of control of the object (i.e. an external person) in some way to induce the unwanted feelings in the recipient and ensure they remain there. Chapter 16 on anger, aggression, and violence picks up this theme, but a more everyday example might be someone who shouts at reception staff in a hospital. This leaves the staff feeling vulnerable and afraid. In this situation, the staff may be experiencing the kind of feelings that were unacceptable to the person.

When someone projects extensively as their typical mode of operating, this can be depleting for the person who may describe feelings of emptiness.

Whilst the mechanism of projective identification can give a person psychological respite from a troubling aspect of their internal world, like all defences, this defensive form is only partially effective. When an intensely unpleasant experience is forcefully communicated to another person, be that a health professional or one's neighbour, by virtue of the corresponding disturbing feelings evoked in the other, they are likely in turn to attempt to return the projections back to the sender in an unprocessed way. For example, by assuming a restrictive or punitive response (as happened with Ben in Clinical Example 2), or by withdrawing the offer of care (see illustration – Figure 2.2).

Figure 2.2 Projective identification without containment. The patient's feelings of inadequacy are projected onto the therapist who identifies with them concretely, rather than reflecting on the interpersonal processes taking place. Illustration by Robert Bangham.

This process can be the basis for deteriorating relationships between service users and staff across a range of settings. The alternative is for staff to make time to stop and reflect on their relationships with patients as the central activity of care.[47] Reflective practice groups offer a space for staff where projective identifications can be recognised, spoken about, and explored – both to reduce unprocessed staff reactions towards patients and to make use of the identifications as a source of information as to patients' experiences (see Chapter 18 on reflective practice groups).

Containment

Projective identification may have a third step, depending on the reflective capacity and training of the therapist and the support of the working environment:

3. The therapist processes and contains the projected contents and 're-projects back into the patient a modified form of the projection'[45]

Point 3 describes a crucial process known as **containment** (see Figure 2.3). This concept was introduced earlier in this chapter (Box 2.2) when discussing parental responses conducive to the infant recognising and managing their feelings.

Figure 2.3 Containment. The therapist undertakes internal reflective work, which allows her to stay with the patient's overwhelming experiences and offer a space to explore these.
Illustration by Robert Bangham.

In psychotherapy, the therapist's role is to reflect on the projections rather than act on them – to notice how one feels when working with a patient, to label states (internally), and to try to understand where a feeling may be coming from. When a patient's projections are received by a therapist, considerable inner effort and work may be required on the therapist's part to prevent either bouncing the feelings back in a reactive way or avoiding noticing the projections. The 'analytic attitude' of a warm neutrality helps the therapist to preserve a degree of objectivity in order to observe feelings and reflect upon them (see Chapter 7). The therapist attempts to modify the aspect of the patient's experience which he now contains 'by direct mental activity of his own going on inside himself'.[45] Bion referred to this internal work of therapists (and parents and other caring figures) as 'alpha-function' – the detoxifying or digesting of painful and difficult affects and experiences. The link to parent-infant dynamics may be helpful here, in how a parent, when holding a distraught baby, uses his or her inner resources to move from the urge to shout 'Just stop crying!' . . . to the parent inwardly naming how he feels. *I'm feeling angry, this is quite an overwhelming experience.* And then perhaps imagining this is something of how the distressed baby might feel – *this is why the baby is shouting* (crying).

From a theoretical perspective, after the patient's projections have been processed by the therapist, then, the therapist 're-projects back into the patient a modified form of the projection . . . The patient then has the benefit of introjecting not only this part of himself but an aspect of the analyst, the understanding part of the analysts' mind which can then become an *internal* resource for the patient in making sense of himself'.[45]

It is helpful to remember that projection happens through a combination of mostly non-verbal signals – facial expression, posture, tone of voice. Therefore, the therapist employs these means too when communicating back to the patient (re-projecting) something about the patient's feelings. Through projective identification, the therapist's emotional state may likely resonate (or be 'contingent') with the patient's. With inner reflection and processing, the therapist takes care to signal (or 'mark') in her facial expression that she is reflecting back the patient's feelings that belong to him, as opposed to the therapist. This is the difference between a therapist communicating to an anxious patient in her facial expression *I can see you're anxious*, which will likely be containing for the patient; as opposed to the therapist communicating via her facial expression *I'm afraid and anxious*, which may give the patient cause for alarm.[48] Most often the containing approach will be achieved through the therapist carrying on being there and remaining interested in the patient whilst resisting 'acting in' by the therapist through acting in a knee-jerk way on the projections. Gabbard, drawing on Carpy, explains the therapeutic potential in the patient seeing that 'the therapist can tolerate difficult internal states that seemed unbearable to the patient'.[13] Of course, one should not take this too far and attempt to tolerate things at any cost – this would not be containing and could end up in unsafe situations for both parties. Being containing does not mean tolerating being maltreated – holding appropriate boundaries is part of a containing approach (see Chapter 5).

Depending on the patient, this 're-projecting back' of processed feelings may also be through empathising with the patient's feelings, talking about what is happening, simply asking a clarifying question, or possibly by making a fuller interpretation when the timing is right.

For example, to return to Andrew from Clinical Example 1, the therapist felt irritated towards him and felt like discharging him as he was requesting. This would have been an easy way forward; however rather than doing this the therapist held on to this feeling and tried to understand where it might come from. The therapist recognised that the way she felt resonated with Andrew's sense of key early figures as being 'criticising' and 'rejecting'. This understanding helped the therapist to formulate (inwardly) about the nature of Andrew's internal world, considering him to have a critical and rejecting object-representation which was now being projected onto the therapist. Through the therapist's inner processing of the projections, she felt a sense of perspective on her irritation and felt less overtaken by it. Instead of discharging the patient, the therapist talked about what might be going on in Andrew's experience.

In summary, it can be seen that as well as being used as a defence, projective identification can be used as a means of communication. If the therapist is able to contain the projections, they can be used as a means of change.

Who Is in the Therapy Room? The Dynamics of the Transference

Transference refers to when the dynamics from a person's inner object world are unconsciously transferred to a present-day relationship. A useful definition comes from Greenson: 'Transference is [. . .] the experiencing of feelings, drives, attitudes, fantasies and defences towards a person in the present which are inappropriate to that person and are a repetition, a displacement of reactions originating in regard to a significant person of early childhood'.[49] In other words, a person relates to another as if the other were somebody from the person's family of origin. Høglend, in his review on research on transference, summarises a contemporary position in recognising the various influences on adult interpersonal functioning and transference, that is, as being determined by 'a multitude of genetic, biological, and interpersonal factors'.[50] Despite this range of influences on transference, which will vary in importance from person to person, transference, Høglend argues, is nevertheless an extremely useful clinical phenomenon as it reflects 'aspects of the patient's personality functioning (regardless of the developmental origin of these patterns)'.[50]

To varying degrees, the dynamics of transference occur in all relationships, not only in the patient-therapist relationship. The object relations theory behind transference was discussed in detail earlier in this chapter. This section focuses more on theoretical aspects of how transference applies in the therapy context. Thinking about the patient-therapist relationship, the therapist may be experienced not wholly as they 'really' are, but partially according to the patient's inner template of what relationships are like (the patient's internal object relations). So, for example, despite in reality a clinician being supportive and interested, the clinician may be experienced as neglectful with the patient feeling un-cared for, if these are the dynamics of the patient's inner objects (see Figure 2.4).

Transference, like the majority of mental life, operates mostly unconsciously. However, in therapy, there is a unique opportunity for a patient to become more conscious of their transference dynamics. Kernberg, an American analyst, says 'transference analysis consists in the analysis of the reactivation in the here and now of past internalised object relations'.[51] In ordinary human relationships the person to whom the transference is made often acts in such a way as to correct the distorted transference perception. However the lack of opportunity to fully reality test in the psychoanalytic situation allows transference distortions to develop more readily and to be seen clearly.[37]

Crucially, the aim of therapy is to not leave it at that – the transference can be a vital window for *understanding* the relational problems that have brought the patient into

Figure 2.4 Transference. A person seeing his doctor. But who is he seeing?
Illustration by Robert Bangham.

therapy in the first place. Furthermore, if supported by a working alliance (Chapter 8) and a secure therapeutic frame (Chapter 5) the therapeutic relationship may allow these problematic situations to be re-worked in the here and now (see Chapter 8 section: 'The Therapeutic Relationship as a Vehicle for Change'). As a counterbalance to this, it is not the case that the only way for therapists to use the transference is to explicitly discuss the dynamics between the patient and the therapist. Most of the time, the therapist's observations about the transference will help with the therapist's own understanding of the patient and inform what approach to take – not necessarily addressing directly the dynamics within the therapy room.

In psychodynamic therapy, the therapist has a professional, relatively warm, therapeutic stance, whilst attempting not to introduce their own personal issues to the therapy (for a full description of a contemporary psychodynamic 'attitude', see Chapter 7). We note that early analytic views on transference (Freud 1914) led to the conception of the 'blank screen' where the therapist was encouraged to reveal as little of herself as possible in order to amplify the transference relationship – this technique is outdated now.

Our view is that the transference is only useful insomuch as it promotes an understanding of unconscious relational dynamics or offers the potential to work these through. If a 'negative' transference is overly intense and there is not a strong-enough working alliance to provide a viewpoint for the patient and therapist to work together and observe, this can interfere with the patient being able to make use of the therapy. It is clearly not useful if the relationship with the therapist is experienced as a concrete repetition of past traumas. A psychodynamic therapist will adjust their approach according to what is most useful to the patient, attempting to manage the level of affect so that it remains in a working range (see 'A Spectrum of Psychodynamic Technique' section in Chapter 7). There is a limit as to what is possible, and some patients do not find the psychodynamic setting to be helpful, connected to a strong negative transference that cannot be thought about in a productive way (see Chapter 9).

Not every interaction between client and therapist is based on transference. This may sound obvious, but it is an important check to ensure that not everything the patient says is interpreted as transference, as it will not be so. The 'real relationship' refers to those aspects of how the patient experiences the therapist that are grounded in reality. Anna Freud suggested that (1954) ' . . . we should leave room for the realization that patient and therapist are two real people of equal status in a real personal relationship to each other'.[52]

Helpful attributes of the therapist – such as their willingness to listen – may, of course, be 'real'. However, even if the patient comments on a 'real' aspect of the therapist, this does not make it a dead end in terms of close listening. The therapist can still be interested in the meaning to the patient of how the therapeutic relationship is experienced. For example, a patient says he likes coming to see the analyst as she is patient and kind – whilst this may in reality be so, the point is to remain curious about what this means to the patient to find a caring, patient, and kind figure. The therapist might inwardly wonder, does this help understand other 'good objects', or is this a figure that is felt to be missing elsewhere? Is the communication defensive in some way, avoiding more complicated feelings towards the therapist, such as feelings of dislike or perhaps attraction towards the therapist? How is this apparently benign figure of the therapist 'used' – to express feelings to and find understanding, or does the patient struggle to make use of a benign figure?

Countertransference

Countertransference was initially described by Freud. He thought that feelings aroused in the analyst in the course of clinical work were a resistance in the analyst towards the therapeutic work, brought about by the analyst's own unconscious conflicts. Therefore, to counteract this problem, Freud recommended that the analyst undergo analysis in order to reduce their resistance.

Unlike his ideas about transference, Freud never got beyond thinking that countertransference was an obstacle. It took later theorists to develop the idea that it could be a useful tool. Heimann (1950) stressed that an analysis ' . . . is not distinguished by the presence of feelings in one partner, the patient, and absence in the other, the analyst but rather the way feelings are acknowledged and worked with. The analyst's feelings far from merely being a source for trouble are more akin to an instrument of research into the patient's unconscious.'[53] Heimann considered that the unconscious of the patient related to the unconscious of the analyst.

Racker (1957) built on these ideas by explicitly linking countertransference with projective identification. He thought that the analyst's countertransference was brought about by his identification with the patient's internal objects.[54] Racker usefully divided countertransference responses into:

- **concordant responses** – where the therapist identifies with the patient's position and feels the same way that he does. This is the basis of feeling empathy and arises from the therapist's identification with the patient's self-representation.
- **complementary responses** – where the therapist is made to feel like the 'other' in the patient's internal world. This reflects the therapist's identification with the patient's object-representation.

The American analyst Joseph Sandler extended our understanding of complementary countertransference responses through his work on 'role-responsiveness'. Sandler formulates that 'the patient will attempt to actualise the self-object interaction, there is a role for the subject and a role for the object and these will be actualised through manipulation of the therapist in the transference through rapid unconscious signals including non-verbal ones'.[37] In other words, the therapist's countertransference may be a response to the patient's transference – the patient unconsciously invites the therapist (and others) to feel and act in ways familiar to the patient from past experiences in relationships. We are focusing here on countertransference in the context of psychodynamic therapy; however, it is worth noting that countertransference phenomena are experienced in all clinicians and indeed in all interpersonal dynamics.

Countertransference feelings may be clear, such as when, during a session a therapist experiences 'that they are not acting like themselves',[13] perhaps feeling angry, or has the urge to be overly placatory, etc. However, like other aspects of our mental life, countertransference is mostly unconscious so its manifestations may be imperceptible, subtle, or easily overlooked by clinicians. More subtle examples might be the clinician not feeling concerned for the patient or being a few minutes late for a session.

A contemporary approach to countertransference is that this comprises two areas:[55]

1. Feelings and impulses that are due to identifying with the patient's projections or being due to a role the clinician is unconsciously invited into by the patient (projective identification). This area is referred to as 'diagnostic countertransference'.
2. Personal reactions that 'belong' to the therapist that are stirred up by the present work with a patient. For example, a clinician consistently felt frustrated when their patients did not 'get better' quickly This might be connected to an unconscious need to 'heal' their patients. These kinds of responses are more due to the therapist's own internal object relations than to the patient's inner world and, if not processed, can be an obstacle to the work.

In reality, the above two areas often interrelate in the ways particular projections from a patient disturb or affect the therapist by virtue of the therapist being a person too with their own inner world and personal life. For example, when a patient projects an intense feeling of inadequacy into a therapist, alongside the 'pure' identification with the patient, the situation is also likely to arouse other feelings and reactions in the therapist. However, if the therapist has insight into their own inner workings, the therapist may be able to register and work through their own personal responses.

As described in the earlier section on Containment, the therapist does not speak directly from her unprocessed countertransference feelings, that is, one would not say '*I feel fed up and want to discharge you*'. Instead, the therapist would use her countertransference feelings to *inform* an understanding of the present dynamic which then influences what she says or does. When a therapist feels provoked or stirred emotionally and is struggling to think, attempting to make an intervention informed by countertransference feelings is unlikely to be received well by the patient. In this common situation it is best to wait and make time after the session is over to reflect on the dynamics, either by oneself or in supervision; and then in a later session to 'strike whilst the iron is cold'.[56]

A countertransference enactment is when the therapist acts on the countertransference feelings as opposed to processing them – sometimes referred to as the therapist 'acting-in'. To various degrees, all clinicians fall into small countertransference enactments at times. O'Shaughnessy explains that limited, partial acting in is inevitable in clinical work.[57] Gabbard refers to this transference-countertransference dimension of treatment as the '"dance" the patient recreates within the consulting room'.[14] The important thing is for clinicians to try and register the situation and reflect on what is happening. A partial countertransference enactment may have a positive impact if it provides an opportunity for an important dynamic to be understood, articulated, and reworked in the here and now.

Small enactments, which can be reflected on by the therapist, should be distinguished from larger therapist enactments, which, if unrecognised, 'interfere with or even halt the therapeutic process'.[57] The latter kind of re-enactments on the part of the therapist are counterproductive, and include boundary violations which are serious (see also Chapter 5). A literal re-enactment ends up repeating the patients' difficulties and trauma in the therapy relationship rather than thinking about them. Taking up the example again of when a patient projects feelings of inadequacy into the therapist – without adequate processing, the therapist may end up acting on these concretely by becoming convinced they are doing a bad job, or referring the patient on prematurely, or by taking it out directly on the patient in some way (e.g. criticising them). With processing, the therapist might think: *Ah, this awful feeling of inadequacy may be something of what it feels like to be the patient.* Or perhaps, *I am being shown an important experience for the patient which is not yet put into words.* Another difficult projection for a clinician to contain is when a patient projects a feeling of hate. If the therapist responds with outward dislike or a punitive response, rather than putting the dynamic into words or even just inwardly reflecting on what is happening, this will clearly be an 'uncontaining' (and potentially unprofessional) response.

Regular supervision is essential to help with reflecting on the transference and countertransference dynamics. Discussions in supervision can help tease out those aspects of the countertransference that derive from what the patient is bringing, and to work out what they represent. Discussion of the countertransference in supervision also helps to reduce countertransference re-enactments by the therapist. This process requires the supervisor to facilitate discussion without straying into personal therapy for the supervisee. Separately from supervision, personal therapy for the therapist is often valuable and is a major part of training to be a psychodynamic psychotherapist.

Outside the 1:1 therapy setting, countertransference theory can provide an alternative perspective for clinicians on their everyday work. Part 4 discusses further common clinician countertransferences and describes ways to promote reflection in clinicians and teams and protection from large re-enactments, including through the use of reflective practice groups. Some healthcare professionals say they are 'not being empathic' if they experience non-benign feelings in relation to their patients, such as feeling dislike, anger, inadequacy, etc. Without a psychodynamic understanding, many practitioners experience emotions like these at work as unwarranted, unhelpful, potentially unprofessional. However, if it can be understood that these responses, when reflected on, might tell us something about the patient's own inner state, then the clinician can begin to make use of a range of countertransference feelings as a source of empathy. Furthermore, having a framework for understanding their own feelings reduces the need for avoidance of feelings (repression). This works the same with clinicians as patients: avoidance of countertransference feelings is more likely to result in feelings intensifying, increasing the chance of acting-in by the clinician as well as stress or burnout.

To summarise:

1. There are countertransference responses in the therapist which continue throughout the treatment and often change over time.[37]

2. Diagnostic countertransference can offer valuable insight into the patient's internal experiences.
3. Personal countertransference stems from the therapist's own objects and may be an obstacle to therapy if the therapist is not conscious of what they are bringing to the dynamics.[55]
4. 'Constant scrutiny by the [therapist] of variations in [her] feelings and attitudes towards the patient' can lead to increased understanding and containment.[37]
5. Small countertransference enactments are inevitable and may indeed be used constructively in therapy work, if reflected upon and appropriately explored.
6. Across clinicians from all fields, psychodynamic therapists included, there is a risk of larger, unhelpful, countertransference enactments, which may go unrecognised. These can be minimised and recognised through personal reflection, supervision, reflective practice, and therapy for the therapist.

The Narcissistic Constellation

This section is a brief introduction to the concept of narcissism. This is an important presentation in clinical work. Narcissism is a constellation of certain relational dynamics and defensive manoeuvres. As such, it draws on and integrates a number of key topics from this chapter so far. Confusingly, the term narcissism is used in slightly different ways by different writers. An understanding of narcissism is also complicated by the fact that there may be quite different outward manifestations of a similar underlying narcissistic dynamic. The topic of narcissism is the central theme in Chapter 14, which discusses the role of more extreme narcissistic dynamics in some people who end up in seemingly stuck situations in inpatient settings. In the present chapter, we refer to narcissism as pertaining to when an individual has several interrelated underlying dynamics: a sense of underlying shame and insecurity with respect to their own vulnerability; a fear of depending on others; a pattern of not relating to others as others really are, but as a projection of part of the individual.

In terms of outward symptoms or manifestations of narcissism, we often observe polarities. An individual may require much in the way of external validation and seem overly concerned about factors which signify success such as wealth or beauty; or conversely, the same individual at others times may move into a position of (apparent) self-sufficiency with a denial of need for others. Another common polarity is in how low self-esteem manifests – an individual may appear (superficially or convincingly) over-confident, somewhat grandiose; alternatively, the same person may present as sensitive, insecure, and anxious, perhaps particularly when a fragile sense of confidence has been wounded.[58] Some people with narcissistic dynamics may be more stable in one pole or another. These polarities can be thought of as different sides of the same coin where an underlying problem is related to an internal sense of inadequacy, emptiness, and shame. As McWilliams explains: 'in every vain grandiose narcissist hides a self- conscious and shame-faced child. In every depressed and self- critical narcissist lies a grandiose picture of what the person could or should be.'[59] To a degree, many of these features may seem familiar to all of us, and 'it should be stressed that there is a continuum ranging from healthy narcissism to pathological as we all to a greater or lesser extent need external affirmation'.[59]

Box 2.8 gives further clinical context to narcissism, drawing on the Greek myth of Narcissus.

Box 2.8 Clinical use of the Narcissus myth

Narcissus was a beautiful but vain young man, who rejected the love of the mountain nymph Echo as he did not think she was good enough for him. As a result of his rejection, she pined away and died leaving only her voice behind. As revenge for his behaviour the god Nemesis condemned Narcissus to become entranced with his own reflection in a pool of water and to fall in love with the beautiful youth he could see there, not realising that it was a reflection of himself. He too died of unrequited love as he was unable to tear himself away from the beauty of his reflection. Thus, the notion of the narcissistic person as being epitomised by an appearance of vanity and self-love was born.

A key clinical use of this myth is its illustration of the difficulty in allowing vulnerability in relationships with others, leading to a closed system which doesn't really allow others in, but provides some security. The myth depicts the costs to oneself of this defensive constellation, as well as the impact on others. The myth starts when Narcissus was a young man, and one wonders what had led him to be vain, self-absorbed, and unable to contemplate a relationship with Echo (see the next section on Developmental Theories). Despite his beauty, a part of him may have developed an intense worry about being unlovable. Narcissus's superior position of 'She is not good enough for me' can be understood as a protection against the unconscious anxiety 'I'm not good enough for her.' Or more plainly, *She'll hate me if she gets to know me.* Perhaps his self-love provided some security – albeit at great cost – from feeling wounded by others.

A presentation of grandiosity and apparent self-love can be understood in that it feels safer to 'invest' in oneself, rather than risk the exposure of showing sincere interest in another person, when previously in development this has been a wounding experience.

Developmental Theories

There are several theories about how narcissistic dynamics may develop and, indeed, the journey may vary between people. According to Freud, pathological narcissism came about when, in the face of disappointment with the real external object, one's emotional investment was withdrawn from external objects and was instead bound up largely in the self. Put very simply, this was responsible for the clinical picture of vanity and need for affirmation seen in some people with narcissistic personal traits.

Following Freud's conception of narcissism, Kohut considers it to be the result of a deficit in the earliest relationships. He thinks that the individual suffers from internal feelings of emptiness due to difficulties in the early parent-infant relationship.[60] If the earliest relationship with caregivers is experienced as being unaccepting and contemptuous of their vulnerability then the infant may learn to hide their vulnerabilities and to regard them as shameful. Winnicott termed the 'false self' where the 'real self' is hidden and protected behind an external façade of acceptability. There is, hence, a fear that if they show their real feelings they will be humiliated or rejected.

A related route to a narcissistic way of being may arise when an individual has been related to as a 'narcissistic extension' of their primary caregivers. One simple description is that of a 'pushy parent' who lacks a sense of having achieved, who puts their child forward to do the achieving to benefit vicariously. If this dynamic dominates the relational scene to the exclusion of more benign interactions, this may leave the child with the confusing message that they are valued not for who they are but for who others would like them to be. (See also, for example, Grosz's essay on 'Why too much praise can be bad for your child'.)[44] The more narcissistically disturbed caregivers can experience their infants as indistinguishable from themselves, who they can end up harming as a proxy for harming themselves.[61]

As a counterpoint to the above, Kernberg emphasises constitutional qualities as being important in the configuration of narcissistic difficulties, perceiving the importance in some individuals of an intolerance of frustration and aggressive impulses as being relevant in the aetiology of narcissism.[60]

In summary, an underlying expectation may be that risking intimacy and trust with another will be overly exposing and result in disappointment or emotional wounding, or a frightening sense of absence or deprivation.

Narcissistic Object Relations

Related to the above developmental experiences, a pattern of object relations can develop where an object-representation sets itself above the self-representation and judges the latter critically for being weak, not valuable, and for having needs and vulnerabilities.[17] This dynamic would then explain the sense of inadequacy and shame as an aspect of the self berates another aspect for being useless and can lead to depressive feelings. The internal object may have a somewhat grandiose, self-sufficient character, having picked up a sense of what a person 'should' be like (*needs are bad and weak, they should be hidden . . . I don't have needs*). This internal object is, in a way, attempting to be protective to the person. The internal object's attacks on the subject's needs and vulnerabilities may feel safer than being exposed to the overwhelming anxiety that to show one's true self and neediness would bring rejection from those one relies on. Or perhaps worse, bring them face to face with a sense of absence of care.

These inner object relations can make sense of certain patterns observed in narcissistic interpersonal relations. As stated, a key dynamic here is an individual's fear of depending on others in the sense of really letting someone into their life and risking showing their personal feelings. And yet, the individual's need for love and approval is still there, in fact made stronger through this subtle closing off to others. Through this conflict, a compromise position can emerge. An individual may emotionally keep others in their life at arm's length through a somewhat pressuring style of relating that invites demonstrations of approval from others ('narcissistic control of the object') rather than risking developing more intimate emotional connections. In this way, those around the person may feel that declarations of love or praise are extracted from them rather than freely given. The free space of the other to give or not give is precisely what the individual fears and is attempting to manage and limit. McWilliams captures this phenomenon as 'their need for others is deep, but their love for them is shallow'.[59] The self-psychologist Kohut uses the term 'selfobject' by which he means people in our lives who support our self-esteem by approving of us and affirming us.

One perspective on Andrew, first described in Clinical Example 1, may be that he is suffering from pathological narcissism. He experienced a distant and difficult relationship with his mother. He has low self-esteem – which really means one aspect of the self holds another aspect in contempt. He has a commentary in his mind telling him he is unlikeable, no one wants him. Understandably this has led him to feel low in mood and at times suicidal as he is actively living with an internal attacking object. Chapters 8 and 12 will explain how these dynamics can be approached in psychotherapy.

An Outline of Psychodynamic Approaches to Change – Theory

In this final section we offer a brief introduction to the multi-layered topic of change. Current thinking is that there are multiple mechanisms of change in psychodynamic therapy that operate synergistically, with greater emphasis on one component or another depending on what is the best fit for each patient.[14] Various ideas are introduced here which are picked up in more detail in several sections throughout this book – we have highlighted where to look for more detail.

Psychodynamic therapy regards symptoms as a starting point for exploration – that is, symptoms indicate that something underlying is going on. A basic premise of psychodynamic therapy is to provide a predictable and containing relationship and a 'therapeutic frame' (see Chapter 5). Within this frame there is a therapeutic space which allows a way in to understanding and noticing what is happening unconsciously and why. What basic needs are not being met; what unconscious (automatic) ways of being in relationships are operating that were adaptive in the past but not now; what defences are employed but may be 'failing'?

The psychodynamic space and the therapist encourage the patient through 'free association' to bring aspects of themselves more into awareness (see Chapter 7). Some patients may talk about their dreams, which can sometimes be worked with to understand aspects of unconscious functioning – the theory of dreaming and a practice for working with dreams is described in Chapter 7. Each person finds something different within the therapeutic frame. Whilst one person might find a sense of freedom and play, another might find the space stifling and clam up, afraid of what the therapist wants from them. The therapist listens outwardly and inwardly to verbal and non-verbal material, observing recurring themes and affects (which may be projected), and noticing patterns in interpersonal behaviour, including in the here and now with the therapist (working in the transference). As Solms explains, the underlying object relations and the learning of 'how to be with the other' cannot be brought to mind directly as they are automatic and in implicit memory: 'Therefore, the analyst identifies them indirectly, by bringing to awareness the repetitive patterns of behaviour derived from them.'[3] The relationship with the therapist can be used as a creative setting for working out how a patient interacts with others and with themself, and how things may go awry in the present day – whilst also allowing new ways of being to be 'tried out' and anxieties about doing so explored and understood. Other vehicles of change include the more supportive elements of therapy, the experience of difficult affects being tolerated and therefore made more tolerable, and the generation of meaning (see Chapters 4 and 6).

It takes considerable time and patience from both parties (therapist and patient) for the patient to be able to become more aware of his inner relationships, patterns of being with others, and psychological defences, never mind contemplating changing these. Anxieties arise with the prospect of changing patterns we are attached to and that were once adaptive. A mourning process may be needed to loosen one's grip on old ways of being and of seeking security (see Chapter 8). Sometimes, old grievances may need to be worked through. These developmental processes and new relational learnings are slow, and explain why, from a psychodynamic perspective, therapy takes time, commitment, and multiple sessions.

Concluding Remarks

Ways of behaving in relation to others can be driven by internal object relationships which operate for the most part unconsciously, that is the patient is unaware of what he is doing. Often these object relationships are longstanding and deeply ingrained. It takes time to recognise what might be going on and much more time to make any change in these patterns of relating. Intellectual insight is often not enough to effect lasting change, and other processes – including new experiences in relationships – are often required.

References

1. Hughes K, Bellis MA, Hardcastle KA et al. The effect of multiple adverse childhood experiences on health: a systematic review and meta-analysis. The Lancet Public Health 2017;2(8):e356–66.
2. Papadopoulos RK. Refugees, trauma and adversity-activated development. European Journal of Psychotherapy & Counselling 2007;9(3):301–12.
3. Solms M. The scientific standing of psychoanalysis. BJPsych Int 2018;15(1):5–8.
4. Suttie I. The Origins of Love and Hate. Harmondsworth, Middlesex: Peregrine Books; 1963.
5. Adshead G, Sarkar J. The nature of personality disorder. Advances in Psychiatric Treatment 2012;18(3):162–72.
6. Gallese V. The 'shared manifold' hypothesis. From mirror neurons to empathy. Journal of Consciousness Studies 2001;8(5–6):33–50.
7. Singer T, Seymour B, O'Doherty J et al. Empathy for pain involves the affective but not sensory components of pain. Science 2004;303(5661):1157–62.
8. Bateman AW, Fonagy P. Handbook of Mentalizing in Mental Health Practice. 1st edition. Washington, DC: American Psychiatric Publishing Inc; 2011.
9. Bion W. The psycho-analytic study of thinking. International Journal of Psychoanalysis 1962;43:306–10.
10. Fonagy P, Allison E. What is mentalization? The concept and its foundations in developmental research. In Minding the Child: Mentalization-Based Interventions with Children, Young People and Their Families. New York, NY, US: Routledge/ Taylor & Francis Group; 2012. pp. 11–34.
11. Fonagy P, Steele M, Moran G et al. Measuring the ghost in the nursery: an empirical study of the relation between parents' mental representations of childhood experiences and their infants' security of attachment. J Am Psychoanal Assoc 1993;41(4):957–89.
12. Winnicott DW. Transitional objects and transitional phenomena; a study of the first not-me possession. Int J Psychoanal 1953;34(2):89–97.
13. Gabbard GO. Long-Term Psychodynamic Psychotherapy: A Basic Text. Arlington, VA, US: American Psychiatric Publishing, Inc.; 2010.
14. Gabbard GO, Westen D. Rethinking therapeutic action. The International Journal of Psychoanalysis 2003;84 (4):823–41.
15. Freud S. Mourning and melancholia. In J. Strachey (Ed. & Trans.). In The Standard Edition of the Complete Psychological Works of Sigmund Freud. London: Hogarth Press (original work published 1917); 1957. pp. 237–58.
16. Rycroft C. A Critical Dictionary of Psychoanalysis. Harmondsworth, Middlesex: Penguin; 1968.
17. Ogden TH. The concept of internal object relations. Int J Psychoanal 1983;64 (Pt 2):227–41.
18. Leiper R, Maltby M. The Psychodynamic Approach to Therapeutic Change. London: Sage Publications Ltd; 2004.
19. Ogden TH. Instinct, phantasy, and psychological deep structure. Contemporary Psychoanalysis 1984;20 (4):500–25.
20. Operationalized psychodynamic diagnosis OPD-2: Manual of diagnosis and treatment planning. Ashland, OH, US: Hogrefe & Huber Publishers; 2008.
21. RCPsych. Psychotherapy, counselling, and psychological treatment in the NHS (online leaflet) [Internet]. 2021; Available from www .rcpsych.ac.uk/members/your-faculties/med

ical-psychotherapy/psychotherapy-counselling-and-psychological-treatment-in-the-nhs

22. Ainsworth MDS, Blehar MC, Waters E et al. Patterns of Attachment: A Psychological Study of the Strange Situation. New York: Psychology Press; 2015.
23. Chopik WJ, Edelstein RS, Grimm KJ. Longitudinal changes in attachment orientation over a 59-year period. Journal of Personality and Social Psychology 2019;116(4):598–611.
24. Freud S. The ego and the id. In J. Strachey (Ed. & Trans.). In The Standard Edition of the Complete Psychological Works of Sigmund Freud. London: Hogarth Press (original work published 1923); 1961. pp. 3–66.
25. Kernberg OF. Some implications of object relations theory for psychoanalytic technique. J Am Psychoanal Assoc 1979;27 Suppl:207–39.
26. Freud S. New introductory lectures on psycho-analysis and other works (1932–1936). In J. Strachey (Ed. & Trans.). In Complete Psychological Works of Sigmund Freud. London: Hogarth Press (original work published 1932); 1964.
27. Di Giuseppe M, Perry JC. The hierarchy of defense mechanisms: assessing defensive functioning with the defense mechanisms rating scales Q-sort. Frontiers in Psychology 2021;12:4728.
28. Cramer P. Anger and the use of defense mechanisms in college students. Journal of Personality 1991;59(1):39–55.
29. Bateman A. Defences mechanisms. In Forensic Psychotherapy: Crime, Psychodynamics and the Offender Patient by Christopher Cordess. London: Karnac Books; 1995. pp. 41–52.
30. OPD Task Force, Kernberg OF, Clarkin JF, Cierpka M et al. Operationalized Psychodynamic Diagnostics (OPD), Foundations and Practical Handbook. Seattle: Hogrefe & Huber; 2000.
31. McWilliams N. Secondary defensive processes. In Psychoanalytic Diagnosis, Second Edition: Understanding Personality Structure in the Clinical Process. New York: The Guilford Press; 2011. pp. 126–50.
32. Vaillant GE. Involuntary coping mechanisms: a psychodynamic perspective. Dialogues Clin Neurosci 2011;13(3):366–70.
33. Lemma A. Introduction to the Practice of Psychoanalytic Psychotherapy, 2nd ed. West Sussex: Wiley Blackwell; 2016.
34. Tynan K. The Life of Kenneth Tynan. Phoenix; 1995.
35. Cramer P. Understanding defense mechanisms. Psychodyn Psychiatry 2015;43(4):523–52.
36. Glover E. The Technique of Psycho-Analysis/Edward Glover. London: Baillière, Tindall & Cox; 1955.
37. Sandler J, Dare C, Holder A et al. The Patient and the Analyst: The Basis of the Psychoanalytic Process. 2nd ed. London: Routledge; 1992.
38. Schafer R. The Analytic Attitude. London: Routledge; 1983.
39. Spillius B, Milton J, Garvey P et al. The New Dictionary of Kleinian Thought. London: Routledge; 2011.
40. Klein M. Envy and gratitude. In Envy and Gratitude and Other Works 1946–1963, Eds. M. Masud, R. Khan. London: The Hogarth Press and the Institute of Psycho-Analysis; 1957.
41. Steiner J. The equilibrium between the paranoid-schizoid and the depressive positions. In Clinical Lectures on Klein and Bion, Eds. Anderson R, Segal H. London: Routledge; 1991.
42. Gay P. Freud: A Life for Our Time. Cambridge: Dent; 1988.
43. Perelberg RJ. Murdered Father, Dead Father: Revisiting the Oedipus Complex. New York, NY, US: Routledge/Taylor & Francis Group; 2015.
44. Grosz S. The Examined Life: How We Lose and Find Ourselves. New York, NY, US: W W Norton & Co; 2013.

45. Hinshelwood RD. A Dictionary of Kleinian Thought. Oxford, England: Free Association Books; 1989.

46. McWilliams N. Projection [Internet]. Encyclopedia Britannica [cited 2022 Jan 9]; Available from. www.britannica.com/science/projection-psychology

47. Hinshelwood RD. Abusive help – helping abuse: the psychodynamic impact of severe personality disorder on caring institutions. Crim Behav Ment Health 2002;12(2 Suppl): S20–30.

48. Bateman A, Fonagy P. Psychotherapy for Borderline Personality Disorder: Mentalization Based Treatment. First Edition. Oxford: Oxford University Press; 2009.

49. Greenson R. The Technique and Practice of Psychoanalysis. New York: International Universities Press; 1967.

50. Høglend P. Exploration of the patient-therapist relationship in psychotherapy. AJP 2014;171(10):1056–66.

51. Kernberg OF, Yeomans FE, Clarkin JF et al. Transference focused psychotherapy: overview and update. Int J Psychoanal 2008;89(3):601–20.

52. Freud A. The widening scope of indications for psychoanalysis: discussion. In The Writings of Anna Freud, vol. 4. New York: International Universities Press; 1954. pp. 356–79.

53. Heimann P. On counter-transference. International Journal of Psychoanalysis 1950;31:81.

54. Racker H. The meanings and uses of countertransference. The Psychoanalytic Quarterly 1957;26:303–57.

55. Casement P. Learning from the Patient. New edition. New York: Guilford Publications; 1992.

56. Pine F. Developmental Theory and Clinical Process. New Haven: Yale University Press; 1985.

57. O'Shaughnessy E. Enclaves and excursions. Int J Psychoanal 1992;73 (Pt 4):603–11.

58. Bateman AW. Thick- and thin-skinned organisations and enactment in borderline and narcissistic disorders. Int J Psychoanal 1998;79 (Pt 1):13–25.

59. McWilliams N. Psychoanalytic Diagnosis: Understanding Personality Structure in the Clinical Process. 2nd edition. New York: The Guilford Press; 2011.

60. Russell GA. Narcissism and the narcissistic personality disorder: a comparison of the theories of Kernberg and Kohut. British Journal of Medical Psychology 1985;58 (2):137–48.

61. Welldon EV. Mother, Madonna, Whore: The Idealization and Denigration of Motherhood. 1st edition. London: Routledge; 2018.

Chapter 3

A Brief Description of the Empirical Basis of Psychodynamic Psychotherapy

Table of Contents

Introduction 51
Clinical Trials 52
Duration of Therapy 53
Ongoing Effect in the Post-Termination Phase 53
Psychodynamic Processes 53
Therapist Influences on Outcome 55
General Therapy Competence and Reflective Capacity 55
The Therapist's Multicultural Competence 56
Therapeutic Alliance in Psychodynamic Psychotherapy 57
Rupture and Repair 58
The Empirical Basis of Transference and Countertransference Phenomena 59
Reflection on Perceptions about the Evidence Base 59
Concluding Remarks 60
References 60

Introduction

There is a growing body of research pertaining to the empirical basis of psychodynamic psychotherapy, with contributions from various angles. These include clinical trials, studies of live therapy sessions (process research), transference and countertransference research. Our aim here is to give a readable and clinically relevant brief description of the empirical basis of psychodynamic psychotherapy, making links to other parts of this book where topics are described with more clinical detail.

We start this chapter with a brief review of the clinical trial evidence in psychodynamic therapy. The chapter then turns to a key question: what is therapeutic about psychodynamic psychotherapy? There are likely multiple agents of therapeutic change in psychodynamic psychotherapy (see Chapter 2, section 'An Outline of Psychodynamic Approaches to Change'). The following sections consider the contribution to psychodynamic therapy outcomes of:

- psychodynamic specific technique
- therapist attributes and characteristics
- the therapeutic alliance.

We have separated these concepts for clarity, though in practice we acknowledge that the above are overlapping areas. What is likely is that both 'therapy-specific' and therapist factors contribute to the outcomes seen, with complex interactions between the different contributions they make.[1] Other 'non-specific' therapeutic factors – including a confiding, reliable setting – are discussed further in Chapter 5.

This chapter does not attempt to discuss contributions from neuro-psychoanalysis although these are important (for a review, see e.g. M. L. Solms's 'The Neurobiological Underpinnings of Psychoanalytic Theory and Therapy'[2]). Findings from attachment research have been integrated into Chapter 2; in particular how the quality of early relationships with caregivers predicts future patterns of relating to the self and others.

Clinical Trials

Psychodynamic psychotherapy is a relational approach to effecting changes in the way the individual thinks of themself and how they experience other people. It also helps them to understand themself in relation to other people, both past and present. The premise is that with this intra-psychic change comes with improvement in self-awareness and the capacity to build and maintain healthy relationships, which, in turn, is associated with symptom reduction.

A Cochrane review of 33 studies of short-term (40 sessions or fewer) psychodynamic psychotherapy for common psychiatric presentations found it was significantly more effective than control conditions such as treatment as usual or waiting list (overall effect size 0.71 for general symptom improvement), with benefits generally increasing in the long term.[3]

Psychodynamic psychotherapy is beneficial in those who have interpersonal difficulties.[4–6] In people with significant relational difficulties, in which pervasive impairments in affective, self, and relational functioning are central, meta-analytic evaluation has shown psychodynamic psychotherapies to be effective treatments.[7]

Mullin et al. found that individuals' quality and level of interpersonal functioning significantly improved with large effect size after psychodynamic therapy and that this was significantly and positively related to the number of psychotherapy sessions attended.[8] The participants' self-reported change in symptomatology was also noted to be significantly related to the changes in interpersonal functioning, supporting the idea that improving relational functioning leads to resolution of the difficulties described by psychiatric presentations.

Studies have shown that in adult women with psychiatric presentations and a history of childhood abuse, psychodynamic psychotherapy is effective in improving symptoms, interpersonal relationships, and social role functioning.[5,6]

Psychodynamic psychotherapy (60 sessions over 18 months) has been found in the Tavistock Adult Depression Study to be effective in people with depression who have not found sustained benefit from previous courses of therapy.[9,10] The study found an improvement in both the symptoms of depression and measures of social adjustment. Another study showed that psychodynamic psychotherapy led to improvement in individuals with PTSD including improvements in interpersonal functioning.[11] A study of women with borderline level psychological difficulties found that psychodynamic psychotherapy improved reflective functioning where dialectical behaviour therapy or supportive therapy did not.[12] For a full review of the efficacy of psychodynamic therapy for people with specific psychiatric presentations, see Leichsenring et al. 2014.[13]

Thus, psychodynamic psychotherapy has a proven beneficial impact on the ability to relate to one's self and to others, which has a positive impact on the individual's experience of themself and the world around them.

Duration of Therapy

A key premise in the field of psychodynamic psychotherapy is that intra-psychic changes take time, and that patterns of relating that developed from a young age and have been present for the predominant part of an individual's life would need a substantial period of treatment to shift. Indeed, a meta-analysis in 2011 by Leichsenring and Rabung of long-term psychodynamic psychotherapy for people with complex mental health presentations found that therapy lasting at least a year or 50 sessions was significantly more effective that shorter forms of therapy (between-group effect sizes ranged between 0.44 and 0.68).[14] This is not to say that shorter durations of therapy are ineffective; the Cochrane review of short-term psychodynamic psychotherapies cited earlier (mean of 12–24 sessions once weekly) showed significant improvement in general, somatic, anxiety, and depressive symptoms, as well as interpersonal problems and social adjustment.

Ongoing Effect in the Post-Termination Phase

A range of studies, including longitudinal studies of psychoanalysis and psychodynamic psychotherapy, have shown that positive changes from therapy are often maintained for years after the end of treatment.[15–21] The improvements seen in the Tavistock Adult Depression Study were noted to be evident not at the end of the therapy but in the follow-up period two, three and four years after the treatment ended. These findings that psychodynamic psychotherapy leads not just to symptom reduction but to interpersonal, social, and relational change and that these changes are long-lasting suggest that underlying intra-psychic change may occur in the therapy, rather than just temporary symptom relief. Psychodynamic psychotherapy focuses on the meaning of experiences, including traumatic experiences in individuals' lives, helping them to integrate them into their sense of self[22,23] and it has been shown to increase self-esteem and decrease feelings of inadequacy,[11] thus addressing the disturbances of self. The experience of the self and the way in which we relate to others can have a substantial connection with the experience of psychiatric symptoms such as low mood, feelings of worthlessness, guilt, anxiety, avoidance, and paranoia. So, we can see how changes in the formation and function of internalised mental representations of self and other that occur through psychodynamic psychotherapy can lead to improvements in the symptoms of psychiatric presentations such as depression, anxiety, PTSD, relational disturbance, and difficulties with eating.

To summarise, psychodynamic therapy is effective for a range of presentations. The chapter now turns to examining research into what makes it an effective therapy.

Psychodynamic Processes

Before considering the relationship between use of psychodynamic processes and outcomes, it is helpful to clarify the therapist processes and activities that characterise psychodynamic psychotherapy.

Blagys and Hilsenroth carried out a review of studies of process research that compared the processes of psychodynamic-orientated therapy with cognitive behavioural therapy.[24] Empirical process research examines therapist activity during sessions, by reviewing recordings or transcripts of therapy sessions and analysing these either qualitatively or with a structured tool such as the Psychotherapy Process Q-set (PQS).[25] Blagys and Hilsenroth identified seven core processes which were particularly emphasised in psychodynamic psychotherapy (Box 3.1). The underlying principles and concepts behind these core processes are discussed further in Chapter 4.

Shedler reviewed the literature about the use of these psychodynamic processes in a range of psychological therapies, and how use of these related to treatment outcome.[26] Core psychodynamic processes (as per Box 3.1) were used in a range of therapy approaches, not only psychodynamic therapy, and were associated with successful treatment outcomes.[27,28] Use of psychodynamic processes that predicted a positive therapy outcome included: experiencing and exploring aspects of mental life that are not initially conscious,[29] an emphasis on discussing the patient-therapist relationship,[30] and discussion of interpersonal relations and links with developmental relationships with early caregivers. Thus, there is evidence to suggest that psychodynamic processes are specifically helpful even when used in other treatment modalities.

Box 3.1 Core psychodynamic processes. Blagys and Hilsenroth (2000)[24]

1. Focus on affect and the expression of patients' emotions.
2. Exploration of attempts to avoid distressing thoughts and feelings, or engage in activities that hinder the progress of therapy (representing exploration of defence and resistance).
3. Identification of recurring themes and patterns in patients' actions, thoughts, feelings, experiences, and relationships (these help to define prominent object relationships).
4. Discussion of past experience (in terms of understanding links between past and present experiences).
5. Focus on interpersonal relations.
6. Focus on the therapy relationship (transference and countertransference).
7. Exploration of patients' wishes, dreams, and fantasies.

A focus on the therapy relationship (number 6 in Box 3.1) – otherwise referred to as 'working in the transference' or 'transference work' – is one area of psychodynamic technique which has been particularly studied. For all patients and particularly for patients with more severe interpersonal difficulties, there is a strong probability that their difficulties will be activated during treatment. This may emerge as difficulties with collaboration, avoidance, dependency, and dropout. Contemporary research and clinical practice emphasise a range of therapist activity under the umbrella of transference work, rather than limiting it to 'transference interpretations'. Høglend defines transference work as 'any therapist intervention that points out, refers to, wonders about, or explains the patient's experience of the therapist and the ongoing patient-therapist interaction'.[31] As such, definitions of transference interventions in research and clinical practice cover a range of dimensions, including:

- encouraging the patient to explore their feelings towards the therapy and therapist and what they imagine the therapist feels about them
- addressing important transactions between patient and therapist

- interpreting 'repetitive interpersonal patterns (including relationships to parents) and linking these patterns to transactions between the patient and the therapist' [32]

Transference is discussed further from a clinical perspective in Chapters 7 and 8. In terms of research, a review in 2014 examined more than 30 studies that investigated the relationship between transference work and therapy outcomes, finding that transference interventions had an active impact on the therapy.[31] Overall, there was a large effect size in favour of transference-based treatments over alternate treatments in terms of interpersonal change and personality functioning. The review suggested that low to moderate use of transference interventions was of benefit, perhaps particularly for people with a higher degree of interpersonal difficulties to begin with. A high frequency of transference interventions (defined as six or more per session in one study[33]) was associated with poorer outcomes. Clinically, high use of transference interventions may reflect a defensive use of transference interventions by a therapist who feels uncertain, deskilled, or helpless in the face of unsettling dynamics or a 'negative therapeutic reaction'.

Transference interventions are not inert, and the approach used in many clinical trials of calculating the average outcomes for patients may mask individual patient differences. For example, in a study analysing recordings of psychodynamic therapy for people with a borderline level of psychological organisation, transference interventions tended to have either a positive or an adverse impact on the therapeutic alliance.[34] This reflects the need to consider any intervention in the context of the therapy as a whole, and to tailor the approach to the individual patient. Perhaps particularly with transference interventions, timing may be important, as is taking care to communicate challenging ideas within a climate of empathy, support, and validation.[35]

Therapist Influences on Outcome

What contribution to therapeutic change is to do with attributes of a particular psychodynamic therapist? A number of variables have been examined in studies, including demographics (therapist age, gender); years of experience and level of skill; as well as a therapist's interpersonal qualities and style.

Across therapy modalities, studies suggest that there is a degree of variability in patient outcomes depending on the therapist. In other words, some therapists have better outcomes than others.[36] In recent studies of a range of therapy modalities, including psychodynamic therapy amongst other approaches, it has been proposed that therapist factors account for between 3% and 8% of patient outcomes.[37,38]

Leichsenring and Rabung's meta-analysis of psychodynamic therapy examined whether years of clinical experience affected outcome and they found that there was no significant effect on outcome of the therapy; similarly, age and gender of the therapist did not appear to significantly affect outcomes.[39] As discussed below, the literature suggests that it is the degree of the therapist's general competence and their reflective capacity, alongside the therapist's multicultural competence, that influences clinical outcomes, rather than the duration of a therapist's clinical experience per se.

General Therapy Competence and Reflective Capacity

A study by Cologon et al. found that reflectiveness in the psychodynamic therapist predicts therapeutic effectiveness.[40] This underlines the importance for psychotherapists in developing self-awareness and self-reflective capacity, something gained through the experience of personal therapy which is a component of many psychodynamic trainings. This also emphasises the importance of professional reflective spaces – such as supervision and reflective practice groups – within which therapists can notice dynamics they are a part of, including emerging enactments with the patient.

In keeping with Cologon et al.'s findings, a study by Nissen-Lie of 70 therapists seeing 255 patients in a psychodynamic outpatient service found that 'professional self-doubt' – that is, a positive reflective capacity in the therapist to question their own assumptions and recognise limitations – was linked to better outcomes.[41] This effect was increased when the therapists had higher 'self-affiliation', defined as 'a stable core of tolerance and nurturance in the personal self'. The authors infer that patients may fare better with therapists 'who can allow themselves to report higher levels of self-doubt in their clinical work because of a more acceptant and less attacking way of treating themselves as persons'. When therapists can inhabit a position where they are comfortable with being fallible (see 'depressive position' in Chapter 2), this may be more containing than a position where the therapist is defensively overconfident which could communicate to the patient that vulnerability and mistakes cannot be tolerated.

Extrapolating from studies on non-psychodynamic approaches, facilitative interpersonal skills have been shown to be causally associated with positive therapeutic outcomes.[37] These include verbal fluency, empathy, and the ability to develop an alliance. A consistent finding from the more general literature is that there is greater variation in treatment outcome between therapists when working with patients who have more severe or complex difficulties.[42]

The Therapist's Multicultural Competence

Hayes, surveying the literature for therapies in general (not psychodynamic specifically), found that some studies suggested an increased risk for premature termination of therapy for clients from ethnically diverse backgrounds compared to white clients, whilst other studies did not find such differences.[43] Historically, the psychodynamic field has been largely silent on considering issues of ethnicity within therapy.[44] More recently, there has been an increase in psychoanalytic discursive papers on therapeutic work when the therapist and client are from different backgrounds (further reading within Knight 2013),[44] and consideration of colonial history and its implications for psychodynamic therapy.[45] This chapter now considers two recent relevant quantitative studies and makes links to clinical practice.

Morales et al. studied 19 psychodynamic therapists working with 144 clients.[46] This USA-based study took place in a university clinic providing low-cost, open-ended, psychodynamic therapy in a culturally diverse community. The study used self-report measurement tools to assess the quality of the therapeutic relationship over the course of therapy and whether this varied according to the client's ethnicity. At session three, there was no difference in how white clients or those from ethnically diverse backgrounds rated the quality of the therapeutic relationship. However, over time, from the patients' perspectives, some therapists were able to facilitate the development of the therapeutic alliance with their white clients but not with clients from diverse backgrounds. In contrast, other therapists had stronger alliance growth with clients from diverse backgrounds than with white clients. A third group of therapists were able to facilitate alliance growth with both groups of clients. A final group of therapists showed no growth in therapeutic alliance with either client group. There was no association between development of the therapeutic alliance and the therapists' own ethnicity.

In the second study under consideration here, Hayes et al. studied 36 therapists' work with 228 clients to investigate whether any observed differences in therapist effectiveness were a function of client ethnicity.[36] Therapy outcomes did not differ between white clients and those from ethnically diverse backgrounds – both groups' symptoms improved. The more detailed findings echoed those by Morales in that some therapists had better outcomes in terms of psychological symptoms when working with clients from ethnically diverse groups than with white clients, and vice versa. These findings were not influenced by other therapist factors, including the therapists' ethnicity, gender, age, or years of experience.

Both Morales and Hayes hypothesise the importance of the therapist's 'multicultural competence' in influencing the variability observed between therapists. Multicultural competence involves an approach and attitude that consists of cultural humility on the part of the therapist, picking up on opportunities to discuss the client's culture and their experiences, rather than avoid the topic. Multicultural competence also entails the therapist having knowledge and sensitivity to the cultural backgrounds of patients, including family systems, traditions, and the socio-political history of that culture.[47] Furthermore, it involves consideration of and reflection on the therapist's own biases and assumptions when working with a patient. In a meta-analysis of 15 studies of therapist multicultural competence, patient-rated measures of therapist cultural competence were strongly positively correlated with better treatment outcomes ($r = 0.38$).[48]

The influence of the therapist's multicultural competence is illustrated by a qualitative study based in New York City, USA of 23 clients from ethnic minority backgrounds who were seeing white therapists.[49] The majority of clients believed that the therapists could not understand key aspects of their experiences and subsequently clients avoided broaching racial and cultural issues in the therapy. However, 70% of participants also expressed feeling that racial differences were minimised if the therapist was compassionate, accepting (i.e. possessed good general therapeutic competence), and comfortable discussing racial, ethnic, and cultural issues (good multicultural competence).

Therapeutic Alliance in Psychodynamic Psychotherapy

The therapeutic alliance refers to the trusting, collaborative, and secure aspects of the relationship between patient and therapist, which allows the patient and therapist to work together to effect beneficial change in the patient. Developing a therapeutic alliance within psychodynamic psychotherapy is discussed from a clinical perspective in detail in Chapter 8. The concept of the therapeutic alliance has been a core part of psychodynamic theory and practice since at least the 1950s,[50] and was discussed in Freud's early work.[51] One could argue, therefore, that the therapeutic alliance within psychodynamic psychotherapy should be considered a specific, rather than a non-specific therapeutic factor.

The formation of a good therapeutic alliance is clinically important because psychodynamic therapy has been found to be more effective in the context of a strong therapeutic alliance.[52,53] Therapists' basic interpersonal skills were found to predict the formation of better patient-rated alliances in both short-term and long-term psychodynamic therapy. Carl Rogers identified a number of core conditions that he proposed as being required for a good therapeutic alliance: congruence, unconditional positive regard, and empathy. More recent studies looking at psychological therapies in general have found that empathy and genuineness are core to the development of a good therapeutic alliance.[54,55]

A study by Heinonen et al. in 2014 examined therapist style and outcome in psychoanalysis (i.e. lengthier therapy with more frequent sessions per week) as compared to psychodynamic psychotherapy. Their findings suggested that there may be differences in emphasis in terms of what is beneficial in therapist style in psychoanalysis versus psychodynamic psychotherapy. With psychoanalysis, there was a suggestion that patients did best when their therapists were highly present (i.e. not aloof) combined with being relatively restrained in giving explicit encouragement and affirmation.[56] It is plausible that this finding might relate to more effective working with the 'negative transference' over the longer term, when therapists take such an approach (see the section 'The Negative Transference' in Chapter 7). This contrasted with psychodynamic therapy, when therapists being somewhat more affirming and encouraging *was* associated with better outcomes.

Rupture and Repair

Progressive growth in the therapeutic alliance, without episodes of friction between patient and therapist, is not the only pattern observed when therapy is successful.[57] Relatively frequently there are ruptures in the therapeutic relationship, particularly when the negative transference comes into play. The idea of rupture and repair within therapy was described by Jeremy Safran (see Samstag and Muran, 2019 for a review).[58] There may be 'withdrawal ruptures', where the patient withdraws or retreats from the work (e.g. missed or cancelled sessions or being distant or silent in the sessions); or 'confrontation ruptures', where the patient makes a complaint or expresses dissatisfaction with the therapy or the therapist (such as when, after a number of sessions, a patient gets in touch with a service to say that they want a change in therapist as they are not satisfied with the way the therapy is going). The withdrawal or complaint is a clear communication from the patient and needs to be picked up and thought about with them. If not addressed and worked through it can lead to premature termination of the therapy or poor outcomes if the therapy continues.

However, if ruptures can be negotiated and repaired within the therapy this may be a transformative process for the patient. As Safran et al. explain, the process of rupture-repair within therapy can 'tap into fundamental dilemmas of human existence, such as the negotiation of one's desires with those of another, the struggle to experience oneself authentically as a subject while at the same time recognizing the subjectivity of the other, and the tension between the need for agency versus relatedness'.[59] In particular, Stiles et al. measured the therapeutic alliance, session by session, in a comparative trial of psychodynamic psychotherapy and CBT for people with depression.[60] They defined a subset of courses of therapy (approximately one-third of the total sample) where there was at least one rupture-repair sequence. Participants in the subset with rupture-repair episode(s) averaged larger gains in outcome measures than in courses of therapy where there were no rupture-repair sequences. In this light, the authors concluded that alliance ruptures 'represent opportunities for clients to learn about their problems relating to others, and repairs represent such opportunities having been taken in the here-and-now of the therapeutic relationship'.

It is important to consider the transference and whether this is influencing the patient's experience of the therapist; for example, as perceiving the therapist as cut off and uncaring, critical, or ineffectual. It is however also vital to recognise the part played by the therapist in the rupture, and whether the therapist has 'acted in' due to a countertransference enactment or if something attributable to them personally has contributed. When there are problems in the therapeutic alliance, therapists who respond by persistently making transference interpretations, without also supportively attending to the patient's feelings and taking a more reparative approach, may achieve poorer outcomes.[61] By contrast, 'a thoughtful exploration of transference issues and alliance ruptures may disprove negative interpersonal expectations and strengthen alliance, self-understanding, and ultimately outcome'.[31]

Resolving therapeutic ruptures is not necessarily straightforward because it involves trying to repair something from within. It is therefore a process that may take some time with movement towards repair followed by further rupture and then back towards repair, with associated feelings of vulnerability and defensiveness evoked in both the patient and therapist along the way. Clinical aspects of this topic are discussed further in the section on 'Rupture and Repair' in Chapter 7.

The Empirical Basis of Transference and Countertransference Phenomena

Transference and countertransference are two key elements of psychodynamic theory. Transference has been discussed in Chapter 2, referring to a patient's patterns of feelings, thoughts, perceptions, and behaviour that 'emerge within the therapeutic relationship and reflect aspects of the patient's personality functioning'.[31] The real characteristics of the therapist will also influence how the therapist is perceived by the patient.

Høglend reviewed empirical studies of patients' relationship patterns within therapy and in their everyday lives.[31] Taken together with neuroscience research on autobiographical relationship episodes,[62] Høglend concluded that:

> '... patients' characteristic patterns of thinking and relating to others show an overlap between relationships outside therapy and the therapeutic relationship. Patients often show several or even many transference reactions over the course of treatment.'

Clinicians' countertransference (for definitions see Chapter 2) can be assessed in a structured way by asking clinicians about their emotional responses to the patients they work with. This can be undertaken clinically in an interpersonal dynamics consultation[63] (see Chapter 19) and also in research. Some studies have found that whilst every therapeutic encounter is different and countertransference is not always identical between clinicians, patterns emerge in staff responses depending on the patient's presentation.[64,65] It perhaps goes without saying that countertransference responses are not limited to psychodynamic clinicians, but are experienced in all clinicians.[66]

The observation that 'average expectable countertransference responses'[64] emerge in relation to the same patient adds weight to the theory that these responses carry meaning. These are important findings as the use of countertransference feelings forms a significant part of modern-day psychotherapeutic technique. It is linked closely to transference, projective identification, and object relations theory, as discussed in Chapter 2.

Reflection on Perceptions about the Evidence Base

There is a view – perhaps less common in recent years – that psychodynamic psychotherapy is not evidence-based and is supported only by conjecture or limited case studies. However, this is demonstrably not the case in recent decades. The psychodynamic field has some responsibility for this perception; historically, psychodynamic clinicians and researchers were slow to adopt modern clinical trial methodology, perhaps related to anxieties about subjecting their beliefs and technique to quantitative evaluation, and concerns about nuance that might be lost in such methods. It is interesting that a misconception about a lack of evidence persists in some areas, despite a wealth of research to the contrary, of which this chapter touches on only a small fraction. From its inception with Freud there has been a divergence in views about the clinical and theoretical value of a psychodynamic approach. It has been hypothesised that the exploration of unconscious processes is exposing and uncomfortable and so evokes defences such as denial; equally, Freud and other early clinicians certainly did not get everything right and much astute criticism has been taken on by the field which has contributed to its evolution into contemporary practice. This emphasises the importance of ongoing support and development of relevant and well-designed research into all the different aspects of psychodynamic psychotherapy.

Concluding Remarks

This chapter has aimed to provide a brief, digestible introduction to the empirical basis of psychodynamic psychotherapy. We provided an overview of clinical trial and meta-analytic literature, the summary being that psychodynamic therapy is helpful for a range of presentations, and there are indications of ongoing benefits in the follow-up period. The chapter drew on psychodynamic process research and on studies evaluating the associations between therapist style and attributes and treatment outcomes.

A chapter like this, in places, artificially deconstructs an overall treatment approach and ethos into seemingly separate elements. In practice, a clinician's approach is integrated and tailored to the patient, recognising that no particular intervention or treatment will be helpful for all patients. Reflecting on the application of research findings to clinical practice, Gabbard encourages clinicians to 'continually monitor the impact of interventions and modify the approach accordingly'.[35]

References

1. Lorenzo-Luaces L, DeRubeis RJ. Miles to go before we sleep: advancing the understanding of psychotherapy by modeling complex processes. Cogn Ther Res 2018;42(2):212–7.
2. Solms ML. The Neurobiological Underpinnings of Psychoanalytic Theory and Therapy. Frontiers in Behavioral Neuroscience 2018;12.
3. Abbass AA, Kisely SR, Town JM et al. Short-term psychodynamic psychotherapies for common mental disorders. Cochrane Database of Systematic Reviews 2014;(7).
4. Plakun EM, Shapiro ER. Psychodynamic psychotherapy for PTSD. J Clin Psychiatry 2000;61(10):787–8.
5. Sachsse U, Vogel C, Leichsenring F. Results of psychodynamically oriented trauma-focused inpatient treatment for women with complex posttraumatic stress disorder (PTSD) and borderline personality disorder (BPD). Bull Menninger Clin 2006;70(2):125–44.
6. Vitriol VG, Ballesteros ST, Florenzano RU et al. Evaluation of an outpatient intervention for women with severe depression and a history of childhood trauma. Psychiatr Serv 2009;60(7): 936–42.
7. Keefe JR, McMain SF, McCarthy KS et al. A meta-analysis of psychodynamic treatments for borderline and cluster C personality

disorders. Personal Disord 2020;11 (3):157–69.

8. Mullin ASJ, Hilsenroth MJ, Gold J et al. Changes in object relations over the course of psychodynamic psychotherapy. Clin Psychol Psychother 2017;24(2):501–11.
9. Fonagy P, Rost F, Carlyle J-A et al. Pragmatic randomized controlled trial of long-term psychoanalytic psychotherapy for treatment-resistant depression: the Tavistock Adult Depression Study (TADS). World Psychiatry 2015;14(3):312–21.
10. Taylor D, Carlyle J, McPherson S et al. Tavistock Adult Depression Study (TADS): a randomised controlled trial of psychoanalytic psychotherapy for treatment-resistant/treatment-refractory forms of depression. BMC Psychiatry 2012;12(1):60.
11. Brom D, Kleber RJ, Defares PB. Brief psychotherapy for posttraumatic stress disorders. J Consult Clin Psychol 1989;57 (5):607–12.
12. Levy KN, Meehan KB, Kelly KM et al. Change in attachment patterns and reflective function in a randomized control trial of transference-focused psychotherapy for borderline personality disorder. J Consult Clin Psychol 2006;74 (6):1027–40.
13. Leichsenring F, Klein S, Salzer S. The efficacy of psychodynamic psychotherapy in specific mental disorders: a 2013 update of empirical evidence. Contemporary Psychoanalysis 2014;50(1–2):89–130.
14. Leichsenring F, Rabung S. Long-term psychodynamic psychotherapy in complex mental disorders: update of a meta-analysis. BJP 2011;199(1):15–22.
15. Blomberg J, Lazar A, Sandell R. Long-term outcome of long-term psychoanalytically oriented therapies: first findings of the Stockholm Outcome of Psychotherapy and Psychoanalysis study. Psychotherapy Research 2001;11(4):361–82.
16. Sandell R, Blomberg J, Lazar A et al. Varieties of long-term outcome among patients in psychoanalysis and long-term psychotherapy. A review of findings in the Stockholm Outcome of Psychoanalysis and Psychotherapy Project (STOPP). Int J Psychoanal 2000;81 (Pt 5):921–42.
17. Monsen J, Odland T, Faugli A et al. Personality disorders and psychosocial changes after intensive psychotherapy: a prospective follow-up study of an outpatient psychotherapy project, 5 years after end of treatment. Scand J Psychol 1995;36(3):256–68.
18. Lampe A, Hofmann P, Gast U et al. Long-term course in female survivors of childhood abuse after psychodynamically oriented, trauma-specific inpatient treatment: a naturalistic two-year follow-up. Z Psychosom Med Psychother 2014;60(3):267–82.
19. Knekt P, Lindfors O, Laaksonen MA et al. Quasi-experimental study on the effectiveness of psychoanalysis, long-term and short-term psychotherapy on psychiatric symptoms, work ability and functional capacity during a 5-year follow-up. J Affect Disord 2011;132(1–2):37–47.
20. Knekt P, Lindfors O, Härkänen T et al. Randomized trial on the effectiveness of long-and short-term psychodynamic psychotherapy and solution-focused therapy on psychiatric symptoms during a 3-year follow-up. Psychol Med 2008;38 (5):689–703.
21. Elkjaer H, Kristensen E, Mortensen EL et al. Analytic versus systemic group therapy for women with a history of child sexual abuse: 1-year follow-up of a randomized controlled trial. Psychol Psychother 2014;87(2):191–208.
22. Krupnick JL. Brief psychodynamic treatment of PTSD. J Clin Psychol 2002;58 (8):919–32.
23. Lindy JD. Focal psychoanalytic psychotherapy of posttraumatic stress disorder. In Wilson JP, Raphael B, eds. International Handbook of Traumatic Stress Syndromes. Boston, MA: Springer US; 1993. pp. 803–9.
24. Blagys MD, Hilsenroth MJ. Distinctive features of short-term psychodynamic-interpersonal psychotherapy: a review of the comparative

psychotherapy process literature. Clinical Psychology: Science and Practice 2000;7 (2):167–88.

25. Jones EE. Therapeutic Action: A Guide to Psychoanalytic Therapy. Northvale, N.J: Jason Aronson; 2000.

26. Shedler J. The efficacy of psychodynamic psychotherapy. Am Psychol 2010;65 (2):98–109.

27. Ablon J, Jones E. How expert clinicians' prototypes of an ideal treatment correlate with outcome in psychodynamic and cognitive-behavioral therapy. Psychotherapy Research 1998;8(1):71–83.

28. Jones EE, Pulos SM. Comparing the process in psychodynamic and cognitive-behavioral therapies. J Consult Clin Psychol 1993;61(2):306–16.

29. Castonguay LG, Goldfried MR, Wiser S et al. Predicting the effect of cognitive therapy for depression: a study of unique and common factors. Journal of Consulting and Clinical Psychology 1996;64(3):497–504.

30. Vocisano C, Klein DN, Arnow B et al. Therapist variables that predict symptom change in psychotherapy with chronically depressed outpatients. Psychotherapy: Theory, Research, Practice, Training 2004;41(3):255–65.

31. Høglend P. Exploration of the patient-therapist relationship in psychotherapy. AJP 2014;171(10):1056–66.

32. Høglend P, Amlo S, Marble A et al. Analysis of the patient-therapist relationship in dynamic psychotherapy: an experimental study of transference interpretations. Am J Psychiatry 2006;163 (10):1739–46.

33. Amlo S, Engelstad V, Fossum A et al. Interpretations of the patient-therapist relationship in brief dynamic psychotherapy: effects on long-term mode-specific changes. J Psychother Pract Res 1993;2(4):296–306.

34. Gabbard GO, Horwitz L, Allen JG et al. Transference interpretation in the psychotherapy of borderline patients: a high-risk, high-gain phenomenon. Harvard Review of Psychiatry 1994;2 (2):59–69.

35. Gabbard GO. When is transference work useful in dynamic psychotherapy? AJP 2006;163(10):1667–9.

36. Hayes JA, Owen J, Bieschke KJ. Therapist differences in symptom change with racial/ ethnic minority clients. Psychotherapy 2015;52(3):308–14.

37. Barkham M, Lutz W, Lambert MJ, Saxon D. Therapist effects, effective therapists, and the law of variability. In How and Why Are Some Therapists Better Than Others?: Understanding Therapist Effects, Washington, DC: American Psychological Association; 2017. pp. 13–36.

38. Baldwin S, Imel Z. Therapist effects: Findings and methods. In Lambert M, ed. Bergin and Garfield's Handbook of Psychotherapy and Behavior Change. Hoboken, NJ: Wiley & Sons; 2013. pp. 258–97.

39. Leichsenring F, Rabung S. Effectiveness of long-term psychodynamic psychotherapy: a meta-analysis. The Journal of the American Medical Association 2008;300 (13):1551–65.

40. Cologon J, Schweitzer RD, King R et al. Therapist reflective functioning, therapist attachment style and therapist effectiveness. Adm Policy Ment Health 2017;44(5):614–25.

41. Nissen-Lie HA, Rønnestad MH, Høglend PA et al. Love yourself as a person, doubt yourself as a therapist? Clin Psychol Psychother 2017;24(1):48–60.

42. Saxon D, Barkham M. Patterns of therapist variability: therapist effects and the contribution of patient severity and risk. J Consult Clin Psychol 2012;80 (4):535–46.

43. Hayes JA, McAleavey AA, Castonguay LG et al. Psychotherapists' outcomes with white and racial/ethnic minority clients: first, the good news. Journal of Counseling Psychology 2016;63(3):261–8.

44. Knight ZG. Black client, white therapist: Working with race in psychoanalytic psychotherapy in South Africa. The

International Journal of Psychoanalysis 2013;94(1):17–31.

45. Thomas LK. Empires of mind: colonial history and its implications for counselling and psychotherapy. Psychodynamic Practice 2013;19(2):117–28.

46. Morales K, Keum BT, Kivlighan DM et al. Therapist effects due to client racial/ethnic status when examining linear growth for client- and therapist-rated working alliance and real relationship. Psychotherapy (Chic) 2018;55(1):9–19.

47. Owen J, Leach MM, Wampold B et al. Client and therapist variability in clients' perceptions of their therapists' multicultural competencies. Journal of Counseling Psychology 2011;58(1):1–9.

48. Soto A, Smith TB, Griner D et al. Cultural adaptations and therapist multicultural competence: Two meta-analytic reviews. J Clin Psychol 2018;74(11):1907–23.

49. Chang DF, Yoon P. Ethnic minority clients' perceptions of the significance of race in cross-racial therapy relationships. Psychother Res 2011;21(5):567–82.

50. Zetzel ER. Current concepts of transference. Int J Psychoanal 1956;37(4–5):369–76.

51. Freud S. On the beginning of treatment: further recommendations on the technique of psychoanalysis. In Strachey J, ed. The Standard Edition of the Complete Psychological Works of Sigmund Freud. London: Hogarth Press; 1913. pp. 122–44.

52. Owen J, Hilsenroth MJ. Interaction between alliance and technique in predicting patient outcome during psychodynamic psychotherapy. J Nerv Ment Dis 2011;199(6):384–9.

53. Høglend P, Hersoug AG, Bøgwald K-P et al. Effects of transference work in the context of therapeutic alliance and quality of object relations. J Consult Clin Psychol 2011;79(5):697–706.

54. Nienhuis JB, Owen J, Valentine JC et al. Therapeutic alliance, empathy, and genuineness in individual adult psychotherapy: a meta-analytic review. Psychother Res 2018;28(4):593–605.

55. Castonguay LG, Hill CE, eds. How and Why are Some Therapists Better Than Others?: Understanding Therapist Effects. Illustrated edition. Washington, DC: American Psychological Association; 2017.

56. Heinonen E, Lindfors O, Härkänen T et al. Therapists' professional and personal characteristics as predictors of working alliance in short-term and long-term psychotherapies. Clin Psychol Psychother 2014;21(6):475–94.

57. Ardito RB, Rabellino D. Therapeutic alliance and outcome of psychotherapy: historical excursus, measurements, and prospects for research. Front Psychol 2011;2:270.

58. Samstag LW, Muran JC. Ruptures, repairs, and reflections: contributions of Jeremy Safran. Res Psychother 2019;22 (1):376.

59. Safran JD, Muran JC. Negotiating the Therapeutic Alliance: A Relational Treatment Guide. 1st edition. New York: Guilford Press; 2000.

60. Stiles WB, Glick MJ, Osatuke K et al. Patterns of alliance development and the rupture-repair hypothesis: are productive relationships U-shaped or V-shaped? Journal of Counseling Psychology 2004;51 (1):81–92.

61. Piper WE, Azim HF, Joyce AS et al. Transference interpretations, therapeutic alliance, and outcome in short-term individual psychotherapy. Arch Gen Psychiatry 1991;48(10):946–53.

62. Loughead JW, Luborsky L, Weingarten CP et al. Brain activation during autobiographical relationship episode narratives: a core conflictual relationship theme approach. Psychother Res 2010;20 (3):321–36.

63. Reiss D, Kirtchuk G. Interpersonal dynamics and multidisciplinary teamwork. Advances in Psychiatric Treatment 2009;15 (6):462–9.

64. Betan E, Heim AK, Zittel Conklin C et al. Countertransference phenomena and personality pathology in clinical

practice: an empirical investigation. Am J Psychiatry 2005;162(5):890–8.

65. Colli A, Ferri M. Patient personality and therapist countertransference. Curr Opin Psychiatry 2015;28(1):46–56.

66. Colson DB, Allen JG, Coyne L et al. An anatomy of countertransference: staff reactions to difficult psychiatric hospital patients. Hosp Community Psychiatry 1986;37(9):923–8.

Chapter 4

An Outline of Psychodynamic Psychotherapy

Table of Contents

Introduction 65
What is Psychodynamic Psychotherapy? 65
Various Slants on Psychodynamic Psychotherapy 68
How Does Psychodynamic Psychotherapy Effect Change? 69
The Exploration of the Past 71
The Healing Power of the Narrative 71
Working Through the Transference 72
A New Relational Experience 72
Insights from Neuroscience: Working with Procedural Memory 72
Practical Considerations 75
Brief Psychodynamic Psychotherapy versus Long-Term Therapy 75
Open-Ended Therapy versus Closed Therapy 75
Can Psychodynamic Psychotherapy be Combined with Psychotropic Medications? 76
Concluding Remarks 77

Introduction

In this chapter, we aim to provide a brief overview of psychodynamic psychotherapy: what it is, how it may bring about change, how long therapy may go on for, and how to combine therapy with medication. We pick up key themes from the previous chapters on history, theory and research, and try and convey the essence of a psychodynamic approach. We hope this chapter will be orientating to what follows in later parts of this book.

What is Psychodynamic Psychotherapy?

Psychodynamic psychotherapy is a type of therapy, derived from psychoanalysis. It is a study of how the mind works, emphasising unconscious aspects of human functioning, the central importance of human relationships, and the 'intricate interactions' among the parts of the mind.[1] The term 'dynamic' is used because these processes and relationships are not fixed but are fluid and changeable.

Psychodynamic psychotherapy and psychoanalytic psychotherapy are both derived from psychoanalysis and throughout this book we will use the first two terms interchangeably as there is no clear distinction between them. According to the literature, the main difference between psychoanalysis and psychodynamic psychotherapy is the frequency of sessions. In psychoanalysis, sessions are held between four and five times per week and psychodynamic psychotherapy sessions between one and three times. In addition, psychoanalysts generally advocate use of the couch by the patient to facilitate their 'free association' (see Chapter 1), whereas psychodynamic psychotherapy tends to be conducted face to face. Other than these factors there is little consensus on the difference between the psychodynamic psychotherapy and psychoanalysis.

As psychodynamic psychotherapy and psychoanalysis have developed over the years there has been a shift in thinking. Messer, a contemporary clinician and researcher, summarises this shift as including a lessening of the view that the prime movers of mental life are aggressive and sexual drives; the advent of ego psychology stressing the importance of ego functions (i.e. the need to adapt to one's present environment, including the use of psychological defences); and the primacy of the human need for relatedness leading to the theory of object relations.[2]

We discuss the goals of psychodynamic therapy at some length in Chapter 6, but a brief summary by Messer is useful at this point: 'The goal is to resolve conflicts, overcome interpersonal problems or repair aspects of the self, leading the patient to feel and function better.' In terms of how the patient feels, 'feeling better', from a psychodynamic perspective, is not as straightforward as walking away from a session feeling happier (although, of course, that might happen too). As we discuss in this chapter and throughout this book, within a containing therapeutic relationship, the psychodynamic process supports a patient to recognise and understand aspects of their inner and interpersonal life that are giving rise to their difficulties. As those of us who have been a patient in psychotherapy may attest, this process of becoming more aware of aspects of oneself may be somewhat discomforting, at least for a while, as we become more in touch with warded-off feelings and come to know more about how we operate in relationships. The patient may feel better, but perhaps through becoming more accustomed to experiencing a range of feelings and motives.

In terms of the practice of psychodynamic therapy, we, as therapists, attend particularly to 'the playing out of transference and countertransference; the centrality of the therapeutic relationship or alliance as a key feature that allows therapy to progress and influences its outcome; the clarification and interpretation of resistance and defence; and the attainment of insight through the exploration of feelings, fantasies, and behaviour'.[2] The therapist draws on a spectrum of psychodynamic technique, including supportive, exploratory and interpretative dimensions (see Chapter 7).

Over the decades, a number of different 'schools' of psychodynamic psychotherapy have evolved from psychoanalysis. We discuss these different slants in the following section of this chapter. Firstly, though, we consider the commonalities across these schools that exist in spite of their differences. To understand the basic principles of psychodynamic psychotherapy, it is important to recognise these commonalities, which are considerable. As we introduced in Box 3.1 in Chapter 3, Blagys and Hilsenroth identified seven core therapeutic processes that are particularly emphasised in psychodynamic psychotherapy and which distinguish psychodynamic from a more cognitive behavioural approach.[3] We will now expand briefly on each of these processes, to try and convey the essence of a psychodynamic approach.

Focus on affect and expression of emotion

This dimension to therapy has its roots in early Freudian psychoanalytic approaches. Breuer and Freud posit that psychotherapy allows 'strangulated affect to find a way out through speech'.[4] The therapist has an 'analytic attitude' and listens closely to the patient, to facilitate a therapeutic space for the patient to 'free associate'. This allows the patient to articulate painful, distressing or seemingly unacceptable experiences rather than suppress or repress them (see Chapter 7). The therapist then supports the patient to explore these emerging experiences, which brings the potential for new associations to form to these experiences and new relational learning to take place. For example, in Chapter 11 on depression, we give the example of how a person may suppress their anger, leading to that person eventually exploding with anger in a way that damages relationships. In therapy, they may discover that communicating what they are angry about before anger builds excessively does not necessarily lead to attacks or criticism, but might be a 'healthy' signal that has meaning. This may lead to the patient learning new ways of interacting with himself and others. As Gabbard and Westen explain, 'From an evolutionary perspective, the function of affect is to guide thought and behavior in ways that foster adaptation, and a chronic tendency to avoid specific affects or affect in general ... leaves the individual without an essential compass for navigating life, and particularly social life.'[5]

Exploration of attempts to avoid distressing thoughts and feelings (representing exploration of defence and resistance)

It is not easy to put distressing thoughts and feelings into speech. Psychodynamic theory and practice are particularly interested in psychological defences and the emergence of these during therapy ('resistance'). Rather than seeing defences as an 'oppositional activity' to be overcome, the psychodynamic therapist explores these with the patient and tries to understand what is happening.[6] When a patient's free association halts (or never gets started) and a defence is encountered, the therapist's focus shifts from facilitating expression of the affect to exploring *what it is* about a particular feeling or situation that the patient needs to avoid. Analysis of how and why a patient 'resists' therapy can help the patient to get to know a great deal about themselves, their history and their interpersonal functioning.

Identification of recurring themes and patterns (these will help to define prominent object relationships)

Psychodynamic therapists observe and seek to understand recurrent themes in what the patient 'brings' to the session (i.e. their narrative of thoughts, feelings, and relationship patterns), in order to gradually define the patient's underlying relational world, that is, their object relationships. Object relations refers to unconscious mental representations of self and other that are 'built up over time and reflect dispositions that arise from innate vulnerability and early childhood experience'[7] (see Chapter 2). The neuroscientific substrate of inner object relationships is discussed later in this chapter, in the section on 'Working with Procedural Memory'. A substantial focus of the middle phase of therapy (see Chapter 8) is supporting the patient to develop insight into how they relate to themselves and others, whilst offering opportunities to explore new ways of being in relationships.

Discussion of past experience

The past is discussed, not for its own sake, but with an eye on the patient's present-day predicaments. Discussion of the past can help the patient to, for example: work through 'stuck' issues from earlier in life, where relevant (see section on 'Key Transitions in Life' in Chapter 2); understand and be compassionate towards present-day ways of being; or come to terms with past losses that continue to affect the patient. In practice, the therapist may facilitate movement in focus between past and present or notice the links between them (see discussion of Malan's triangles in Chapter 7).

Focus on interpersonal relations

From a psychodynamic perspective, a patient's difficulties arise substantially out of the nature and quality of the relationships they form with others (and with themselves), hence the detailed interest on relational processes within psychodynamic therapy.

Focus on the therapy relationship (transference and countertransference)

Shedler writes, 'the essence of psychodynamic therapy is exploring those aspects of self that are not fully known, especially as they are manifested and potentially influenced in the therapy relationship'.[8] The therapy relationship is central to the psychodynamic approach. There is not one way that the therapy relationship is used, but many. This is a large topic that is explored throughout this book, in particular in the sections 'Working with the Transference' (within Chapter 7) and 'The Therapeutic Relationship as a Vehicle for Change' (within Chapter 8). In brief, this focus ranges from paying attention to the therapeutic alliance, to the therapist observing how the patient relates to the therapist to inform an emerging formulation, to transference interventions, to making use of the countertransference to pick up on what the patient is projecting. The therapy relationship can provide a setting where the patient can explore new ways (or 'procedures', see 'Insights from Neuroscience: Working with Procedural Memory', later in this chapter) of interacting with himself and others.

Exploration of wishes and fantasies

The psychodynamic therapist shows curiosity and interest in whatever the patient brings, including their wishes, fantasies and dreams. Exploration of a person's dream and fantasy life can add an additional dimension to understanding themselves. Freud famously hypothesises that 'the interpretation of dreams is the royal road to a knowledge of the unconscious activities of the mind'.[9] We elaborate an approach to working with unconscious communications such as fantasy and dreams in Chapter 7.

To summarise, a reasonable conclusion is that all forms of psychodynamic psychotherapy draw on these core processes to a greater or lesser extent.

Various Slants on Psychodynamic Psychotherapy

Over the years, various 'schools' of psychodynamic psychotherapy have evolved with different slants on theory and treatment approach. Chapter 1 outlined the evolutions in approach of a number of UK-based clinicians, including Melanie Klein as well as the 'middle group' of Balint, Bowlby, and Winnicott. We will not cover these again here, but will mention now an influential development in the United States. Beginning in the 1960s, Kohut developed 'self psychology' to treat patients who we would now regard as experiencing narcissistic difficulties. He disagreed with Freud on a number of important points. Kohut thought that narcissism was not always a problematic trait and considered a degree of narcissism to be necessary to develop good relations with the self and with others. In self psychology the 'self' is a central concept, and it is thought that a 'good-enough environment' is essential for a child to be able to develop a healthy sense of self. If this does not happen, self-psychologists suggest that a person relies on external people as the only way to feel good about themself. These other external people are called 'selfobjects'. In self psychology, it is considered that therapist empathy is important as the therapist is needed to provide a different type of object to be internalised by the patient.

A common way of conceptualising the range of slants within psychodynamic psychotherapy is between a 'contemporary Freudian' approach at one end of a spectrum and a 'relational psychodynamic' approach at the other. A contemporary Freudian approach emphasises the importance of core Freudian concepts, with some contemporary modifications and extensions of his theories.[10] Ego psychology, developed by Hartmann in the United States in the 1940s, was such a development, the main evolution being a lessening of emphasis on instinct, conflict, and drives and more emphasis on supporting the ego's ability to function and adapt.

A relational psychodynamic approach, by contrast, combines an emphasis on interpersonal relationships (from interpersonal schools of psychoanalysis) with the object relations tradition, in particular the concept of internalised representations of self and other.[11] This approach retains connections to aspects of Freud's approach, but departs from others, particularly Freud's early instinct and drive theories.

Different schools of thought place different emphasis on the relative importance of external versus internal events in the aetiology of a person's difficulties, and on whether aggression is more 'primary' or arises more as secondary to frustration of needs by 'deficits' in the environment. We agree with Leiper and Maltby who suggest that for many contemporary psychodynamic practitioners, these debates seem less important now than they used to: 'the external and internal worlds are now thought of as existing in a dialectical interplay'. Some psychodynamic therapists' practice is more closely linked to one particular contemporary psychodynamic 'school' or another, whilst other therapists are more integrative, adapting their approach depending on the patient.

It is also helpful to recognise that certain modern psychodynamic approaches are manualised, that is, based on a manual which defines a specific theoretical approach and practice. These approaches were often initially designed around a specific presentation such as depression or borderline dynamics, with subsequent wider adoption.[7] They are usually time-limited with a well-defined structure to the phases of therapy. Table 4.1, adapted from Yakeley,[7] summarises some of the main manualised forms of therapy delivered in the UK which are influenced by psychodynamic psychotherapy.

How Does Psychodynamic Psychotherapy Effect Change?

Following on from the practice of psychodynamic psychotherapy, in order to understand this approach better, we now turn to the different theories on how it works, with the caveat that there is currently no consensus on the modes of action. Gabbard and Westen's contemporary position, which we adopt in this book, in that there are likely to be multiple modes of therapeutic action within psychodynamic therapy which interrelate,

Table 4.1 Main psychodynamic therapies available in the UK's National Health Service

Therapy and key clinician(s) associated with its development (year of development)	Core features	Selected clinical indications
Interpersonal therapy Klerman (1996)	This is a brief structured therapy emphasising current interpersonal relationships. Four foci – grief, disputes, deficits and role transition	Depression
Psychodynamic interpersonal therapy Hobson (1985) and Guthrie (1991)	Consists of humanistic and interpersonal elements. Has seven components – explanatory rationale, shared understanding, staying with feelings, focus on difficult feelings, gaining insight, sequencing interventions and making changes	Depression, somatisation
Dynamic interpersonal therapy Lemma (2010)	Brief focused therapy based on distillation of evidence-based manualised psychodynamic approaches, incorporating object relations, attachment and mentalization theory. Focus is on the patient's interpersonal and affective functioning in the 'here and now' of the session	Depression, anxiety
Cognitive analytic therapy Ryle (1982)	Brief therapy which integrates psychoanalytic and cognitive techniques, emphasising patient's relationships. Constructs formulation of difficulties with the patient using 'reciprocal role procedures'. Identifies the defence mechanisms maintaining them – 'traps, dilemmas and snags'	Developed originally for people with neuroses and people with marked relational difficulties with 'borderline' dynamics. Now used more widely
Mentalization-based therapy	Based on attachment theory and integrates psychodynamic, cognitive	Developed originally for the treatment of people with 'borderline' dynamics;

Therapy and key clinician(s) associated with its development (year of development)	Core features	Selected clinical indications
Bateman and Fonagy (mid 2000s)	and relational components. Focus on enhancing mentalization which is the ability to reflect on one's own and others' state of mind	has wider applications
Transference focused psychotherapy Clarkin and Kernberg (mid 2000s)	Consists of individual therapy two or three times a week based on psychoanalytic object relations theory. Focus is on the reactivation and interpretation of the patient's split-off internalised object relations in the transference	Developed for use with people with marked difficulties in relationships, including people with 'borderline' dynamics

Adapted from Yakeley 2014,[7] reproduced with permission from Cambridge University Press.

rather than a single one.[5] However, for clarity, it can be helpful to artificially separate out different possible modes of action. The following headings are adapted from Lemma:[12]

The Exploration of the Past

As described previously, one of Freud's earliest theories of change was that insight could be gained by bringing to the surface traumatic memories which had been repressed. This is likely to be the model that many new therapists have in mind when thinking of psychodynamic psychotherapy and yet is probably the least representative of modern practice. It is certainly true that we are interested in a patient's past experience but not because the past can be altered nor because it can necessarily be blamed for the patient's current situation. Furthermore, through developments in neuroscience, it is now recognised that 'memories are not direct replicas of the past *per se* . . . memory undergoes a complex process of reconstruction during retrieval' and is influenced by a person's present mood state and context.[13] Knowledge of a patient's recollections of childhood is helpful as it can be used to understand and predict how they might form current relationships, including with their therapist. As we have described in Chapter 2, the dynamics of the past can be recreated (unconsciously) in the present.

The Healing Power of the Narrative

Here a narrative is created where exploration of past experiences is considered an important aspect. Patients can experience relief through forming a more coherent narrative of their life, integrating and making sense of various past experiences.

Working Through the Transference

As discussed in Chapter 2, the patient unconsciously projects aspects of himself into the therapist (transference), which may evoke responses in the therapist (countertransference). Using her observation of the transference and drawing on her countertransference, the therapist uses transference interventions to support the patient to be more aware of his projections. She does this using accessible language and in a reflective, open-minded manner (see Chapter 7). In this way the patient may be able to take back his projections. We can use more technical terminology and say this represents the patient moving from 'paranoid-schizoid' to 'depressive position' functioning and in this way the patient becomes more in touch with reality (see Chapter 2 for explanation of these terms).

A New Relational Experience

In the psychotherapy world there is some disagreement as to how the therapy relationship can effect change. Do we as therapists become a transference object, 'thereby allowing the patient to examine patterns of relating in the here and now'?[12] Alternatively, do patients get better 'through involvement with an emotionally responsive therapist who provides a new interpersonal experience that disconfirms negative expectations of others'?[12] Advocates of the latter approach consider it to be important that the patient can find in the therapy relationship a new and different experience which can be internalised by the patient (note, this does not mean the therapist deliberately striving to be an 'ideal' figure, nor does this mean the therapist letting go of a psychodynamic frame with its boundaries). In clinical practice, the two approaches – exploring the transference *and* discovering in the therapy relationship new ways to be – can work synergistically, as we describe in Chapter 8 (in the section 'The Therapeutic Relationship as a Vehicle for Change').

Insights from Neuroscience: Working with Procedural Memory

To recap from Chapter 1, in early psychoanalysis it was postulated that painful memories were kept out of consciousness by repression but that they found expression through neurotic symptoms, dreams, or parapraxes (slips of the tongue). Since then, research into the neuroscience of memory has progressed and there have been some interesting developments. In brief, there are a number of different types of memory system, as depicted in Figure 4.1.

Sensory memory refers to the brief retention (less than a second) of information from touch, sound and vision. Working memory refers to the temporary storage and manipulation of information for complex tasks such as understanding language, learning and reasoning.[15] Focusing specifically on long-term memory, there are two main memory systems: declarative memory (also called explicit memory); and non-declarative memory (also called implicit memory).

Declarative memory is where a person is orientated to themselves, events and facts. The word declarative in this context refers to specific, explicit memories that can be consciously recalled or 'declared'. This type of memory orients us in the world and is not thought to fully develop until around two to three years of age due to the immaturity of the brain systems which mediate this type of memory.[12] Declarative memories can be experienced consciously but require retrieval to become conscious.[16] There are two types of declarative memory. Episodic memory refers to our ability to 'recall and re-experience specific episodes from one's personal past'.[17] Semantic memory is our memory for facts and general

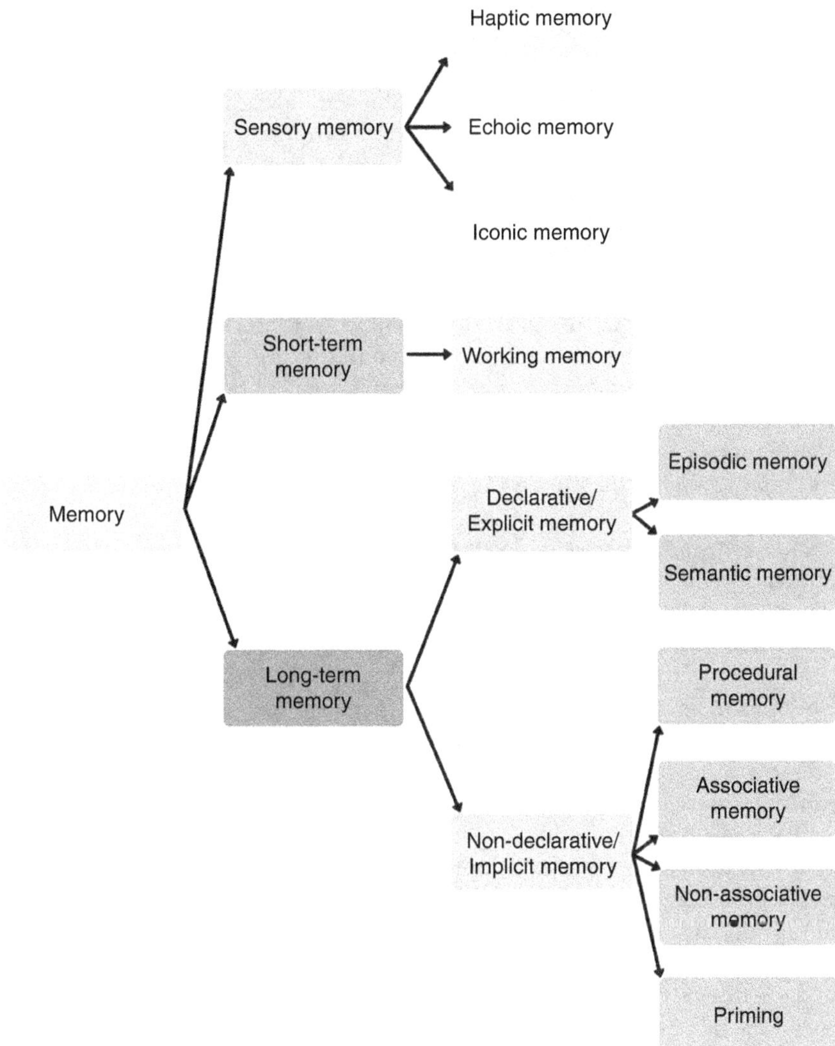

Figure 4.1 Memory classification.
Image from Camino and Güell 2017,[14] reproduced under Creative Commons Attribution License (CC-BY 4.0).

knowledge about the world. It is thought that mechanisms of repression operate partly through brain systems that actively inhibit retrieval of declarative memory.[12,18]

The term non-declarative refers to memory that is accessed unconsciously (i.e. without being 'declared'), and includes memory that may manifest implicitly through certain skills and abilities, or through how a person interacts in relationships. Non-declarative memory consists of four different components, all of them unconscious. We will focus here on two components of non-declarative memory, procedural and associative memory. We don't know for sure, but it is thought that procedural memory is particularly important in the young infant.[12] Procedural memory is non-verbal and non-symbolic. Procedural memory is involved with 'how to do' something, for example how to ride a bike. Importantly this is the main memory system involved in 'how to be in a relationship', although it is likely that the other memory systems also have a role in influencing relationships in older children and adults. This use of procedural memory means that early templates of how relationships work are deeply unconscious yet influential on our everyday lives. These templates are not directly accessible to conscious thought – they have not been 'repressed' as they were never conscious in the first place. Of course, procedural memories continue to form in older children and adults.

Associative memory refers to 'the storage and retrieval of information resulting from an association (i.e., resulting from an association with other information)'.[14] It is likely that many patterns in relationships reflect both 'implicit procedures and associations'.[5] Emotional memory is a sub-type of associative memory. Emotional memory is the process whereby a feeling is evoked by a specific situation. Under extreme stresses such as overwhelming trauma, episodic memory may not be laid down, but there may be emotional memory, and memory of the physical experience of the event (the latter as part of procedural memory).[19]

In adults, as Lemma describes, declarative and non-declarative memory systems interact. For example, constant conscious repetition 'can transform a declarative memory into a procedural one. Likewise, repeated avoidance of particular thoughts or feelings may result in the associated behaviour becoming automated (i.e. procedural)'.[12]

Lemma goes on to explain that procedural memories 'cannot be directly translated into conscious memory and then into words: they can only be known by inference',[12] that is, by observation of interpersonal behaviour. During therapy, these relational templates from procedural memory are re-enacted (played out) in the transference which brings habitual, unconscious ways of relating to the fore. In this *indirect* way, they can be made more conscious, in order to evaluate and modify them. Furthermore, the therapy relationship provides an opportunity for the patient to experience with the therapist new kinds of interaction. If these new kinds of interaction are repeated multiple times, this may lead to the patient learning new procedures of being with others and oneself, that is, new procedural memories forming. This latter mode of change does not rely on verbal interpretation, but more on 'the importance of the quality and the nature of the interactions between the therapist and patient that bypass language itself'.[12] We find this contribution from neuroscience helpful in clarifying the clinical approach described above under the heading 'A New Relational Experience'. (Chapter 6 discusses the role of associative memory networks in a process of therapeutic change.)

Until more research clarifies further the modes of therapeutic action, it would be reasonable to assume that different patients, with help from their therapists, will discover their own way of using therapy. The so-called non-specific therapeutic factors – including the formation of a positive therapeutic alliance – are also important for therapeutic change (these are discussed in Chapters 6 and 8). With some patients, change will be more about making sense of the past, with some it will be more about working in the transference, and with others it will take the form of discovering a new relationship. It is likely that over a course of therapy, all of these modes of action will be important, and also it is likely that different modes of action will predominate in different phases of the therapy.

Practical Considerations

In this final part of this overview chapter, we cover a number of practical considerations to do with psychodynamic therapy.

Brief Psychodynamic Psychotherapy versus Long-Term Therapy

Contrary to popular belief, most psychodynamic therapies carried out in the UK and the USA are relatively brief[20,21] and research has demonstrated that these briefer therapies are effective.[22,23] Generally, we consider a brief therapy to be between 10 and 20 sessions, although this is not a hard and fast rule. Nor do sessions need to be weekly, so a brief therapy can stretch over a longer period of time than might be expected by the number of sessions.

How does a brief therapy differ from a longer term one? According to Dewan et al., specific characteristics of a brief therapy include planning, that is, they are brief by design and not by default and they are focused, with the aim being to achieve smaller change rather than broad personality change.[24] Although this aim may seem modest, we can bear in mind that even a small change in a patient's symptoms and interpersonal functioning can lead to a significant improvement in quality of life. For example, a small change in someone's functioning may make the difference between a person not quite managing to hold down a relationship to just being able to stay in a supportive relationship.

Specific emphases in technique in the briefer therapies include a focus on promoting a positive therapeutic alliance. There is also an emphasis on explicitly identifying the ways in which a patient relates to others and themself that are not helpful in the present day. Then the therapist and patient actively explore ways to manage these relational patterns.

However, brief therapy is not for everyone. It is useful for patients with problems that have a relatively recent onset and who are highly motivated. Patients who have severe difficulties in interpersonal relating or who have more chronic conditions are unlikely to do well with a brief therapy. This is because there will not be enough time to develop trust, develop a formulation, and work things through. As Solms explains, 'the establishment of new procedural memories is a *slow* process.'[25] For these patients, brief contact may carry a risk of making things worse through forming and then disrupting an attachment before meaningful change can take place.

Open-Ended Therapy versus Closed Therapy

Open-ended therapy means that there is no decision at the beginning of therapy as to when it will finish. This mean that ending occurs when the patient feels ready to finish his therapy. For Freud, the goal of psychoanalysis was to convert neurosis into 'ordinary human misery', meaning that there is no magical end point when a patient will feel completely better. Therefore, in practice, the therapist plays an active role in supporting the patient to think through when it is the right time to finish. External factors can also play an influence on when to finish therapy, such as moving house, changing job, retirement, and so on.

Closed therapy means that the duration of therapy is agreed at the outset. Often the end date remains a focus throughout the work, especially in a brief therapy. Once an ending has been agreed it is important to keep to the original arrangement, otherwise the therapist is at risk of enacting boundary transgression. This holding of the frame can be difficult, especially if the patient seems to regress, which can be the case when faced with an ending. Good supervision and support are invaluable in this situation. This book focuses more on closed therapy, which is more common for newer therapists and those working in a publicly-funded setting.

Can Psychodynamic Psychotherapy be Combined with Psychotropic Medications?

We know that psychotherapy can effect change, so can combining therapy with medication result in greater change? Research suggests that a combination of the two may be better than for psychotherapy alone, especially in patients with moderate to severe symptoms.[24] Clinically, for example, psychotropic medication can be used to improve biological depressive symptoms which might otherwise prevent a patient from being able to make use of therapy.

The addition of medication during therapy is not without complications, however. Dewan et al. elegantly paraphrase Freud's 'a cigar is not just a cigar' replacing this famous quote with 'a pill is not just a pill'.[24] What this means is that both patients and their therapists have their individual conscious and unconscious thoughts as to the meaning of medication (see the Clinical Example below). Considering the patient in the first instance, the addition of medication might be experienced by the patient as the therapist thinking them weak and unable to cope or, on the other hand, not prescribing may be experienced by the patient as the therapist being neglectful or depriving. These experiences can, of course, hopefully be articulated as part of the therapy and worked through. In their paper on the placebo effect, McQueen et al.[26] state that 'medicines often have special emotional significance for patients that goes way beyond any realistic appreciation of their physical effects . . . medicines may be invested with notions of food, nourishment and care (Tutter 2006)[27] or in more paranoid contexts, poisoning'.

A therapist might withhold the possibility of medication due to their unconscious feelings of omnipotence or may advise prescription of psychotropic medication in response to countertransference difficulties of feeling helpless and inadequate. Both these positions may be better explored during supervision rather than acted upon straight away. Of course, even if countertransference feelings are implicated this does not mean that it is incorrect to prescribe.

Clinical Example A pill is not just a pill

A young woman Ms A., with poorly controlled diabetes, was referred for psychodynamic assessment as she had not responded well to a previous psychological intervention and antidepressant medication. A psychodynamic assessment elicited that she had experienced her father as a controlling and aggressive man who she had feared and disliked, and she had rebelled against him from her early teens onwards. Further exploration elicited that she had unconsciously equated the regime of insulin taking and attendance at endocrine clinics as being controlling. This experience of feeling controlled had aroused rebellious and oppositional tendencies in her, leading to poor diabetic management.

The same dynamic had happened with the previous therapist when they 'agreed' tasks to undertake in between sessions, and this opposition increased when the previous therapist suggested that Ms A. commence antidepressant medication. Once this was recognised and discussed with Ms A., she became better able to distinguish between her early adverse experience and her experience of current health professionals who were trying to help her.

If medication is indicated, then we need to work out how this should be prescribed. In our experience, prescribing usually works better if carried out by a different person to the therapist as the act of prescribing can interfere with the unfolding of the therapeutic relationship and make it more complicated. Moving from a two-person to a three-person relationship can however increase the potential for splitting, especially if the patient's characteristic defensive processes already involve splitting, as with the dynamics of borderline states of mind (see Chapter 13). In the latter situation, good communication between the therapist and prescriber is essential. There may in fact be the potential for positive therapeutic change if the therapist and the prescriber can work together and act in a consistent way, thus providing what may be a new experience of a 'parental couple' working together and holding the patient in mind.

Finally, it is of interest that when general clinicians (i.e. non-psychotherapists) are seeing patients but not providing formal therapy, the importance of the therapeutic relationship remains highly significant. A study found that during the treatment of depression using imipramine, over 9% of the variation in self-reported outcome was due to the psychiatrist providing the treatment. The effect of the psychiatrist was nearly three times larger than that for medication.[28] No matter what treatment was prescribed, psychiatrists had a better outcome if they adopted behaviours which promoted a positive alliance.

Concluding Remarks

In this chapter we have described an outline of psychodynamic psychotherapy, drawing on themes from the preceding chapters on history, theory, and research. Psychodynamic psychotherapy is a large subject with a long history and evolution from psychoanalysis, and we have attempted here to give an overview of the essence of a psychodynamic approach. We acknowledged the variation in approaches within the overall field of psychodynamic therapy, from more Freudian to more relational, and between non-manualised and manualised approaches. We also introduced contemporary contributions from neuroscience – particularly in understanding and working with procedural memory. Finally, we discussed practical considerations in terms of therapy duration and the use of medication. We hope that this will be orientating for later chapters which go into various dimensions of psychodynamic psychotherapy in more depth.

References

1. Messer SB, Kaslow NJ. Essential Psychotherapies, Fourth Edition: Theory and Practice. New York: Guilford Publications; 2019.
2. Messer SB. Psychoanalytic and psychodynamic therapies: long term and short term. In Cautin RL, Lilienfeld SO, eds. The Encyclopedia of Clinical Psychology. New York: John Wiley & Sons, Ltd; 2015. pp. 1–9.
3. Blagys MD, Hilsenroth MJ. Distinctive features of short-term psychodynamic-interpersonal psychotherapy: a review of the comparative psychotherapy process literature. Clinical Psychology: Science and Practice 2000;7 (2):167–88.
4. Breuer J, Freud S. On the psychical mechanism of hysterical phenomena: preliminary communication from studies on hysteria. In The Standard Edition of the Complete Psychological Works of Sigmund Freud, *Volume 2: Studies on Hysteria.* London: Hogarth Press; 1893. pp. 1–17.
5. Gabbard GO, Westen D. Rethinking therapeutic action. The International Journal of Psychoanalysis 2003;84 (4):823–41.

6. Schafer R. The Analytic Attitude. London: Routledge; 1983.
7. Yakeley J. Psychodynamic psychotherapy: developing the evidence base. Advances in Psychiatric Treatment 2014;20(4):269–79.
8. Shedler J. The efficacy of psychodynamic psychotherapy. American Psychologist 2010;65(2):98–109.
9. Freud S. The Interpretation of Dreams. London: Hogarth Press (original work published 1900); 1953.
10. Wolitzky D. Contemporary Freudian psychoanalytic psychotherapy. In Essential Psychotherapies, Fourth Edition: Theory and Practice. New York: Guilford Publications; 2019. pp. 35–70.
11. Curtis R. Relational psychoanalytic/ psychodynamic psychotherapy. In Essential Psychotherapies, Fourth Edition: Theory and Practice. New York: Guilford Publications; 2019. pp. 71–108.
12. Lemma A. Introduction to the Practice of Psychoanalytic Psychotherapy, 2nd ed. Chichester: Wiley Blackwell; 2016.
13. Brenneis CB. The analytic present in psychoanalytic reconstructions of the historical Past. Journal of the American Psychoanalytic Assoc 1999;47(1):187–201.
14. Camina E, Güell F. The Neuroanatomical, Neurophysiological and Psychological Basis of Memory: Current Models and Their Origins. Frontiers in Pharmacology 2017;8.
15. Baddeley A. Working memory. Science 1992;255(5044):556–9.
16. Gabbard GO. Long-Term Psychodynamic Psychotherapy: A Basic Text. Arlington, VA: American Psychiatric Publishing, Inc.; 2010.
17. Hudson JA, Mayhew EMY, Prabhakar J. Chapter 3 – The development of episodic foresight: emerging concepts and methods. In Benson JB, editor. Advances in Child Development and Behavior. London: Elsevier: 2011.
18. Schmeing JB, Kehyayan A, Kessler H et al. Can the neural basis of repression be studied in the MRI scanner? New insights from two free association paradigms. PLoS One 2013;8(4):e62358.
19. McWilliams N. Secondary defensive processes. In Psychoanalytic Diagnosis, Second Edition: Understanding Personality Structure in the Clinical Process. New York: The Guilford Press; 2011. pp. 126–50.
20. Baldwin SA, Berkeljon A, Atkins DC et al. Rates of change in naturalistic psychotherapy: contrasting dose-effect and good-enough level models of change. Journal of Consulting and Clinical Psychology 2009;77(2):203–11.
21. Olfson M, Marcus SC. National trends in outpatient psychotherapy. American Journal of Psychiatry 2010;167 (12):1456–63.
22. Lambert MJ, Hansen NB, Finch AE. Patient-focused research: using patient outcome data to enhance treatment effects. Journal of Consulting and Clinical Psychology 2001;69(2):159–72.
23. Castonguay L, Barkham M, Lutz W et al. Practice oriented research: approaches and applications. In Handbook of Psychotherapy and Behavior Change. New York: Wiley; 2013. pp. 83–133.
24. Dewan MJ, Steenbarger, BN, Greenberg, RP, eds. The Art and Science of Brief Psychotherapies: An Illustrated Guide, 2nd ed. Arlington, VA: American Psychiatric Publishing, Inc.; 2012.
25. Solms ML. The Neurobiological Underpinnings of Psychoanalytic Theory and Therapy. Frontiers in Behavioral Neuroscience 2018;12.
26. McQueen D, Cohen S, John-Smith PS et al. Rethinking placebo in psychiatry: the range of placebo effects. Advances in Psychiatric Treatment 2013;19(3):162–70.
27. Tutter A. Medication as object. Journal of the American Psychoanalytic Association 2006;54(3):781–804.
28. McKay KM, Imel ZE, Wampold BE. Psychiatrist effects in the psychopharmacological treatment of depression. Journal of Affect Disorders 2006;92(2–3):287–90.

Chapter 5

Framing a Psychodynamic Space

'Psychotherapy has to do with two people playing together. The corollary of this is that where playing is not possible then the work done by the therapist is directed towards bringing the patient from a state of not being able to play into a state of being able to play.'
(Winnicott 1968)[1]

Table of Contents

Introduction 79
Early Encounters with the Setting 81
On the Way into a Session 81
The Analytic Setting 82
Allowing a Psychodynamic Encounter to Unfold 84
The Edges of Sessions 85
The Limits of Therapy 85
Professional Boundaries and Violations 86
Concluding Remarks 87

Introduction

The present chapter focusses on the concept of framing a psychodynamic space. This is the basis for other aspects of psychodynamic therapy to come into play (see Chapter 7 on technique). People come to therapists in various states of mind. Some people have histories of neglect and may carry expectations of something similar happening to them in the therapy room. Some may be looking for help with long-term difficulties. Others may be acutely distressed and not know why. Others still, may come to therapy at the behest of others and may themselves be sceptical about what therapy could offer them. If we think about times when we have been a patient – such as being in hospital, going to the doctor worried about a symptom, or perhaps if we have been in therapy ourselves – we can connect to the swell of anxieties, uncertainties, and psychological defences that may characterise a person's interactions with health services. How we as clinicians present ourselves and organise the caring environment is crucial for a space to be created – or *framed* – where something therapeutic can happen in relation to these initial anxieties.

Winnicott writes about parents creating a 'holding environment'. This refers to a certain quality of receptive and predictable interactions that parents build up in relation to their infants, allowing the infant to feel physically and emotionally held. If this environment is good-enough (not perfect), the developing infant may be able to make use of these interactions with his caregivers to begin to make sense of his own mind and feelings. Clinicians have a similar task in creating a safe 'therapeutic frame' (sometimes referred to as the 'analytic setting') when patients present in distress and looking for help, or present as defended against their distress and their need for help.

The psychoanalyst Michael Parsons compares a therapeutic frame with entering a theatre, a religious building, or a playground.[2] A boundary is crossed, which allows the potential for something different to occur on the inside compared to the outside. On the way into a psychodynamic therapy session, a patient may encounter aspects of a therapeutic frame through the reliable way the meeting is set up, a regular pattern to session times and duration, the therapist's non-judgmental interest in all aspects of the patient, and the opportunity to talk about themself in the presence of an attentive clinician. The patient may then feel secure enough to begin to explore things. What can unfold inside the frame is a 'reliable and professional relationship, where old patterns may be repeated, but can be thought about and understood in a way that frees people to change'.[3]

A key underpinning facet of the psychodynamic therapist's practice is tuning in to the emerging transference (how the patient relates to and experiences the therapist) and the countertransference (the therapist's responses to the patient). This involves the therapist developing a capacity to carefully observe and listen to the patient, whilst also attending to and considering her own 'inner instruments' (her own feelings, impulses, ideas/associations).[4] A reliable therapeutic frame puts up some scaffolding and allows the therapist to be in a frame of mind where they can notice how the patient uses the therapeutic space, as well as listen inwardly to their own responses and associations to the encounter. Parsons calls this state of mind the 'internal analytic setting'.[2] The frame provides the therapist with a structure which allows them to adopt a sense of relative neutrality, both internally and relationally (see Chapter 7 for more detail on the 'The Psychoanalytic Attitude'). It is against this relative neutrality that the patient's idiosyncrasies are brought into relief and, through this, made available for understanding. Conversely, if the frame is not reliable, then the therapist cannot discern the patient's personal style and peculiarities. The patient's relational dynamics, once noticed, can be explored within the therapy sessions and may become the main focus of the work itself. Does a patient, for example, use the space easily in a straightforward way, or do they come late and find it hard to talk? Does the offer of the therapist's attention evoke feelings of vulnerability in the patient, perhaps leading to defensive manoeuvres such as closing off or going on the attack? Is the therapist experienced as neglectful, or as a harsh and critical figure?

The American psychoanalyst and educator Glen Gabbard observes that notions of 'frame' or 'boundaries' may imply an unthinking rigidity. This is a misunderstanding of what is intended. Rather, the edges of the sessions are intended as 'an envelope within which the therapist can be empathic, warm and responsive [. . .] the boundaries in therapy create a safe and secure context within which therapist and patient can enter a "play space" where feelings, perceptions, thoughts and memories can be played with and be explored'. The therapist should, 'above all, be a human'.[5] The boundaries are not created with an expectation that the patient will always hold them, but rather that if they are not set out it is impossible to explore what might be behind them being shifted. Take for example, a patient who misses a couple of appointments after a particularly difficult session in which issues around bereavement emerged. If a frame has not been established, it is harder to explore with the patient why they felt the need to subsequently cancel.

In this chapter, we examine various considerations that go into framing a psychodynamic space, organised roughly in sequence as they might be encountered by a patient.

Early Encounters with the Setting

Creating a therapeutic frame starts before a patient arrives at the service for the first time. From the first communications, a psychodynamic approach attempts to convey that what is on offer is a relationship where time can be taken to stop and think, and where realistic expectations are set up about what is available. In practice, this is done through careful attention to written or verbal communication with the patient in the setting-up phase. This includes explaining the therapist's intention about the initial meeting(s) – usually an opportunity for a consultation with a psychotherapist as opposed to long-term treatment starting straightaway (see Chapter 9 on Assessment and Formulation). The therapist takes care to use straightforward, jargon-free language, and is warm whilst also being measured in tone and realistic about what can be offered.

Even before the first appointment, a patient's concerns and relational dynamics might start to emerge in the ways they relate to the service; for example, by insisting on being seen outside of normal working hours, or by being very compliant and deferential with arranging the appointment, by repeatedly changing or cancelling appointments, or perhaps through becoming offended at some aspect of the initial correspondence. Clinicians try and think carefully about what these communications might signify and how, or indeed whether, to respond. Taking time at this point to consider the possible underlying factors at play helps the clinician to avoid reacting in extreme positions such as being punitive (e.g. prematurely discharging a patient after they miss a single appointment) or over accommodating (e.g. seeing a patient at 9pm when the service is set up to run safely from 9am to 5pm). The therapist will also try and be reflective about what she may have brought to the interaction, rather than assume it is all about the patient. Even at this early stage, the therapist is intending to convey some important things to the patient about the psychodynamic frame: a focus on reflection before action; and the balance that the therapist is trying to strike – neither being prematurely gratifying nor withholding.

On the Way into a Session

The psychoanalyst and writer Thomas Ogden describes how the build-up to the initial encounter with a psychodynamic therapist can be a time where anxieties, fantasies, and internal objects may surface and become noisier.[6] This intense period has the potential for new insight and change as pre- or un- conscious aspects of the patient's life become more accessible. The leading edge of anxieties emanating from a patient's inner object relations may surface on the walk from the waiting area to the therapy room. For example, a patient in the corridor might say: *'I'm so sorry I'm late, you must be very busy.'* These opening 'moves' may contain valuable information about the patient's ways of navigating the world. The therapist respects the potential meaning of corridor interactions and, with tact and within the privacy of the clinic room, may ask further about these. 'On the way in, you apologised for being late and expected me to be busy – can you say more?'

The clinician's approach of gathering these corridor anxieties and exploring them more fully once in the room does not mean that the therapist stays steadfastly mute in response to anything the patient says on the way in. Depending on how apprehensive the patient feels, a mute response from the therapist could be far from 'holding'. Instead, in the corridor, the clinician tries to find a way to tactfully acknowledge something of the communication, without going into matters when there is not yet the privacy to do so properly.

We need to adapt to the nature of the patient's anxieties and their developmental level of organisation (see Chapter 9). Some patients need light conversation on the way to the therapy room to be put at relative ease and keep anxieties within a tolerable limit. This sort of humane responsiveness can make all the difference for some patients between leaving therapy early and being able to come to sessions. With other patients, it may be fine just to listen on the way in without saying much. Patients' requirements for 'corridor interaction' can change over time.

The Analytic Setting

In preparing for a session, the therapist arranges the room so the layout is consistent from week to week. The therapist turns off their phone and, if working in a building with others, may put an engaged sign on the door to ensure privacy and protected time for the patient without interruptions. It is often easier for people to have new or difficult discussions when they share the same space but are not directly facing each other – think about two people in the front of a car in conversation on a long journey. Likewise, positioning therapy chairs at around a 45-degree angle allows easy movement between free gaze and relaxed eye contact. It is useful to have one or two clocks in the clinic room near both parties' natural eye lines.

Although it can feel tempting for the therapist to note down key moments or insights at the time, this might be distracting and mean that the therapist is not fully available during the session. In addition, a patient might notice what is written down and what is not, and thus may modify their narrative. Therefore, in the vast majority of situations, the therapist will not take down notes during sessions. However, after sessions, the therapist writes a formal entry for the record and might also write session transcripts in anonymised form for training purposes.

An unreliable setting is depicted in Figure 5.1.

Figure 5.1 An unreliable setting. The door is ajar, the therapist looks distracted, and the effect on the patient is palpable.
Illustration by Robert Bangham.

The situation in Figure 5.1 is clearly not conducive to a therapeutic encounter unfolding. By contrast, to create a therapeutic frame, the therapist tries their best to be reliable. In practice, this includes giving adequate notice about appointment times, being aware of the start and end time of sessions, giving notice about planned breaks in therapy, and being clear about the length of the course of therapy being offered or explaining if the contact could be open-ended. The therapist explains that therapy is a confidential space, whilst also acknowledging the limits to this if the patient poses a significant risk towards themselves or others. All this is about creating a predictable, familiar setting which is conducive to an analytic encounter unfolding (see Figure 5.2).

A consistent session duration means patients know how long they have with the therapist – this may sound basic, but this predictability can help an anxious patient explore new and unsettling areas. Many people feel more secure if they know they are not going to be closed off unexpectedly. Equally, it can be containing to know that the exposure of a session won't go on for ever, that it will draw to a close after a predictable time. Most psychodynamic sessions run for either 50 or 60 minutes, which for many people allows enough time for something to unfold but is not too long to be overly tiring.

If a patient is embarking on something obviously distressing close to the end of a session, it may be helpful for the therapist to mention that they are conscious of there being only a few minutes left, and that it may not be possible to go into this fully in the present session – though there would be time the following week. This can avoid a sudden stop and conveys the notion of future sessions, possibly allowing the patient to feel held in the therapist's mind.

Sometimes, a patient may ask a question once the session has finished, or as they are packing up to leave the room. If this question does not realistically require urgent attention, it may be more containing to try and keep the anxieties within the usual envelope of the session and to say something like, '*Can we respect this question and make proper time to look at this next week.*'

If something comes up right at the end of the session that requires immediate attention – such as significant concerns about risk – time must be taken to explore this, and appropriate steps taken if needed. If it becomes a pattern for concerning situations to come up in this way, then this can then be looked at within the therapy to try and understand why this is so. For example, is it a way of avoiding separation; is a situation being repeated whereby the

Figure 5.2 The reliable external features of the therapeutic frame help to create a steady and containing environment for therapeutic work.
Illustration by Robert Bangham.

caring figure of the therapist is unconsciously invited into a position of either ignoring the patient or showing extra care; or might the patient feel too vulnerable if important matters were brought up earlier in a session and given more exposure?

Being a reliable therapist is not the same as attempting to provide 'perfect' care. This is both impossible and clinically undesirable. When circumstances emerge which are out of the therapist's control (e.g. a short notice cancellation due to illness) then the therapist apologises, and tries to understand how the patient might be feeling (see also sections on 'Rupture and Repair' in Chapters 3 and 7).

The therapist tries to be reflective when a patient does not come to sessions. Rather than viewing a missed session as a sign of a person 'not engaging' and discharging them, instead a therapist would try to think about what the missed sessions might signify for the patient. The way a person comes or doesn't come to sessions, or attends late or early, shows us something about how they *are* engaging with offered care. Most people who come for therapy have difficulties in the way they relate to others, particularly in caring relationships, so ambivalence about coming to sessions is expected and working through this can be part of the therapeutic process.

For good clinical care, the therapist will need at times to draw on their core clinical training and skills. One does not stop being, for example, a doctor, nurse, psychologist, or social worker when one become a psychodynamic therapist. So, when appropriate, the therapist will, for instance, explore the patient's current risks, assess the severity of a depression, or liaise with other professionals as required.

Allowing a Psychodynamic Encounter to Unfold

After the creation of a therapeutic frame, the patient is invited to start: to try to put into words what comes into their mind and to talk about what they are experiencing, whatever it is. The therapist listens closely to the patient, with interest and curiosity. Particularly as therapy progresses, the psychodynamic therapist may also use more 'expressive' (i.e. 'interpretative') approaches – this comes alongside the practice of close listening and 'following' (see Chapter 7 on technique).

Patients may come to therapy with a conscious idea of a problem they wish to address. However, when allowed the opportunity to explore, many patients quickly find themselves expressing different and unexpected themes, as unconscious thoughts, feelings, impulses, and conflicts emerge. It may transpire that the initial 'problem' the patient was seeking relief from was a signal that something was remiss in the patient's internal world (see Clinical Example 1). Alternatively, the initial 'presenting complaint' may in retrospect turn out to be a more palatable displacement of the 'real' issue. To take an example from Freud, a patient may not come to therapy for help with feelings of guilt. Instead, he may feel ill.[7]

Clinical example 1 **Realising underlying issues**

Mr McLeod, a man in his fifties, came to therapy with a conscious wish to address the feelings of anxiety he experienced whenever he left his house. However, with the space to just talk and see where things went, Mr McLeod discovered what was really troubling him was a sense of not knowing what he wanted in life. He experienced a dawning realisation that he had never taken the time to ask himself this question. With time to talk and explore things, his anxiety receded, without a direct focus on this symptom. The initial anxiety was a signal that something was wrong.

The Edges of Sessions

The borders between one place and another are often interesting places. In therapy too, interesting information can emerge around the edges of sessions. Often the first few minutes or even seconds can be revealing (see Clinical Example 2). Similarly, the very end of a session, as the patient is leaving, can contain important interpersonal observations.

Clinical Example 2 Hanging up a jacket

Aaron came to his first therapy session. He seemed comfortable enough in the waiting room and walking along the corridor to my room. But as soon as he entered the room, he looked awkward and out of place. He was worried about where he should sit and was apologetic about hanging his jacket up on one of the pegs, as if he had done something wrong.

When Aaron sat down and started talking the atmosphere returned to the comfortable mood of the waiting room and corridor. After some months of working together, Aaron's central issues gradually emerged in words – his deep sense of never really belonging anywhere, and a history of being adopted in early infancy.

In retrospect, something of this experience was observable in the opening of the first session, as demonstrated in Aaron's anxiety about taking his place in the room with me. The observations from that first minute aided in the understanding of his situation and the subsequent work of putting things into words.

The Limits of Therapy

Another aspect of the therapeutic frame concerns the limits of therapy. In all services there will be limits in terms of resources, operating hours, and therapist availability. At times it may be necessary for the therapist to explain, humanely yet clearly, what roles she is and is not able to fulfil. For example, depending on the background and realities of a service, a clinician will be able to fulfil the role of therapist but not necessarily that of nurse or social worker. This reality may draw varying degrees of 'negative' transference – perhaps evoking feelings of rejection or dispelling a notion of being 'rescued'. However, when supported by a good therapeutic alliance, these realistic limits allow the potential for such dynamics to be put into words and understood.

Nancy McWilliams, psychologist and psychoanalyst, writes about how, when working with patients who struggle between poles of separation or engulfment with others, the therapist may experience a pressure to go the extra mile, perhaps through attempting to provide the care the patient feels has always been missing. For example, by regularly extending sessions, or carrying out tasks for the patient that are outwith the therapeutic role or the therapist's abilities. According to McWilliams, the therapist will have to tolerate being told off by the patient for having 'rigid, selfish rules', but clinically the patient is likely to do better when the therapist can hold on to the agreed, realistic limits and boundaries. Furthermore, when a therapist's limits are not explicit a patient's actions may escalate 'until they find the ones which have been unstated'.[8]

Limits which need addressing at an early stage include threats of violence or sexual advances from the patient. These pose risks to both parties, as well as undermining the patient's therapy. Consulting with a colleague or supervisor is helpful to work out how to address these situations. The clinician's approach is often a combination of 'boundaries plus understanding', that is, addressing the boundaries that are needed for both parties' safety, alongside attempts to understand what the patient is communicating through their actions.[9] This often defuses the need to act the situation out.[10]

It is important that these realistic limits and boundaries do not grow arms and legs and restrict the therapist's warmth and interest within a session. Some clinicians have a concern that they should not move from their chair to bring the patient a glass of water if this is requested, nor look at a photograph, artwork, or another possession the patient has brought in, as this would somehow be 'departing from the frame'. So, to clarify, it *is* part of a contemporary psychodynamic approach to be interested in what the patient brings to the session, be that showing you a letter or a photograph or an item they have brought with them. These interpersonal events may of course carry a great deal of meaning and communication, and the therapist can and should consider this dimension. It will likely be appropriate to bring a glass of water if it is requested. This act might signify that the patient is seeking a more concrete experience of care. Such partial enactments, as described further in Chapter 2, are inevitable and provide a way in to understanding interpersonal dynamics. To labour the point, bringing a glass of water, and reflecting (perhaps inwardly) on this, is a different way of responding to a patient's thirst than buying them bottles of mineral water to take home or giving the patient money to spend on drinks.

Professional Boundaries and Violations

We cannot leave the topic of setting the frame without discussing the important issue of boundary violations by the therapist. For example, the latter therapist who buys bottled water for the patient is moving into the territory of a therapist boundary violation. Boundary violations by clinicians and therapists can occur in any field of work, and it is a sensible position to realise that none of us, as clinicians, are immune to this potential. Acknowledging that all boundary violations by clinicians are serious, some writers have conceptualised these as being on a spectrum of severity, with a 'smaller' boundary violation potentially leading on to further and more serious violations.[11] A boundary violation on the part of a clinician is likely to bring harm to the patient, even if the patient does not feel disturbed at the time. There may be harm to the patient through direct psychological effects or via damage to future trust in caring professionals, and there may also be reputational damage to the profession. There is a marked power imbalance between therapist and patient which may affect a patient's capacity to agree or disagree to what a therapist asks of the patient, and the therapist has to realise this and accept that anything other than a professional relationship is neither possible nor ethical.[12]

There are many reasons behind a professional boundary violation, and we can only briefly introduce this important topic here. Boundary violations may be in the emotional, financial, or sexual realm. Within psychodynamic therapy (as with other professional relationships), at times there may be an 'idealising transference'[13] where 'the therapist's character is distorted and imbued with idealised attributes that reflect the patient's unmet developmental longings'.[12] Without reflection and supervision to process the associated countertransference, a therapist might fall into the trap of attempting to enact the love or care that the patient feels he has been missing, rather than the therapist recognising these dynamics and attempting to help the patient to understand his feelings and their meaning while being clear about the therapist's professional role and limits. Equally, a professional boundary violation may be more to do with the clinician's own personal issues. Frequently, these two areas overlap, with boundary violations being more common at a point in the clinician's life when they are more vulnerable, such as being recently bereaved, in conjunction with a clinical situation that carries powerful interpersonal pressures. The management of a professional boundary breach is beyond the scope of this book, other than to outline the principle of seeking senior advice immediately when there is a concern, taking immediate steps to protect and support the patient, and involving the professional's local service and regulatory body for investigation. It is also likely to be a difficult time for the professional involved who will need appropriate support.

Concluding Remarks

This chapter has outlined how a therapist might go about establishing a space which a patient might start to use therapeutically. As discussed, the notion of a therapeutic 'frame' is useful but is misunderstood if the word is taken literally to mean an unbending rigid approach or an adherence to rules for their own sake. 'To frame' – used as a verb – perhaps conveys the creative and attitudinal elements of this concept more accurately than the 'frame' as a noun which emphasises the external manifestations.

References

1. Winnicott DW. Playing: its theoretical status in the clinical situation. Int J Psychoanal 1968;49(4):591–9. Copyright © 1968 Institute of Psychoanalysis, reprinted by permission of Taylor & Francis Ltd, on behalf of Institute of Psychoanalysis.
2. Parsons M. Raiding the inarticulate: the internal analytic setting and listening beyond countertransference. Int J Psychoanal 2007;88(Pt 6): 1441–56.
3. RCPsych. Psychotherapy, counselling, and psychological treatment in the NHS (online leaflet) [Internet]. 2021; www.rcpsych.ac.uk /members/your-faculties/medical-psychotherapy/psychotherapy-counselling-and-psychological-treatment-in-the-nhs
4. Sternberg J. The therapist's inner instruments. In Infant Observation at the Heart of Training. London: Routledge; 2015. pp. 43–60.
5. Gabbard GO. Long-term Psychodynamic Psychotherapy: A Basic Text. Arlington, VA: American Psychiatric Publishing, Inc.; 2010.
6. Ogden TH. Comments on transference and countertransference in the initial analytic meeting. Psychoanalytic Inquiry 1992;12 (2):225–47.
7. Freud S. The Ego and the id. In Strachey J. (ed. & trans.). In The Standard Edition of the Complete Psychological Works of Sigmund Freud. London: Hogarth Press (original work published 1923); 1961. pp. 3–66.
8. McWilliams N. Psychoanalytic Diagnosis, Second Edition: Understanding Personality Structure in the Clinical Process. 2nd ed. New York: The Guilford Press; 2011.
9. Craissati J, Minoudis P, Shaw J, et al. Working with offenders with personality disorder, A practitioners guide. Ministry of Justice, National Offender Management Service; 2015.

10. Lemma A. Introduction to the Practice of Psychoanalytic Psychotherapy, 2nd ed. West Sussex: Wiley Blackwell; 2016.
11. Sarkar SP. Boundary violation and sexual exploitation in psychiatry and psychotherapy: a review. Advances in Psychiatric Treatment 2004;10 (4):312–20.
12. Hook J, Devereux D. Boundary violations in therapy: the patient's experience of harm. BJPsych Advances 2018;24 (6):366–73.
13. Kohut H. The psychoanalytic treatment of narcissistic personality disorders. Outline of a systematic approach. Psychoanal Study Child 1968;23:86–113.

Chapter 6

The Goals of Psychodynamic Psychotherapy

'... *much will be gained if we succeed in transforming your hysterical misery into common unhappiness* ....' Freud and Breuer, Studies in Hysteria. (1895) [1]

Table of Contents

Introduction 89
Initial Phase Goals 90
Promotion of a Therapeutic Alliance 91
Middle Phase Goals 91
Final Phase Goals 92
An Alternative Way of Looking at Goals in Psychodynamic Psychotherapy 93
Symptom Relief 93
Life Adjustment 94
Structural Personality Change 94
Procedural Goals 95
Goals from a Neuroscience Perspective 95
Complications 95
Concluding Remarks 96

Introduction

There are several schools of psychotherapy which have overlap, but also differences in theoretical orientations; these have been briefly described in Chapter 4. These theoretical differences lend richness in terms of conceptualising what goals a therapist is aiming for during therapy but inevitably add a degree of complexity as to what these goals might be. This complexity around goal definition can be seen right at the start of the development of psychotherapy. For example, it is often thought that Freud developed his analytic method with no goals in mind, however, as can be seen from the quote above, Freud did have aims for his treatment, aims which are also explicit in his statement 'Where id was, there ego shall be' (i.e. increasing awareness of and agency in one's inner life and relations with others).

As other schools developed from psychoanalysis, they emphasised differing goals. For example, a Winnicottian therapist might work towards a reduction in false-self functioning, a Kohutian therapist might look for reorganisation of the self with a corresponding lessening of reliance on external selfobjects, and a Kleinian therapist might aim to reduce persecutory anxieties with a reintegration of projected parts of the self in order to function better.[2]

Some therapists advocate that the only goal of therapy is to analyse the patient, a position drawn from Bion (1967) where he says that 'the purest form of listening is to listen without memory or desire'.[3] Some theorists have taken this to mean that each session should be approached with no memory of what has gone before and with no desire to change anything. Leiper and Maltby describe this goalless position as being 'wise nonsense'.[4] They go on to explain that although the idea of approaching a session with no memory or desire might seem nonsensical, there is a rationale behind it. A person coming into therapy will be aware of their conscious difficulties but they will also have a number of unconscious ones of which they not aware, and which may even be in conflict with the conscious difficulties. Thus neither the therapist nor the patient can initially know what the goal of a particular therapy may be and they will need to work patiently together until things become clearer.

The experienced psychodynamic therapist therefore will not initially agree specific goals with their patient as they may be incorrect or only partially correct.

However, whilst having a good clinical rationale, this apparently goalless position may not necessarily feel helpful to the patient, to the therapist, or to managers responsible for developing healthcare systems. In addition, to carry out effective research on psychodynamic psychotherapy there needs to be clear criteria for what is being measured so, at times, we need to be able to identify clearly defined goals.

We can see that there is a tension between these two positions, the first being to solely analyse the patient and the other to have clearly formulated goals. To try to resolve this tension it can be helpful to think that the goalless state is initially necessary to provide the conditions where later on conscious and unconscious goals can emerge and be recognised by the patient and therapist. Or as Cooper puts it 'goallessness and free association are both tactics for reaching the strategic goals of identifiable change in inner and outer life'.[2]

Keeping this tension in mind we go on to describe some of the goals in psychodynamic psychotherapy and we use a simple schema which divides goals into those which are non-specific to psychodynamic psychotherapy and those which are more specific. Generally the non-specific goals tend to come into play earlier in a therapy and the specific goals later; however, it should be stressed that this is a bit of an artificial divide as some of them will need to be met across the whole time frame of a therapy whilst under certain circumstances the more specific goals may need to be attended to sooner. For example, if a patient comes to therapy and quickly develops a strong negative transference response to the therapist, it may be necessary in the early stages to interpret this negative transference, even though this is a specific goal. This interpretation would be necessary to try to develop a reasonable therapeutic alliance to enable the patient to continue in therapy.

Initial Phase Goals

Goals to be worked towards in the beginning phase of therapy tend to be generalisable across all forms of psychotherapy and thus are less specific to psychodynamic psychotherapy. Although termed 'non-specific' or 'common' factors, they are important. For instance, complex transference interpretations will not help a patient if he has already dropped out of therapy due to the therapist not paying sufficient attention to non-specific aspects, such as being empathic. Psychodynamic psychotherapy can initially seem confusing and frustrating and developing these factors can help both the patient and therapist to settle in.

Laska et al. summarise common factors in therapy as follows:

- *An emotionally charged bond between therapist and patient.*
- *A confiding, healing setting in which therapy takes place.*
- *A therapist who provides a psychologically derived and culturally embedded explanation for emotional distress.*
- *An explanation that is adaptive and is accepted by the patient.*
- *A set of procedures and rituals engaged by the patient and therapist that leads the patient to enact something that is positive, helpful or adaptive.*[5]

Chapter 5 has discussed how to frame a space in order to develop many of these non-specific factors – in particular, the creation of a confiding and containing setting for therapy. In terms of explanations for emotional distress, a key focus of psychodynamic therapy is attending to the patient's feelings and allowing space to both experience and also understand these. Chapter 7 on technique covers the more 'educational' aspects of explaining and working with distress.

Research has yet to fully determine just how important common factors are to outcomes in psychotherapy compared to more specific psychodynamic factors. This is not a surprising finding as research has yet to determine how therapy works; there is much evidence to show that it does, but there is less evidence on how. Some researchers believe that therapeutic change is effected largely through the operation of the non-specific common factors and others think that the specific factors are necessary.

These so-called common factors will be at play across all phases of therapy although they will vary in importance depending on what stage the therapy is in. For example, explanation of the rationale for therapy is more likely to be important at the beginning of a therapy whereas the emotionally charged relationship will be necessary across all stages and may become more intense towards the end.

Promotion of a Therapeutic Alliance

Another goal of psychodynamic psychotherapy, and a more specific one, is to foster the therapeutic alliance. There are many definitions of this, but it can be reasonably defined as 'the non-neurotic rational reasonable rapport which the patient has with his therapist and which enables him to work purposefully in the analytic situation'.[6]

Numerous studies have demonstrated the importance of a good therapeutic alliance to satisfactory outcome, and research has also demonstrated a moderately strong relationship between dropout and a weak therapeutic alliance.[7,8] For more detailed information, see Chapter 2 on empirical evidence, and for those curious about how to promote a positive therapeutic alliance this will be explored in the Chapter 8 section on 'Developing a Therapeutic Alliance'.

Middle Phase Goals

The set of goals and concepts listed below will be expanded upon in Chapters 7 and 8, but in brief they are important for the middle phase of therapy and include:

- Look out for and explore the transference.
- Monitor therapist countertransference.

- Use the emergence of transference and countertransference responses to inform formulation of the patient's object relations.
- Link the patient's object relations with external current relationships.
- Work with resistance and understand how the resistance demonstrates the patient's habitual defences.
- Promote capacity for self-analysis.

These are illustrated in the clinical example below.

Clinical Example 1 Middle stage goals

Audrey was referred with symptoms of depression and anxiety. On exploration, it transpired that these symptoms had been precipitated by a change at work. Audrey had previously worked for many years alongside a female manager she had experienced as sympathetic, but had recently been moved to a different department where she was working with an older male manager. This was technically a promotion, but not experienced by Audrey as such.

She described feeling that that she would not be able to succeed in her new role at work and was afraid that she would come across as 'stupid'.

Describing her early childhood relationships, Audrey felt that her father had been critical and undermining of her, comparing her abilities unfavourably to her younger brother.

During the initial stages of therapy all seemed to go smoothly and her male therapist worked hard at showing empathy, warmth, and understanding, thus aiming to promote a therapeutic alliance, an initial phase goal.

After some months of therapy, Audrey began to worry that her therapist thought she was inadequate and stupid (*a transference*). The therapist himself began to think that she wasn't doing as well as he had initially hoped and began to think that other therapists in his supervision group had better patients than him (*evoked countertransference*).

With the help of supervision, he recognised this as being a familiar relationship constellation to the patient (*internal object relations*) and was able to talk to her about how she may have been experiencing him. She admitted that she thought he was critical of her and that she had been thinking of dropping out of therapy. Exploration of this dynamic between them allowed her to see that what she was thinking was not accurate and had been based on a misinterpretation when she thought he had seemed bored during one session (*exploration of transference*). Following on from this admission she was able to see that she was experiencing her new manager in the same way, thinking, with no concrete evidence, that he thought she was stupid.

The therapy also explored what her perception of the therapist and others as being critical of her meant for her and what it stirred up (*working with the transference*).

Eventually she became aware that she experienced inner thoughts that undermined her; this inner dialogue was barely perceptible yet was persistently telling her that she wasn't as good as anyone else. After leaving therapy, when she was feeling anxious she was often able to think about what was happening internally and became on the lookout for when this 'inner voice' was activated (*capacity for self-analysis*).

Final Phase Goals

The goals for the final stages of therapy are as outlined above in the beginning and middle phases of therapy with two important additions. The patient (and therapist) needs to be able to deal with the ending of therapy and ideally the patient needs to learn how to mourn the loss of the good object of the therapist. This requires the patient to be able to separate from the therapist without feeling as if the relationship is rubbish or that all that has been gained is completely lost.

Paradoxically, if a therapy has gone well, it can be difficult to manage the ending, sometimes for the therapist as much as the patient. It can be difficult for a patient to leave a therapy relationship that has been experienced as helpful and caring, and a therapist too can find it hard to end with a patient who has been gratifying to work with.

The goal here is to manage the ending in a good-enough way without resorting to acting out on the part of the patient or the therapist. Examples of acting out might take the form of unthinkingly extending the number of sessions or the patient dropping out of therapy sooner than planned.

Mourning and loss will be described in more detail in the chapter on phases of psychotherapy (Chapter 8).

An Alternative Way of Looking at Goals in Psychodynamic Psychotherapy

Westenberger-Brueur (2006) describes another useful way to think about goals in psychodynamic psychotherapy.[2] She divides goals into four sections with no section being any more important than another, as she considers them all to work in tandem. They are:

- Changes in symptoms and complaints
- Changes in life adjustment
- Changes in personality structure
- Realisation of procedural goals.

We now go on to describe these in more detail.

Symptom Relief

Patients enter therapy for a number of reasons. However, they usually seek help for symptom relief; it is relatively unusual for a patient to seek therapy because of difficulties in relationships, either with themselves or with others. They are more likely to present with feelings of depression, anxiety, problems with substance misuse, and other symptoms. One early goal is to try to understand the symptom in light of the patient's habitual relational style. For example, a person may present with depression but on exploration of his important relationships it may become clear that he has a repeated history of rejecting others in his life, pushing them away due to a fear of intimacy. Thus, his depressive feelings are consequent on feeling isolated and lonely. Another patient may present with substance misuse and be found to have substantial difficulties regulating emotional states leading to alcohol use when feeling rejected and lost.

Clearly, symptom relief is not specific to psychodynamic psychotherapy but, contrary to what some believe, Westenberger-Brueur argues that it is intrinsic to the model. From the very beginning of the psychoanalytic endeavour, Freud postulated that symptoms came about from the interplay between unconscious and conscious processes with the symptom being the compromise formation between the consciously unacceptable idea and the build-up of tension in the unconscious.

To continue with Freud's ideas, he wrote more specifically that the goal of treatment had been reached 'when two conditions have been approximately fulfilled: first that the patient shall no longer be suffering from his symptoms and shall have overcome his anxieties and his inhibitions: and secondly, that the analyst shall judge that so much repressed material has been made conscious, so much that was unintelligible has been explained, and so much internal resistance conquered that there is no need to fear a repetition of the pathological process concerned'.[9]

It follows that in the early stage of therapy it can be useful for us to take a clear history of symptom development, including when they started and what was happening in the patient's life at that time. It is important to try to get under the symptom, as it were, to understand triggers and to help the patient connect their important relationships with what they are feeling and any symptoms they may have.

For example, on assessing a patient with depression, careful enquiry may discover that this feeling is consequent on a recent loss of some kind. Further investigation may reveal that the patient had been hospitalised as a child for long periods of time, sensitising them to separation and loss. These unconscious painful feelings of abandonment having been reawakened by the more recent loss.

Life Adjustment

Many patients will come to therapy with the conscious goal of alleviating problems with life adjustment. For example, people who have suffered childhood sexual abuse or other childhood trauma often present with psychological symptoms but also describe long-term difficulties making and sustaining relationships. They often have problems with parenting, difficulties relating to authority figures at work, or difficulties with intimacy and vulnerability. These can be seen as an understandable response to adverse early childhood experience resulting in understandable difficulties with trust. A very reasonable goal would be better adjustment in this area.

Thus, early goals in therapy are to link the patient's presenting symptoms with relationship patterns, current life circumstances, and events from the past.

Structural Personality Change

This tends to be a goal for the middle and ending phases of therapy rather than early on and we can see that this has been achieved if we can observe that the patient has new and different kinds of relationships with others and with himself.

Taking the example of Audrey (from Clinical Example 1), by the end of her therapy she reported a better working relationship with her male manager as she was able to see him more as he really was rather than the person she feared he would be. She was also happier within herself, recognising that internally, in her mind, she had not treated herself very kindly over the years. During therapy she discovered she had an aspect of herself, which operated mostly unconsciously, and which considered herself stupid and useless. This aspect had been activated in relation to the change at work where she was required to relate to an older man. If one part of the self is telling another part that it is useless then this is likely to arouse feelings of anxiety and depression (see Chapters 11 and 12). Structural change can therefore be seen here as Audrey has a different relationship between aspects of herself and with others.

Other indicators of structural change are more access to emotional life and a more fluid use of defences with less reliance on archaic defence mechanisms and a shift towards more adaptive ones.

Procedural Goals

This section relates to the use of techniques and processes specific to psychodynamic psychotherapy which are required to effect change. These are:

- Promotion of free association.
- Develop transference relationship and monitor countertransference.
- Manage boundaries and resistances.

These are all discussed further in Chapter 7.

Goals from a Neuroscience Perspective

According to Gabbard and Westen (2003), almost all therapists, even those using different theoretical models, show an underlying consistency in that they all have as a goal the altering of unconscious associative networks.[10] The theory of memory is a rapidly expanding science and is not fully developed; the following section is intended to be read alongside the section 'Insights from Neuroscience – Working with Procedural Memory' in Chapter 4, as they are complementary.

As described in Chapter 2, internal representations of the self and others are not things stored in memory but are connections formed among mental units such as memories, sensations, and emotions.[10] By the time a patient attends therapy these associative links have been repeated many times and are subsequently strong.

One aim is therefore to try to modify or 'weaken' these links.[11] For example, Audrey expected her therapist to be bored by and disinterested in her when she felt vulnerable. She had strong associative links between her internal representation of a 'boring self' in relation to a 'disinterested other' if she showed her vulnerability. By repeatedly exploring and reflecting on this dynamic in the therapy, this link became weaker.

At the same time as this weakening is occurring, links between more adaptive mental representations need to be formed in a new associative network. In therapy, by allowing the patient to explore different kinds of interactions to those he expects, there is the potential for new associations to form. Using the example of Audrey – because her therapist was consistent in keeping the frame, was empathic, and recalled important material from week to week, Audrey was able to develop a new association between a 'vulnerable self' and a 'concerned and helpful other', as opposed to 'vulnerable self' and 'disinterested other'. As expanded on in Chapter 8 (section 'The Therapeutic Relationship as a Vehicle for Change'), the therapist treads a path between neither colluding with the patient's expectations of them nor brushing the expectations away either (avoiding the 'negative transference'), as the latter would leave the problem 'out there' and mean that the relevant underlying memory networks were not activated and hence not in a state amenable to change.

Complications

Finally, a word of warning. As mentioned in the Introduction and in the section on 'Symptom Relief', although some goals are conscious, in the background there may be other quite unconscious ones and this applies to therapists as much as patients. Therapists can be driven by factors out with their own consciousness. For example, a need to heal can be bound up with an archaic object relationship, perhaps connected to experiences of being brought up by a depressed parent; or perhaps to compensate for unconscious feelings of guilt around infantile aggression. These issues are not likely to be problematic if therapists are aware of them; otherwise, they may become depressed if their patients do not respond to therapy or they may engage in boundary transgressions in a superhuman effort to make their patients 'well'. These issues can hopefully be explored in the therapists' own personal therapy or to a lesser extent in supervision.

Setting goals, even conscious ones, can further be complicated by being influenced by the therapist's own socio-economic background. In our role as a clinical supervisor, we have often attempted to bring to light a dynamic whereby a trainee is trying to make a patient change to fit in with their own ideas of what a successful life would look like.

As we have outlined earlier in this chapter, patients too have both conscious and unconscious goals for their therapy. Some patients, whilst consciously seeking change, may unconsciously need to hang on to their symptoms, perhaps to demonstrate to others just how unwell they are or perhaps out of a need for vengeance (see Clinical Example 2).

Clinical Example 2 Emergence of an unconscious goal

During therapy Mr Brown proved remarkably resistant to trying anything new, even though his life appeared empty and wretched. Rather than engaging in ever-increasing efforts to promote change, his therapist began to explore the dynamic of Mr Brown's reluctance to change. After reflection, Mr Brown stated that he would not allow himself to feel better because that would mean his father, who he felt had treated him badly (but was now dead), would have 'got away with it'. This feeling was so intense that Mr Brown was adamant that he would change nothing that caused him pain even though his father was no longer around to witness his suffering.

Thus, in opposition to his conscious goal of feeling less depressed, Mr Brown's unconscious goal was to continue his life of suffering.

In *The Ailment*, Main (1957) writes about the strong unconscious pull some patients have towards sadomasochistic relationships, going on to describe how masochism can actually become sadistic.[12] This might sound improbable until as a therapist one has had the experience of feeling persecuted by being with a patient who will not improve, no matter how much effort is expended in trying to help them.

Concluding Remarks

In this chapter we have discussed how a key psychodynamic approach is to allow treatment goals to emerge as therapy unfolds, rather than prescribe these beforehand. In tension with this, we have outlined several overarching goals for psychodynamic psychotherapy which integrate therapy process and outcome, following the approach of Westenberger-Brueur. Finally, we have commented on the therapist's unconscious goals, including perhaps a need to heal, and the need for personal reflection for the therapist to prevent issues emerging for themself or their patients.

References

1. Freud S, Breuer J, Bowlby R et al. Studies in Hysteria. UK ed. Penguin Classics; 2004.
2. Westenberger-Breuer H. The goals of psychoanalytic treatment: conceptual considerations and follow-up interview evaluation with a former analysand. The International Journal of Psychoanalysis 2007;88(2):475–88.

3. Bion W. Notes on memory and desire. Psychoanalytic Forum 1967;2:271–86.
4. Leiper R, Maltby M. The Psychodynamic Approach to Therapeutic Change. London: SAGE; 2004.
5. Laska KM, Gurman AS, Wampold BE. Expanding the lens of evidence-based practice in psychotherapy: a common factors perspective. Psychotherapy (Chic) 2014;51(4):467–81.
6. Greenson RR. The working alliance and the transference neurosis. The Psychoanalytic Quarterly 1965;34(2):155–79.
7. Martin DJ, Garske JP, Davis MK. Relation of the therapeutic alliance with outcome and other variables: A meta-analytic review. Journal of Consulting and Clinical Psychology 2000;68(3):438–50.
8. Horvath AO, Symonds BD. Relation between working alliance and outcome in psychotherapy: a meta-analysis. Journal of Counseling Psychology 1991;38 (2):139–49.
9. Freud S. Analysis terminable and interminable. Int J Psycho-Anal 1937;18:373–405.
10. Gabbard GO, Westen D. Rethinking therapeutic action. The International Journal of Psychoanalysis 2003;84 (4):823–41.
11. Gabbard GO. Long-term psychodynamic psychotherapy: a basic text. In Long-Term Psychodynamic Psychotherapy: A Basic Text. Washington, DC: American Psychiatric Pub.; 2010.
12. Main TF. The Ailment. British Journal of Medical Psychology 1957;30(3):129–45.

Chapter 7 Psychodynamic Psychotherapy Technique

Table of Contents

Introduction 98
Core Psychodynamic Attitude and Approach 99
The Psychoanalytic Attitude 100
Working with Unconscious Communication 104
Working with the Transference 106
The Negative Transference 108
Using the Countertransference 109
Working with Rupture and Repair 111
A Spectrum of Psychodynamic Technique 112
Support/Affirmation 114
Empathy 114
Information Giving 114
Exploration and Elaboration 115
Clarification 115
Confrontation 115
Interpretation 116
Working Through 119
Working with Resistance 121
Concluding Remarks 125

Introduction

Freud compared psychotherapy to the game of chess, with the psychodynamic frame (see Chapter 5) being the equivalent of setting up the chessboard and agreeing something of the parameters of play.[1] How therapy then progresses is absolutely specific to any particular patient-therapist pair, just as every game of chess unfolds differently. It follows therefore that the skills required to be a psychodynamic psychotherapist are difficult to learn without having the experience of being a therapist and yet trainee therapists may understandably be reluctant to learn 'on the job' as they may fear not doing it well.

To try to address this concern, by way of introduction, we describe three tasks which, if followed, are likely to make a good start to any therapy: firstly, to carefully create a therapeutic frame with a patient, including explaining and agreeing the 'boundaries' of a session (i.e. including when and where sessions are to take place); secondly, to try to maintain the frame; and finally, to pay close attention to what the patient talks about. As Sublette and Novick explain, 'as a therapist you will spend much time listening and observing. Your chances of maintaining a strong rapport with the patient will be improved if you devote yourself to what the patient is saying.'[2] Devote seems like a strong word to use but is a good one. It is informative to see how both patient and therapist respond to these tasks, and it is interesting to observe how the therapeutic frame is used by the patient and indeed by the therapist too. What does the patient say during the session and, as importantly, how does he say it? A basic premise of psychodynamic psychotherapy is that everything that goes on during the session may have meaning, including emotions that are evoked in the therapist and how the therapist responds to these.

Clinical Example 1 Everything may mean something

A trainee psychiatrist working with a patient was being supervised along with her peers in a supervision group. To the supervisor, the patient seemed very engaged and brought interesting and relevant material to the sessions. The trainee however felt that her patient was uninteresting compared to the patients her peers were treating and she felt unsatisfied and bored. The supervision group members were supportive of the trainee but also agreed with the supervisor that the patient was indeed engaged. The supervisor encouraged the trainee to hold on to her feelings of disinterest and to resist the temptation to probe and ask interesting questions in order to 'spice things up'. Towards the end of the therapy the patient related a poignant story of how when she was a little girl she would come home from school, brimming with excitement about what she had done that day, only to experience her mother as being disinterested and subtly discouraging of her daughter's accounts. This description shone a light on the therapist's feelings of boredom as it could be understood that this mother-daughter dynamic was being replayed in the therapy and could be explored with the patient. The key point here is that the therapist's feelings that her patient was boring had meaning.

Starting psychodynamic psychotherapy with a patient is often anxiety-provoking for both parties and may leave a new therapist feeling deskilled. Learning a new style of working can add to a feeling of being at sea. It is perfectly understandable to feel anxious going into any therapeutic situation, no matter how experienced a therapist you are. It may be reassuring to the therapist starting out to know that although the anxiety can, and indeed should, remain, the sense of feeling deskilled and somewhat lost will lessen over time.

Psychodynamic technique is a large topic, and we have, somewhat artificially, organised it into several sections to make it easier to digest. We start with a description of a core psychodynamic attitude and approach – this sets a tone at the start of therapy, runs throughout, and provides an ethos and approach on which other aspects of technique can build. We then discuss working with the dynamics of transference and countertransference, this approach being one of the distinctive characteristics of psychodynamic therapy. Next, we outline a spectrum of psychodynamic technique, ranging from more supportive to more 'expressive' techniques such as interpretation. In the final sections of this chapter, we discuss working through and approaches to working with resistance. These latter approaches tend to be more useful in the middle and end phases of therapy, but it should however be noted that most of these techniques may be required at any point during the therapy.

Core Psychodynamic Attitude and Approach

In this section, we first consider the 'analytic attitude', which refers to aspects of the therapist's general approach and manner, before then exploring the linked topic of unconscious communication and free association. We make a few preliminary remarks on free association at this point, as it is helpful for understanding the rationale behind the analytic attitude.

A key skill which therapists should try to adopt from the outset is in encouraging the patient to 'free associate'. So, at the beginning of a session, rather than introducing a topic for discussion, a therapist might say '*where would you like to start today?*' and encourage the patient go on from there. This technique is linked to Freud's 'fundamental rule', where he encourages patients to say 'whatever comes into their heads, even if they think it unimportant or irrelevant or nonsensical . . . or embarrassing or distressing'.[3] We note that this is by no means an absolute rule, and there are times when the therapist may introduce a topic for discussion – for example, if something important is being avoided that needs to be raised, or to address something the patient is doing that is detrimental to their therapy.

The importance of encouraging free association is that it is a way of accessing unconscious ideas, thoughts, wishes, feelings, and so on. This does not mean that the therapist is inactive, however. Most patients who have not previously been in therapy may well find it a strange and potentially unsettling experience having someone focus exclusively on them for a full 50 or 60 minutes. Some technique and a way of listening attentively are needed on the part of the therapist to enable the session to unfold spontaneously without falling back on familiar ground of taking a formal history. We will come back to this again under the heading 'Unconscious Communication', after looking first at the analytic attitude.

The Psychoanalytic Attitude

Lemma, Roth, and Pilling in their competency framework characterise the analytic attitude as being, 'a particular way of listening: the therapist empathises with the client's subjective experience while at the same time being curious about its unconscious meaning, rather than trying to solve problems or give advice'.[4] They go on to explain that keeping a reflective and interpretative mode 'conveys to the client, even if painfully, that difficult states of mind can be reflected upon with another person'.

There are three aspects to the analytic attitude: *neutrality*, *anonymity*, and *restraint*. These terms are useful to a degree, but it is important they are understood in a relative sense, not be taken literally.[5] Sometimes these qualities are mistakenly considered to be the same as Freud's early notion of the therapist acting as a mirror or a 'blank screen'; however a blank screen technique is not considered helpful or good practice in modern psychodynamic psychotherapy. Use of a contemporary analytic attitude with these three aspects is considered to be necessary both to pick up unconscious communications from the patient and to allow the transference relationship to develop.

Relative Neutrality

Neutrality (sometimes referred to as being non-judgmental) is not about being inactive or indeed uncaring, but rather is an attempt not to influence the patient in any particular direction. The reason this is important is because patients often present for therapy with conflicts or more frank splits in their functioning (see Chapter 2). Whilst a patient may express a conscious desire to achieve a certain outcome, another, perhaps more unconscious, aspect may not want that outcome at all. Kernberg (2016) puts this another way, defining neutrality as 'the analyst not taking sides in the patient's activated internal conflicts, remaining equidistant . . . from the patient's id, ego and superego and from his external reality'.[6]

We as therapists need to appreciate that we cannot decide what is right for the patient in terms of how they live their life, only the patient is able to decide that. Our task is to allow the patient to recognise the different dimensions of himself well enough to make informed choices (see Clinical Example 2).

Clinical Example 2 Neutrality and non-judgmental inquiry

Male patient: '. . . so that's why I felt so sad last week. Oh, this is irrelevant, sorry for going off on one. . .'

On close inspection of this snippet from a therapy session, it appears that two aspects of the patient are operating in quick succession and in conflict with each other:

- 'So that's why I felt so sad last week.' An aspect that was talking to the therapist about feeling sad.
- 'This is irrelevant, sorry for going off on one.' Another aspect that dismissed the feeling of being sad and then apologised to the therapist.

Here the invitation is to side with one position or another. However, if we consistently attend to one side of a conflict only, it will leave the other side untouched. As Mark Edmundson puts it, 'Any part of the self [that is] denied expression is bound to erupt – or at least assert itself – in ways that will be harmful to the individual'.[7] Therefore, the patient and therapist need to acknowledge and get to know the various dimensions of the patient's inner world in order to deepen understanding of the patient's internal conflicts. In the example here, the therapist went on to attend to both voices coming through:

It sounds like there is more than one thing going on here. It sounded to me like a part of you was expressing feeling sad. And another part of you felt that was irrelevant. How did you experience this?

Of course, being non-judgmental and neutral is an impossible ideal – the therapist is never truly neutral; what type of intervention they make and which part of the patient's narrative they focus on is likely to reveal something of the therapist's own goals (see Chapter 6), not to mention the therapist's own biases and interests. Furthermore, aiming to be non judgmental should not be confused with being inert as a therapist or passive. Gabbard clarifies that 'psychodynamic psychotherapy should not be labelled as "non-directive". It is frequently necessary for the therapist to direct the patient's attention to things that are being avoided.'[5]

Relative Anonymity

Here, the therapist tries to be 'as unobtrusive as possible and tries to retain a more neutral, relatively anonymous stance towards the client' – it is, after all, a space for the patient. Such an approach 'prioritises reflection and interpretation over action'.[4] Over time, we as therapists find a way to be ourselves, to be emotionally available whilst not over-disclosing information about our private lives. Again, it needs to be stressed that the latter does not mean being cold and aloof. Gabbard observes that novice therapists are more likely to be too cold rather than too warm, perhaps being influenced by images embedded in wider culture of a cold, detached, analyst. This is to be guarded against. In practice, the therapist's office, choice of pictures, way of dressing, and other clues all present a picture of what they may be like as a person. This cannot and should not be avoided and it is unlikely that these factors would provide enough of a picture of the therapist to preclude transference reactions to form.[5]

Asking questions of the therapist is common, especially in the earlier phases of a therapy. This may make the therapist feel uncertain as to how to respond. Generally, there are two categories of query. Firstly, questions concerning professional matters, which can be answered openly; for example, what are the qualifications of the therapist or what is the cost of therapy. Secondly, personal questions which ought not to be answered, such as, is the therapist married, do they have children or do they hold religious beliefs.

To slightly contradict the above advice, however, we consider that no question is without meaning, even a 'legitimate' one. One way of dealing with a question is to say something like '*I will answer your question in a moment, but first could we explore what may be behind it?*' Questions of a more personal nature could be responded to by saying '*I can understand why you might be interested in whether or not I may have children; however, I wonder what might be behind your question?*' This might then, depending on the context, lead on to a tentative interpretation such as ' ... *Perhaps you are worried that I might not be able to relate to the difficulties you are experiencing with your teenage son* ... '

An approach of relative anonymity frees up the patient to project onto (and into) the therapist. Through the process of projection (see Chapter 2), the therapist can then be experienced in a number of ways by the same patient at different points in the therapy. Different aspects of the patient's internal object relations are brought to light, and therefore made available for consideration and understanding. This is the basis for the transference response. As the transference develops organically, the therapist neither brushes it away when it arises nor accepts it uncritically. In this way, the therapist conveys respect for the patient's experiences of the therapist as being something important to be explored and reflected on. If all goes well, the patient will discover and learn over time, through experience, that the relationship with the therapist does not necessarily fit all the patient's predictions (see section on Transference in this chapter and Clinical Example 1 about Audrey in Chapter 6).

With the therapist's help, an observing position, also called the 'third position', needs to be achieved by the patient. Lemma et al. explain that the therapist needs 'to stand back from the interaction with the client so as to reflect and comment on it, thereby helping the client gain understanding of how they relate to others'.[4] This position allows the possibility for the patient to observe the transference situation and reflect upon it, otherwise the therapy could just be experienced as a concrete traumatic repetition of past relationships. Of course, at times during therapy, the therapist is likely to be experienced somewhat concretely 'as' the patient's critical mother, for example. This might happen a number of times before the therapist and the patient can notice and think about this.

Therapists need to allow themselves to be affected by their patients and their ailments and distress. This is an important point and necessary because sometimes trainees feel it is unprofessional to be affected by the patient or feel things about them. As Lemma at al. explain, 'rather than being aloof, the psychoanalytic / psychodynamic therapist should be actively engaged and emotionally attuned to the client's subjective experience: they are a participant in the therapeutic process and will experience strong feelings in response to the client's communications'.[4]

The boundary around the therapist's personal details is distinguished from times when patients may ask if the therapist is familiar with a certain film, book, or computer game. This may be a prelude to using the subject matter to express something by analogy or association:

[Midway in a session, the patient has been talking about suppressing feelings]

PATIENT: Do you know the film The Work?

THERAPIST: Yes, a bit. What's coming up for you about it?

PATIENT: Well, the bit where the prisoner suddenly breaks down in tears, I wish I could do that . . .

Such territory can often be rich and helpful to explore, and might have unnecessarily been shut down had the therapist declined to say if they had or hadn't seen the film. Even if the therapist isn't familiar with the topic raised, they can still take an interest in what the patient made of it. These conversations may allow movement into a playful space (analogous to the use of music-making or art materials in arts therapies) that can free something up from a two-person intensity. Depending on the situation, links might later emerge to the therapy situation or to the patient's interpersonal relationships outwith therapy.

Relative Restraint

This final aspect of the analytic attitude concerns not excessively gratifying the patient's conscious or unconscious wishes for care beyond the limits of the therapeutic frame. Examples of what might be considered excessive gratification by the therapist include:

- trying to show they are the longed-for figure a patient has been seeking
- buying the patient items or gifts
- trying to be overly reassuring and moving squarely into an advice-giving mode rather than exploring anxieties.

To put this into perspective, Gabbard points out that a 'total absence of gratification would result in losing the patient. Unless the patient gets something from the therapist, the therapy is unlikely to continue . . . Therapists provide a good deal of gratification in simply listening in a humane and warm way to the patient's concerns.'[5]

Rather than excessively gratifying the patient's wishes, the therapist tries to supportively explore and talk about these interpersonal pressures and dynamics so they can be understood and processed. People frequently enter therapy with a fantasy that they will be fixed or cured by the therapist. A related fantasy is that the therapist has all the answers of how to live the perfect life. Smith described the '*golden fantasy*' as 'a wish to have all of one's needs met in a relationship hallowed by perfection'.[8] When this fantasy is in operation the therapist may feel a great pressure to offer help and advice. However, on reflection, how is the therapist really to know what is best for a patient seeking help? Rather than being nudged by the patient to enact the golden fantasy, it would be kinder and more therapeutic for the therapist to help the patient mourn the fact that all their desires cannot be gratified by one single relationship. This gives the patient the opportunity to learn about living in the real world with its limits and frustrations.

If the therapist is repeatedly 'invited' by the patient into an advice-giving role, it may be helpful to explain the therapist's rationale: '*I think I may be more useful to you in the long run if I try and help you to work out what you need, even though this is frustrating for you.*'

This may be followed up by further exploration or a tentative interpretation. For example, with a patient who seemed afraid of making mistakes, the therapist enquired: '*I'm interested in your asking me what you should do . . . is there perhaps a worry about making decisions, to know what is best for you? Maybe we could explore this . . .'*

Closely linked to excessive advice-giving is the excessive giving of reassurance. Feeling drawn into being overly reassuring can be a therapist's response to feelings of helplessness and despair. It follows that these feelings may be being projected into the therapist by the patient. Therapists may experience a strong urge to tell a patient that everything will work out for the best, or that their problems may not be as bad as they fear. However, this temptation to reassure can be understood as the taking up of an omnipotent position – how does the therapist know that things will work out? Clearly, they do not.

Overly reassuring statements can feel to the patient as if the therapist is not taking their problems seriously or that the therapist is unable to tolerate their distress. This may cause the patient to hold back in the therapy for fear of damaging or upsetting the therapist. In other words, reassurance is not necessarily reassuring. It may well be more containing to explore these difficult feelings. Looking at the following patient statement:

'I am so worried that this therapy is not going to help me, I feel so depressed and frustrated and I worry my wife will leave me . . .'

The therapist's attempt at reassurance might look like: *'I am sure it will all work out fine, she has never left you before . . .'*

A more reflective response could be: *'I think it is very hard for you to have these feelings of sadness and frustration and I can understand you would be worried about driving people away. I wonder if we can think about what it is that is making you feel this way?'*

As hopefully will be becoming clearer, an analytic attitude can, sometimes fairly quickly, open up quite striking and unexpected conversations. These conversations can bring to the surface previously unconscious dimensions of a person's life. The next part considers unconscious communication in more detail.

Working with Unconscious Communication

One goal of psychodynamic psychotherapy, which we introduced in Chapter 6, is to make that which is unconscious conscious. In the context of the kind of conversations that an analytic attitude gives rise to, we now consider three main ways of picking up and working with unconscious communication: by using the patient's *narrative* alongside their *free association*; by exploring their *ways of relating*; and by *analysing dreams.*

The patient's *narrative* is what they talk about in the session. The patient may appear able to talk spontaneously and freely, or may find speaking difficult and the session feels stilted and awkward. As a therapist, we need to take an active interest in what the patient is actually saying, but also try to think about what other things they may be communicating too; in other words, what might be behind what they are talking about. This is linked to the concept of *free association*, which we introduced earlier, which was initially developed by Freud. He advised patients to follow his 'fundamental rule' in order to access preconscious (i.e. just beneath the surface) or unconscious material. In a modern version of this 'rule', the patient is encouraged to speak freely and what they talk about is listened to carefully by the therapist who is trying to understand underlying thoughts and phantasies and what the transference may be at that point in time (see Clinical Example 3). The term for this is analytic listening. It can be helpful for the therapist to try to notice how they are feeling and responding internally to what their patient is talking about (countertransference) as this can provide vital information about unconscious communications.

Clinical Example 3 Listening to the patient's free association

Early on in her therapy, Ms Y spoke about how, after her previous session, she found herself gazing longingly at some cream cakes in a bakery window. She wanted one very much, but felt greedy and guilty about this.

In the therapist's mind, the idea of 'cream cakes just out of reach' captured a central dynamic for this patient. She had always felt deprived and as if good care was just out of reach. The vignette also illustrated her tendency to deprive herself of nourishment; she seemed to compulsively care for others, whilst depriving herself of good things. She was stick-thin and miserable. Here, this single incident encapsulated some key themes at play in this patient's internal world. The exploration and elaboration of this dynamic with the patient proved a fruitful area of the work.

Observing how the patient *relates to others* is another way of accessing unconscious aspects of a patient. Therefore in a session it can be useful to note not only what the patient is saying but how they are saying it and what impact this has on the therapist. For example, a patient of one of the authors – Mrs S – tended to talk loudly and angrily, even though she was describing seemingly ordinary matters, and came across as hostile and threatening. When this was tactfully pointed out to Mrs S, she was astonished as she considered herself to be downtrodden and subservient. She was completely unaware of how she could project the fearful and cowed part of herself into others, making them feel intimidated by the way she spoke. This kind of interpersonal focus is picked up later in this chapter in the section on working with the transference.

The final approach is *dream analysis.* During Freud's topographical phase of psychoanalysis, he asked patients to bring fantasies and dream material to their analysis. He theorised that the content of unconscious repressed fantasies could be expressed (in disguise) in the form of dreams, parapraxes (slips of the tongue), symptoms, or acts of creativity. More about Freudian dream theory is described in Box 7.1.

Many patients bring dreams to therapy. A standard approach to exploring a dream is to start with the manifest content presented by the patient; and then from there, to work towards deeper layers of meaning, seeking to understand the patient's disguised wishes,

Box 7.1 Freudian dream theory

According to Freudian dream theory, the dream which is remembered upon wakening is referred to as the manifest content. 'Dream work' carried out by the individual during sleep consists of the transformation of dream material from the latent (i.e. unconscious) content to the manifest content. Freud postulated that dream work is necessitated by the continuing need during sleep to censor unacceptable or overwhelming wishes and feelings and, through this process, to preserve sleep. He considered dreams to be 'sleep's guardian'.[9] The level of censorship achieved during dreaming is less than during waking life. Therefore the analysis of dream material represents a route into the patient's unconscious internal world. In modern thinking, dreams are not just considered to be a product of repressed fantasies but reflect in symbolic form fears, conflicts, and, in the case of PTSD, an attempt to overcome and master traumatic experiences.[5]

fears, and conflicts. This is a joint endeavour between patient and therapist. The therapist encourages the patient to free associate to (i.e. expand on) the various dimensions and elements of the dream (such as a scene, or a prevailing mood, or a theme); all the while, the therapist is using analytic listening to inform what she says or does. As Bollas puts it, the aim is to discover 'what the dream itself evoke[s] in the mind of the dreamer'.[10]

In object relations theory, aspects of a dream can be thought of as representing internal objects and the relations between them. For example, a sleeper who dreams of being chased by a frightening killer might be understood as having an internal relationship whereby a frightened part of the self is threatened by a sadistic other part. Perhaps this would be evidenced in waking life as the patient's self-destructive behaviours such as self-harm, risky sexual behaviour, drug use, and so on. In this way, dreams can provide a way in to talking about important aspects of the patient's life, both internal and external.

To summarise, by listening analytically, the therapist attempts to tune into the patient's unconscious communications. The therapist is alert to the different streams of communication, from the conscious, more-surface levels to depth. Lemma sums it up: 'the bulk of our analytic work . . . thus becomes a matter of symbolic decoding'.[11]

Working with the Transference

'We all bring something to a new encounter . . . we transfer'.
(Høglend, 2014)[12]

We have mentioned an interest in the dynamics of the transference several times thus far in this chapter, and we now take up this important theme in more detail. We explained the theoretical aspects of transference in some detail in Chapter 2 (section 'Who Is in the Therapy Room? The Dynamics of Transference'). To recap briefly, transference refers to the patient's 'patterns of feelings, thoughts, perceptions, and behaviour that emerge within the therapeutic relationship and reflect aspects of the patient's personality functioning'.[12] Other aspects of the patient's experience of the therapist will reflect what the therapist is actually like (the 'real relationship'). The subset of all the patient's feelings towards the therapist that represent the transference often originate in early developmental experiences and, as such, are 'misplaced' in the present in the relationship with the therapist. Transference feelings can often be understood as the patient projecting their internal 'object-representation' onto the therapist (see Clinical example 4, Part 1). At other times in the transference relationship, the patient might project their internal 'self-representation' onto the therapist (see Figure 8.2 in Chapter 8).

Clinical Example 4 – Part 1 Early intense negative transference

Coming from a deprived area, John, was referred with a history of depression. He was sent an appointment quickly and was seen, on time, in a suitable therapy room. The first thing he said as he was shown into the room was that he hoped that he wasn't going to be given the 'f***ing runaround'. This was said in an aggressive and prickly manner.

The transference was immediate – John felt he was in the presence of someone who was not going to care for him or treat him with respect. On exploration of his childhood history, he described having a lot of brothers and sisters. By John's account, his mother had been unable to cope with all her children and he had been put into care. Care placement after care placement had broken down and his experience was of being passed from pillar to post. Latterly the placements broke down due to his aggressive and hostile presentation.

The therapist tried to explore the negative transference he had developed towards her by trying to slow the interaction down, allowing him space to explore his feelings about what was happening as well as exploring his perspectives about the consultation process and therapist.

John's recollected experience of receiving care in his past was that his parents had been rejecting and negligent. Thus, in spite of being offered a reasonable experience in clinic, his unconscious fear was that the therapist would give him the 'runaround'. His Fantasy was that she would be neglectful and depriving too, like others from his past. He then behaved as if this was *actually* the case, in the process creating a new relationship that was heavily influenced by his expectations.

As a result of the analytic attitude described earlier, patients undergoing psychodynamic psychotherapy are more likely to develop intense transference feelings than patients in other types of therapy. This should always be taken into consideration with patients who have particularly persecutory internal objects such as with John. When these persecutory objects are projected onto a therapist, it may make this type of work especially challenging for both parties. There can, however, be a lot to gain from working in the transference. Indeed, a recent study of psychodynamic therapy suggests that patients with worse interpersonal functioning and less helpful object relationships, on average, benefit more from transference interventions compared to those patients with better functioning.[12] This makes sense as patients with less helpful ways of relating and with internal worlds that function with difficult objects are more likely to project these and to develop problematic transference relationships. On the other hand, some of these patients might find a more explicitly structured model of therapy, in which the transference may be less likely to be stimulated, to be more tolerable for them. Assessing who is likely find benefit from psychodynamic work is discussed more fully in Chapter 9.

As has been shown in Chapter 2, the phenomenon of transference can show us how a patient's internal world, including their predominant object relationships, is configured. As these are unconscious, the patient (like all of us) is often unaware of how he relates to other people. Psychodynamic psychotherapists work alongside the patient to discover what it is he does in relation to the therapist; because what is happening within the therapeutic relationship is likely to be happening with others in the patient's life. A transference intervention might look like the following:

> *'This may be difficult to hear but I wonder if you are experiencing me as being dismissive and rejecting, especially as I have just cancelled a* session?'
>
> Depending on how the patient responds, the therapist might then go on to explore the patient's experience of himself: *'How does this leave you feeling?'*

If it is possible to help the patient to recognise a stereotyped relational pattern, as enacted within the here and now of the transference relationship, this can be a moment of significant therapeutic opportunity. The freedom conferred by this kind of insight may pave the way for the patient to develop new ways of relating in their lives outside of therapy. Returning to John from Clinical Example 4 – Part 1, he was mistrustful of others and aggressive towards them due to his expectation that they would reject him. This dynamic led other people to avoid contact with him as his demeanour was off-putting and made them feel uncomfortable. Sadly, this only confirmed to him that people were rejecting and uncaring, thus strengthening his internal world view. In this way, his internal world configuration gets recreated in his actual world; it becomes a self-fulfilling prophecy. This dynamic was alive in the therapy room – thus posing both a challenge, but also an opportunity for John to develop insight into his difficulties and discover new ways of relating to himself and others.

Contemporary research and clinical practice within psychodynamic psychotherapy emphasise a range of therapist activity under the umbrella of transference work, rather than limiting matters to 'transference interpretations' (see Box 7.2). (This topic is discussed further from a research perspective in Chapter 3, in the section on 'Psychodynamic Processes'.)

In general, transference interventions are thought to be more beneficial if used sparingly during a session, with higher use of transference interventions being associated with poorer outcomes (see Chapter 3). There are various schools of thought on how much and how early to analyse the transference, and it clearly should depend on what is most useful for each patient (this is discussed further in the section on 'Interpretation' later on in this chapter).

This process of elucidating and working with the transference may sound relatively straightforward. However, it needs to be emphasised that in the therapy room there are two people, both of whom have internal worlds and internal object relationships. This may make the therapeutic situation complicated and confusing – hence the need for a supervisory process (Chapter 10).

The Negative Transference

A negative transference refers to when the patient experiences the therapist as being exceptionally unhelpful, useless, or even persecutory. This can feel difficult, or even intolerable, for both parties. People choose to become therapists for a number of reasons, sometimes due to reparative drives derived from past childhood experiences, both conscious and unconscious. Therefore, some therapists feel a particularly strong need to be a 'helpful and good therapist', in order to placate their own internal objects. This can make working in the negative transference a particular challenge for some of us.

When any therapy is under the influence of a pronounced negative transference, the therapist can be tempted to prove that the patient's negative view of her is wrong by trying to

Box 7.2 Dimensions of transference work used in research studies and clinical practice[13]

1. The therapist encourages exploration of thoughts and feelings about the therapy, therapist, and the therapist's style and behaviour
2. The therapist encourages the patient to discuss how they believe the therapist might feel or think about the patient
3. The therapist addresses transactions in the patient-therapist relationship
4. The therapist includes themselves explicitly in interpretive linking of dynamic elements (conflicts), direct manifestations of transference, and allusions to the transference
5. The therapist interprets repetitive interpersonal patterns (including relationships to parents) and links these patterns to transactions between the patient and the therapist

be ever more understanding and more caring. Understandable though this response may be, it is unlikely to succeed as no therapist is able to offer perfect care and, even if they could, this would not be helpful to the patient as it limits the opportunity for mourning the loss of the ideal. A psychodynamic approach is, instead, to offer the potential for the patient to forge new associations and ways of being, through encountering something of the problematic relational dynamics in therapy – but discovering new ways that relationships can function compared to predictions. Mitchell summarises this as discovering 'something new from something old'.[14] This can then enable the patient to extrapolate how he may also do this in other areas of his life. (The reader is directed to section on 'The Therapeutic Relationship as a Vehicle for Change' in Chapter 8, which expands further on this topic.)

Working in the negative transference takes patience and understanding on the part of the therapist (and the patient too) and can be dispiriting and tiring. Here, supervision can be invaluable in helping the therapist to tolerate periods of working in the negative transference where they may feel they are making little progress, through making sense of the interpersonal dynamics and providing support in processing and tolerating the countertransference.

Using the Countertransference

Working with the transference is intertwined with using the countertransference. The theoretical concept of countertransference has already been described in Chapter 2. To briefly recap, the countertransference refers to two, interrelated, areas: firstly, the therapist's feelings that are due to identifying with the patient's projections; secondly, personal reactions that 'belong' more to the therapist that are stirred up by current work with a patient.

As described in more depth in Chapter 2, Racker usefully subdivided the first area of countertransference responses (i.e. therapist responses linked to the patient's projections) into two forms.[15] There are *concordant* responses – where the therapist identifies with the patient's position and feels the same way that he does. And *complementary* responses – where the therapist is made to feel like the 'other' in the patient's internal world.[16]

The countertransference can inform the therapist about the present relational dynamics between the patient and the therapist (see Clinical Example 4 – Part 2). Furthermore, processing and reflecting on the countertransference is essential in bearing the emotional demands of working in the transference, as mentioned earlier.[17]

Clinical Example 4 – Part 2 **To illustrate countertransference: John continued**

The predominant feeling evoked in me when seeing John was irritation. I felt I had done a good job by attending to his referral in good time and I felt cross that he did not acknowledge this. I did not like to recognise this feeling in myself, but it was there. After our first meeting he cancelled the following two sessions at short notice. At this point my usual practice would be to write to ask him to contact me if he wished for another session. However, I found myself sending him a further date and time for an appointment. On reflection this was partly to try to compensate for feeling dismissive and angry with him and partly to try to make up for his childhood history of deprivation. This would be an example of a small countertransference enactment. This means I acted in response to feelings generated in me by John, rather than reflecting on them and trying to understand them with him. Interestingly he did not attend this session, though did telephone again asking for another appointment. Ultimately, it was me who, in John's own words, was given 'the runaround' and who ended up feeling rejected and deprived. This is an example of projective identification.

Eventually, John did attend a second appointment. Although he expressed a wish not to undertake longer-term therapy, we continued to meet for several more sessions. These provided an opportunity for him to reflect on the dynamics that had become alive so quickly in relation to his contact with me. The door was left open for him to seek a re-referral again in the future, should he wish to consider exploring things in more depth.

In practice it can be hard to recognise when countertransference due to a patient's projections is at play. A useful way to identify when a therapist's feelings are being evoked by a patient is to consider whether or not the therapist would *expect* to be feeling a particular way. If they have not slept well or perhaps are preoccupied with personal matters, it is likely that they will feel tired or anxious no matter how a patient is presenting. However, if all is generally going well in life and these feelings are being experienced under particular circumstances with a patient, it is possible that projective identification is taking place (see Chapter 2). In this situation, the therapist's feelings can be used to identify and understand the feelings the patient may be unconsciously trying to avoid, as well as the positions that others may be 'invited' into by the patient.

By way of example, when working with Mrs S (the patient who shouted at the therapist without realising it – see section on 'Working with Unconscious Communication'), the therapist had the experience of feeling intimidated and afraid to speak in case she said the wrong thing. This would not be the therapist's usual state of mind so, using the principle of the 'internal supervisor',[18] she came to the conclusion that these feelings may in fact represent a split off part of the patient, a frightened and cowed part, which Mrs S had unconsciously projected into the therapist as it was intolerable for Mrs S herself to feel it. The therapist then became identified with this projected aspect and experienced it as countertransference.

Conceptualised in this way, the phenomenon of feelings being evoked in the therapist by a patient can be considered to be a useful tool rather than something to be avoided. However, as is often the case, the theory is more straightforward than the practice. Sometimes projected feelings are so powerful that it can be difficult to think at all and it can be hard to understand what may be happening in the therapy session. One useful way of dealing with this situation is to comment on it: '*It feels as if there are quite strong feelings coming up just now, I think it might be helpful if we stopped to have a think about what might be going on.*' At other times, countertransference feelings are hard to notice or may go unnoticed, and it is worth remembering that countertransference, like most of mental life, operates predominantly unconsciously (see Clinical Example 5).

Clinical Example 5 **An absence of concern in the countertransference**

A lack of concern in the countertransference can be hard to register at the time. For example, in A&E in the middle of the night, a trainee psychiatrist was assessing a man who had recently taken an overdose. The patient wished to go home and did not appear distressed. He spoke pleasantly about his plans for the next few days in a way that left the doctor feeling nothing in particular. His troubles were behind him, he said. The doctor left the patient to write up her notes. It was then that her insides twisted with anxiety as she realised that the patient's lack of concern could be, in fact, a particularly concerning sign that indicated a severe lack of concern for himself and his own life. The doctor realised that the patient may have projected his *lack of anxiety* into her so that she had not taken his presentation as seriously as it warranted. When she went back to the patient to explore things in more depth, it transpired that the patient did in fact have well-formed plans to end his life – in the patient's current state of mind, he was not bothered whether he lived or died.

Some common countertransference feelings are difficult to bear – such as feeling inadequate, useless, cruel, or depriving – perhaps especially so if a therapist is motivated by particularly strong reparative drives of their own. It is important to try to reflect on countertransference feelings in order to understand what they may represent in terms of the patient's internal world and object relationships and then to talk to the patient about this understanding – or, putting this another way, giving back to the patient their projections in a more manageable form. This processing on the part of the therapist is known as *containment*.

Small countertransference enactments (i.e. acting on the countertransference without reflection and processing) are inevitable to a degree and, if reflected on afterwards, are simply part of the therapeutic process (see Chapter 2). When countertransference feelings go unrecognised and unprocessed, this may result in therapists inadvertently assuming unhelpful positions towards the patient that can bring about an escalation in the patient's difficulties. As stated earlier, supervision can provide a space in which the therapist's feelings can be described, processed, and some sense made of what is generating them and how this may be dealt with. Reflective group settings such as reflective practice groups or Balint groups have an important role here too (see Chapter 18).

Working with Rupture and Repair

A 'rupture' is a threatened breakdown in the therapy relationship and can take place at any time during therapy. As described in Chapter 3, a rupture is often due to an interaction of transference and countertransference phenomena, where both patient and therapist may have contributed to the situation. The ways that a patient has of defending themselves and interacting with the therapist may have brought up countertransference feelings in the therapist, who, for their part, has acted on these rather than contained them. The hope is that a positive therapeutic alliance, along with the preparation that patient has been given in the consultation phase, is strong enough to keep the patient in therapy so that what is happening can be put into words as opposed to being acted upon. If the therapist and patient can work together to repair the rupture, this may actually be productive for the therapy (see Chapter 3). The key points of psychodynamic technique around rupture and repair are:

- If a patient has stopped coming to sessions, in a reflective way, consider efforts to try and encourage the patient back to sessions (whilst also respecting aspects of the patient that may not wish to come).
- Talk about what is happening with the patient. Ideally early on when we sense that a rupture may be developing but, if not, then once the patient is back in dialogue.
- Don't get defensive but be curious about what has happened.
- If there has been a countertransference enactment, then apologise and acknowledge our part in things breaking down. Some patients may value the therapist's humility in apologising when the therapist has made a mistake, and this can be a model for the

patient, demonstrating that making mistakes is part of being human and doesn't have to come with shame or persecution.

- Try and empathically explore what has been happening for the patient, and how they experienced things when we did something 'wrong'.
- When things are a bit 'cooler' emotionally we can try and help the patient to understand possible links between the present situation, when this has occurred elsewhere, and what underlying issues have been stirred up.

The following clinical example may illustrate these principles:

Clinical Example 6 Example of a rupture-repair

A psychiatric trainee was 8 months into a one-year therapy working with Jan. Due to being on night duty the trainee had to cancel a session and had neglected to remind her patient the week before. Jan had come to his session as usual and waited the full 50 minutes in the waiting room before reporting to the receptionist in a state of upset and anger saying he no longer wished to attend therapy as he felt so let down by his therapist.

Following supervision, the doctor contacted the patient by letter apologising for her mistake and asking him to attend at his usual session time to try to work out a way of going forward if at all possible.

Jan agreed to attend and initially presented in an angry and distressed state, but calmed down somewhat when the doctor acknowledged her mistake and apologised again. Later in the session, the therapist was able to explore with the patient why he had not spoken to the receptionist sooner but had waited alone in the waiting room for the full 50 minutes. He became tearful and responded by telling the therapist how the situation had reminded him of the joint custody arrangements made following his parents' separation. On days when his father was supposed to pick him up from school, he would often forget or be late, leaving Jan waiting alone in the playground. He had a vivid memory of looking through the school railings, anxiously waiting for his Dad, never being sure if he would come or not.

The therapist was able to empathise with his sadness and anger and was also able to make the link with the transference feeling of being at the mercy of an unpredictable and absent father/therapist.

The therapy continued until the end of the year with the patient making good progress into how he tended to be passive in relationships, not voicing his needs, with the result that he often felt let down and neglected.

To summarise, the clinical scenarios described in these sections on working with the transference and countertransference serve to illustrate the ways that a patient's internal world can be activated and made clearer in the here and now of the therapeutic situation. It needs stating that there is no point activating these ways of relating unless there is a way of managing them and putting these dynamics to therapeutic use. To this end, we outlined various approaches to working in the transference and using the countertransference.

A Spectrum of Psychodynamic Technique

In this section, we consider the question of what the psychodynamic therapist's approach might be at any given point in a session. Leiper and Maltby identify that, 'one of the challenges of psychodynamic practice . . . is to identify from all the possibilities available what is the most salient, most helpful, most facilitating of change at any given time.'[19] There are several, complementary ways to approach this question.

Leiper and Maltby, in advising therapists as to what may be most facilitative to the process of therapy, go on to suggest that 'this is often achieved through choosing to focus on the clearest connections that can be made with the main difficulties or conflicts the client is experiencing in her life'.[19] An important way of making clear connections and getting to what matters is through exploring the patient's affects and attempts to avoid affects (see also Chapter 3, Box 3.1). This involves the therapist trying to follow the affects in a session and their intensity. When the therapist is faced with several affects or possible avenues to pursue, Ogden advises the therapist to try to tune into and understand the 'leading edge of anxiety ... the principal source of the disruption' at any given moment.[20] There is a balance to be struck between, on the one hand, things becoming too intellectual and flattening affect so the session feels lifeless; and, on the other hand, promoting so much affect that the patient becomes overly distressed and unable to think.

Various psychodynamic writers since the 1970s have conceptualised psychodynamic technique as ranging from the more supportive to the more 'expressive' (i.e. interpretative) (Box 7.3).[21] This can be orientating for clinicians. We note that not all comments or techniques fit neatly into this idea of a spectrum of technique, and concerns about what technique to use when 'should not interfere with spontaneous conversation as it unfolds in the therapeutic dialogue'.[5]

Box 7.3 A spectrum of psychodynamic technique, drawing on various authors [5,21,22]

Interpretative interventions (including transference and extra-transference interventions)

Therapeutic 'confrontation'

Clarification

Exploration and elaboration

Empathic validation

Support and affirmation

In this list, more supportive interventions are listed lower down, more expressive interventions are higher up.

In very general terms, supportive techniques help develop the therapeutic alliance and may be particularly useful in the earlier stages of therapy whereas the more expressive techniques, such as interpretation, tend to be more helpful once the therapy is more established.

This is however an oversimplification and much depends on the individual patient. Techniques from all parts of the spectrum may be useful in all phases of therapy. Sometimes a 'deep' interpretation early on in therapy (or indeed in the assessment phase) might feel very containing to a patient and may give them an experience of being really understood. In other cases, a patient may develop a negative transference almost immediately and it may be necessary to explore and interpret this quickly in order to prevent the therapy from breaking down (Clinical Example 4). Other therapies may never or only rarely require a transference interpretation as they progress well with a good therapeutic alliance.

Sublette and Novick provide helpful 'pearls', distilled from clinical practice and the psychotherapy literature, for consideration by the novice therapist. These suggestions map reasonably well on to the spectrum of technique in Box 7.2, and provide guidance as to whereabouts on the spectrum a therapist might be at various points in a session:

- You will spend most of your time listening and observing ...
- You cannot help the patient unless you can empathise with him ...
- Clarify anything that seems vague, unusual or unclear to you ... [We would add a caveat to this which is that one task of therapy might be to sit with 'not knowing' and feeling confused – sometimes for long periods of time.]
- Confront the patient concerning behaviours that emerge as detrimental ...
- Interpret sparingly. The most essential areas for interpretation are behaviours that threaten the integrity of the therapy in any way ...
- Be prepared to revise all your comments depending on the patient's response ...
- You will make mistakes – this is fine and can even be useful ... [2]

We now look at the interventions mentioned in Box 7.2 in more detail.

Support/Affirmation

Support and affirmation are often useful in the beginning stages of a therapy and can help to promote a good therapeutic alliance. Support is implicitly provided by the reliability of the therapist and the regularity of the contact as well as through the implicit acceptance of all parts of themself that the patient brings. Using regular 'ums' and 'aahs', as well as 'mild interjections or grunts, demonstrate that the analyst is still present, alive, listening, following and trying to understand'.[23]

Examples of encouragement might be saying something along the lines of '*You tried something different there*' or '*I can see that you are struggling to stick with exploring this when it is difficult for you.*'

Empathy

Put simply, this means trying to understand a patient's experience and to communicate to them that they have been understood. Here the therapist tries to immerse herself in the patient's experience. In order to do this, it can be helpful to consciously think – how would I feel if this was happening to me? This can help to understand what the patient is going through and can help to frame empathic responses, for example '*I imagine that you would feel upset and worried by that ...*'

Information Giving

Information giving is a technique which does not fit neatly in the spectrum in Box 7.2. Information giving might be advising on the natural history of a depressive episode or the stages of mourning. It may also take the form of explaining the link between symptoms such as depression or anxiety and difficult interpersonal or even intrapersonal relations.

Psychoeducational interventions are used in psychodynamic psychotherapy but may look a little different to those used in other mental health specialties. One instance of a psychoeducational intervention would be discussing with someone who has a history of childhood sexual abuse that it is perfectly understandable that they have developed defences of mistrust and avoidance of vulnerability and dependence on other people – as these defences would have served them well in the past. It would be important to go on to explore how relevant these defences are to the person's present life – is the person operating as if the external threat is still present, when in fact things may have changed in the external world? Are the person's defences bringing difficulties now? The latter questions move into exploration/elaboration, illustrating how, in practice, the session unfolds organically rather than staying rigidly in one place on the spectrum of technique.

Another possible psychoeducational intervention might be to discuss with a patient, at an appropriate time, how his use of drugs could be conceptualised as a way of extinguishing painful feelings; and that it might be helpful to try to work out what these feelings might be in order to try to sit with them.

Exploration and Elaboration

Encouraging exploration and elaboration by the patient – in the middle of the spectrum in Box 7.3 – is usually where therapists and patients spend much of their time in sessions. This overlaps with several core approaches already discussed, including the core psychodynamic attitude, encouraging the patient to free associate, exploring affects, and being interested in how and why affects are avoided (i.e. exploring defensive processes).

Clarification

Another helpful 'pearl' described by Sublette and Novick is to 'be stupid'.[2] On the face of it this may seem like a strange instruction to a therapist but what they mean by this is, don't assume you know what is going on, and do maintain an attitude of curiosity. This attitude of curiosity demonstrates to the patient that we are really thinking about them and what they bring to the session. If we allow ourselves to be genuinely curious, then the patient might, with time, develop their capacity for openness and curiosity about themselves. Often novice therapists experience feelings of incompetence, which are usual when learning a new skill; however, these feelings can influence the therapist into feeling awkward generally about not knowing and this can inhibit asking ordinary questions. Other times, an overvaluation of interpretative work can lead therapists to downplay other core techniques which actually are very important in terms of the therapeutic process. It is worth bearing in mind that competence does not mean all-knowing.

Clarification can range from a relatively simple question like '*when did you say this happened*?' to more complex questioning which is outwith social norms and can feel uncomfortable for both therapist and patient. It can be helpful if a therapist develops a way of asking difficult questions that demonstrate interest and empathy even if the enquiry may not feel altogether comfortable for a patient. Examples might be: '*I wonder what it was that led you to do that?*', '*any idea what that might have been about?*', '*what might have been behind your comment*', and so on.

Confrontation

This intervention is not about being argumentative as one might think from the common use of the word. Instead, it refers to pointing out to a patient something important they are doing which they are overlooking or avoiding, so that it can be acknowledged and further understood (see Clinical Example 7).

Clinical Example 7 Therapeutic confrontation

A patient, Julie, who tended to be very placatory but who also had a history of aggressive self-harm, started to bring her therapist small gifts just before a break. When the therapist drew attention to this, Julie admitted that the gifts were intended to disguise her angry feelings about being abandoned (an example of the defence mechanism 'reaction formation'). Julie was aware of her feelings but found them unpleasant and difficult to express and she worried about how her therapist would respond to her anger and frustration. Hence the gifts could be seen as a way to avoid anything uncomfortable coming up in the room. This behaviour could also be recognised in her everyday life. During therapy Julie was able to recognise that this was unhelpful to her because her true feelings could not be explored with people in her life and so could not be resolved.

This therapeutic confrontation took the form of, *'I'm not sure if you are aware of this but I have noticed that you tend to bring me a gift just before we are due a break. I wonder what might be behind this?'*

Therapeutic confrontation is particularly relevant in the here and now of therapy. When therapeutic confrontation is to do with something happening between the patient and therapist, this forms part of the range of therapist activities that come under the umbrella of 'transference work', which we discussed earlier in this chapter.

During sessions, patients often talk about their current lives and relationships and inevitably there is a degree of subjectivity in their descriptions One of the tasks of the therapist is to offer a different viewpoint of their behaviour and their way of being – this is the third position described earlier. In this way, confrontation can offer the patient, in the here and now, information about themselves in a very immediate and real way. These discoveries may not always be pleasant, so making interventions of this nature requires sensitivity and a good therapeutic alliance, otherwise the patient can feel criticised or persecuted.

Interpretation

There can be a lot of anxiety generated around psychodynamic interpretation as it is sometimes considered to be the gold standard technique of psychodynamic psychotherapy and certainly it is one of the basic components of psychodynamic technique.[6] A simple description of an interpretation is that it consists of bringing something to a patient's awareness that they were previously unaware of. This is achieved through the translation of the patient's unconscious communication as it is expressed through their narrative, free association, dream material, and relational dynamics.[11] An interpretation is a hypothesis, it is not intended to be an absolute truth and should be couched in a tentative manner such as, *'I may be wrong but I wonder if . . .'* This allows the patient to agree or disagree with it. Even if a patient does not seem to respond well to an interpretation this does not necessarily mean it is incorrect (although it may be), it may just have been badly timed.

As when an interpreter translates a foreign language, the interpretation of unconscious material can never be completely accurate as it will be influenced by whoever is doing the interpreting. What is more important than absolute accuracy is that the interpretation is conveyed in a respectful manner and that the therapist is always open to being corrected.[11] Winnicott provides the encouraging advice that 'it is comparatively rare for a patient to be hurt by wrong interpretations made in a genuine attempt to use what is presented, the mistakes in omissions being due to the limits that belong to all human endeavour'.[24] It should be helpful for a novice therapist to note that a patient is unlikely to be harmed by an incorrect or a poorly timed interpretation as long as it is couched in a tentative and empathic manner.

What Is an Interpretation For?

There are several possible intentions of an interpretation. Firstly, 'at its simplest, one of the functions of an interpretation is to convey to the patient that his communications, however incoherent or confused are meaningful ... many interpretations serve the function of validating the patient's experience'.[11] Secondly, an interpretation can convey to the patient that he is not alone. Thirdly, as raised earlier, an interpretation can also provide a different perspective, the so-called third position. Patients often enter therapy with deeply ingrained ways of relating to others which are not always helpful and of which they are unaware. Interpretation can be used to tactfully point out these patterns of relating, along with a hypothesis of what might be underlying the pattern. Used in this latter way, interpretation overlaps with therapeutic confrontation – it is a question of what depth would be most helpful to put into the intervention. An interpretation would go beyond just pointing out an aspect of the patient's interactions. To illustrate, let us go back to Julie from Clinical Example 5, where the therapist drew attention to how Julie tended to buy the therapist gifts before breaks in therapy. In an interpretation, the therapist might start with the same approach as confrontation: '*I wonder what might be behind this ...?*' but then add an interpretative dimension such as, '*... and wonder if it is linked to me going away? I remember you saying how you can feel abandoned if your partner goes away for the weekend.*'

In practice, a good interpretation needs to be well-timed for the patient to be able to work with it. Sometimes an interpretation may be accurate but the patient is not yet ready to take it on board. But how is a therapist to know when the timing is right? There is no hard and fast rule about this. Sometimes, it may be helpful to make an interpretation when the unconscious issue in question is alive in the room and so more accessible for the patient to grasp. For other patients, making an interpretation when the emotion in the room is running high may result in the interpretation being taken literally (i.e. lacking an 'as if' quality), or being felt as intrusive or unhelpful; for these patients, it may be best to 'strike when the iron is cold'.[25] In part, it is a matter of trying it out, to tentatively make a suggestion about what the therapist thinks might be going on, and then noting the response by the patient. Interpretations using phrases such as '*this may be wrong but I wonder if ...* ' give the patient the experience that the therapist is thinking about him and, in addition, leave the way open for him to disagree.

In terms of transference interpretations (which are but one form of interpretation), a rule of thumb is that if the patient is attending sessions consistently and exploring issues openly, there is probably little to be gained from making transference interpretations. This is in keeping with Freud's advice to wait to interpret the transference until the transference brings resistance to the therapeutic process.[1] Freud introduced this caution to guard against any tendency in the therapist to 'regard it as a special triumph to fling these "solutions" in [the patient's] face at the first interview'.[1] A more Kleinian approach might be to interpret the transference earlier on.

When there are issues arising within the therapy relationship such as an early therapeutic rupture, it is important to try and put what is happening into words and to try and work it through. This may include the use of interpretation. For example, '*I wonder if you are finding it difficult to get here on time because the therapy is making you feel exposed and vulnerable?* Depending on the particular situation, the therapist might continue, '*... and perhaps this reminds you of times in the past when your vulnerability has been used against you?*'

As Lemma writes, 'A good interpretation is simple, to the point and transparent.'[11] It is helpful to demonstrate to the patient where the interpretation has come from and to show the workings of the therapist's mind – this is what is meant by 'transparent'. One of the goals of therapy is to foster the ability of self-reflection and analysis, which means to be able to think about oneself and one's actions in order to generate meaning. With the use of a good interpretation, the therapist can model this.[11] There is little point in peppering the session with clever interpretations – even if they are accurate, this does not help the patient to think for himself and to reflect on his states of mind and responses to them.

According to Malan, following the affect in a session very closely will help the therapist to determine if an interpretation has meaning for the patient.[26] He says that if the interpretation has hit home there will be a deepening of the rapport between the therapist and patient and, in addition, a further elaboration of material in the narrative which confirms its utility. A conscious agreement without these confirmatory factors may simply be a demonstration of a compliant patient. By contrast, conscious disagreement, but with further unconscious elaboration, may signify an accurate intervention. Therefore a useful means of determining whether an interpretation has meaning is to listen hard to what the patient talks about after it has been made.

Types of Interpretation

There are various forms of interpretation. An interpretation may involve the therapist 'pointing out connections between different phenomena when the patient does not see the linkage'.[5] At other times, it may be about using the countertransference to tentatively explore warded-off affects. We now describe two forms of interpretation in more detail: extra-transference interpretations and transference interpretations.

Extra-Transference Interpretations

Sometimes called 'reconstructive interpretations', extra-transference interpretations make a link between the patient's current life and his recollections of experiences as a child. They explicitly make a connection between the patient's interactions outside the session and with his accounts of family experiences when growing up. For example, '*I think you are worried about your boss taking advantage of you and potentially abusing you because this connects with some of your experiences of your father when you were a boy that you were telling me about.*'

Transference Interpretations

This type of interpretation references the here and now and explicitly comments on the patient's relationship to the therapist. These can help the patient to become more aware of the way he is relating to the therapist (and possibly therefore with others). The content of a transference interpretation is inferred from what the patient talks about during a session, the manner in which they talk about it, and generally what kind of atmosphere is created. Patients can say the same thing in a very different way and the therapist needs to be able to take this into account. A transference interpretation might look something like the following:

'*I wonder if you are worried that I will be impatient and angry with you when we talk about painful experiences that you have had in the past. Perhaps that is why you have found it difficult to attend our sessions on time and why, when you are here, you feel anxious and find it difficult to speak.'*

Note here that the therapist outlines the steps she has taken to get to this interpretation.

Lemma states 'A reconstructive interpretation locates the origin of the patient's behaviour firmly in the past . . . By contrast a transference interpretation is bolder: it invites the patient to examine his emotional reaction, however uncomfortable or distressing in the immediacy of the therapeutic relationship.'[11] This can be anxiety-provoking, both for the patient and for the therapist, partly because this is outside usual societal norms for talking to each other. However, a transference interpretation, being both immediate and affect laden, can bring significant insight for the patient which may give him the necessary tools for change.

The distinction between these two types of interpretation can be further illustrated by Malan's work and his two triangles, which we describe in the following section on working through.

Working Through

The range of techniques just described rarely work immediately and any change is likely to be transient. Working through refers to the repetitive process within therapy sessions of supporting the patient to get to know how he relates to himself and others, and being able to use this insight to explore new ways of relating (see also Chapter 8, section on the 'Middle Phase of Therapy'). Malan devised two triangles as an aid to supporting the therapist in making links across the patient's ways of relating in different situations, as a psychotherapy session unfolds (see Figure 7.1). These triangles can help in working out what the transference is, what the corresponding countertransference is, what a patient's underlying object relations are, and thus support the process of working through.

The first triangle is known as the 'triangle of defence'. This triangle is closely linked to the conflict model described in Chapter 2 and describes the way in which hidden feelings

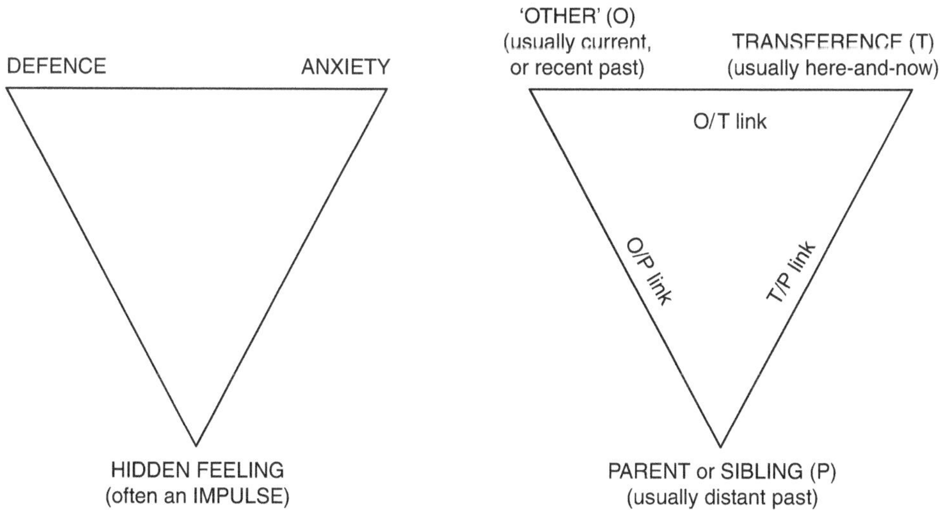

Figure 7.1 Malan's triangles. Triangle of defence (left); triangle of person (right). Reproduced from Malan (1995)[26] (under STM permissions guidance).

(often an impulse) cause anxiety which in turn leads to defensive manoeuvres on the part of the patient (Chapter 11 on anxiety expands further on this). These hidden feelings are associated with the patient's internal objects.

The second triangle is the 'triangle of person'. The three tips of the triangle represent the *Other*, the *Therapist,* and the *Past.* Patients usually seek therapy due to problems they are experiencing in their current lives. These problems can be symptoms which have arisen as a consequence of difficult relationships, or the presenting problem may be a more clear-cut relational one. These current life problems are represented by the *Other* tip of the triangle. Generally in therapy it tends to make sense to the patient if the therapist explores this area during initial sessions.

To illustrate the triangle of person, consider Andrew, the 45-year-old dentist, described in Chapter 2. The therapist initially explored Andrew's depressive feelings, finding out at what point they had arisen in relation to his current life and exploring anything that tended to increase them. In response to this exploration Andrew described feeling undervalued and criticised by his wife for not doing better in his career, and undermined by his manager who he felt did not like him. This activity on the part of the therapist represented exploring the *Other* tip of the triangle.

The *Past* tip relates to the patient's sense of their childhood experience. Here in the case of Andrew, he had felt he was an unwanted child and had experienced his mother as being openly critical and rejecting of him, favouring his older sister.

Thus an extra-transference/reconstructive interpretation might take the form of linking the current difficulties Andrew is experiencing with his manager and wife (Other) with his sense as a child of feeling rejected in his relationship with his mother (Past). This would be an Other-Past link.

This example demonstrates how the triangles can be used to structure a session – the therapist can listen out carefully for themes that come up time and again, or for repeated descriptions of difficulties in relationships. They can then consider which area(s) the narrative refers to and, where appropriate, make interventions linking two or more points of the triangle.

Returning to Andrew again from Chapter 2, as therapy progressed he became increasingly convinced that his therapist did not like him and did not wish to work with him. He began to write her frequent letters in illegible handwriting which were frustratingly difficult to read, seeking reassurance that the therapist valued and wanted to continue working with him.

Here it may have been tempting to offer reassurance to Andrew that he was liked. However, this would have driven his anxieties underground and also would have missed a valuable opportunity to tactfully point out (i.e. make an observation) about how he habitually related to others, that is, as if others would not like him and potentially would be rejecting of him. This dynamic afforded an opportunity for another side of the triangle to be linked – Andrew's expectations of being disliked and rejected by the therapist with his experience of the past in relation to his mother. This would be an example of a transference interpretation where the Transference-Past link is made.

Lastly, a link can be made between the *Other* and the transference as there seems to be a clear correspondence between how Andrew experiences his wife and how he has been relating to the therapist. As we can see, over time in therapy, we may identify the same central relational dynamic emerging in all three corners of the triangle (Figure 7.2). This points to the patient's underlying mental representations of self and other which manifest across all three

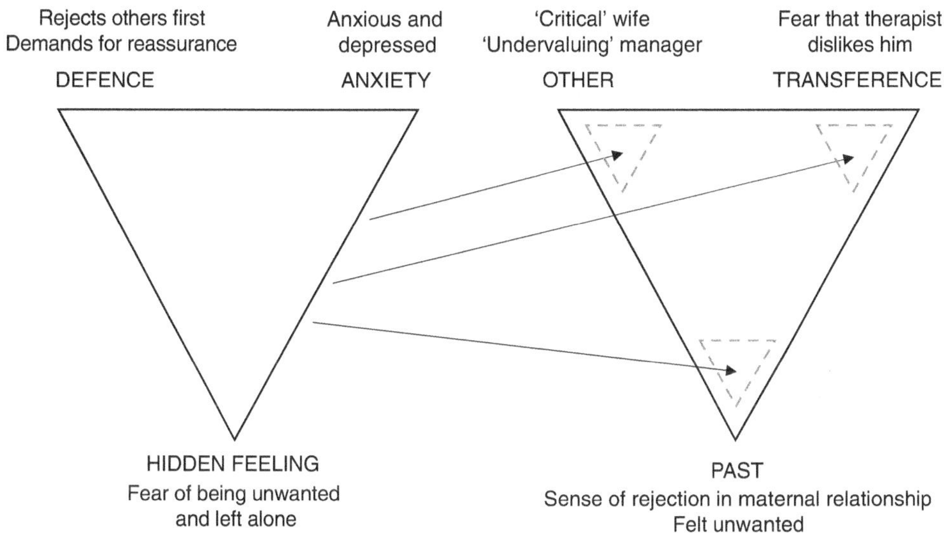

Figure 7.2 Formulation for 'Andrew' using Malan's two triangle approach.
Adapted from Leiper et al. (2004)[19] and Molnos (1984)[27] with permission from SAGE and Wiley. Copyright SAGE (2004) and Wiley (1984).

tips of the triangle of person. Figure 7.2 follows the approach of Molnos in combining the two triangles – the arrows represent how the key dynamics of conflict in the first triangle may manifest across all interpersonal settings.[27]

Malan's triangles provide one way to help the therapist (and therefore the patient) to organise and make sense of what might seem initially like a confusing tangle of narrative, feelings, symptoms, defences, and so on. It can also provide some direction for what the therapist might attend to at a given point in a course of therapy. For example, if a person's defensive processes might be apparent (the top left point in the triangle of conflict), but not their feelings, the therapist might listen out in particular for feelings or explore with the patient about what is driving their defences. The triangle of person might support the therapist to make an interpretation that involves making links between how the patient operates in a similar way in two or more relationships settings – that is, this paves the way for the patient developing insight into recurring interpersonal patterns and his role in unconsciously bringing these about.

Working with Resistance

In this final section, we address how to work clinically with the phenomenon of resistance (for definition and theory of resistance, see Chapter 2). In brief, resistance refers to when the patient's defences are activated during the course of therapy, as a result of what is happening in the work. Resistance might occur at any point in therapy. The themes in this section could be read alongside Chapter 8, in particular the section on 'The Middle Phase of Therapy'.

As most of us realise, it is difficult to change. Sometimes it seems obvious that a person's current way of functioning is causing misery and yet there is a draw to old patterns of behaviours in spite of all evidence that they are unhelpful. Those of us who have experienced therapy ourselves will also have struggled to do things in a different way. But why is this the case? It is considered that there are several different reasons but one major underlying factor is that it can feel very risky indeed to try new ways of relating as this can mean making oneself vulnerable and may also require giving something else up. A succinct way of putting this is 'better the devil you know.' Leiper and Maltby, drawing on Fairbairn,[28] explain that our present modes of relating reflect a compromise 'created with difficulty in the past; however painful, [these modes] were the best we could do in the circumstances … Even bad relationships provide a subtle sense of safety and connection in the world.'[19]

Resistance has sometimes been misunderstood as being a hindrance to therapy, with a related misunderstanding being that attempts should be made to bypass or break through it. However, remembering that resistance is the manifestation of the defence mechanisms a patient uses, it follows that, as all patients have defence mechanisms, all patients will show resistance at some point in their therapy. Exploring how a patient demonstrates resistance, and understanding where it has come from, offers valuable information as to their way of operating in interpersonal relationships. Or as Gabbard puts it, 'perhaps the most important principle is to regard resistance as a phenomenon that reveals rather than conceals. We might regard resistance as the way that patients show us who they are. Patients must do psychotherapy in the way they must do it not the way that we think they should do it. Resistance is not "bad" behaviour on the part of the patient.'[5]

Often it is fairly straightforward for a patient to cognitively recognise their problems and to understand where they have come from, but in order to change their current way of relating, much repetition is required in the therapy. The repetition required when working with resistance is closely linked to the process of working through as described in the previous section. Conceptualising this need for repetition in the work of change is to understand that to give up habitual ways of being requires the work of mourning for the loss of the old self and old object relationships (see Chapter 8, section on 'Mourning'). This takes effort and time because giving up old ways of relating brings up feelings of anxiety and sadness, even if the current ways of relating are in some aspects problematic for the patient.[19] Technically this task requires that the therapist is holding and empathic, as previously described, but at the same time is able to be adequately distanced to be able to note what is going on.

Resistance may seem to emerge spontaneously or may be more clearly connected to what is happening in the therapy process, sometimes occurring during or immediately after a particular intervention. As such, the therapist needs to be prepared at any point to turn their attention to resistance. For some, if not all, patients, resistance accompanies developmental change at every step of the way.

Greenson (1967) provides a useful summary strategy for working with resistance[29], adapted below:

- Note the fact that the patient is resisting and what it is that they are doing.
- Ask yourself, and explore with the patient, what is being kept at bay, what function does the resistance serve? For example, what affect, loss, or idea is the patient trying to avoid?
- Think together about why the patient needs to do this and empathise with the patient's predicament.

During the beginning stages of therapy there are a number of ways resistance can be seen. For example, a person may, unconsciously, turn things around and ask the therapist a lot of questions or seek advice, as a protection against the vulnerability of becoming 'a patient'.

There may also be long silences in the session or alternatively a lot of talking with no space to think. Usually, these resistances will settle once the patient gets used to the setting, especially if the therapist follows the basic principles of therapy and attempts to keep a therapeutic frame and its boundaries. However, some resistances persist, and it is important to try to address them (see Clinical Example 8).

Clinical Example 8 Anna: Working with resistance

We now take up again the example of the psychiatric nurse, Anna, mentioned in Chapter 2 (Example 3), at a point midway through the year of therapy. Anna understood intellectually how her way of hiding her struggles was driving her into depression, but she was in no way prepared to let slip the role she portrayed to the outside world of the dependable, solid carer. She said she was 'never going to be vulnerable again'. Her defences (repression of her own needs for care) were strong, her resistance to change evident and understandable given her sense of family dynamics as a child.

Change was facilitated through an ongoing process of empathising with her anxieties. This included the therapist acknowledging how frightening it felt for her in the present day in terms of exposing unmet needs; and acknowledging the fear of the unknown and unfamiliar. In a session two-thirds through the year, the therapist spoke with her about how, on the one hand, Anna wished new ways of relating were possible, and noted that she had come into therapy looking for change. Whilst, on the other hand, the therapist recognised just how much she was also holding on to tried and trusted ways of being and didn't want to let these go. She seemed to feel understood by this. The session after this, Anna returned looking a bit lighter. It seemed this understanding allowed her to feel contained and, somewhat paradoxically, mobilised a capacity to do things differently.

A turning point was when she was able to risk letting her boss know something of her inner struggles and found that this was met with sympathy and a solidity, as opposed to her boss collapsing in the way she had experienced people doing in the past.

The following are some common ways that resistance can outwardly manifest, along with discussion of possible ways the therapist might respond.

Flight into Health

This is when a patient tells you that they feel better, even though they have only attended a small number of sessions and nothing obvious has changed. If this happens, we might try to explore further with the patient what is happening both in their outside life and in the therapy. Are there still problems present? The patient is likely to feel comforted that they no longer have symptoms, but if their underlying issues are unchanged, this symptom relief is unlikely to last. The therapist therefore attempts to make sure that if the patient decides to leave therapy that they do so having some insight into any ongoing issues.

Silence

Silence can often be anxiety-provoking for a therapist. It can evoke a clinical dilemma in which the therapist does not wish a silence would go on for too long, but at the same time does not want to be too directive. It can be helpful to share this dilemma with the patient – '*You are not speaking much today and I'm not sure if you would like us to be quiet together for a while . . . or if there is something you would like to speak about but are finding it hard to get started.*'

Timekeeping

Sometimes a patient may be late to a session for good reason, but sometimes a pattern of lateness becomes clear. If this seems to be happening, try to identify what the actual pattern is and then bring this to the attention of the patient. It can also be helpful to monitor the countertransference evoked in the therapist when the patient is late and use this to frame an intervention (see Clinical Example 9).

In practice, if a patient is late to a session, the therapist should keep to the agreed session time, tempting though it may be to extend it, especially if the reasons for lateness seem to be compelling. Depending on circumstances, the therapist might say something along the lines of:

'*I appreciate there are real practical reasons why you may be late today. And I wonder whether there may be other reasons too*?' Or, the therapist might explore what it is like for the patient having a shorter session (e.g. the patient might feel relief, or guilt, or short-changed).

This way of intervening addresses both the outside life of the patient as well as the underlying resistance, which can make exploring the resistance more acceptable to the patient.

Clinical Example 9 **Emily: A late arrival**

Emily, a patient whose initial presentation was via a dramatic suicide attempt, had outlined fantasies of harming herself at the end of one session and had turned up 30 minutes late for the next one. During those 30 minutes her therapist had felt frightened and panicky. This countertransference gave the therapist a possible insight into the awful feelings her patient may have been experiencing in relation to separations.

Using her countertransference feelings to inform her, the therapist tentatively explored with Emily how she might be experiencing the session endings. The patient agreed that she felt desperate in between her sessions. Talking with her about this helped to increase the positive therapeutic alliance leading to the possibility of sensitive exploration of Emily's actions on others. This was able to give the patient a better insight into how her behaviour impacted on others and illustrated why she found it difficult to maintain good relationships with people. Note that the therapist did not discuss her own feelings directly in an unprocessed form but used them to consider what might have been getting projected into her.

Missed Sessions

Thinking about missed sessions, there may be differences between a session which has been cancelled by prior arrangement, as this is sometimes unavoidable, and one which is missed with no word. Unexpectedly missing a session can be a sign of an active resistance by the patient. If this happens, it can be a good idea to contact the patient to let them know that the therapist was sorry the patient wasn't able to make their session and to encourage them to attend next time. It should be noted that this is not a hard and fast rule and practice varies according to different therapists and the needs of the specific patient. Additionally, it can be helpful to note the emotional impact of any cancellation, lateness, or missed session on the therapist as, again, this may provide valuable information about the patient's internal world.

Acting Out

Freud (1914) writes that 'we may say that the patient does not remember anything of what he has forgotten and repressed but *acts* it out. He reproduces it not as a memory but as an action; he repeats it without of course knowing that he is repeating it.'[30]

Acting out is used to describe events that occur outwith the analytic setting and can be considered to be a form of resistance in that the patient is doing something active rather than observing and reflecting on themselves. By way of example, a patient, who was angry about a comment her therapist had made during the session, subsequently got into an argument with a bus driver on the way home.

Acting out is often connected to the transference. However, a note of caution – not everything that happens outside a session is connected to the transference. It can be annoying to the patient and come across as false and lacking in empathy if a therapist tries to relate everything back to themselves.

Resistances in the Terminal Phase

Often the ending of therapy can evoke separation anxiety which can bring up ambivalent feelings in the patient. These can be unconsciously defended against as they can feel unacceptable to the patient and instead are manifested in resistance. Behaviours derived from this resistance include missing sessions, a return or worsening of the patient's original symptoms, and finding it difficult to find things to talk about. Patients might also try to find an immediate replacement therapist, either seeking one out on their own or requesting an immediate onwards referral. This can be seen as an attempt to avoid painful feelings of loss or abandonment. These feelings should be explored well before the planned ending of the therapy in order to give the patient the opportunity to mourn their loss. This is discussed further in the section on the 'Ending Phase' in Chapter 8.

Concluding Remarks

This chapter has outlined psychodynamic psychotherapy technique, ranging from the more supportive end of the spectrum to the more expressive (interpretative). This includes the utilisation of transference and countertransference to elucidate internal object relations along with how to use interpretation and other approaches to bring these to the attention of a patient. It is important to understand and consider technique across the spectrum in order to develop a working alliance, to address resistance, and to work with the patient to discover and rework old ways of relating, both to others and to himself. The utilisation of technique in psychodynamic psychotherapy is significantly influenced by the associated underpinning theory and should be tailored according to the requirements and peculiarities of each patient at each point in the therapy.

To conclude, as Leiper and Maltby put it – 'Old ghosts are invoked and let loose in the transference in the hope that they can be laid to rest.'[19]

References

1. Freud S. On the beginning of treatment: further recommendations on the technique of psychoanalysis. In Strachey J, editor. The Standard Edition of the Complete Psychological Works of Sigmund Freud volume 12. London: Hogarth Press (original work published 1913); 1958. pp. 122–44.

2. Sublette ME, Novick J. Essential techniques for the beginning psychodynamic psychotherapist. Am J Psychother 2004;58 (1):67–75.
3. Freud S. Freud's psychoanalytic procedure. In The Standard Edition of the Complete Psychological Works of Sigmund Freud volume 7. London: Hogarth Press (original work published 1953); 1904. pp. 249–56.
4. Lemma A, Roth A, Pilling S. The competences required to deliver effective psychoanalytic/psychodynamic therapy. Research Department of Clinical, Educational and Health Psychology, UCL; 2008.
5. Gabbard GO. Long-term psychodynamic psychotherapy: a basic text. In Long-Term Psychodynamic Psychotherapy: A Basic Text. Washington, DC: American Psychiatric Pub.; 2010.
6. Kernberg OF. The four basic components of psychoanalytic technique and derived psychoanalytic psychotherapies. World Psychiatry 2016;15(3):287–8.
7. Edmundson M. Death of Sigmund Freud: Fascism, Psychoanalysis and the Rise of Fundamentalism. London: Bloomsbury Publishing; 2008.
8. Smith S. The golden fantasy: a regressive reaction to separation anxiety. Int J Psychoanal 1977;58(3):311–24.
9. Freud S. The Interpretation of Dreams. London: Hogarth Press (original work published 1900); 1953.
10. Bollas C. The Evocative Object World. New York, NY: Routledge/Taylor & Francis Group; 2009.
11. Lemma A. Introduction to the Practice of Psychoanalytic Psychotherapy, 2nd ed. West Sussex: Wiley Blackwell; 2016.
12. Høglend P. Exploration of the patient-therapist relationship in psychotherapy. AJP 2014;171(10):1056–66.
13. Høglend P, Amlo S, Marble A et al. Analysis of the patient-therapist relationship in dynamic psychotherapy: an experimental study of transference interpretations. Am J Psychiatry 2006;163 (10):1739–46.
14. Mitchell SA. Influence and Autonomy in Psychoanalysis. New York: Routledge; 1997.
15. Racker H. The meanings and uses of countertransference. The Psychoanalytic Quarterly 1957;26:303–57.
16. Sandler J. Countertransference and role-responsiveness. International Review of Psycho-Analysis 1976;3(1):43–7.
17. Carpy DV. Tolerating the countertransference: a mutative process. Int J Psychoanal 1989;70 (Pt 2):287–94.
18. Casement P. Learning from the Patient. New edition. New York: Guilford Publications; 1992.
19. Leiper R, Maltby M. The Psychodynamic Approach to Therapeutic Change. London: Sage Publications Ltd; 2004.
20. Ogden TH. Comments on transference and countertransference in the initial analytic meeting. Psychoanalytic Inquiry 1992;12 (2):225–47.
21. Leichsenring F, Steinert C. Towards an evidence-based unified psychodynamic protocol for emotional disorders. Journal of Affective Disorders 2018;232:400–16.
22. Bateman A, Holmes J. Introduction to Psychoanalysis: Contemporary Theory and Practice. London: Routledge; 1992.
23. Rycroft C. A Critical Dictionary of Psychoanalysis. Harmondsworth, Middlesex: Penguin; 1968.
24. Winnicott DW. The Value of the Therapeutic Consultation: Written in 1965. In Winnicott C, Shepherd R, Davis M, editors. Psycho-Analytic Explorations. London: Routledge; 1989. pp. 318–24.
25. Pine F. Developmental Theory and Clinical Process. New Haven: Yale University Press; 1985.
26. Malan D. Individual Psychotherapy and the Science of Psychodynamics. 2nd edition. Oxford: Butterworth-Heinemann (Elsevier); 1995.
27. Molnos A. The two triangles are four: a diagram to teach the process of dynamic brief psychotherapy. British Journal of Psychotherapy 1984;1(2):112–25.

28. Fairbairn WRD. Psychoanalytic Studies of the Personality. London: Routledge & Kegan Paul; 1952.

29. Greenson R. The Technique and Practice of Psychoanalysis. New York: International Universities Press; 1967.

30. Freud S. Remembering, repeating and working-through. In Strachey J, editor. The Standard Edition of the Complete Psychological Works of Sigmund Freud volume 12. London: Hogarth Press (original work published 1914); 1958. pp. 145–56.

Chapter 8

The Overall Structure of Psychodynamic Therapy

Table of Contents

Introduction 128
The Early Phase 130
Developing a Therapeutic Alliance 131
Close Listening 133
Allowing a Formulation to Unfold 134
The Early Phase in Practice 135
Middle Phase 136
The Formulation in Action 137
The Therapeutic Relationship as a Vehicle for Change 139
Working Through 140
Mourning 142
Late Phase (Separation) 143
A Basic Principle – Talk about the Ending 144
Transference and Countertransference Work 145
Ending, What Ending? 145
Gratitude 146
When Therapy Has Not Been Helpful 147
Endings and Borderline States 147
Post-Termination Phase 148
Concluding Remarks 149

Introduction

It is one of the remarkable but also unsettling characteristics of psychodynamic psychotherapy that its course is not rigidly predetermined, so that things can emerge in therapy that neither the therapist nor patient could have anticipated. What focus the work takes and what therapeutic approaches are most useful for each patient need to be discovered along the way. This does not mean it is impossible to give direction or that there is no structure to therapy. We could continue the analogy (from Chapter 7) to chess, where there are countless possibilities of future moves, albeit contained within the structure of the game. Despite this, guides are available, many of which may organise play into the dynamics of the opening, the mid-game and the endgame. Likewise, in psychotherapy, there are many paths that the therapy can take, but it is also possible to offer guidance and outline the general phases it may follow. In this chapter, we aim to provide orientation to clinicians who are embarking on their first courses of therapy. We integrate theory and technique to offer a longitudinal perspective on how matters can play out over a course of therapy.

As a very rough guide, in a course of time-limited therapy, the early, middle and late phase each last approximately one-third of the overall time. This chapter provides a general guide to what issues and tasks are more likely to surface at various points in the work, but several clarifications are important. Phases tend to blend into each other, rather than being clearly demarcated like acts in a play. Furthermore, a focus that is usually associated with one particular phase may emerge at any time. For example, the patient's anxieties about leaving the therapist are described in the section on the late phase, but, in reality, these concerns may emerge at any point. Additionally, for a proportion of patients, the work may stay in what feels like an early phase throughout much, if not all, of the work for various reasons – for example, due to a strong defensive structure or instability in their current life – and they may not yet be able to undertake the 'working through' typical of the middle phase.

There are differences and overlaps between open-ended work and time-limited work. In time-limited work, especially in briefer courses of therapy (less than six months), the therapist needs to stay very conscious of the number of sessions available, and often needs to guide the therapy along using more structure. With open-ended work there is more time and space to allow things to unfold organically, but spontaneity and space are still very much part of brief therapy too. It is a question of degree. Sometimes in publicly funded open-ended therapy (i.e. when the patient does not pay a fee), there comes a point in the work when the patient may miss sessions as part of avoiding dealing with their problems. According to O'Neill, this can happen because the patient is (unconsciously) investigating whether or not therapy is limitless and grounded in the realities of time and value.[1] The therapist will need to address this to prevent the therapy becoming, in the words of Freud, 'interminable'. When this particular dynamic can be articulated and sufficiently worked though in sessions, this can be steadying for the patient and bring about 'a new seriousness thereafter in the level of the patient's involvement in the treatment'.[1] This chapter will focus mainly on time-limited work, typically, weekly sessions over 6 to 18 months. In our experience, this is the usual arrangement for therapists who work in publicly funded services and those at the start of their career.

A schematic overview of a course of therapy is depicted in Figure 1. Of course, in reality, therapy is much messier than this; not least, because some patients leave therapy earlier than planned. As Leiper & Maltby explain, the purpose of imagining a simplified model in this way is to enable us 'to see the work as a whole, something which is not always easy to do when in the midst of it'.[2]

The process of therapeutic change has been summarised by Freud as 'remembering', 'repeating', and then 'working through'. In the early sessions, key tasks for the therapist are creating a therapeutic frame (see Chapter 5), developing a 'working alliance', and being interested and curious towards the patient, their life, and inner world. A therapeutic (or 'working') alliance refers to the forging of a trusting, collaborative, and secure dimension to the relationship between the patient and therapist – this is discussed further in the section 'Developing a Therapeutic Alliance', below. In this early phase, some patients feel initial symptom relief and release (sometimes referred to as 'catharsis'), and a sense of hope as they begin to put into words their underlying difficulties ('remembering') and develop a clearer sense of what is going on. In the middle phase, characterised by 'repeating' and 'working through', the work can come alive as old patterns come to the fore and the patient and therapist attempt to understand and explore the strong

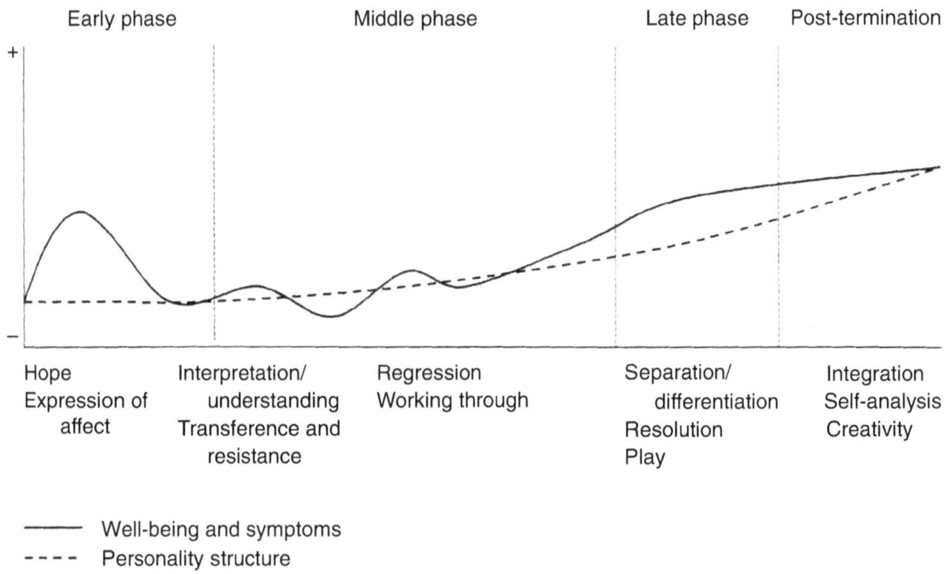

Figure 8.1 Idealised course of psychodynamic psychotherapy. The words underneath the graph illustrate common processes and phenomena associated with therapy in its various phases. These processes reflect particular interactions between patient and therapist (such as working through or attending to the emerging transference). In terms of emphasis, some of these processes refer more to the therapist's activity (such as interpretation), and others more to the patient (such as self-analysis in the post-termination phase).
Adapted from Leiper et al. 2004[2] and Wolberg 1977[3] with permission from SAGE and Elsevier.
Copywrite SAGE (2004) Elsevier (1977).

attachments to well-established defences and ways of relating. The late phase can be a productive period where concerns from the middle phase may come to life even more clearly. Attention is given to the process of separation from the therapist and the various tasks that go with this, such as coming to terms with the limitations of what is possible in therapy. Finally, in the post-termination phase, patients may experience ongoing development as changes in their underlying mental structures (i.e. their ways of experiencing self and other, and associated defences) brought about in therapy make themselves felt in their everyday lives and relationships.

The Early Phase

The early phase is typically about 'remembering'. Through interactions with a therapist who is listening and receptive, the patient can bring to mind and put into words aspects of themselves, their history, and their relationships with others that hitherto may have been out of their awareness. This may account for the observation that many patients feel some relief and improvement during the early phase.[2]

This section on the early phase of therapy can be read alongside the chapter on creating a therapeutic frame (Chapter 5) and the chapter on technique (Chapter 7) which cover core approaches used early in therapy and the 'analytic attitude'. The present section will focus on three important aspects of the early phase of therapy: developing a therapeutic alliance; close listening; and developing a psychodynamic formulation.

Developing a Therapeutic Alliance

The therapeutic alliance has been defined by Zetzel as 'the consistent, stable relationship which will allow the patient to maintain an essentially positive attitude to the psychoanalytic task when the conflicts revived in the transference neurosis bring disturbing wishes and fantasies close to the surface of consciousness'.[4] Freud considered that the patient needed to observe themself as if they were another person and that this was a necessity if therapy was to be successful. This phenomenon can also be seen as an aspect of the therapeutic alliance. The quality of the therapeutic alliance is a strong predictor of a good therapeutic outcome.[4]

Some people come to therapy with an idea or wish that they could somehow get rid of or 'cut out' unwanted aspects of their psyche, that is, aspects of their mind or personality. This is a developmentally 'archaic' way of attempting to deal with anxieties. However, not only is this impossible, but if this idea is pursued by the patient, it could well make them feel worse about themselves. This is because the underlying needs arising from the unwanted aspects of their mind will not be addressed; furthermore, an internal dynamic of wanting to get rid of aspects of oneself is likely to give rise to feelings of dislike about oneself and a sense of being unwanted. For these patients, the therapist aims to contain these troubling experiences, to understand them, rather than get rid of them. The therapist tries to form an alliance with the patient, more specifically with the observing aspects of the patient, to work together in a shared aim to try and understand these troubling experiences.

The therapist cultivates the therapeutic alliance by their availability, interest, reliability, and warmth. This is the basis of any therapeutic work. Furthermore, the therapist conveys support through their empathic, non-judgmental approach. A reasonable therapeutic alliance allows the patient and therapist to work together and means that the relationship can survive 'in spite of the strong and often negative emotions that may surface during treatment'.[6] A common school of thought is that a good therapeutic alliance is a prerequisite for more interpretative techniques to be useful to the patient, including working in the transference.[5] However, a recent study suggests that working in the transference (see Box 3.2 in Chapter 3), if done sensitively and skilfully, may actually bring the most benefit when there are current difficulties in the therapeutic alliance – perhaps as the negative transference seems real to the patient and not abstract[7] (see also Høglend 2004[8] and Chapter 7 for further discussion about therapeutic alliance and working in the transference).

A therapeutic alliance may be formed easily with some patients. However, this may take longer and require considerably more attention when working with someone whose internal world lacks a benign figure (i.e. when someone lacks a sense that others or the self could have good qualities). It is a fundamental thesis of this book that the therapist adapts their approach to each patient, whilst retaining the core principles of psychodynamic theory and practice. Crucially the therapist has to consider the developmental level (or levels) that the patient is functioning at (see Chapter 9, section 'Organisation of the Internal World'). A quieter, 'uncovering' style suits many patients with a more neurotic developmental organisation.[6] This contrasts with work with people operating at a borderline developmental level, where the emotional intensity may be high for both parties. In this situation, the therapist has to be quick-thinking, transparent in their communication about mental states, responsive, and clear in demarcating the boundary between the patient's and the therapist's mental state (see Chapter 13). Psychodynamic work with people with a more psychotic developmental organisation may be possible for experienced clinicians, with some adaptation in therapeutic technique, and where the patient is sufficiently supported within their external environment. Interested readers are directed to McWilliams[6] and Lucas.[9] (Please note, 'psychotic' in the psychodynamic sense has a somewhat different meaning to the psychiatric use of the term – see Chapter 9 for explanation of the psychodynamic meaning.)

Exploring the in-session process is an important way to deepen the therapeutic alliance. This includes the therapist noticing changes in the patient's affect from direct observation and from countertransference experiences, and commenting on these sensitively, for example:

- *'Did you notice how the feeling seemed to change a minute ago from x to y? What was happening then?'*
- *'You looked teary when you spoke about . . . '*
- *'I'm aware we're talking about these really serious things. But it's as if we could be talking about something really light – how does it feel for you?'*

Not only can this facilitate a deepening in rapport, as the patient may feel that they have really been listened to, but often these subtle changes in affect signal something that is going on for the patient beneath the surface. Attending to these subtle changes can help promote a patient's interest in and awareness of their inner workings.

The therapist also takes an interest in the here-and-now situation of the patient's experience of being with the therapist:

- *'What is it like talking to me about this?'*
- *'You said earlier you were worried about talking to me about feeling miserable . . . what is it actually like?'*

At this stage, this is not necessarily about interpreting the transference, but about demonstrating an interest in the patient's subjective experience, and facilitating open expression and dialogue.

Certain approaches can be unhelpful to the development of the therapeutic alliance (Box 8.1).

One might understand the points in Box 8.1 as relating either to an overly cold and strict approach to the analytic attitude, or to the opposite problem of the therapist not bringing enough structure and not setting boundaries (see also Box 8.2).

Box 8.1 Therapist approaches which can hinder development of a therapeutic alliance. From Ackerman et al. (2001).[10]

Being inflexible

Failing to structure the session

Over-structure of the session

Inappropriate self-disclosure

Inappropriate use of silence

Unyielding transference interpretations

Superficial interventions

Box 8.2 The therapist's manner

A therapist striving for ideal care will likely sooner or later fall to the opposite pole in the patient's experience as an ideal position is unsustainable and splits experiences into extremes of 'good' and 'bad'. Furthermore, a therapist who, for personal reasons, needs to be experienced as wholly good is likely to make it harder for their patients to get to know, articulate, and process the relational dynamics they bring (such as expectation of others as absent, frightening, aggressive, and so on). If a therapist is hasty to imply, *'oh no, that's not me'*, it closes the door on being able to reflect on how these dynamics are alive in the here and now. In fact, when a therapist ducks the negative transference by insisting they are 'good', the patient is likely to feel invalidated because their experience of the therapist is being dismissed.

It is easy to go too far the other way too, and for the therapist to be too cold. As early as 1935, Suttie criticised Freud as having a 'taboo on tenderness' in the therapeutic relationship, with anxieties on the part of the therapist leading to an overly passive and reserved technique.[11]

In our view and practice, rather than having a manner at one extreme or another, the therapist takes a steady, relatively warm approach. Of course, due to the transference, this does not mean that the therapist is necessarily experienced in this way. As therapy goes on and projections are processed and able to be 'taken back' by the patient, a more realistic picture of the therapist may emerge in the patient's mind – referred to classically as the 'resolution of the transference neurosis'. The therapist does not have one fixed manner, but the degree of outward activity, transparency, and support on the part of the therapist is tailored to what is most useful for each patient (see earlier discussion in 'Developing a Therapeutic Alliance' about developmental level of the patient and adaptations in therapist style).

For those patients who are desperately seeking an ideal in the therapist, rather than attempting to provide an ideal, what may be more useful in the long run is a benign, consistent (rather than all-perfect) therapist who provides a relationship where the loss of the ideal can be mourned rather than denied, and where new but good-enough ways of being can be discovered.

Close Listening

What do patients find in psychodynamic therapy? The opening of every course of therapy is a journey of discovery for each patient and their therapist. The therapist should aim for spontaneity and a capacity to be surprised, and develop a respectful stance, which acknowledges the individuality of each patient. The therapist encourages the patient to elaborate on what they are saying, is curious about underlying feelings, enquires about people that are spoken about and how the patient feels in relation to them, and is interested in how the patient relates to themself.

This approach offers patients the experience of being listened to attentively (Ogden 1992).[12] As a result, the patient may also begin to question, perhaps for the first time, well-established patterns of relating that hitherto appeared unremarkable.

The therapist listens and takes an interest not only in the patient's words, but also how they are said: the themes that emerge and what content tends to be joined or separated; the various moods and colours of the session; whether the patient's words and feelings match or conflict, as when a patient says they feel fine but with a sad voice and slumped posture. In parallel, the therapist pays attention to the nature of the transference relationship and how they feel and react inside (countertransference). Michael Parsons compares this kind of listening – where the therapist listens both outward and inward – to the process of reading poems.[13] The analogy may also extend to music. We listen to the notes, but may also be affected by them. Both sources are necessary to take in the meaning of a song. The therapist might also observe:

- What is not being spoken about. For example, the therapist may notice in session six that the patient has not said a single thing about their father and that this absence may turn out to be very relevant.
- What seems to the patient so ordinary to the point of being ignored, but seems extraordinary and significant to the therapist.

This sounds like a lot, and it is! Whilst this kind of listening does, indeed, require concentration, if we try too hard, as when a musician or athlete gets too tense, we cannot 'play' (i.e. listen, be responsive) and be available to the patient. So, like a musician or athlete who practises beforehand, but then sets this practice aside to be in the moment, the therapist too tries to combine directed attention to the patient with a receptive state of mind that is open to being surprised.

An empathic approach refers to an ongoing process of showing interest in the patient's experience and demonstrating a desire to understand. This includes exploring the patient's recurrent patterns of feeling and acting, and developing an understanding of how and why they arose. Ways of being that appear 'disordered' now may have once provided some order (see Chapter 2, section on 'Accommodating to the World as We Find It').

In this phase, to varying degrees, the patient's experience moves beyond talking and feeling listened to by the therapist. As a result of the psychodynamic space provided and the therapist's containing responses, the patient, too, may gradually develop an ability to listen to himself.

Allowing a Formulation to Unfold

The nature of the relationship that the patient forms with the therapist, and the therapist's countertransference, provide key information about the patient's internal world and relationships. A picture (or formulation) usually emerges as to the internal relationships, conflicts, and associated affects and defences that underlie the patient's problems. Understanding the past and present dynamics provide a map which can help to orientate the patient and allow them to work out where they came from, where they want to go, and why they keep getting lost.

As discussed in Chapter 4, from a neuroscience perspective, interpersonal patterns derive partly from procedural memory (i.e. 'how to' do something memories). Procedural memories are 'hard to learn and hard to forget'.[14] Hence, the psychodynamic focus on allowing ample time and repeated opportunities to become more aware of the emerging formulation. Furthermore, procedural memories cannot be brought directly into consciousness, but we can become aware of our habitual ways of being in relationships through inference, that is, from careful observations of our interpersonal behaviour.[15]

The generation of meaning is an important task of therapy as it is one route to effecting change.[2] Feelings of pain and distress can seem very arbitrary. If these feelings are seen to have meaning, they can feel more tolerable. In addition, we are able to take on more personal responsibility if we can understand our motivations better. This gives us the possibility of reflecting on situations, rather than merely reacting to them. Contemporary therapists hold that meaning is actively constructed between patient and therapist and does not simply reflect an objective state of affairs. It is a construction of a new story.

There is now a move away from the theory that there is an objective truth to be found in 'reconstructing' the patient's past and that such an endeavour would be therapeutic *per se*. The understanding of a person's history and past experience can help in working out a map of how the patient has reached their current predicament and in helping them treat themselves in a kinder fashion. Alongside this however, a major focus for psychotherapists is on present-day dynamics and in mobilising the patient's sense of ownership of their life and decisions. Leiper and Maltby make the crucial point that, 'It is easy for the therapist to attend to what has conditioned her client's ways of being' and to neglect the person's current active agency and role in maintaining patterns. Such a therapeutic trap 'runs the danger of providing the client only with an intellectual rationalisation for her actions,' and 'lacks the capacity to promote change'.[2]

Many contemporary therapists, therefore, concentrate their therapeutic efforts on the formulation and interpretation of the patient's *current* representations of himself in relationship with other people, and the patient's *current* conflicts.[15]

In the very earliest sessions, a provisional formulation may help guide the therapist in what they attend to in the sessions. This can allow space for the patient to make discoveries for themselves, with the therapist acting as facilitator. This way, the patient will feel more ownership of the work and of their life as opposed to feeling that they are working with a therapeutic guru who will be irreplaceable once the therapy ends. When the patient is working towards a new insight that the therapist can already detect, it can be tempting and narcissistically gratifying for the therapist to 'steal the cherries' and get in there first. However, it will be more useful to let the patient discover the cherries for themself.

The Early Phase in Practice

To illustrate how the early phase of therapy might play out, here are three brief examples:

1. For a withdrawn woman, who functioned well at work, the opening sessions had a constrained, tight feel. The patient hinted at troubling issues that she wanted to talk about, but then would clam up into silence. Within a supportive working alliance, the patient began to put into words worries about damaging others and how she could view herself as somehow defective. At points of emotional difficulty, the therapist noticed how the patient could veer off into abstractions. Central therapeutic approaches in these opening sessions were to allow a story to unfold whilst taking an interest in the patient's defensive (protective) moves into abstraction; and, as her anxieties about being close to others emerged more clearly in the therapy room, to find tolerable ways to talk about these so they could be better understood.
2. A young man came for his session, very well-built, dressed for the gym. He spoke openly but superficially about his past and his troubles in the present – in particular his infidelity with every woman he had been with, how he would just walk out, and his sense that people would 'probably leave [him] anyway'. He repeatedly said that his employer had sent him for therapy but how he himself didn't really want to come. Interestingly, the therapist felt, in the countertransference, a sense that the patient was wasting her time and had an urge to discharge him. At other times he spoke about his poor body image and bulking up at the gym to try and compensate – these moments felt different to the therapist, who felt a sense of the patient's vulnerability. For this patient, the early focus was

acknowledging and exploring his ambivalence about being in therapy. If ignored, the therapist felt the chance of the patient stopping therapy without warning would be high. The therapist recognised the importance of forming a collaboration with the patient, a place from which they could both work together to understand things – as it seemed that the patient's object relations were probably characterised by a highly rejecting and dismissing dynamic along with fairly strong defences against feeling vulnerable.

3. A lady in her late 50s opened the sessions with a stream of anxieties, all running one into the other. It was hard for the therapist to follow the content. The therapist realised that attempting to clarify each thing the patient said seemed to result in more confusion and anxiety. Rather, the therapist felt a key task was to attend to fundamental processes of emotional containment and to try and let the patient know she had heard how overwhelming things could feel for her. With this approach, the patient then became tearful and sad – seeming both to feel understood by the therapist, but also sadness in relation to experiences that were coming to the surface. Interestingly, the therapist did at times feel quite overwhelmed by a deluge of material and unable to listen, whilst at other times felt quite cut off. The therapist held on to these countertransference observations, unsure as yet what, if anything, they might mean.

The work carried out in the early phase on facilitating insights and developing the formulation will potentially pave the way to more experiential processes of change. In order for old patterns to be weakened, newer, or perhaps moderated, object relationships need to slowly develop and consolidate alongside old patterns. This is discussed in the section on the middle phase of therapy.

Middle Phase

During the middle phase, often the formulation becomes more alive and less abstract. With this developing insight, the mid-phase frequently sees a person repeating old patterns, sometimes holding on to them more strongly than when they arrived in therapy ('Resistance' – see also Chapter 7).

As noted in Chapter 2 on theory, there is a gap between insight and change. Our underlying ways of interacting with ourselves and others can be modified, but do not necessarily change quickly as an adult. Implicit memory systems (see Chapter 4) – which are the neuroscientific correlate of our inner objects and procedures of how-to-be-with-the other – are not readily updated. Psychological dynamics – including defences, resistance, and difficulties with mourning also serve to keep the status quo. Furthermore, there is the draw to what we perceive as familiar: 'The core of our experience is inextricably tied to the relationship to an internal other' (Leiper and Maltby 2004 drawing on Fairburn 1952).[2] In early development, we form relationships with whoever is there, including with frightening, dangerous, or neglectful external figures if that is all there is. These relational experiences – interacting with constitutional and social factors – come to shape our internal object world and become the norm. Leiper and Malby go on to explain that change, 'in either our sense of identity or our ways of connecting with others, is a threat to the opposite pole of the self-other relationship'.[2] The prospect of changing or loosening the patterns of our inner object relations can bring considerable anxieties. This includes a fear of change: *It will be even worse over there, in the unknown. At least I know the old way of being.*

An increase in resistance is therefore an expected and normal defensive reaction to the first tremors of structural change (see section on 'Structural Personality Change' in

Chapter 6). This may be a sign that someone's internal world has become unsettled by the therapeutic process. For a person with well-honed and trusted defences and patterns, shifts in their internal world are often unsettling emotionally. They may feel worse before they feel better. This is depicted in Figure 1, with an increase in symptoms at the start of the middle phase.

This turmoil in the middle phase presents an opportunity. The underlying memory traces and associations are more labile and hence potentially more open to revision through developing insight, new relational experiences, and mourning.[16] These repetitive processes – which entail hard work – are what is meant by 'repeating' and 'working through'.

This section on the middle phase can be read in conjunction with the closely related topics of resistance, rupture and repair, and working with the transference and countertransference (all in Chapter 7 on technique).

The Formulation in Action

The process of a patient getting to know more closely their key object relations, as identified in the formulation, involves experiencing and reflecting on them many times and from many angles. In the middle phase, repeated patterns of relational dynamics may come up week in and week out in different guises, based on what is happening in the patient's current life and in therapy. The therapist supports the patient to recognise and familiarise themselves with their own particular dynamics. As this happens, the formulation tends to become refined and feel more solid and less intellectual. Links to recollections of childhood experiences contribute to a compassionate understanding of how underlying object relationships evolved (see Malan's triangle in Chapter 7).

A full formulation may identify several key object relationships. In time-limited therapy, for pragmatic reasons, the therapist often concentrates the work on one or two key object relationships. As introduced in Chapter 2 on Theory, different sides of an object relationship will be projected in different circumstances. At this point in the chapter, we will now concentrate on a single object relationship, the different aspects of which (i.e. the self- or object- representation) get projected or identified with. This is depicted in Figure 8.2.

To bring Figure 8.2 into clinical practice, we will use the example of Ralph (Ralph is also discussed in Chapter 12).

Clinical Example Ralph: Part 1

Ralph, a man in his 50s, sought therapy as he felt 'constantly miserable, bitter'. He was single, had 'no friends', and had worked for many years as a train conductor. He saw himself as a 'shit magnet' and couldn't work out why people treated him badly when he always held himself 'correctly'. He recalled that, growing up, he experienced his father as a violent man who could also be highly critical towards Ralph. In the opening session, Ralph criticised the therapist – Mr Richards – for being 'slow off the mark' and described the building in which they met as 'shabby'.

Through work in the early phase, it transpired that Ralph's internal world was characterised by an internal object which was hostile and contemptuous in relation to a demeaned part of the self that felt useless.

In the early sessions, Ralph spoke about how he expected hostile treatment from others and how this left him feeling useless and insecure (this corresponds to the topmost situation in Figure 8.2). He began to become more curious about this, as opposed to it just being 'the way it is'. Ralph used the therapy space to think about this recurring experience, how it played out at work, in relationships, and the family circumstances in which it arose as a child.

During the middle phase of the work, Ralph spoke more about long-standing experiences of an internal critical 'voice' leading to another part of himself feeling criticised and useless. In the therapy sessions, Ralph became more familiar with how an aspect of himself (the object-representation) treated other aspects of himself (the self-representation) in a hostile way – this is the lower-most situation in Figure 8.2.

The therapist also noted that at times Ralph assumed a criticising and demeaning position towards others, including towards the therapist, as in his opening criticisms about the therapist and the clinic building (this is the middle situation in Figure 8.2). At times, the therapist felt hurt or angry and he began to think that these identifications could lead others around Ralph to react to him in an unsympathetic way. The therapist started to consider how this latter scenario could begin to be articulated in a way that would be helpful for Ralph – this is picked up in part 2 of this clinical example.

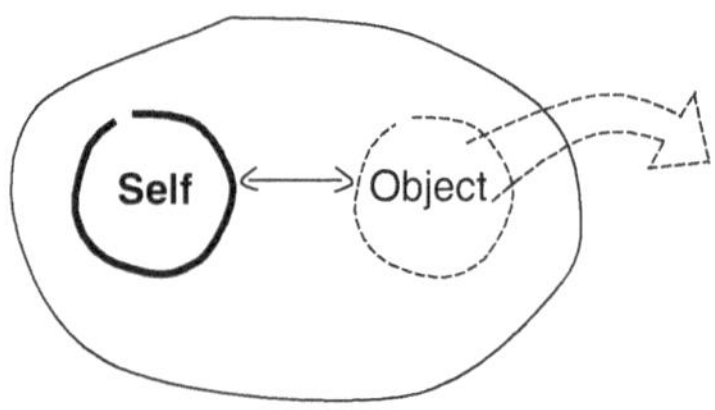

Projection of the object-representation.
In this situation, a person's internal object-representation is projected onto others. The individual is more identified with their self-representation.

For example, in a patient with a criticising object-representation, this would come through in narratives of experiencing others as criticising, with the individual himself feeling useless.

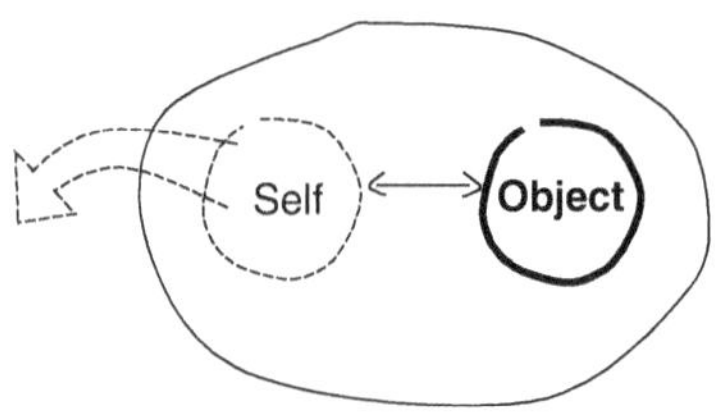

Identification with the object-representation.
In this situation, a person takes on the role of their internal object-representation. Their self-representation is projected into others who may be 'invited' into the latter's position.

To keep with the same patient, he now criticises others who may then feel somewhat useless. The individual treats others in the same way he feels others treat him.

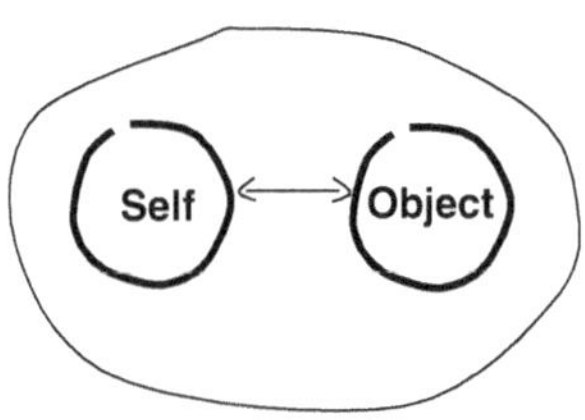

How we relate to ourselves
In this situation, the most prominent dynamic is how the individual is relating to himself, without others featuring strongly.

This might come through in the individual's criticising inner dialogue, evoking a feeling of uselessness.

Key. Self = self-representation; Object = object-representation; [projection arrow] = projection;
Bold font and outline indicates representation(s) the individual is currently more identified with

Figure 8.2 Different ways that the same object relationship can manifest.

These different manifestations of the same object relationship can initially seem to a patient like disparate areas of their experience, but, with reflection, often they can be helped to understand the links. The psychodynamic approach works on the basis that a person needs multiple encounters with their core object relations in their various manifestations and permutations, intellectually and experientially, for these to become noticeable to the person and to allow for new learning.

For clarity, we have separated out these three expressions of an internal object relationship (as per Figure 8.2); and indeed, often one of these dominates the scene at a given point in time. However, at other times, the reality is more complex as the underlying object relationship colours the current relational scene in multiple ways. For example, when working with Ralph, at times in the sessions it appeared to the therapist that Ralph experienced the therapist as a criticising figure putting him down; whilst Ralph was also disappointed with what the therapist had to offer; all the while experiencing an internal 'voice' castigating himself for his own 'deficiencies'.

This mobilisation in the here and now of therapy of old learned patterns opens the possibility for these to be modified and for new ways of relating to develop. A reasonable and realistic aim may be for the patient to contemplate a loosening of attachments to these 'old' objects or ways of being – in a climate of compassion towards these objects – while simultaneously exploring new experiences and new ways to relate to self and others.

The Therapeutic Relationship as a Vehicle for Change

'Something new from something old'
(Mitchell 1997)[17]

So, when therapy is beginning to set something in motion, how might new object relationships develop and old objects be revised? Freud puts it strikingly: 'It is impossible to destroy anyone *in absentia* or *in effigie*'.[18] What he means by this is that a here-and-now experience in the room with the therapist is required for new learning. The therapeutic setting allows the patient to make predictions about how the therapist will feel and react – whilst the therapist encourages reflection on these expectations. The therapist treads a path of neither colluding with the predictions (this would be a too literal enactment of the object relationships and unhelpful) nor brushing them away as this would leave the problem 'out there', or '*in effigie*'. Gabbard summarises this important point of technique by explaining, 'What is crucial is that the analyst (or analytic situation) is not only different from an object from the past but in some respects similar to it.'[16] Current thinking would tend to regard the therapeutic situation – with its overlapping elements of transference, 'real' relationship, and the working alliance – as offering a new relational experience, which is influenced by the past rather than being a replica of it.[5]

From a neuroscience perspective, the patient needs to find an experience similar enough to their inner objects for underlying memory networks to become activated and labile, yet different enough to allow them to be revised.[16] Mitchell calls this process, 'something new from something old'.[17]

Psychodynamic therapy can provide a distinctive experience through tolerating and containing the relational dynamics that a patient brings. Therapists use their psychodynamic training to 'hold' and put into words the interpersonal pressures and dynamics between therapist and patient. The patient 'habituates to the anxiety with repeated visits to the therapist, who does not react in the way that the patient anticipates'.[5] This can allow change in the patient to take place in their unconscious links between key affects, beliefs, and representations that have become associated through experience.[16] For example, if a patient has learnt that expressions of anger lead to rejection by others, it may be a novel and influential experience to gradually encounter something different in the relationship with the therapist. Such new learning will be more visceral and powerful when this discovery arises out of (tolerable) transference expectations that the therapist might reject the patient if they expressed anger. This is more fruitful than the therapist insisting that they would be perfectly fine if the patient expressed anger. In the latter case, the patient may (or may not) be reassured, but the learning would not be as experiential, and, consequently, fewer new associations would be made. (See Chapter 12 for a longer clinical example of working in the transference.)

Clinical Example Ralph: part 2, six months into the therapy

Building on their previous work, the therapist began to tactfully draw Ralph's attention to how he (i.e. Ralph), at times, identified with the contemptuous aspects of himself, and located the useless and demeaned feelings in others, that is, how Ralph could put others down. Ralph replied that he didn't know what the therapist meant. Taking a (metaphorical) deep breath, the therapist said, 'Well, I'm thinking of times – like in the first session when you commented on the building being shabby and me being slow.' The therapist tried to be supportive and bring meaning to what was difficult for Ralph to hear: 'I think at these times, I'm holding those vulnerable feelings we've been talking about that you struggle with – I think these feelings are very important ones for you.'

This interpretation was hard for Ralph to hear and he felt somewhat upset, but held by the therapeutic alliance, he was able to stay in therapy and explore the emotions that came up. Ralph appeared conflicted – moving between doubling down on his criticisms of the therapist and acknowledging a more vulnerable side of himself.

For Ralph the therapy provided an alive encounter with a central relational dynamic for him – that of someone putting the other down – but with a key difference. Through 'holding' the action, slowing it down, and reflecting on the dynamics, this brought the potential to navigate a different way through this relational situation compared to usual, and to form new associations and learn new relational patterns. In one session, Ralph reflected that he knew he could 'go on the attack when actually [he] felt frightened . . .'

In these ways, over the course of therapy, the patient may create a modified experience of being with the other. This allows their existing unconscious associational networks to become weaker, and new associations and procedures to form, which are more adaptive to the present day (see also Chapter 6). If the patient's underlying relational templates have changed, the new learning originating within the therapeutic relationship may play out in other relationships in the patient's life. This kind of transference work – whilst clearly serious at times – can also be playful and involve humour and personal discovery.

Working Through

This section commences with the continuation of the case of Ralph – who had seemed to be doing well . . .

Clinical Example Ralph: part 3

Whereas Ralph had previously taken pride in what he saw as his high 'moral standards' to which he held others and himself to account, for brief periods during therapy he had started to consider the harm this was causing to his internal and external worlds. In a session eight months into therapy, this caused a feeling of crisis. Had the way he had been living for decades 'been completely wrong'? When Ralph returned for the following session, it was as if he was in the full grip of his original presenting relationship patterns. People were idiots, he had been wronged, and he was just a magnet for bad treatment.

At this stage, Ralph seemed to be resistant to changes in his internal world. It would appear that Ralph would have much to gain from change, such as having better relationships with others and with himself, and consequently feeling less depressed. However, such change might also result in loss to him. In order for people to develop new ways of relating to others, old patterns will have to be loosened, though not necessarily totally discarded. As Leiper and Maltby put it, 'renunciation is at the heart of the process of working through'. In practice, it is not an easy course to loosen one's grip on tried and tested ways of being in relationships; they serve a considerable defensive/protective function and are deeply ingrained so one can rarely just decide to move on. One's feelings as well as thinking need to be involved.

Realising that an old way of being may be causing problems and that new ways may offer a solution, can be difficult for many of us. A great deal may have been invested in the old ways over the years. Ralph, who had placed a lot of pride in his 'high moral standards', now was attempting to come to terms with the fact that this stance, in the present day, was actually destructive to both himself and others. For Ralph, to relinquish his way of seeing others as 'idiots' and his position of 'rightly criticising them' would require the painful work of him recognising his own role in inadvertently turning others against him, as well as recognising his own fallibilities. However, if he was able to explore this, with the support of his therapist, it could open up new and healthier ways for him to be in relationships.

From a dynamic perspective, a person develops these ways of relating, which, though they are ultimately constraining, serve to manage their anxieties. As discussed in Chapter 2 on Theory, the patient originally developed these relational patterns to provide a sense of security in relation to troubling, 'insoluble' experiences, even if these were 'incomplete solutions'. A person in the middle phase of therapy may feel conflicted – to risk loosening these attachments to familiar ways of being may feel unthinkable, even dangerous; whilst, at the same time, a slight loosening of the old ways provides a glimpse of change that may feel creative and freeing, and even playful. The therapist and the patient may have to examine the nature of object relationships and associated defences many times in sessions in order to understand their ongoing influence. The therapist helps the patient to recognise the differences between then and now. In tandem, there is the potential within the therapeutic relationship to risk departing from the usual script and to try out something new out of something old.

For example, with Ralph, over time, it became clearer that his putting down of others (and himself) served as a sort of protection against a wounding experience of feeling put down and attacked by others. It felt exposing and vulnerable to risk not immediately 'going for the attack button', as he called it. The therapy setting provided an opportunity to play with this idea and try it out.

Mourning

'Only a loss that is experienced can be mourned.'
(Raphael-Leff, 2019) [19]

Mourning is the process of coming to terms with the loss of something. Commonly this refers to the loss of someone through death or separation, but there are other kinds of losses too. These include:

- coming to terms with the limitations of old ways of being in relationships and loosening our attachments to them[2]
- coming to terms with disappointments in life and in therapy
- letting go of a fantasy that one's early life experiences can be changed. This may include grieving for the lack of yearned-for experiences
- the loss of time 'wasted' through avoidance and defensiveness
- letting go of a wish to do with an ideal concept of a marriage or relationship
- letting go of a wish to be more 'successful' or better at something
- the loss of the therapist in the late phase

Recurrent mourning processes, some more significant than others, are essential for us to enjoy and find meaning in the good-enough realities that life and relationships may offer.[20] Mourning involves experiencing and accepting the reality of the loss and facing painful, sad, and often conflicted feelings. An understanding of the process of mourning can help patients and therapists navigate this slow and awkward journey.

Coming to terms with the loss of something or someone important in one's life, whether the relationship was complicated or otherwise, is a gradual, cyclical, repetitive process and takes time and work. One may approach and then avoid acceptance of the loss many times. Someone may experience anger, rather than sadness or grief. There is often ambivalence about whether one wants to come to terms emotionally with a loss, or even accept that something has been lost in the first place (denial). Loss is not the sort of thing one can 'get over' in a few sessions – at least, not in any meaningful way. Psychodynamic therapy can provide a setting where the dynamics of mourning can be understood, supported, and empathised with.

A person's relationship with what is lost is never completely severed – that would be unrealistic and represent a manic denial. However, over time the relationship may evolve, and become more circumspect. As Leiper and Malty explain, 'Detachment comes bit by bit and is likely to be prolonged; the experience of loss is, as it were, divided into manageable elements without a clear ending to this process.'[2] When thinking about the loss of old ways of being in relationships, space may emerge for new patterns and new people.

It may seem a stretch to compare mourning the loss of a person who has died to a mourning process to do with relaxing one's grip on a long-held way of operating in the world; but both are losses, and the psychological processes have similarities. Many patients are familiar with mourning as a process that takes time and necessitates experiencing painful and ambivalent feelings. This explanation may make sense to patients, normalise their journey and experiences, and convey a realistic sense of a time frame for long-lasting change as opposed to a quick fix.

Late Phase (Separation)

'An ending is perforce shaped by what preceded it.'
(Holmes 1997)[21]

When a process of separation takes place within a caring relationship, both parties approach this with a range of preconceptions and anxieties, influenced by previous experiences of separation and loss. With patients who have a history of profound loss, the dynamics of loss are likely to be more intense in connection to the therapist in this period. If the patient's anxieties around separation can be articulated with the support of the therapist, the late phase can be a time of positive development for the patient.

To illustrate, a parent who can tolerate their child leaving home communicates that they can tolerate separation. This allows the child to go on their way and discover what is to come. This shows trust in the child that they can develop, make mistakes and survive them. Similarly, the patient may find a sense of containment and solidity through finding a therapist who is able to talk about feelings surrounding separation, yet remain steady (see Clinical Example 'Paul', below). This may implicitly communicate to the patient that they are acceptable as they are and that the therapist has confidence in them.

Clinical Example Paul: late phase dynamics

Paul was a 25-year-old man who had been in therapy with Dr Jones for 16 months. As a young boy, Paul had lost his mother – his parents had separated and, by his account, his mother moved to a different country, and they had had no contact since. Paul had found some benefit from the therapy and was beginning to form relationships with people which weren't based on them needing to be perfect (this had been Paul's previous pattern in relationships, which inevitably led to disappointment). In a session two months from the end of therapy, Paul asked Dr Jones if she could continue the sessions beyond the planned 18-month period. Paul was in an anxious state of mind, saying that therapy was the only thing helping whilst everything else has been a disappointment. Dr Jones felt a strong pull to offer Paul an additional couple of months, but Dr Jones thought she had better take stock and think things through first.

In Dr Jones's group supervision session, the group wondered if something important was being communicated to Dr Jones through Paul's anxious request for more sessions, perhaps something about his underlying feelings of others never providing enough. Dr Jones tuned in to her countertransference feelings that she wasn't giving enough, which she realised was behind her urge to offer more sessions. It gradually emerged that, rather than acting by extending the sessions, the task here was to try and explore these dynamics within the remaining sessions and empathise with Paul's position and feelings. Dr Jones realised that she had been avoiding tackling feelings of disappointment and loss that Paul felt about the ending of therapy, and that this very topic was of central importance for Paul in his life. By thinking rather than doing, there was the possibility for integration of the good experiences of therapy alongside the disappointments – if successful, this would be a new experience in relationships for Paul.

The late phase of therapy can be a very productive period. The ending and separation process may be: a catalyst for change; facilitate the identification with a good-enough figure; or help the patient on their journey in tolerating imperfections and disappointments, freeing them up to make use of available relationships in the real world. The realities of therapy sessions coming to an end may bring underlying issues more clearly into the transference relationship, offering the potential for these to be further understood and addressed.

Some patients have a fantasy that the therapy will go on for ever, or that the therapist has a special capacity to cure them, and the patient need only pour out their difficulties and wait for things to get better. Sometimes the shock of the ending phase can serve to dispel these fantasies. The impending reality of the ending can bring a sense of 'ok, I'm going to have to actually do something about my issues, then'. This realisation can instigate a process of issues being addressed, as well as facilitating a sense of the patient being their own person who is separate from the therapist (see Chapter 2, on Winnicott's concept of the value of discovering the limits of a good-enough caring figure who sometimes 'gets it wrong').

Some contemporary therapists question the terminology 'ending phase' or 'termination' of therapy on the grounds that it conveys something overly final and an absolute and permanent break. Pedder suggests a more helpful analogy is that of an adolescent leaving home – he may need to leave and return several times, before finally being able to move out.[22] Furthermore, whilst terms like 'the ending' reflect how it can feel for some patients at points in the late phase, they do not capture the fact that therapy effects may persist after face-to-face contact stops. We have used the term 'late phase' in the section heading to reflect this discussion, although we also use the language of 'ending' at times, as we feel this conveys the important limits to the work.

An in-depth discussion of when to stop sessions with open-ended work is beyond the scope of this book (see Lemma for a full discussion).[15] In time-limited therapy, the duration of therapy is decided at the consultation phase, thus, the ending is 'there' at the beginning of the work.

A Basic Principle – Talk about the Ending

It is important to discuss the upcoming separation and explore what emotions and meanings this situation evokes (see Box 8.3). If this has not already arisen, then, in general, it is helpful to start this exploration from approximately half to two-thirds of the way through the work. The emotional significance of the separation usually becomes clearer as the therapy progresses into the final months.[15]

With many patients, much of the work around ending consists of mourning that things are not perfect and that therapy cannot solve everything. If discussion about the ending of sessions is avoided, there is a risk that either the patient's underlying feelings are not brought into the light, or the feelings may come out in the final session, which is insufficient time for working through. The therapist may need to raise the topic of ending regularly in

Box 8.3 Basic principles in the late phase (after Lemma)[15]

- Explore the patient's reactions to the ending
- Put into words feelings and fantasies
- Express and normalise affect – sadness, anger, loss
- Explore how earlier situations colour the current experience in the therapy. This is an opportunity for recurrent patterns that are evoked by the upcoming separation to be thought about with the therapist and understood

the last phase, for example, 'I'm aware we have a couple of months left to meet' or 'we only have three sessions to go . . . '.

Transference and Countertransference Work

The reality of impending separation from the therapist may stir up important, unresolved relational issues, which come more clearly into the dynamics of the transference relationship. These commonly include dynamics of rejection, abandonment, neglect, or hanging on to an ideal of never-ending perfect therapy. If held by the therapeutic alliance, which offers containment and understanding, the ending phase of psychodynamic therapy provides further opportunity to understand and work through 'stuck' patterns in relationships. The major benefit of this kind of work is that it is not in the abstract 'out there', it is happening in a modified form 'in here' with the therapist in the actual session.

Many patients will not be able to communicate their feelings about the ending directly in words, so they may emerge unconsciously in other ways – for example, by missing sessions; in talking about a figure in their life who has let them down; through dreams; by subtle changes in how they treat the therapist; through projecting feelings which may be picked up as changes in the countertransference.

The therapist's countertransference feelings may become more intense in this period. Depending on the therapist's own internal world and attachment style, and the nature of projections from the patient they are working with, there may be a range of responses. The therapist might feel:

- a sense of loss at the ending of therapy
- or a sense of relief
- or a sense of being deficient or a bad clinician
- or as if they are abandoning the patient
- that the therapy does not matter to the patient and so ending does not really matter

These countertransference experiences potentially contain vital information about the patient and the situation but require processing to make sense of the meaning of these responses. It can be useful for the therapist to bring up how they feel in relation to the work, in supervision or in a reflective practice group.

Privately, and without impinging on the patient's space, endings may provide the opportunity for a parallel working through for us as therapists. Reflecting on endings can help therapists to come to terms with being an ordinary and good-enough therapist, and letting go of a drive to offer extraordinary therapy. A fantasy of bringing 'perfect mental health to every patient' can be persecutory for a therapist and make it hard to take pride in what can realistically be offered.[23]

Ending, What Ending?

Some patients appear completely unfazed by the upcoming ending of therapy. Even with exploration, they may not be aware of feeling very much about it. Patients with more detached attachment styles (see Box 4 in Chapter 2 on 'Bowlby and Attachment Theory') may have learnt not to notice their own feelings, never mind express them. The therapist can 'listen in' to their countertransference for possible information about the patient's warded-off feelings. For therapists in this situation, it is important not to collude that nothing matters, as this leaves any underlying feelings untouched. This may be more common in therapists who themselves tend to a more detached style of relating.[21] Instead, the task is to try and address what is happening. For example:

Therapist: I wonder if it may be risky for you to consider if there is anything behind 'feeling fine'?

Or perhaps the therapist may make an interpretation, building on repeated explorations of key dynamics in early phases of the work. The therapist might speak directly to the patient to the best of her understanding:

Therapist: You don't feel anything about this. What's in my mind is . . . no wonder you wouldn't feel anything. This is the main thing we've spoken about over the months. About how you learnt over the years to not show your feelings, even to yourself. I think something similar is happening again here with me.

Gratitude

Some patients *are* aware of a sense of loss about therapy ending. Here, the therapist and patient can try and work out together what has been of value which they are anxious about losing. According to Kleinian thought, gratitude stems from the gratification the other has provided.[24] Whilst this may be uncomplicated for many of us, for those with more deprived and disturbed histories, the ability to feel that another has provided something valuable may be a discovery made in therapy in relation to the therapist. It has implications for future development, as gratitude forms the basis for appreciating and taking in what people outside of therapy can offer. This in turn opens up a way to allowing oneself to be appreciated by others, as well as valuing oneself. Hence, when a patient experiences and expresses gratitude to the therapist, it is important that the therapist receives this warmly.

Impending separation can provide an impetus for the patient to try and establish in their life outside of therapy things they found helpful within the therapy. Of course, not everything about the therapy will be able to be recreated identically in everyday life. This would be to deny the loss of the therapist, but some aspects can be sought out and developed. Links to life outside therapy may already have taken root in the earlier phases of therapy, and the anxiety of the ending may serve to accelerate this process.

For some patients who have in fact derived benefit from the work, what may initially surface is not recognition of value, but angry feelings towards the therapist, who may be charged with providing nothing good. It may be possible to get behind this anger and for the patient to realise that his anger and upset signify that he is going to miss something about the therapy that has been of value.

A common expression of gratitude can be demonstrated by the patient bringing the therapist a gift during the ending phase, most commonly in the final session. We advise following Gabbard's humane and grounded approach to gifts.[5] In general, inexpensive gifts can be accepted with thanks, and the therapist can then try to explore any meaning attached to the gift. As well as a communication of gratitude from the patient or a wish to give something back, the gift might serve to avoid more difficult feelings such as anger towards the therapist. Occasionally, a gift's function may be – not always consciously – an attempt to pressure the therapist into doing something for the patient. If the therapist is unsure about whether to accept a gift, the therapist can explain that they need to discuss it with their supervisor first or check on any organisational policy.

When Therapy Has Not Been Helpful

Of course, no therapy is effective for everyone. Some patients do not find the psychodynamic approach helpful. It is, however, important to differentiate this from scenarios which may superficially appear similar. Namely, when a patient devalues therapy because they are angry about it ending; or when there are dynamics related to deprivation and vulnerability, which can make acknowledgement of having been dependent on the therapist very difficult.

If, after reflection, the conclusion is that psychodynamic therapy was not a good fit for the patient, then a main task for the therapist is to be able to discuss this with the patient, with his best interests and the principle of 'do no harm' at the centre. This can be easier said than done as therapeutic 'failures' can be narcissistically wounding for clinicians. We, as therapists, should take care to avoid taking things out on the patient and blaming them for not getting better, or inappropriately prolonging therapy for our own needs.

This is also a time for the therapist to reflect honestly on the efficacy of time-limited therapies for a patient, even if the courses of therapy undertaken have been relatively lengthy in duration (i.e. a year or more). If the clinician observes that the patient has had several courses of therapy over the years, but things are getting progressively worse, then they need to reflect. Does the patient need to discover a 'good object' in the first place? (For an explanation of 'good object', see Chapter 2, section 'Development of the Internal World'.) Holmes writes, 'One can only be securely separate if one feels attached in the first place'.[21] For more disturbed patients who have not internalised a good object of any kind, the ending of contact with professionals may be experienced concretely as another trauma, resulting in immediate seeking of another clinician and in cycles of disrupted attachments. It may be more helpful going forward for the patient to have one consistent figure for many years, if indeed this is possible to arrange. Rather than formal therapy with a fixed term, the 'treatment' may be therapeutic contact over a longer period of time (for more on this idea, see Chapter 17).

On a rare occasion, we may consider extending a brief contract to something more long term if psychodynamic therapy has been a good fit, but in retrospect, the duration of therapy offered was clearly insufficient for the patient's degree of structural or relational difficulty and need. This would only be offered after much reflection and discussion in supervision. For example, for Ms R, who was sexually abused by a parent and who operated at a borderline psychological level, in retrospect, the three-month course of therapy offered had been too short. Three months barely allowed a secure attachment to form before it was due to be broken. Disturbing memories and topics had arisen, but with insufficient time for processing or developmental change. All was left up in the air as the last few sessions approached. In this situation, the therapist, after reflection with her team, discussed this frankly with Ms R. The therapist and Ms R agreed mutually that it would be helpful, after the three months of therapy, for Ms R to have a review session with the clinician whom Ms R initially saw for consultation. Following this, Ms R went on to undertake 18 months of therapy which she found helpful. The ending of this course of therapy was still difficult with a pressure to extend it. However, the more solid working alliance and the longer duration of therapy meant the limits were experienced as containing, with therapy ending as planned.

Endings and Borderline States

As the end of therapy approaches, some patients move into an 'archaic' but familiar state of mind, where they experience themself and others as having either wholly good or wholly bad attributes. They experience therapy as 'nothing' because it wasn't 'everything'.

There is no 'as if' quality in this state of mind, and the patient cannot hold on to good and bad aspects at the same time (splitting). The therapy may be, in the heat of the moment, rendered useless, and the patient may feel they are in the presence of a deficient, useless, or abandoning figure; in other words, they have (hopefully temporarily) 'lost' their therapist and they may feel frightened and angry. This relational dynamic may be the central predicament that brought the patient into therapy in the first place. Sometimes, patients can go round and round therapies, services, and relationships as nothing lives up to the ideal.

Whilst this sort of situation may have come up earlier in therapy, often the realities of the ending resonate with the patient's inner predicaments relating to loss, not feeling loved, or abandonment. As a consequence, these become more alive. In the countertransference, the therapist might feel that they, or the patient, are not good-enough, or this dynamic may be displaced on to the service or the therapist's supervisor. Alternatively, the therapist and the work may be idealised. Idealisation may feel very different to when the work is experienced as totally useless, but reflects the same underlying defence of splitting.

Sometimes there can be a temptation to alter boundaries in response to the unsettling interpersonal dynamics that are stirred up around the ending phase. McWilliams observes that when the therapist extends themselves beyond the agreed limits in the hope of making up for the patient's hardship, people in a borderline state may become more disturbed, regressing, and escalating problematic behaviours until limits are found.[6] Through the therapist withstanding and containing the patient's experiences, the patient may gradually develop a sense of perspective in relation to what is happening.

In this way, the patient may be able to move from a state of mind characterised by extremes (paranoid-schizoid position) to one where the ambiguity and the ordinariness of things can be tolerated (depressive position). Moving into the latter, more integrated, position can bring feelings of sadness and grief, as well as feelings of guilt for the hurt caused to others through attacking their imperfections. But alongside this, there is the potential for more authentic, stable, and ordinary relationships. When people can tolerate the disappointment of ordinary mixedness of the therapy and the therapist (i.e. the good and the bad), and let go of the ideal, it can free them to experience others more as they really are, with both good points and imperfections. It can also help them to make use of the good-enough care actually available from others, and to establish a benign object in their own mind. These themes of letting go of an ideal and tolerating the ordinary are also common in many patients in the late phase, not just those whose main way of psychological functioning is at a borderline level.

Post-Termination Phase

The process of separation from the therapist can set in motion for the patient a taking-in of beneficial aspects of the therapy and therapist. After the actual sessions have stopped, the patient may realise and be able to take more ownership of the role they played in their therapeutic journey and have to play going forward – a taking back of projections from the therapist. Out in the real world, the patient can discover what inner capacities have developed during the therapy. People also discover what situations they continue to find difficult and, indeed, if these prove significantly problematic, they may find their way back into therapy again at some point in the future, or perhaps consult the therapist again for a one-off or series of meetings.

Therapists working in public sector services are usually required to write a summary letter to the patient's referrer at the end of therapy. Without over-disclosure of intimate and personal session material, this letter can contain information about the therapy, what kind of approaches the patient found helpful and not helpful, as well as thoughts about what may be useful for the patient in the future.

As noted previously, extending therapy in an unreflective way as the ending approaches or referring on immediately for further therapy, whilst well-intentioned, might short-circuit the ending process and deprive patients of the post-termination phase. The months and sometimes years after the last actual session are part of the process itself – a space and opportunity for patients to apply what they have found useful in therapy to their everyday lives. If someone's underlying relational world and how it is organised has changed, then the benefits in terms of a person's relationships may play out over a longer timescale. The process of therapy ending also helps people to come to terms with where they are up to and what therapy is and is not capable of achieving. In summary, through the therapy sessions ending, the work continues as the patient's journey continues. In the ending is a beginning.

Concluding Remarks

This chapter has attempted to describe an arc of what psychodynamic psychotherapy may be like. Whilst we cannot do justice to the variations in how therapy can unfold and to the individual character of the work with each person, this chapter can provide a general framework. This chapter provides some orientation to Part 3 of the book, which offers further clinical examples, following patients from the beginning to the end of therapy.

References

1. O'Neill S. Process Facilitation in Psychoanalysis, Psychotherapy and Social Work. 1st ed. London; New York: Routledge; 2018.
2. Leiper R, Maltby M. The Psychodynamic Approach to Therapeutic Change. London: Sage Publications Ltd; 2004.
3. Wolberg LR. The Technique of Psychotherapy. 3rd ed. New York: Grune & Stratton; 1977.
4. Zetzel ER. Current concepts of transference. Int J Psychoanal 1956;37 (4–5):369–76.
5. Gabbard GO. Long-term psychodynamic psychotherapy: a basic text. In Long-Term Psychodynamic Psychotherapy: A Basic Text. Washington, DC: American Psychiatric Pub.; 2010.
6. McWilliams N. Psychoanalytic Diagnosis, Second Edition: Understanding Personality Structure in the Clinical Process. 2nd ed. New York: The Guilford Press; 2011.
7. Høglend P, Hersoug AG, Bøgwald KP et al. Effects of transference work in the context of therapeutic alliance and quality of object relations. J Consult Clin Psychol 2011;79(5):697–706.
8. Høglend P. Exploration of the patient-therapist relationship in psychotherapy. AJP 2014;171(10):1056–66.
9. Lucas R. The Psychotic Wavelength: A Psychoanalytic Perspective for Psychiatry. New York, NY: Routledge/ Taylor & Francis Group; 2009.
10. Ackerman SJ, Hilsenroth MJ. A review of therapist characteristics and techniques negatively impacting the therapeutic alliance. Psychotherapy: Theory, Research, Practice, Training 2001;38 (2):171–85.
11. Suttie I. The Origins of Love and Hate. Harmondsworth, Middlesex: Peregrine Books; 1963.
12. Ogden TH. Comments on transference and countertransference in the initial analytic

meeting. Psychoanalytic Inquiry 1992;12 (2):225–47.

13. Parsons M. Raiding the inarticulate: the internal analytic setting and listening beyond countertransference. Int J Psychoanal 2007;88(Pt 6):1441–56.
14. Solms M. The scientific standing of psychoanalysis. BJPsych Int 2018;15(1):5–8.
15. Lemma A. Introduction to the Practice of Psychoanalytic Psychotherapy, 2nd ed. West Sussex: Wiley Blackwell; 2016.
16. Gabbard GO, Westen D. Rethinking therapeutic action. The International Journal of Psychoanalysis 2003;84 (4):823–41.
17. Mitchell SA. Influence and Autonomy in Psychoanalysis. New York: Routledge; 1997.
18. Freud S, Strachey J, Freud A et al. The dynamics of transference. In The Standard Edition of the Complete Psychological Works of Sigmund Freud: Early Psycho-Analytic Publications. Vol. 12, 1911–1913. London: Vintage; 2001.
19. Raphael-Leff J. Pregnancy: The Inside Story. London: Routledge; 2019.
20. Steiner J. The equilibrium between the paranoid-schizoid and the depressive positions. In Clinical Lectures on Klein and Bion, Eds Anderson R, Segal H. London: Routledge; 1991.
21. Holmes J. 'Too early, Too late': endings in psychotherapy – an attachment perspective. British Journal of Psychotherapy 1997;14(2):159–71.
22. Pedder JR. Termination reconsidered. Int J Psychoanal 1988;69 (Pt 4):495–505.
23. McWilliams N. Psychotherapy in a Pandemic [Internet]. 2020; http://web.tiscali.it/cispp/mcwilliamsPANDEMIC.htm
24. Hinshelwood RD. A Dictionary of Kleinian Thought. Oxford, England: Free Association Books; 1989.

Chapter 9

Psychological Assessment and Formulation in Psychodynamic Psychotherapy

'In every consulting room, there ought to be two rather frightened people: the patient and the psychoanalyst. If they are not both frightened, one wonders why they are bothering to find out what everyone knows.'
(Bion 1974)[1]

Table of Contents

Introduction 151
Early Infantile Experiences 154
Understanding Defence Mechanisms 155
Organisation of the Internal World 157
Patterns of Object Relations 158
Thinking about Formulation 159
Concluding Remarks 160

Introduction

Nowhere is Bion's assertion more pertinent than in a psychodynamic consultation. At the start of any experience of psychotherapy is a period of consultation, of getting to know the patient and whether the therapy will be right for them. This is an experience of two people having feelings about being in a room together and trying to make some sense of this. The consultation is likely to be the first experience the patient has of a psychodynamic way of thinking, and it has the potential to be an experience of being deeply heard and understood. Traditionally this was referred to as 'an assessment for psychotherapy' but increasingly the way this process is framed is changing. The term 'assessment' and what was called 'assessment for suitability for psychotherapy' evokes an idea of judgment and that the patient has to pass a test or meet a set of criteria in order to be allowed access to a hallowed and restricted resource only available to the privileged few. In the NHS this is often mysteriously referred to as the offer of 'long-term therapy' which, in a resource-poor NHS of short-term interventions and early discharges, seems like a holy grail.

There has traditionally been an idea that through the assessment we can determine who will and who won't do well in psychodynamic psychotherapy and that certain characteristics make some people more 'suitable' for this type of therapy than others. In 1964 William

Scofield coined the term YAVIS.[2] This stands for 'young, attractive, verbal, intelligent, and successful' and refers to a group of characteristics that were said to be preferred by clinicians assessing for psychotherapy. He proposed that individuals with these traits have a greater capacity to develop a positive therapeutic relationship with the therapist, leading therapists to assume that these individuals would achieve better outcomes in the therapy. It has been suggested that there is a bias towards preferentially accepting these patients into psychotherapy. Scofield also hypothesised that the unconscious motivation for this is that there is a desire in the therapist to work with patients who will do well in therapy in order to support the therapist's view of herself as competent and successful. This however perpetuates a sense that psychodynamic psychotherapy is a 'special' therapy that is only for certain 'special' individuals. It is now clear that this idea of the criteria that predict a better outcome in and greater suitability for therapy is a fallacy. Several large-scale studies have examined predictors of outcome of psychotherapy and have found that baseline variables were poor predictors of outcome.[3] It is also worth noting that, for men from African and Caribbean backgrounds, referral rates from general practitioners to inpatient mental health services were found to be lower than average, with rates of referral from the criminal justice system being higher than average.[4] Furthermore, there is some evidence that men from African and Caribbean backgrounds are less likely to receive psychotherapy and are more likely to be admitted to, secluded, or restrained on secure psychiatric wards.[4] We need to consider whether we have racial biases at consultation. When we think of the YAVIS patient is this a white patient? In the UK, psychotherapy has traditionally been a largely white, middle-class profession and it needs to be carefully considered whether there is then an unconscious valence for people considered to be similar to the therapist. This is something that we need to have an awareness of, reflect on, and actively address.

So, if we can't rely on a set of characteristics or criteria that determine whether someone will be able to gain from psychotherapy, how do we go about determining who we work with and who would be better served by a different approach? This is where the experiential nature of a psychotherapy consultation comes into its own. In the consultation period, the aim is to give the therapist an experience of the internal world of the patient and the patient an experience of what the therapy will be like. A consultation over a series of meetings may even give the opportunity of developing a patient's capacity to do the therapeutic work. The consultation is not just an assessment of the patient's characteristics and history, it is a psychotherapeutic encounter, and vital to this is the therapist's experience of the interaction and their capacity to use this to develop a formulation of the individual's specific difficulties. First of all, it is useful to think about why the patient has been referred or sought psychotherapy and, in particular, why now? Is it about a move towards something or a move away from something? We can find instances where the referrer is seeking to discharge or 'get rid' of a patient and uses a referral to psychotherapy to make this more palatable to themselves and to the patient, as opposed to those situations where psychotherapy is felt to be a potentially important and beneficial intervention for the patient. Equally, the patient might be seeking to move away from or 'get rid' of disturbing or painful feelings and experiences rather that moving towards exploring and understanding them.

The consultation is a complex process that often starts before the patient even enters the room. From the moment that the appointment is set up and an idea of the consultant forms in the mind of the patient, the relationship begins. The patient's phantasy may be of a benign authority who will offer understanding and support, but it may also be of a persecutory, critical figure who will keep them from the precious support that they need. In the current age, we also have to consider that the patient may, having received the appointment, search for us online and they might know or think they know something about us from what they find. For example, a patient who searched the internet for the therapist's name and, having found information about a different person with the same name, became convinced he knew details of the therapist's family and professional relationships, which in fact were not correct. However, even before the ubiquity of the internet and social media, patients created narratives about their consultants' lives outside the consulting room. There was a patient who was convinced that she had identified my car as being the expensive red sports car that was parked outside the department. This was very far from the reality of my old and slightly battered hatchback which was parked several streets away.

The contact frequently starts in the run up to the consultation (see also Chapter 5, section on 'Early Encounters with the Setting'). The patient may call up anxiously to check the details of the appointment. They may cancel at the last minute or even arrive extremely early and be sitting vigilantly in the waiting room as the consultant arrives in the building. With a psychodynamic way of thinking, we can understand that these behaviours are not random or entirely due to external events. Having an idea of unconscious processes means that we can understand these behaviours as communications and take into consideration how they make us feel – are we irritated at the cancelled appointment, or relieved? Do we feel wrong-footed by the patient who is there looking at us as we arrive for work, or intruded upon and exposed? This is all information for us to understand the patient and can inform our formulation of how they relate to and experience others. Examining our countertransference helps us get an insight into the transference.

Clinical Example 1 Ms Clarke

In order to set up a consultation appointment with Ms Clarke, the departmental administrator called and left a message on her answerphone. She didn't attend the stipulated appointment. When subsequently sent a letter asking her to contact the department should she wish to arrange a second appointment, Ms Clark contacted the service to say that her old phone had been stolen so her number had changed, and she didn't receive the original phone message about the first appointment. The consultant therefore asked the administrator to offer her a second appointment, but again she did not attend. The consultant had a nagging concern that the appointment letter hadn't been sent and contacted Ms Clarke direct. It emerged that she hadn't received the letter with the second appointment. The consultant's feeling was that she had been negligent by not ensuring that Ms Clarke received the appointments and she felt guilty. The experience that was evoked in the consultant was that she had not been attentive enough in making sure that the setting up of appointments went smoothly, a feeling of not being there to make sure everything was okay and that help was offered when needed.

What emerged in the consultation was that Ms Clarke's parents had separated when she was very young. She lived with her mother and sister who was 12 years older, and it was a struggle. When she was six her mother left, and they had no further contact with her. She was cared for by her sister from then on. She said that her mother didn't care enough to stick with them when things were hard. When Ms Clarke was 14, her sister had gone on a trip that Ms Clarke was supposed to attend, but Ms Clarke cancelled at the last minute and did not join her sister. She was subsequently informed that her sister had been in a car accident, and she died a few days after the accident.

We can see how this initial contact with the consultant could have repeated an experience of neglect and abandonment, but due to her reflection, the consultant was able to 'stick with it' despite things not being easy to continue the care of Ms Clarke. It would have been easy to have discharged her and walked away after she failed to attend the initial appointments. Also, the feeling evoked in the consultant of guilt at not offering care when needed, echoed not just Ms Clarke's experience of her mother, but her feeling of guilt for not being there to offer help when her sister was injured and dying.

There are a number of excellent texts that describe the areas that are important to cover when seeing someone for a psychodynamic consultation.[5] Garelick sets out an approach to the consultation in which the initial appointment consists of a more open psychodynamic encounter where the patient is allowed space to bring whatever material they choose, facilitating free association.[6] It allows an opportunity for the consultant to examine the nature of the experience with the patient in the here and now and to reflect on this, to develop a sense of the affective quality of the interaction without having to gather information or try and follow or reconstruct a narrative. In the second and subsequent consultation there is then opportunity to find out more about the patient's background and fill in any gaps in the narrative. This helps to give a sense of how the patient frames their experience, how they describe their various relationships, and what their experiences are of external situations, both historical and current. Garelick notes that history-taking has an added function in that it implicitly indicates to the patient that their current difficulties derive from past experiences and that making links between present and past is important and enlightening. However, gathering all the finer details of the patient's history is not the central aim of the consultation, and what is equally important and informative is what they chose to tell you – their narrative, *how* they tell you, their experience of sharing these things with you, and what they leave out. A good psychiatric history undertaken by the referrer or a questionnaire that has been completed prior to the consultation may be a useful complement to the consultation. These additional sources may document the factual details of the person's history, leaving you freer to hear their story and focus on the experience with them in the room without being overly concerned about getting historical information. It allows you to be aware if they miss out or gloss over important events, experiences, or relationships, and to be curious about this with them.

Early Infantile Experiences

Asking for an early memory allows us to get a sense of early infantile experiences and can give a glimpse of the internal object relationships. For example – a woman who described a memory of being on holiday and on a horse ride seated in front of her father, held by him, reflected perhaps an oedipal wish to be in a high-up position, paired with her father with no mother in sight; or a young man who brought a memory of not being told certain details about an important family event, the description of which the consultant found confusing and hard to piece together, potentially reflected an early experience of confusion and fragmentation. Of course early infantile relationships will not be remembered clearly, if at all, or necessarily 'accurately' (see Chapter 4, section 'The Exploration of the Past') but, using the early memory in concert with descriptions about the patterns of relational experience, we can often infer something about how early experience may have influenced the patient's present-day object relationships. Asking the patient for a dream can also give an insight into their unconscious and internal world. Hannah Segal gives a lovely example of how a dream can give a clear picture of someone's internal experience.[7] A male patient, who was a naval officer, described dreaming of a pyramid at the bottom of which was a crowd of rough sailors with a heavy gold book on their heads. On top of the book stood a naval officer of the same rank as him on whose shoulders stood an admiral. The admiral seemed to place great pressure from above and the group of sailors pressed up from below in a way that was felt to him to be equally awe-inspiring. Having described the dream, he said 'this is myself, this is my world'. Through exploration of the dream and the patient's associations, a narrative emerged of how he was pressed by the force of his instincts from below and the prohibitions of his conscience from above, with the gold book representing a golden road which he tried to keep to in between them. We can see reflected in the dream how the main defence mechanism, by which he managed, was repression. He subsequently identified the admiral as symbolising his father who, later in the therapy, could be understood as not being as aggressive or pressuring as in his phantasy. This reflected how he projected his aggression into his father, the introjection of whom formed his superego.

Understanding Defence Mechanisms

The unstructured nature of the consultation experience may be anxiety-provoking, and this should be monitored and managed, not leaving the patient in too much anxiety. It does however give an idea of how the patient would manage the apparently unstructured nature of psychodynamic psychotherapy. The consultation provides a safe space to look at how the patient responds to anxiety or frustration, and what defences they use to manage these. It allows us to see whether they can tolerate and appreciate an experience of being heard and understood and make use of this, or whether they experience this as persecutory or exposing, and mobilise defences such as denigration, contempt, splitting, or projective identification to manage this. Do they become paranoid or attacking? Do they raise a complaint about the consultant being inept or negligent? One way to observe this is to see how the patient manages between consultation appointments. For example, a young man, following an initial consultation, took to his bed, was unable to get up to attend an important family gathering, and missed out on an opportunity to repair a fractured relationship with his father. Or a patient who contacted the service to complain that the consultation had been traumatic and intrusive, and that it had left him very disturbed. The latter said that he had contacted his GP, who he had a good relationship with, and been told that the way that the consultation was conducted had been inappropriate. This would be an example of possible splitting, which could be explored with the GP. Thus, the patient's response to initial appointments can give us a clue to the anxieties and responses that an exploratory approach might stir up in the patient.

It is useful to see whether the patient blocks out the experience of the session, forgets what was talked about, or if they can think about what was discussed and bring back questions, thoughts, and associations. There was a young woman who had over a number of years been seen for consultations for psychotherapy, but some external reason or other always prevented her from then going on to enter a course of therapy. In the current consultation, the consultant was therefore unsure about the patient's wish to really look at herself in therapy and noted in the consultation that the patient remembered very little of her childhood. However, she returned to the second consultation and said that after the first appointment she had contacted her mother to find out more of the details of her childhood and she spoke about these. She went on to make good use of the psychotherapy. It is usually a positive sign if the consultation evokes curiosity in patients about themselves.

There are also patients who don't come back to second appointments; or those who become more fragmented; or resort to methods to get rid of the feelings evoked such as through self-harm, excessive alcohol or drug use, or attending their GP to request medication. This highlights the importance of ascertaining the likelihood of the patient becoming unwell or destabilised during psychotherapy. The process of psychotherapy can open up areas of a patient's experience that they have been cut off from and it can stir up difficult and destabilising memories and emotions. It is useful to anticipate that a patient may have a period of becoming destabilised and unwell during the course of the therapy as their defences are lowered, so it is helpful to establish how unwell they have been at their worst – and particularly in recent years – and whether they have had periods of severe depression, suicidality, or psychosis. This may indicate that psychotherapy is not the right intervention for this individual, or at least at the current point in time.

Bion highlighted that 'the analytic experience, in spite of all the appearances of comfortable couch, comfortable chairs, warmth, good lighting – it is in fact a stormy emotional experience for the two people . . . the analyst is supposed to remain articulate and capable of translating what he is aware of into comprehensible communication. That means that he has to have a vocabulary which the patient might be able to understand if given a chance to hear what the analyst has to say. It sounds absurdly simple – so simple that it's hard to believe how difficult it is.'[8] The work of the consultation is intense and demanding for both patient and consultant. It is anxiety-provoking and exposing for patients and they will enlist their familiar defences in order to protect themselves. Crick, however, also notes that as consultants we may seek unconsciously to defend ourselves against the difficult nature of this work by distancing ourselves from the patient and feeling detached and all-knowing, and that the disturbance is all located in the patient; we may shift to a stance of diagnostic assessment or maternal care.[9] There can be a pressure to offer a solution, answer, or diagnosis rather than staying in the mess and confusion of a patient's fragmented internal world. However, confronting these feelings and putting them into words can be deeply relieving to the patient.

Given that the psychodynamic consultation is an encounter, which will in all likelihood create anxiety and a sense of vulnerability in the patient, we can expect to see defences emerging in the moment-by-moment interaction. We may notice the operation of these when there is a sudden change in topic or vagueness in what the patient is describing, moving to discuss the external reasons for a problem, or going into excessive detail (see Chapter 2 for further discussion about defences). It is useful to pay attention to what was being talked about just before these defensive changes came into play. This might give us some clue as to what the anxiety or painful experience is behind the defence. If we pick up on these defensive manoeuvres, then we can interpret both the defence and the underlying anxiety and gauge the patient's response and whether they can reflect and elaborate on what the consulting therapist has interpreted. If the defences become more entrenched or the patient shows regressive behaviour, it suggests that an uncovering of defences through a process of psychotherapy might not be indicated, as they serve a function of protecting the patient from disintegration. Hinshelwood describes how the process of psychotherapy is to try out hypotheses with the patient.[10] We build up a formulation of the patient's internal world by watching the fate of our interpretations or hypotheses. It is worth a note on the importance of attending to cultural considerations as they come into the consultation. What might be seen as defensive from one cultural perspective may reflect a cultural norm in others, and we must remain mindful of and curious about this.

Organisation of the Internal World

A useful frame for considering how an individual might respond in psychotherapy is to consider what the level of organisation of their internal character structure is. This may be mainly on the neurotic, borderline, or psychotic level. People who function predominantly on a neurotic level tend to be more integrated. This means that they tend to have an agentive sense of self (i.e. a sense of agency in their life) with a capacity to reflect on their inner experiences such that their internal difficulties can be worked through. There is good differentiation between the self and other and between reality and phantasy with a coherent and stable sense of identity and self-representation. They have the capacity to be aware of both an experiencing and observing self, which underpins self-reflection. Similarly, there tends to be a more rounded and reality-based perception of others. Individuals who function at a neurotic level tend to rely on 'neurotic' or 'mature' defensive processes, with repression being the main defence. They can also use archaic defences, but these are not so prominent and there is greater flexibility in their defensive functioning.

With borderline organisation there is less distinction between the internal psychic experiences and external events. The capacity to work through struggles internally is impaired and thus, they are mainly acted out in the interpersonal sphere. There is an experience of a distressing lack of a coherent sense of self and the self-experience can be very inchoate. Because of this discontinuity and inconsistency, when regressed they can experience psychotic-like phenomena such as hearing voices, seeing things, or feelings of paranoia or persecution. In non-regressed states their reality testing is fine and they can present as being well and without apparent difficulties. The defences are of an archaic nature and involve omnipotence, denial, splitting, and projective identification. The experience of the other is generally highly influenced by projection and there can be a limited perception of the other as they are in reality. Equally, although there is a concept of there being a separate self and other, it can at times be hard for these patients to clearly distinguish between a sense of self-identity and other due to the level of projection that occurs. They can lack the 'reflective function' that allows them to understand their own and others' experiences, feelings, and behaviour; or, in other terms, they struggle to 'mentalize'.

Individuals who have a psychotic organisation present with a high degree of fragmentation. Interestingly, Freud described the psychotic process as being akin to a bandage placed over the psychic fracture in an attempt to fix it. There is a loss of symbolic function where the 'as if' quality of experience is lost. Thoughts and phantasy become concrete and real, internal and external have no distinction and therefore the ability to delineate reality falters. Fear and confusion predominate. With the loss of distinction between reality and phantasy, internal and external, continuity of self and other, there is a loss of the capacity for self-reflection. People with a psychotic level of organisation tend to use primitive or preverbal defences such as withdrawal, denial, omnipotent control, idealisation and devaluation, splitting, projection and introjection, and somatisation. These defensive processes protect the individual from archaic anxieties such as of annihilation and 'nameless dread'.

While I have described these organisational structures as distinct, they are not mutually exclusive, and individuals can exhibit more than one level of organisation. In some individuals there may be a psychotic area in an otherwise neurotic character structure. This can be hard to discern in the limited number of sessions of a consultation. For example, a young woman presented as very depressed following the death of her parents and of her son. What emerged was that she was in a psychotic state of merger with her dead child and parents and spent all her time feeling that she had to keep them alive by keeping them constantly in her thoughts, not throwing away any of their belongings, and keeping things exactly as they were when they died, to the point where she had become completely removed from life.

Patterns of Object Relations

A useful framework for picking out the relational dynamic is the tripartite structure of psychodynamic formulation. This was first described by Karl Menninger[11] and later expanded by Malan.[12] It consists of seeing common patterns within the descriptions of the patient's past experience reflecting early infantile object relations, their experiences in current life situations, and the experience in relation to the consultant (see Malan's triangles in Figure 7.1 in Chapter 7).

Clinical Example 2 Marco

Marco was man in his 30s who had been referred for psychotherapy as he had become very anxious and withdrawn. He was noted by the referrer to have an extremely close and protective relationship with his mother. This had been the case ever since his father had left them when he was a child after having been physically abusive to his mother. He was seen for a consultation and was accompanied by his mother. He was initially extremely anxious and appeared sullen, looking down, and pulling his cap down to cover his face. The consultant tried to open things up with him by gentle enquiry but with little success. After a time she suggested that perhaps if Marco attended alone next time, it would help him feel freer to talk. He did so and Marco seemed to be more relaxed and described his difficulties, how he hated it if his mother went out with friends. He talked of how he would become frustrated and enraged if she went on a date with a man. He described how he would spend most of his time at home, rarely leaving the house. He had very few friends but he did have one female friend who he was very close to. He had recently become upset by the fact that this friend had developed a romantic relationship with a man from her work and they were spending quite a lot of time together. Marco had become very angry with his friend and they had argued. He gave her an ultimatum saying it was him or the new boyfriend. As the consultation went on the consultant became aware of a feeling of connection with this disturbed but intelligent young man. She felt that she had been able to establish a good and trusting relationship with him where Marco openly discussed his difficulties and complex relationships in a frank and honest way. She thought that she would be able to offer him something therapeutic. After the session the consultant reflected on what had happened and how there seemed to be a repeated pattern of a very close and 'special' relationship between Marco and a woman – his mother, the friend, and the consultant – where the presence of a third was felt to be bringing in something disturbing or harmful and so had to be excluded. This is depicted in a diagram, following Malan's triangle format, in Figure 9.1.

We can see how a common relationship runs through all three areas of the patient's life – past, current external, and in the consultation – as there is an internal figure or relationship that is retained and repeatedly projected into others. When we see the repetition of a particular relationship in these three spheres, we can reasonably assume that this represents a picture of an internal object-relationship, lived out continually and repeatedly in the patient's experience over the course of their life.[10] Different sides of the object relationships will be externalised in different situations. It is useful to hold in mind the idea of a single relationship with an object, the different aspects of which get projected or identified with (this concept was introduced in Chapter 8, section 'The Formulation in Action').

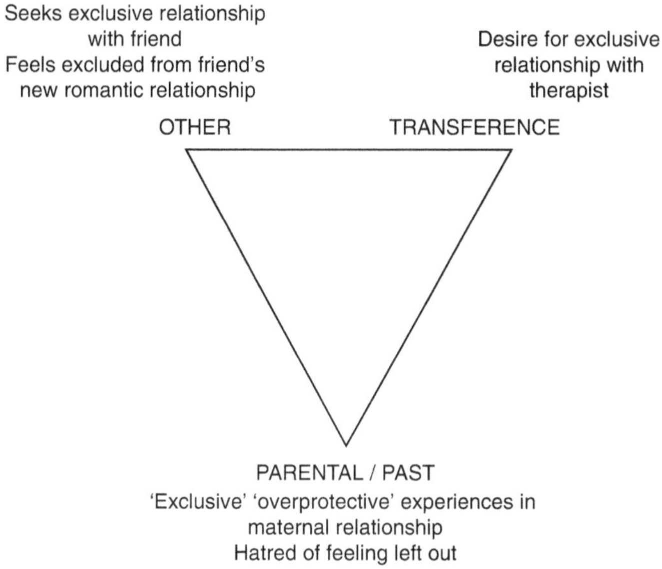

Figure 9.1 Formulation diagram for Marco
Based on the 'triangle of person' formulation format of Malan (1995) [12]

Thinking about Formulation

A central question that needs to be considered when we come to doing a consultation is, what is the core difficulty for the patient? What is it they want to be different? Does the patient want to feel better, to simply get rid of the painful or discomfiting feelings that they experience, or do they have a sense that there is something in them that needs to be understood and to change in order for there to be positive changes in their life? This will guide us as to whether psychodynamic psychotherapy is an approach that will help them with these difficulties. Another question to ask is, are they in a place where there is space for internal change through the therapy? There are some reasons that the latter may not be the case. These include a lack of sufficient stability in their external situation such as significant problems with housing, poverty, and debt which mean that simply surviving is a preoccupation; a degree of reliance on drugs or alcohol that precludes being able to think and reflect, or a pattern of use which brings concern for the patient's health or survival should substance use increase during therapy as they become less defended; issues around dependency whereby the patient did not find previous psychodynamic therapy helpful, and where a concrete desire to be ideally cared for overtakes the capacity to reflect on this situation and its difficulties.

Through the process of consultation, we can come to a formulation or understanding of the patient's difficulties. A useful question to ask oneself when constructing a formulation is – can I represent this patient's internal world for myself? As Lemma noted, the focus or the emphasis that a particular consulting therapist gives to certain aspects of what the patient brings, and how they bring these together to construct the formulation, will be influenced by their particular theories and what these lead us to pursue or not with the patient.[5] The formulation is a picture of the patient's internal world constructed from the hypotheses tested in the consultation.

Concluding Remarks

The consultation is a process in which there is the development of an understanding of the patient and their particular difficulties. It provides an opportunity for the patient to experience a space in which they are listened to and thought about in a unique way in an effort to open up a new way of seeing themself and to see if psychodynamic psychotherapy is right for them. When deciding about whether psychodynamic psychotherapy is right it is important that the patient is in contact with the fact that often the therapy can be a painful and difficult process that involves self-examination and confrontation with the less admirable aspects of the self. It is not a place to go where you will be soothed and the painful feelings dissipate to leave you happy and carefree. As Freud suggested, 'We do well if we can turn neurotic misery into ordinary unhappiness'.[13] The person must be open to looking into themselves and seeing whatever they might find there, out of a desire to be able to do something differently and to work on themselves. A good consultation doesn't necessarily lead to an offer of psychotherapy. If, however, the consultant has been able to maintain a therapeutic approach and to continue to function and think about and with the patient – or regain their ability to think when this has been lost, what Bion termed 'continuing to think under fire' – and if the patient has had a meaningful experience of feeling understood and of understanding something – then it is a successful endeavour. The patient's decision to enter psychodynamic psychotherapy or not can then be based on this experience rather than being something that they are granted a place in by the 'expert' consultant.

Finally, while the process of consultation and formulation is generally something that is developed between and for the patient and consultant, it can also provide a useful tool to other healthcare professionals who are working with the patient such as the GP or mental health team. This is discussed further in Chapter 19 on consulting to the clinical team.

References

1. Banet AG, Bion WR. Interview. Anthony G. Banet interviews Wilfred R. Bion. Group & Organization Studies 1976;1(3):268–85.
2. Schofield W. Psychotherapy: The Purchase of Friendship. New Brunswick & Oxford: Transaction Books, 1986.
3. Caligor E, Stern BL, Hamilton M et al. Why we recommend analytic treatment for some patients and not others. J. Am. Psychoanal. Assn. 2009; 57(3); 677–94.
4. Keating F. African and Caribbean men and mental health. *Ethnicity and Inequalities in Health and Social Care.* 2009; 2(2); 1–12.
5. Lemma A. Introduction to the Practice of Psychoanalytic Psychotherapy. Chapter 5. W. Sussex: John Wiley & Sons, 2016.
6. Garelick A. Psychotherapy assessment: theory and practice. Psychodynamic Psychotherapy, 1994; 8(2); 101–16.
7. Segal H. Phantasy. In Introduction to the Works of Melanie Klein. Routledge, 1978.
8. Bion WR. 1977. In Bion in New York and Sao Paulo: And Three Tavistock Seminars. Harris Melzer Trust, 2019.
9. Crick P. Selecting a patient or initiating a psychoanalytic process? Int. J. Psychoanal. 2014; 95(3); 465–84.
10. Hinshelwood RD. Psychodynamic formulation in assessment for psychotherapy. British Journal of Psychotherapy, 1991; 8(2); 166–74.

11. Menninger K. Theory of Psychoanalytic Technique. London: Imago, 1958.
12. Malan D. Individual Psychotherapy and the Science of Psychodynamics. 2nd edition. Oxford: Butterworth-Heinemann (Elsevier); 1995.
13. Freud S, Breuer J. The Standard Edition of the Complete Psychological Works of Sigmund Freud, Vol. 2, Studies on Hysteria, 1895. Strachey J, Freud A, eds. London: Hogarth Press and the Institute of Psycho-analysis; 1955.

Chapter 10 Some Reflections on the Supervisory Process

'We claim no authority ... we require no direct agreement from the patient, nor do we argue with him ... In short, we conduct ourselves on the model of a familiar figure in one of Nestroy's farces – the manservant who has a single answer on his lips to every question or objection: "It will all become clear in the course of future developments."' (Freud 1937)[1]

I will start with a vignette from my own training experience. A patient who was rather placating in manner had the following dream:

> *A man goes away and comes back wearing second-hand clothes, claiming that they belong to him.*

Although at first it seemed to both of us that the man might well be him, as I thought about it more I started to recognise that associations to the man in the dream led to me – in other words this was my patient's experience of my supervision. Namely, I go away to somewhere else and return wearing someone else's interpretations (the second-hand clothes) whilst claiming that they belonged to me.

Now what I want to focus on here as regards this vignette is this: it tells us something about what psychoanalytic work is **not**. It is not 'giving interpretations to patients' in the same way that a doctor might give medicine to patients. I think all of us 'believe' this, and yet, as with many things of this nature that we 'believe', it is surprisingly difficult to function in such a way that is consistent with our own beliefs. I think there are various sorts of pressure functioning at different levels – within our own minds, in the patient's mind, and also at an institutional level, which effect a kind of degradation of psychoanalytic work to the point where the thought-providing quality of understanding, which is mobile and dynamic, degrades into static dogma and ritualistic practice.

Understanding, then, which is a core of our work, is not something that can be simply *given* but something that the patient and analyst *discover*. I think that some of my best work takes place when, as I go to say something, it changes almost whilst I'm in the act of saying it. As if at that moment or in that process I move from an action – 'making an interpretation' – to understanding something or discussing something (I think this is related to Bion's description of the move from paranoid-schizoid to depressive position taking place inside the analyst). It is as if at this moment one moves to a kind of 'oh yes, now I see' – moving from a state where the interpretation which, though 'correct' (plausible), is saturated with countertransference and so is more an *action*. Speaking here ('interpreting') is merely the outward sign of that process.

For example, being about to say to a patient 'you feel that I'm very angry with you' (the implication being 'but of course I am not'). Here, interpretation is an action both to convince a patient and the analyst that of course the analyst isn't angry. Now that is different to moving to a position where one can understand or see why there is a pressure to communicate to the patient (and myself) what a kind and nice person I am. One hears something of this action quality of interpretation in the language that we use when speaking of our work – I am referring to expressions such as 'interpreting to the patient' or 'I took it up with him', 'confronting the patient with . . . ', 'I can see I needed to make a transference interpretation'.

I think that understanding often takes place when one is moving away from the position of interpretation as *action* and moving towards the position of the interpretation as the outward expression of a discovery.

Understanding then is an *emergent* function, not something that is *given,* yet of course to get to that state we have to do a lot more.

The process I am describing here, where thought-provoking ideas (discoveries) are degraded into ritualised practices, is very related to what Tom Main described in his paper 'Knowledge, learning and freedom from thought', where he described how (in institutions) yesterday's thought-provoking idea becomes tomorrow's dogma.[2]

Main called this a move from an ego function to superego function; a move from possessing an idea to becoming possessed by an idea. New ideas are very often threatening, whether it be at the level of the institution or of an individual mind. The growth-promoting functioning of interpretive work is inevitably always under threat and this is an ingredient of certain types of countertransference experience. One might think of the therapist, who gives apparently plausible interpretations but without enthusiasm or conviction, and so lives out the experience of being a depressed mother who provides what she thinks a baby needs in a dutiful way.

My reason for focusing on these issues here is because I think an important site of this degradation of growth-promoting thought takes place at the site of the transmission of knowledge from one generation to the next – and a prime location for this is at the interface of supervision.

I suspect many supervisors have had the uncomfortable experience of last week's interesting understanding turning into this week's ritual procedure, as the interpretation is given dutifully and reported in the supervisory hour. This is one of the reasons I often get very anxious in supervisions when supervisees write things down. I always fear that they might read what they've written and make energetic attempts to remember it (which is of course different from them remembering something of the supervision in the session because now it makes sense).

It is, I think, a well-established fact that a deep understanding of our patient arises from a full recognition of the transference situation. Understanding is the aim of our work, and the transference happens to be the central location of that understanding. Yet this thoughtful idea, this conception of our work, easily slips into something that looks the same but is, I believe, entirely different. It becomes degraded into a kind of fetish which I call 'giving the transference interpretation'. This is being given not as a sign of understanding, but a ritualised procedure serving to deal with anxiety, placate the supervisor, and which replaces understanding. Many times, I have heard sessions where one can sense, as the session is read out, a mounting anxiety in the therapist that they haven't *yet* made a transference interpretation – and it is already halfway through the session! The therapist then makes a 'transference' interpretation which is not the result of understanding, they do not connect with it, but it is more out of duty to the received paradigm. It is a pseudo-transference interpretation. It is easy for an atmosphere of triumph to enter supervisory seminars where either the supervisor or other participants will 'show' the therapist that they have 'missed the "transference"'.

This problem of the degradation of thought into dogma occurs with many good ideas in psychoanalysis. For example, I think John Steiner's work with borderline patients led to a very thought-promoting distinction between 'analyst-centred and patient-centred' interpretations. He suggested that when dealing with patients suffering from borderline states, it is often much easier to explore the patient's mental contents in projected form, focusing on the patient's experience of the analyst rather than insisting that these are the patient's thoughts, the latter being often experienced by the patient as a forceful re-projection into the patient. I've come across a number of occasions, however, where this kind of understanding has become a kind of injunction – 'this is a borderline patient and so I know I can't make any patient-centred interpretations but only analyst-centred interpretations'.

Reaching for certainties often starts as a result of anxiety and this is inevitable in all of us. However, it can acquire a kind of life of its own and this is quite damaging.

I would now like to turn more fully to the supervisory process. The meeting between supervisee and supervisor is inevitably located with a complex framework – supervisor, supervisee, patient, psychoanalytic allegiances, and so on. The supervisor is not only there to help the work move forward, but also as an educator and to some extent as an agent of the institution.

This setting provides fertile soil for the processes I have been describing. It is clear and, I don't think it is helpful to disown this, that generally a supervisor has considerably more knowledge and experience than the supervisee, but this does not mean that necessarily the supervisor would have managed the case much better than the supervisee, but supervisees find this very hard to believe. This can extend to an idealisation, which becomes a source of persecution. The result is that the supervisee spends much of the session not thinking about their patient but about how much better their supervisor would be doing. On many occasions, having understood a kind of enactment in a good supervision, I know the supervisee leaves believing 'of course that would not have happened to him'. Yet, later in the day, I find myself making exactly the same type of mistake.

This idealisation cannot be easily got rid of. And there is another kind of ritual, which I think supervisors easily get drawn into and I include myself here – of a kind of compulsive confessional mode to try and show the supervisee how unideal we are. I think supervisees see through this quite easily.

So, what is the principal aim of supervision? I think we aim to help the supervisee think about the material and to try to be aware of the processes that prevent this. For this to happen, I think it is very important to distinguish a supervisory session from an analytic session. Yet one is also trying to maintain something of an analytic attitude. Understanding of material presented is often accompanied by the recovery of interest and enthusiasm for the work and this often takes place when the transference/countertransference situation can be understood. The supervisee, to some extent when they bring material from a session, also embodies the relationship between themself and the patient. I mostly prefer to hear written detailed sessions but sometimes this can become, I think, a way of evading an understanding of the nature of the relationship and so, on occasion, I ask supervisees to put aside their notes and just to talk about the patient. This however can also be subject to the idealisation and used as a way of not having to make notes!

One should avoid making it too much of an aim, so to speak, to find out about the psychotherapist's countertransference, it should more be something that is discovered. In my experience, it is rarely discovered through directly asking psychotherapists about how they feel about the patient.

One often discovers aspects of the countertransference when thinking of the patient during the day, in quite private moments. For example, I remember seeing a patient in a supermarket who I hadn't seen for many years and who, at first, I didn't recognise. I had an impulse to run towards this man and say 'Hello, I haven't seen you for ages,' in an exceedingly friendly manner. What struck me about this was that I hadn't been aware before of just how warmly I felt about the patient. I am struck by the feeling of dread that takes over me as regards one patient – and the disturbing ease when it comes to another, when thinking of having to cancel a session.

A colleague of mine dreaded seeing his patient at the tennis club where they were both members. In fact, he tried to avoid going to the tennis club on occasions when his patient would be there. I had assumed this was because the patient was a better tennis player than he was and that he found this rather humiliating. But I hadn't actually asked him why he hated seeing his patient at the club. When I eventually did ask, it emerged that what my own colleague couldn't stand was seeing who his patient always played tennis with. He always played with a man referred to by some as the 'club psychopath' who was well-known for picking up women, having sex with them, and dropping them.

It turned out that there was a typical pattern in this patient's analysis, which now could be seen more clearly. The patient would for a while seem very involved with his analysis and then, in the next session, there would be a sudden radical change in the atmosphere, the patient becoming distant and mocking. My colleague then realised just how much he hated what one might now think of as a psychopathic part of the patient who was always luring him (the patient) away from the good understanding. When the patient, so to speak, teamed up with this part of himself, the analyst was abandoned.

Sometimes one finds something of these more private experiences in supervision in the ways the supervisee comes to represent aspects of the patient in their functioning in the supervision – in a parallel process. However, again, this is not something that we can insist happens but, when it does, it can be very revealing. Looking back at my first vignette it could also be seen that in repeating my supervisor's interpretations I had maybe become identified with a part of the patient who was very dutiful and tended to do what he was told to do.

Example

A female who I am currently supervising (T) had in treatment a young French man B, who was very dominated by his mother with whom he was in contact with every day. He seems quite unable to escape his mother's intrusiveness and yet also stimulates it, through a certain secretiveness. On the other hand, he also dreads feeling excluded and his secretiveness, as well as his provoking the intrusiveness, projects the feeling of exclusion into his object. He often relates accounts of events to his therapist but not making things quite clear and the therapist tends to respond by asking him lots of 'clarifying' questions. Through asking questions she lives out the role of the mother who can't bear to be left out. This pattern would occur particularly when the patient was talking about a girlfriend – he wouldn't be clear which girlfriend he was talking about, whether it was a serious girlfriend or not, what had taken place between them, etc.

T was about to start her second training case and over the preceding few weeks she and I had tended to spend a few minutes discussing the second case in a chatty and informal manner (this actually had nothing to do with me as she was taking the case to another supervisor). She had told me on a number of occasions that the new case, G, was a very interesting artist and she was clearly very excited by the prospect of taking on this patient. She started one supervision by telling me that she had now started the new case, it was going OK, and she conveyed a certain enthusiasm for her patient (which was lacking from the case she presented to me). She then, apologetically, informed me that she hadn't much material to present. There had been a bank holiday, which meant one cancelled session; she had not had sufficient time to write up the other sessions – as she saw her new case G only 15 minutes after B left (i.e. leaving little time for writing up). Before she started with G, she had plenty of writing up time for B.

She then presented a session which had a rather dead quality. The interpretations in a way seemed reasonable but lacked any conviction and sounded rather dutiful. The material presented contained an account of the exciting time that B had enjoyed with his new girlfriend over the bank holiday weekend. He informed his therapist that he went back to his girlfriend's house and she 'was all over him'. But he didn't seem to communicate anything as to how he regarded this new relationship. The therapist over the course of the session suggested that the patient was trying to get her to ask him questions, that he was rather absent from the session, and the patient appeared to respond in an apparently insightful way, even at one point saying, 'that's just what H (the girlfriend) says, that I've gone off in my mind'.

Although this may have been right, the function of this sort of comment seemed to me to be more of a way of including the therapist in a dutiful way, again without much enthusiasm or conviction.

The patient mentioned a dream in which he went on a plane journey to Paris (Paris was associated with excitement – he was from the suburbs) in a slightly dishevelled state with his trousers unbuttoned; he then buttoned himself up as he got off the plane.

I thought that this exactly conveyed something of the atmosphere of the session. He had had an exciting unbuttoned-up weekend with his girlfriend, but the session with his therapist was buttoned up and restrained.

As we discussed this, the therapist suddenly said, rather nervously but with real conviction, that she does feel – she couldn't quite catch the word – but then said 'jealous, I feel jealous of his girlfriend'. She then added that she feared the patient might suddenly leave therapy.

We were then able to reconstruct the situation along the following lines – the therapist T had, without being quite aware of it, felt angry at being continuously excluded by this patient and this had been going on for some considerable time. She was enacting this by getting together with her new patient in an exciting way and, through doing so, was excluding B. The rather braced up and stiff relationship with B paled into insignificance when compared to an exciting new patient. This had been enacted by spending some of her supervision time discussing the new patient and more concretely through having the new patient displace B in terms of her having no time to write up her session.

Of course, unwittingly, I had been a support to this enactment through my involvement in the second case which, as I said, had really nothing to do with me. I recognised that I had been rather jealous of the new relationship with the exciting new patient, with presumably an interesting supervision session with her new supervisor, and seemed to have ended up, a bit inappropriately, involving myself in it.

Now this understanding, including the enactment, was helpful, I think, to me and to my supervisee. I do think that it is important that there is an atmosphere which can allow such things to evolve, and when such parallel processes are discovered, they are usually very helpful. However, one cannot insist that such parallel processes happen. They just do.

Conclusion

I have tried in this brief chapter to discuss how although we have certain beliefs about the analytic process, they are hard to sustain. Burnyeat, a philosopher, has discussed what he calls the 'fragility of belief' and refers to a famous Platonic dialogue where although an individual accepts Socrates's position and believes it to be right, they find themself quite unable to carry it through or act in accordance with it. It is as if the minute Socrates isn't there, this belief dissolves in his mind.

Interpretations, as I understand it, reflect change as much as they cause it: very often a change internal to the analyst. To confuse the understanding that a good interpretation both represents and communicates, with the words of the interpretation itself, is a kind of concreteness. Although many of us, I suspect, accept this – it is a hard position to sustain with our patients – and particularly hard, I am suggesting, to sustain in supervision.

Psychoanalysis has been described as an impossible profession; the other familiar impossible professions are law and education. Given that the supervision is an attempt to increase analytic understanding, that it is also educational, and further that the supervisor represents the institution and has some legislative and governance function, one can see that being a supervisor turns out to be a combination of three impossible professions.

Reference

1. Freud S. Constructions in analysis. In Strachey J, editor. The Standard Edition of the Complete Psychological Works of Sigmund Freud volume 23. London: Hogarth Press (original work published 1937); 1964. pp. 257–69.
2. Main T. Knowledge, learning, and freedom from thought. Psychoanalytic Psychotherapy 1990;5(1):59–78.

Part 3: Application for Mental Health Presentations

Chapter 11 Psychodynamic Approaches to Anxiety

Table of Contents

Introduction 171
Sense of Self and Anxiety: The Importance of Containment 173
Encountering Archaic Anxieties 174
Anxiety Linked to Fear of Separation and Loss 176
Anxiety as a Signal of Internal Conflict 178
Anxiety Arising from a Critical Internal Object 179
The Therapist's Experience of Anxiety in the Therapy Room 180
Concluding Remarks 182

Introduction

We all know what it's like to be anxious. It's a common state of mind (and body) that we experience from time to time, whether preparing for a job interview, meeting new people, driving home on a nearly empty tank, or living through a global pandemic. All of these situations can lead to anxiety, which can be expressed physically, emotionally, and in our thoughts and behaviours. In a physiological sense, our body responds by activation of the autonomic nervous system. This can cause us to experience palpitations, breathlessness, nausea, and sweating (to name a few). In addition to physical symptoms of anxiety, we can feel frightened, low in mood, irritable, or perhaps even excited or hopeful. In terms of cognitions, we may ruminate, catastrophise, and have difficulty concentrating. From a relational point of view, we might withdraw from or, conversely, cling to others. Some writers, drawing on a model of core emotional needs, contrast panic anxiety with fear.[1] To explain these two concepts further: the classic fear response – to either fight, flee, or freeze – is understood as a reaction to situations that are perceived as dangerous to our physical or psychological survival (see Chapter 2, Box 2.1, and also Chapter 16 for the relationship between fear and anger), whereas panic anxiety is more to do with separation from our loved ones or a worry about this happening. From an evolutionary point of view, anxiety can be helpful. It can motivate us not only to protect ourselves but to solve problems, to create, develop and thrive in a world that continues to present us with potential hazards.

The situations we have mentioned are temporary, for the most part. We tend to experience relief from our anxiety when we fill up our car or when the job interview is over. When the source of anxiety has dissipated our heart rate slows, our anxiety will settle, our mood may lift, our mind may allow us to think about other things, and we establish our usual forms of contact with those close to us. However, this is not always the case. For patients who may seek psychodynamic psychotherapy for anxiety states, this state of mind and body is more chronic. Instead of passing, it may linger and incapacitate. This can become problematic and lead to difficulties in functioning. For these patients, anxiety may be preventing them from developing and sustaining relationships, fulfilling their creative potential, and experiencing what the world has to offer.

For some patients who seek psychodynamic therapy, anxiety *may* be the presenting difficulty. For others, the primary concern may be about relationships with the self and others, and then during consultation they speak of an underlying sense of dread, worry, fear, and apprehension. Some patients may arrive already prepared with questions: *Where do these panic attacks come from? What is it about being in social situations that makes me want to retreat?* For others, these questions have not yet crystallised, but the therapist's hope is that the therapeutic process will stimulate curiosity about the nature and origin of the anxiety.

There is often something about the quality of anxiety that feels unknown, inexpressible. Despite this uncertainty, in early sessions there are often accounts of difficulties in early experiences with caregivers – experiences of environments which felt less than secure; experiences of significant others as unavailable or abandoning; a sense of a parent who was anxious, depressed or emotionally dysregulated. Something *is* known, yet the link between what is known and unknown is buried.[2]

Perelberg states that 'Freud emphasises the notion of a signal that is a response by the ego threatened with an experience of danger. It is a reaction to a traumatic situation . . . The signal refers to a danger already experienced in the past.'[3] Anxiety therefore may be alerting us to both a conscious, external threat in the present (e.g. being stranded due to an empty petrol tank) and to something unconscious related to earlier threatening experiences – is the nearly empty tank a representation of something internal?[2] Perhaps the patient ends up in recurring situations where they find themselves lacking and feeling empty.

It is important to note that for patients who experience anxiety that feels overwhelming and that impairs functioning, this will be expressed in various ways. A psychodynamic approach to anxiety is not disorder-specific; anxiety can and usually is present to varying degrees in all patients who are seen for psychodynamic psychotherapy. Equally, a person's symptoms may not have reached the threshold for a clinical 'disorder', however this does not negate distress.

Freud wrote in *Inhibitions, Symptoms and Anxiety* that we want 'to find something that will tell us what anxiety really is, some criterion that will enable us to distinguish true statements about it from false ones. But this is not so easy to get. Anxiety is not so simple a matter.'[4] The psychodynamic literature on anxiety is vast, owing perhaps to its diffuse and complex presentation, as Freud hints. This complexity arises partly because patients may experience anxiety at multiple developmental levels (see Box 11.1); this is particularly likely if there are ongoing experiences of trauma or deprivation in the external environment.

Box 11.1 A developmental hierarchy of anxiety (adapted from Gabbard)[5]

Anxiety can be conceptualised in terms of developmental level. Archaic anxieties – disintegration anxiety and persecutory anxiety – are associated with early developmental distress in an undeveloped self. As an infant develops, different anxieties may be experienced. In the following list, anxieties that occur later in one's development are higher in the list and more archaic anxieties are lower down:

Anxiety arising from a critical internal object

Fear of loss of love of the object

Fear of loss of the object (separation anxiety) (depressive anxiety)

Persecutory anxiety

Disintegration anxiety

Anxieties developed in each developmental phase will not necessarily be outgrown forever but can be re-evoked at any stage in life.[5] This chapter expands on the forms of anxiety in this list in later sections.

The various schools of psychodynamic thought each bring a depth and a perspective to the understanding of anxiety. This chapter will outline some psychodynamic approaches to understanding anxieties using clinical material to illustrate these concepts. We start with the core concept of containment and then discuss various forms of anxiety, moving from the developmentally more archaic (sometimes referred to as 'primitive') to those arising later in development.

Sense of Self and Anxiety: The Importance of Containment

Clinical Example 1 Alex: feeling dread but not knowing why

Alex was referred for psychodynamic psychotherapy with a long-standing history of generalised anxiety symptoms including restlessness and irritability. He also described waking in the morning with a sense of dread and feeling that he had no understanding of what this was about. During assessment he spoke of being aware that during his childhood his mother had been diagnosed with a 'personality disorder' and that she struggled to understand and regulate her own emotions as well as his. As he grew up, he learned what to do to keep her feeling happy and settled and what would cause her distress. However, he felt that there had been little room to understand himself.

Bion presents us with the notion of 'nameless dread', which he described in *A Theory of Thinking* (this concept was introduced in Box 2.2 on 'Bion and Containment' in Chapter 2). In short, this refers to a state of dread that Bion surmises may arise in the infant if the primary caregiver is consistently experienced as unable to take in, understand and make meaning of the infant's experiences. The result is that feelings and experiences become devoid of meaning and the infant is left in this confusing, unknowing, anxiety-filled state.[6] Killick notes that:

> Fear of disintegrating is a normal infantile anxiety which seeks containment within the symbiotic environment. If this is uncontained, the anxiety, plus the experience of the

> absence of containment, is reintrojected. A 'no-breast' is established in the inner world, a 'wilfully misunderstanding object' that strips experience of whatever meaning it has.[7]

Winnicott similarly describes anxiety as emerging due to repeated failures in the dynamics of caregiver–infant attunement and an overall sense of lack of a 'holding environment'. He states:

> With 'the care that it receives from its mother' each infant is able to have a personal existence, and so begins to build up what might be called a continuity of being. On the basis of this continuity of being the inherited potential gradually develops into an individual infant. If maternal care is not good enough then the infant does not really come into existence, since there is no continuity of being; instead the personality becomes built on the basis of reactions to environmental impingement.[8]

If we link these concepts to Clinical Example 1, we might infer that Alex was seeking to discover an understanding of himself as an individual. His sense of himself in the world appeared to have developed out of a concern to react to and predict his mother's emotional states. This particular patient responded well in therapy to a predictable, reliable, and containing frame. He was able to make use of the therapeutic space to start to open up and talk about his thoughts and feelings. He described a particularly close relationship with an aunt, who would often take care of him. She noticed when he was withdrawn and had made time for him, taking him under her wing and allowing him space to 'just be'. The internalisation of a good containing object from childhood had allowed him to make use of the therapist and the containing frame in a fairly straightforward way.

Encountering Archaic Anxieties

When disturbed and traumatic early experiences are coupled with a lack of 'good enough' containment, anxieties might present in more archaic forms. Within psychoanalytic and psychodynamic literature, we find mention of these as *persecutory anxiety* and *disintegration anxiety*. Gabbard notes that persecutory anxiety relates to Klein's observation of the paranoid–schizoid position in which 'persecuting objects from outside will invade and annihilate the patient from within'.[5] (The concept of the paranoid–schizoid position was introduced in Chapter 2 in the section on 'Movement between Defensive 'Splitting' and a More Integrated Position'.) Klein related this (and to some, this is controversial) to innate aggression within the infant. Klein's views on aggression and anxiety are captured in Box 11.2. Disintegration anxiety, in contrast, is described as 'the fear of losing one's sense of self or boundedness through merger with an object or from concern that one's self will fragment and lose its integrity in the absence of mirroring or idealising responses from others in the environment'.[5]

Whilst a contemporary psychodynamic approach may not accept Klein's conceptions to the letter, her articulation of the dynamics and feel of these experiences of annihilation, persecution, and disintegration can be orientating for the therapist when listening to patients with archaic developmental anxieties.

The following example is simplified to illustrate the presentation of anxiety related to a very early developmental stage (see Clinical Example 2). In reality (as with all patients) the presentation was multi-layered with the patient experiencing difficulties at multiple developmental levels. What was of note with this patient was that the anxiety was felt mostly by those who came into contact with him (neurologist and therapist) rather than by the patient himself. The therapist's responses to anxiety will be discussed in more detail later in the chapter.

Box 11.2 **Melanie Klein's theoretical views on aggression and anxiety**

Klein stated that from birth 'anxiety originates in the fear of annihilation'.[9] For Klein, the fear of annihilation originates from innate aggressive impulses (the notion of a 'death instinct') within the infant. The Kleinian infant experiences conflicting feelings between a draw towards life (loving instincts) but yet a pull towards deathly instincts (aggression and destructiveness). The tension feels unbearable and so these feelings (both good and bad) are split and projected into external objects – the 'good' and 'bad' breast, later the mother. The infant then is subject to what Klein calls *persecutory anxiety*, which is the experience of the projected aggression as coming from the external object. For example, the breast that is not immediately available to satisfy hunger is experienced by the rudimentary ego as dangerous.

Later when the infant comes to understand that the 'good' and 'bad' breast (mother) are one and the same, the anxiety becomes a *depressive anxiety* – a fear that the infant has harmed this loved 'other' through his phantasied destructive attacks. Over time, if the parental figures are sufficiently attuned to the infant, giving the infant the projections back in a processed and containing way enough of the time, the infant can get to know that the parent can not only survive these attacks but can help the infant manage and understand difficult feelings. However, where there is a lack of attunement between care-giver and infant, the infant may experience ongoing anxieties and may be predisposed to developing various psychopathologies, especially if exposed to trauma or other disturbances.[9,10]

Clinical Example 2 **Brendan: a young man with unexplained collapses**

Brendan was a mature student studying chemistry. He was in his late twenties and had been experiencing sudden collapses since his teens. No physical cause had been found for these sudden periods of apparent unconsciousness. His general practitioner referred him to a psychotherapist.

When he was a couple of months old, his mother was admitted to hospital for several months after becoming severely depressed and suicidal. This was a pattern that was repeated several times throughout his childhood. When this happened, he stayed with his maternal grandmother who he described as 'strict and no-nonsense'.

He had been under the care of a neurologist who had kept on seeing him despite there being no neurological cause for his symptoms. The neurologist explained to the psychotherapist that she had kept seeing Brendan because 'I felt worried about him, he reminded me of my son and I wanted to make sure he would be ok.' The neurologist noted that as she began talking to the young man about discharging him, these collapses became more frequent.

At consultation with the psychotherapist, Brendan did not appear anxious, however he spoke of recurring nightmares in which he would find himself lost in desolate landscapes. He would wake with a huge adrenaline surge and find it difficult to get back to sleep. He wondered if it was perhaps his tiredness that contributed to the collapses.

Over an extended consultation period, the therapist noticed a pattern emerging. The patient would describe his experiences in a calm and unperturbed manner, whilst she found herself feeling tremendously anxious about him, even when not at work. She recalled the neurologist's feelings towards the patient, which were similar – there was a sense of really wanting to 'hold on' to him. In her own supervision, she speculated that he needed someone to hold his anxious and unbearable feelings because he felt he was unable to manage them himself. Reflecting on these dynamics and his developmental history, the therapist and her supervisor hypothesised that at a very early age he may have experienced a sense of disintegration in relation to feeling insufficiently contained or a sense of an inconsistent holding environment.

Brendan received two years of therapy due to the recognition that longer term work might be needed in order to establish a containing therapeutic relationship in which he could learn to rely on the therapist to help him understand and process feelings and experiences. Over the course of the therapy the patient began to become more curious about his experiences and his dreams. He began to notice a theme in his dreams of having to fight for life and feeling terrified. Looking back on his childhood, he reflected that he was constantly in a state of tension, worrying that his mother might die.

As the work progressed and he could talk about his feelings more, his collapses lessened. When the end of the work approached, his collapses intensified for a period of time. However, he was able to openly discuss his fears about the separation and if he could 'survive' on his own.

Anxiety Linked to Fear of Separation and Loss

Mark Solms, psychoanalyst and neuropsychologist, notes that anxiety and depression have roots in the same separation-distress response in the brain. In the acute phase of becoming separated from a caregiver, there is panic and an anxiety response. If the separation continues and there is a loss of the caregiver, this becomes despair, which Solms observes is the phenotype for depression.[11] This echoes earlier work from Bowlby's seminal paper on separation anxiety in which he details his observations of young children admitted to hospital. Bowlby describes three phases that may be observed in reaction to the separation from their parents – protest, despair, and finally detachment. He links the protest phase to separation anxiety and the despair phase to that of grief and mourning.[12] Both authors recognise anxiety as the response to the threat of being separated from or losing the object (i.e. the external primary carer), whereas depression (despair) can occur from the ongoing experience of loss, where hope that the object will return has gone. This will be discussed further in Chapter 12 on depression.

In contrast to Klein's view on the inherent aggression of the infant (mentioned in Box 11.2), Fairbairn's view is that aggression in the infant arises due to frustration or deprivation in the early relationships and is not innate. Where Freud spoke of our instinctual drives as pleasure-seeking, Fairbairn described humans as object- (relationship) seeking first and foremost.[13] Fairbairn describes that the nature of the relationship with caregivers changes over the course of the infant's development, beginning with an infantile dependence where the caregiver is not felt to be separate, and moving towards a mature dependence where relations are with 'separate and differentiated objects, loving and loved'.[14] For Fairbairn, separation anxiety thus occurs in this process of differentiation between the self and the object (i.e. the caregiver).[14] This is a normal process and the anxiety can be worked through if the infant has internalised 'good enough' objects and has a supportive external environment. However, if early relationships have been experienced as unreliable or fraught with anxiety, this process of differentiation and separation can become difficult. Celani, commenting on Fairbairn, notes:

> Every decision the child makes is an attempt to maximize his attachment to his desperately needed objects. He has no alternative but to reject or accept his object—an alternative which is liable to present itself to him as a choice between life and death.[15]

Fairbairn's idea of attachment seems to resonate with Bowlby's protest phase discussed above – that when the infant is faced with 'emotional deprivation,' there is not a turning away from the object (at least initially) but in fact 'increased attachment'.[16] Clinical Example 3 demonstrates this. (For further on Attachment Theory, see Chapter 2, Box 2.5.)

Clinical Example 3 **Amir: feeling anxiously responsible for others' happiness**

Amir presented with anxiety symptoms which he had been experiencing since his twenties. Now, in his early forties, he had tried various forms of therapy and medication, all of which had been helpful to a certain extent. However, he still described waking daily feeling anxious and unable to shake these feelings. Another reason which precipitated his referral was ongoing anxiety related to the desire of having a baby. He and his wife had been trying to conceive for a number of years and were in the process of seeking fertility advice. He felt upset that his wife was having to endure different tests and medications. Linked to this anxiety, he often felt responsible for ensuring other people's happiness, and experienced devastation when he felt that others were disappointed in him. He spoke of his work as a social worker which he was passionate about, often working protracted hours to try and repair situations for his clients.

Amir described early experiences of living with an unpredictable father and an anxious mother. By Amir's account, his father, although reasonably affectionate, could became chaotic and violent when stressed. His father eventually left when Amir was six (his younger brothers were four, two, and one) and did not stay in touch. His mother's response to this was to 'get on with it, make the best of a bad situation', busying herself and rest of the family. Amir described this busyness as extreme and meant his mother became more and more unavailable. As she became more unavailable, he tried harder to please her and help her out. He described himself as a bit of an entertainer for the family, recalling that he would cheer up his little brothers by doing funny impersonations and magic tricks.

In therapy, Amir was very likeable. He was warm, open, and funny, telling amusing anecdotes which the therapist often laughed along with, somehow forgetting what they were there to do and what the patient had really come for. In his own supervision, the therapist reflected on his sense of emptiness and loss of role after Amir had left the sessions. His supervisor thought about this and how it brought to mind Amir's role as 'the entertainer' for his family. The therapist wondered if perhaps there was something about Amir being entertaining in the sessions that meant they both became blind to seeing what was underneath his blitheness.

Over months, he was able to open up about his fear that he had somehow caused his father to leave and that his mother had been left disappointed with him. He had often worried that she might leave too and so he felt a responsibility to make her (and his brothers) happy again. He was able to reflect that there was also conflict about the process of becoming a father. He feared that his wife would leave him if she did not become pregnant, but also (like his mother) she might become less available to him if a baby arrived.

There was an underlying fear that he was 'not enough'; that if others saw him as he was, they might be disappointed or leave. To compensate, he had to become funny and charming and ensure that he was always meeting their needs. This was also explored in transference work, through exploring his anxiety that he needed to entertain the therapist to keep him there. Over the course of therapy, he was able to discover experience of an 'other' that he did not need to entertain or support, who did not leave. This allowed him the space and safety to consider alternative perspectives of himself.

Anxiety as a Signal of Internal Conflict

As mentioned in the introduction, there are many routes to anxiety. This section discusses the notion of anxiety as a signal of some form of inner conflict. Freud's view of anxiety developed over time. In his early thinking, he speaks of anxiety as a symptom related to unfulfilled instinctual (usually sexual) impulses.[14] As his thinking and work developed, he shifted in this view with the development of his topographical model of the mind. He explains that when unacceptable impulses arise, they are forced out of consciousness to preserve socially acceptable norms and that anxiety symptoms result due to repression of these instincts.

He takes these ideas further with the introduction of the structural model; anxiety becomes not only a symptom but a signal (see also Chapter 2, section 'Internal Conflict'). With the development of the concept of the id, ego, and superego he introduces us to an internal world in which conflict may exist between different parts of the self. He writes of the id that acts in accordance with the pleasure principle, seeking instant gratification at any cost.[17] The superego – an accumulation of internalised rules and demands based on morals, societal norms, and parental values. And finally, the ego that tries to balance the demands of both id and superego, whilst hoping to experience pleasure and avoid pain.

Freud posits to us that anxiety can function as a signal of some sort of unconscious threat or danger. Rycroft explains that signal anxiety refers to 'that form of apprehensiveness which alerts one to internal changes which might disturb one's equanimity'.[18] This signal results in the ego taking 'some action . . . to avert the threat posed by the conflictual aspects of the self or ambivalent state of mind. The "solution" is to avoid conscious acknowledgment of the threat.'[17] In order to maintain a sense of equilibrium and decrease this internal tension, the ego employs defences to prevent the conflict from coming into consciousness. Whilst we may not refer frequently to the id and superego in daily clinical language, Freud's ideas laid a foundation which is essential to the understanding of anxiety – that we may have desires, feelings, and wishes that come into conflict with other parts of ourselves. There may be a fear that if we acknowledged these instincts to ourselves or others (especially those we are in meaningful relationships with), something catastrophic might happen, as shown in Clinical Example 4.

Typically for Freud, when his clinical theories evolved, he would often not fully renunciate the previous version of the theory in question, perhaps as he felt that both old and new versions captured something about the dynamics of life (which are not always neat and straightforward). So it is with Freud's contributions to understanding anxiety. We have both the idea that anxiety is a symptom resulting from repression of needs or other aspects of ourselves; *and* the notion that anxiety communicates (signals) the need for repression of a conflict. In our experience, both theories have clinical utility.

Clinical Example 4 A university student: an example of anxiety related to defences no longer 'working'

A student was criticised by her tutor at university in relation to a recent placement she had completed. She thought she had worked hard and performed to the best of her ability, so she was surprised by the criticism, but thanked her tutor for his critique as he was clearly more experienced than her. Her friends commented that they thought the criticism was harsh and they had noticed his tendency to bully before, but the student felt sure he had been acting in her best interests. Later that evening, she found herself feeling a sense of dread and had a panic attack out of the blue. Her friends had asked her out for dinner, but she cancelled following the panic attack.

So how might we understand this? In relation to her tutor, there may be a desire to respond with rage or even hatred. However, there might also be a part of her that feels she could work harder and do better if she doesn't want to fail. In order to maintain balance internally and to quell these conflicting parts, there is reaction formation of the aggression into more 'positive' feelings in order to conceal the hostility.

If we were to focus a lens on her past experiences, we would find that she experienced her father as a punitive and demanding figure who expected good behaviour and high academic achievements, or she would 'have to fend for [her]self'. She took a role of accepting his punishments with no protest and with promises to try harder. This was something she learned from her loving but anxious mother. We might imagine the conflict and anxiety around having to conceal angry feelings in order to maintain security and her place within the family.

If, as Freud suggests, these defences operate unconsciously, we might then wonder how someone like this presents with anxiety symptoms. We might think of anxiety as arising when our defences are no longer serving us. What seemed to happen in this situation was that her friends' comments brought to the edge of her consciousness something she was defending against – a struggle with a bullying paternal figure and her rage about this. The result was a feeling of anxiety and avoidance of her friends, that is, those who might bring this situation to her attention again. This student began to experience more regular panic attacks and social anxiety, which interfered with her ability to go to university and spend time with her friends. She was referred for psychodynamic psychotherapy where she was able to start to address what was underlying her anxieties.

As discussed in Chapter 9, defences tend to vary in relation to developmental level. For someone who is primarily functioning at a borderline level, splitting and projective identification may be the principal ways of managing anxiety. However, for someone whose functioning is at a more neurotic level (as in Clinical example 4), there may be use of more mature defences such as displacement, reaction formation, or intellectualisation to quell anxiety. This does not preclude someone who generally functions at a more neurotic level from sometimes functioning with more archaic defences.[19]

Anxiety Arising from a Critical Internal Object

We might find that a patient brings experiences that predominantly communicate guilt, feeling 'bad', shame, worries about not being 'good enough'. There might be a sense of hesitancy and caution when it comes to being in relationships and experiencing the world – a fear of getting things wrong or failing. They may feel stuck, finding it difficult to play, or be creative.[20]

Depending on the theoretical standpoint, we could describe this as the patient having a particularly punitive superego (Freudian), or anxiety coming from an 'internal saboteur', otherwise referred to as a critical internal object (object relations theory). Although these two viewpoints are not synonymous, they are complementary. They offer the proposition that the patient's sense of self can become subject to an excessively harsh, demanding, and punitive internal object. When this occurs, the patient's sense of self can become squashed and diminished under the pressure of this internal oppressor (see Clinical Example 5).

Clinical Example 5 Ella: a woman experiencing anxiety and somatic symptoms

Ella was seen for a psychodynamic consultation following referral from her GP. She was in her late twenties and had been experiencing anxiety around her health, often presenting with varying somatic complaints for which no organic cause had been found.

In consultation, Ella spoke of her mother also suffering with chronic physical health problems for as long as she could remember. Her mother remained essentially bed-bound and required help with daily tasks such as washing and dressing. Ella was the youngest of four siblings, with three older brothers. She recalled that from a young age she was the main carer for her mother due to being the only other 'woman' in the house. This became a way of life for her. Gradually her elder brothers all left home – travelling, moving in with partners, exploring the world. She continued to live at home with her parents, caring for her mother. There was a sense that she was expected to be helpful, to care, to be 'good'.

Initially in her therapy sessions, there were long silences and a sense of her being very controlled, often retelling experiences in a clipped way without emotion or expression before trailing off into silence again. The therapist commented that perhaps it felt uncomfortable for her to have this much freedom for herself and was curious to know how it felt having to give so much space and time to her mother. This seemed to relieve some tension and allowed Ella to discuss a bit more freely what this experience of caring for mother was like for her. She would talk of her predicament – on the one hand feeling it was her duty to help out at home, but on the other hand tentatively wondering what living her own life might be like.

When the therapist took breaks for holidays, the patient would often talk about how lonely she had felt and how difficult it had been without the sessions. The therapist's countertransference was of feeling guilty for having fun and freedom when the patient was feeling miserable, but also of feeling frustrated and trapped by the patient. The therapist came to realise that she was being given an experience of being in the patient's shoes. Ella longed to go and live her life and have fun and felt furious with her mother but also guilty about this. There was a sense of a harsh internal object that deemed her own desires as selfish and her anger as unjustified. (The anger was an unacceptable feeling which was converted into a somatic symptom.)

The therapist was able to use her countertransference as a way of exploring feelings the patient might have had about the therapist's absence, and the links between this situation and Ella's interpersonal situation at home. Over the course of a year, Ella was able to trust that the therapist was offering a space that the patient could use to talk about her feelings, including her anger, and explore them with a freedom without feeling she was being 'selfish' or 'unreasonable'.

With a moderation of her internal critic, coupled with internalising a more benign way of relating to herself, Ella was gradually able to contemplate what she wanted out of life, without being overtaken by feelings of guilt. This led to her being able to separate somewhat from the self-sacrificing caring role and explore more her own wishes and desires.

In this way, we can see how different developmental levels of anxiety coexist and interact, that is, anxiety related to both a critical internal object and to separation are present. This example is compressed, and we have focused more on her anxiety in relation to a critical inner object.

The Therapist's Experience of Anxiety in the Therapy Room

As discussed elsewhere in this book (Chapters 2 and 7), noticing our countertransference responses when with a patient is extremely important. Developing an understanding of the transference and countertransference can help us to appreciate the nature and developmental level of the anxiety.

In this chapter we have looked at various forms of anxiety, and the clinical examples have shown how countertransference responses differed with each patient. We may consider anxieties as roughly corresponding with different stages of development. At the beginning of this chapter, we gave consideration to archaic anxieties (persecution or fragmentation) which correspond to an undeveloped self, whereas anxieties arising more from a critical internal object may relate to a more mature self. Betty Joseph describes this helpfully:

> . . . our patients use us rather differently if they are more integrated and the anxieties on the whole more related to others as real people; anxieties which contain a fear of loss, concern, guilt, a desire to put right, and a desire to get themselves right; these patients are therefore nearer to what Klein has called the depressive position . . . In the transference, therefore, we tend to feel . . . less invaded, and there is more possibility of introjection and of communication to and about the patient as a whole; there is less pressure on the analyst to act out in the transference.[21]

With Brendan (the young man with unexplained collapses in Clinical Example 2), whose anxiety was of a primitive nature, there was limited capacity to tolerate his own anxiety. Instead of experiencing and bearing anxious feelings, there was an unconscious projection of his anxiety into those who came into contact with him. If he was not able to make contact with someone who could hold these projections, these intense feelings became so unbearable that he *literally* collapsed. The countertransference responses for his neurologist and therapist show that they were carrying the anxiety for the patient. What perhaps was most therapeutic in this situation was the reliable, containing nature of the therapeutic relationship over the course of a long-term therapy. Gabbard notes that change can occur via the relationship through ' . . . internalization of function, in which the patient develops the capacity to perform a hitherto external function, as when a patient learns to self soothe through repeated experiences of soothing by the therapist'.[22]

I mentioned earlier that some patients may be consciously aware of their anxiety and have a desire to make sense of its origins. That being said, Joseph also notes that we 'have to expect that our patients will use us to some extent to avoid anxiety, rather than, as we might ideally wish, to understand it'.[21] With Amir (Clinical Example 3), the therapist found herself laughing along with his entertaining jokes, caught up in something collusive which avoided a deeper exploration of the anxiety. In the words of Edna O'Shaughnassey, they had gone on an 'excursion'. O'Shaughnassey explains an excursion as a flight from emotional contact.[23] In this case the therapist used her countertransference to reflect on her loss of separateness from the patient, her transient lack of ability to observe and think. The therapist used interpretation to show the patient how he was slipping into a familiar role in the sessions as a way of stopping her from (in his perception) thinking badly of him.

For Ella (Clinical Example 5), there was the presence of an internal critical object that restricted her ability to 'live life'. In therapy, this was initially shown in her difficulty to 'play' in the therapeutic space. Gabbard notes one facet of the therapeutic relationship that can be helpful, in relation to a patient who has a highly critical internal object, is the potential for the patient to 'begin to internalize the therapist's interested, exploratory stance toward material previously experienced as shameful or otherwise "bad", or . . . internalize[s] a more explicitly temperate attitude toward his impulses or actions'.[22] The therapist used an interested and explorative stance, which implicitly communicated to the patient that desires, feelings, and wishes could all be thought about rather than be pushed down and hidden (see also Chapter 12 for other therapeutic approaches for working with someone with a critical internal object).

Concluding Remarks

I want to go back to Freud's quote at the beginning of the chapter that '. . . anxiety is not so simple a matter' as a reflection on the diffuse and complex nature of anxiety.[4] It has not been the intention of this chapter to provide an exhaustive analysis of anxiety but to shed some light on some psychodynamic approaches to thinking about anxieties. We have thought about how difficulties in containing processes between caregiver and infant early in the infant's life may predispose to the persistence of archaic anxieties. We have explored the nature of separation and loss in relation to anxiety, and finally we have reflected on how internal conflict and the role of a critical internal object can bring about anxiety. The clinical examples illustrated how the wider variation in anxieties may present in therapy, and the last section focused on how the therapist may experience and respond to these different anxieties.

References

1. Solms M. The neurobiological underpinnings of psychoanalytic theory and therapy. Frontiers in Behavioral Neuroscience. 2018;12.
2. Glick R, Roose S. Anxiety as signal, symptom and syndrome. In Simpson H, Neria Y, Lewis-Fernandez R et al., eds. Anxiety Disorders Theory, Research and Clinical Perspectives. London: Cambridge University Press; 2010. pp. 50–59.
3. Perelberg R. The riddle of anxiety: between the familiar and the unfamiliar. The International Journal of Psychoanalysis. 2018;99(4):810–27.
4. Freud S, Strachey J, Freud A et al. The Standard Edition of the Complete Psychological Works of Sigmund Freud. Vol. 20, An Autobiographical Study, Inhibitions, Symptoms and Anxiety, Lay Analysis and Other Works (1925–1926). London: The Hogarth Press and the Institute of Psychoanalysis; 2001.
5. Gabbard G. Psychodynamic Psychiatry in Clinical Practice. 5th ed. Washington, DC: American Psychiatric Press; 2000. p. 259.
6. Bion W. The psycho-analytic study of thinking. International Journal of Psychoanalysis. 1962;43:306–10.
7. Killick K. Soundless screaming: psychotic anxiety and analytic containment. In Kiehl E, ed. Copenhagen 2013: 100 years on: Origins, Innovations and Controversies Proceedings of the 19th Congress of the International Association for Analytical Psychology. Daimon Verlag; 2014.
8. Winnicott D. The theory of the parent-infant relationship. International Journal of Psychoanalysis. 1960;41:585–95.
9. Klein M. On the theory of anxiety and guilt. In Klein M, Isaacs S, Heimann P et al., eds. Developments in Psychoanalysis. London: Routledge; 1989. p. 276.
10. Hinshelwood R. A Dictionary of Kleinian Thought. London: Free Association; 1991.
11. Solms M. Link between depression and anxiety [Internet]. University of Cape Town, Centre for Innovation in Learning and Teaching. 2017 [cited 28 April 2022]. www.youtube.com/watch?v=XEG1rkx4oBc
12. Bowlby J. Separation anxiety. The International Journal of Psychoanalysis. 1960;41:89–113.
13. Fairbairn W. Psychoanalytic Studies of the Personality. Tavistock Publications Ltd. London: Routledge. Kegan Paul Ltd.; 1952.
14. Quinodoz J. The Taming of Solitude: Separation Anxiety in Psychoanalysis. London: Routledge; 1993.
15. Celani D. Applying Fairbairn's object relations theory to the dynamics of the

battered woman. American Journal of Psychotherapy. 1999;53(1):60–73.

16. Celani D. Fairbairn's Object Relations Theory in the Clinical Setting. New York: Columbia University Press; 2010.
17. Leiper R, Maltby M. The Psychodynamic Approach to Therapeutic Change. London: SAGE Publications Ltd; 2004.
18. Rycroft C. A Critical Dictionary of Psychoanalysis. London: Penguin Books; 1995.
19. McWilliams N. Psychoanalytic Diagnosis: Understanding Personality Structure in the Clinical Process. New York: Guilford Publications; 2011.
20. Britton R. Sex, Death and the Superego. London: Routledge; 2019.
21. Joseph B, Feldman M, Bott Spillius E. Psychic Equilibrium and Psychic Change. London: Routledge; 1989.
22. Gabbard G, Westen D. Rethinking therapeutic action. The International Journal of Psychoanalysis. 2003;84(4):823–41(832).
23. O'Shaughnessy E. Enclaves and Excursions. The International Journal of Psychoanalysis. 1992;73:603–11.

Chapter 12

The Psychodynamics of Depressing/Depressed States

Table of Contents

Introduction 184
Theory of Depressing/Depressed States 185
Depression as a 'Basic Emotional Response' 187
Dynamics of Loss and Abandonment (an 'Anaclitic' Dynamic) 188
Dynamics of Internal Criticism (an 'Introjective' Dynamic) 190
Other Feelings in Depressing/Depressed States besides Low Mood and Sadness 191
Therapeutic Working with People with Depressing/Depressed States 192
General Principles 192
Therapeutic Working with Dynamics of Loss and Abandonment 193
Therapeutic Working with Dynamics of Internal Criticism 196
Concluding Remarks 198

Introduction

Paul Hoch, psychiatrist and educator, poses a key question: are different people with depression 'the same clinically, do they have the same psychodynamics, and do they respond in the same way to therapy?'[1] In response, we suggest that the dynamics of depression are various – that is, there are many ways of being depressed – and that present-day experiences of depression may arise out of a range of difficulties first felt in early relationships. We will highlight common developmental themes and therapeutic situations amongst people who experience depressing/depressed states. In particular, we will expand on two common clinical constellations in some detail: the first, a pattern to do with dynamics of loss and abandonment; and the second, a tendency to harsh self-criticism, which leads to a devaluing of oneself and others. The reason we use the phrase 'depressing/depressed' state is to capture the dynamic nature of depression, as opposed to conceptualising depression as a passive state of affairs when someone 'just is' depressed. From a psychodynamic view, this is an active and *dynamic* situation, where an aspect of someone's internal world is depress*ing* in some way to that person, leaving them feeling depressed. This chapter approaches the external manifestations of depressing/depressed states not as a discrete 'disorder', but more as a 'basic emotional response' that signals that something is amiss in an individual's world which requires attending to and addressing.[2]

It should be said at the outset that these broad, general principles, though providing a helpful framework, are in tension with the core psychodynamic aim of focusing on what is unique about each patient and jointly discovering with them their own, particular set of object relations and psychological defences.[3] Interacting with psychodynamic factors, an individual's particular social circumstances and constitutional factors combine to a depressing/depressed situation that is unique to them.

In terms of how people with depressive relational dynamics respond to therapy, whilst there may be commonalities in a general psychodynamic approach, the nub of therapeutic work cannot be prescribed in advance but varies for each person and needs to emerge and be discovered along the way. In contrast to a 'disorder-centred' approach, which sees the problem in terms of illness, a psychodynamic approach offers the potential to understand the meanings and the relationships that sit behind symptoms of depressing/depressed states, locating feelings as part of an active internal world.

The relational dynamics discussed in this chapter are commonly observed in people who present with symptoms of depression but are not exclusive to this. How an individual manifests and manages their underlying relational dynamics varies, influenced by a multitude of factors including what cluster of defences is the best 'fit' for a person at each stage in their life, and whether they are functioning at a neurotic, borderline, or psychotic level (see Chapter 9, section 'Organisation of the Internal World'). Indeed, a person might become depressed at one point in their life and, at another, restrict their eating, yet their underlying object relations would be expected to be similar at both points. As such, many of the themes raised in this chapter will be relevant for a range of people, not just those with depression.

Theory of Depressing/Depressed States

Certain social situations – including adversity, poverty, and inequality – increase the likelihood of someone becoming depressed, not only because of the higher exposure to stress, but also due to the added strain these circumstances put on early and later relationships.[4] Biological, including genetic, factors can play a significant role too.[3]

Moving on to psychodynamic theory, Fonagy summarises a contemporary psychodynamic understanding of depression as an 'outgrowth of current life difficulties arising out of painful and continuing ambivalence first felt in relation to those of the greatest emotional significance to the patient early in the course of his/her development'.[5]

Given a therapeutic space, many patients give accounts of how – starting long before overt depression – they experienced 'everyday' relational stresses and disappointments as wounding, which resulted in upset, hurt, outrage, or aggrievement felt for days or much longer. This phenomenon is sometimes referred to as 'narcissistic vulnerability'.[6] In the early phase of therapy, a patient's narrative can unfold to reveal how perceived disappointments, criticisms, or injustices relate to inner dynamics of abandonment or criticism, exposing vulnerable aspects of themselves. These inner dynamics may have been present, in some form, since early development.[7] An understanding may be reached of how – perhaps due to accumulating 'injuries' to one's fragile esteem – depression eventually ensued. (We note that this general account is not exclusive to the development of depression, but is common in different outward presentations of mental distress such as difficulties with eating, use of substances, obsessive thoughts, etc.)

In people who present in a depressed state, early developmental difficulties can take many forms but two common themes centre around the experiences of loss and abandonment; and/or feeling criticised and devalued.[8] These are expanded on in later sections of this chapter. Whilst one theme or another may dominate the clinical picture, they may also coexist. Indeed, 'the combination of emotional or actual abandonment with parental criticism is particularly likely to create depressive dynamics'.[9]

These kinds of early developmental experiences, especially if prolonged and coupled with the lack of a trusted person to confide in, may lead to the relational difficulties being adopted internally by the individual, rather than being spoken about and expressed. In other words, a person's internal world starts to become coloured by the painful interpersonal dynamics experienced. For example, a child may develop a representation of others as undermining their sense of self and self-worth. These kinds of internal object relations may be adaptive at the time they developed – by bringing predictability to experiences or a sense of control (see Box 12.1). However, the internal dynamics may persist into adulthood and be difficult to update, even if external conditions change. As well as affecting the person's present and future relationships with others in the external world, a depressing/depressed relationship operates intra-psychically in the way the internal object relates to the internal subject – where one aspect of the self is depressed by another.

McWilliams elaborates, 'the internalised object does not have to be a person who in reality was hostile, critical or negligent (though this is often the case [. . .]) for the patient to have experienced the object that way and internalised such images'.[9] The child's lens, whilst perceptive in many ways, may be imbued with their own private inner world, which

Box 12.1 Adverse childhood experiences and the internal world

As described by Fairburn, in some individuals with histories of maltreatment, the other person or situation at the source of the disturbance can be idealised, with all the 'bad' attributes being located within the individual themself.[10] 'I had a happy childhood' – or the lack of recall of early memories – is a common account in people whose early experiences have in fact been very disturbing. This form of defensive manoeuvre can serve to protect the child from overwhelming distress, as the defence moves the source of the distress from an external person whom the child is dependent on, to being located internally and hence feeling more under control and less frightening. In other words, a situation such as a sense that 'I depend on someone who hates me' – is converted to something more like 'I drain others, I'm bad' or 'I drove her away'. Ferenczi describes similar dynamics in child abuse, where the child may 'identify with the aggressor' and feel bad and responsible, as a defence against a more disturbing situation of recognising that they have done little wrong and an adult, who they may also love and depend on for survival, is abusing the relationship.

Whilst taking ownership of the fault may feel more bearable at the time, if this accommodation persists, it has consequences for how the child holds himself in esteem and might predispose to a depressed response (or other ailments) later in life.

Readers may relate to this dynamic in miniature in thinking about when something seriously goes wrong in one's life that was out of our control. We may jump to 'It's my fault, I did something wrong' with a feeling of guilt, as a protection against the more unsettling possibility of 'there may have been little I could have done to prevent this unfortunate situation from happening'. As McWilliams remarks, humans can prefer 'the most irrational guilt to an admission of impotence'.[9]

brings personal colours and sensitivities to how others are experienced and responded to. Equally, in some cases, the character of someone's internal object relationships may be strongly shaped by real events and traumas. Even with the latter situations, a key therapeutic task is to keep a person's sense of interest and agency in their own present-day functioning, with an understanding of how past experiences link to present-day difficulties.

Psychodynamic theorists have developed overlapping theories about the dynamics of depression (see Box 12.2).

Box 12.2 Selected psychodynamic theories about the dynamics of depression

1. Anger directed inward (Abraham, 1911) [11]
2. Unresolved early losses and failure to mourn (Freud, 1917) [12]
3. Early insecure attachment meaning that present-day losses may reactivate feelings of being unlovable and the absence of others (see Chapter 2, Box 2.4, 'Bowlby and Attachment Theory')
4. Living for a dominant other that restricts vision of other approaches to living (Arieti, 1977) [13]
5. Prolonged helplessness in relation to another who is depended on, leading to depression as a 'basic emotional response' (Sandler, 1987) [14]
6. Narcissistic injury (Busch, 2009) [6]
7. Yearning for others but expecting abandonment (an 'anaclitic' dynamic, Blatt 2012) [2]
8. Internal relations characterised by a criticising and demanding object-representation in relation to a self-representation that strives for an ideal but feels inadequate (an 'introjective' dynamic, Blatt 2012) [2]

Rather than seeing the above as competing theories, clinically, it may be more helpful to understand these as complementary and overlapping. There is not one dynamic for all, nor is there necessarily one 'depression'. In terms of overlap, some of the theories consider very similar territory, but with slightly different theoretical viewpoints and terminology. For example, a thread to do with unprocessed loss coupled with a sense of others as absent, weaves its way through Freud's conception of failure to mourn, Bowlby's early insecure attachment, and Blatt's yearning for others but expecting abandonment. The remainder of this section on theory expands on three of the more recent theoretical perspectives in Box 12.2, which capture complementary dimensions: Sandler's conception of depression as a 'basic emotional response', and Blatt's two clinical pictures. We survey and integrate some of the other theories along the way.

Depression as a 'Basic Emotional Response' (Number 5 in Box 12.2)

When faced with a distressing experience, such as a loss, maltreatment, or repeated criticism, an individual's initial response may be 'protest' or 'fight'.[14] A child may feel angry, and scream and shout to get attention. An adult, who feels taken advantage of by a colleague, may feel anger which spurs them on to try and resolve things.

But what if a child, in their relationship with someone on whom they depend, cannot resolve troubling issues, for example, those of loss and abandonment, or feeling devalued and criticised? Furthermore, what if the child cannot end the relationship or distance themselves from it, nor has anyone to confide in for support and containment? In other words, what if he or she feels helpless and alone with their troubles? This is 'painful ambivalence' – when the relationship is both needed but also associated with some kind of protracted painful experience.[14]

Whilst a wide range of feelings and responses arise in someone with depressive relational dynamics, these frequently include a pattern of depressed affects (e.g. low mood, sadness); a withdrawal of drives (inactivity, loss of appetite); and a resignation to the status quo. This pattern can be understood as a 'basic emotional response' that serves as a signal to the individual or to others – to whoever will listen – that something is remiss in an individual's world that requires attending to and addressing.[2,14] According to Luyten and Blatt, this depressive response signals that a significant discrepancy exists between an individual's basic need for emotional and physical safety and security (or other needs) and their current predicament where these needs are not being met. As well as an attempt at communication, this basic emotional response – common to a degree in some other animals – is hypothesised to provide some relative psychological and physical protection when feeling helpless in the face of overwhelming anxieties.[4] Sandler notes that this line of thinking can be taken too far and he cautions against elevating depression as being something to be revered or as something that is uncritically 'useful'.[14]

Dynamics of Loss and Abandonment (an 'Anaclitic' Dynamic, Number 7 in Box 12.2)

Freud noted the importance of early losses as conferring a vulnerability for a person to become depressed in later life. This strand of thought has been developed by subsequent clinicians and put into a contemporary relational framework.[2,7] An early loss – such as the loss of a parent through death or estrangement – may dispose a child to develop a self-representation characterised by a sense of being left (an 'abandoned self'[3]) in relation to an unavailable or abandoning object-representation. Possible experiences arising from the self-representation include sadness, loneliness, and longing for an absent or unavailable other. This depiction is sometimes referred to as an 'anaclitic' depression.[8] 'Anaclitic' means leaning on – referring to the dynamic of longing for someone to lean on, but expecting the other to be absent or unavailable.

By no means do all children who experience early loss develop an anaclitic pattern of internal object relations. It is not just the loss that is relevant but how it was dealt with. The presence of a good-enough relationship with another parent or caring figure is protective. If a child can express their loss and feel understood by someone else, the loss can begin to be mourned. 'Depression is the opposite of mourning'[9] – from a theoretical perspective, if a person can grieve, they may be less likely to become depressed by the loss.

Conversely, 'a family atmosphere where mourning is discouraged' or where grief is frankly denied, can lead to a child developing beliefs that grief and 'needs for comfort are destructive'.[9] This makes a path towards a depressive internal dynamic more likely. Rather than the child being able to process what has happened, the child may be more likely to accommodate their experiences through identifying with the source of the distress and so taking it inside.

Apart from loss by death or estrangement, there are other routes to someone developing a relational world characterised by unavailability or loss. For example, if primary carers are experienced by the child as significantly withdrawn – perhaps related to the use of substances and/or mental distress themselves – this might predispose the child to feeling insecure in later relationships, bringing expectations that others will similarly be distant or disinterested[15] (see Chapter 13 for clinical examples along these lines).

A person who is afraid of abandonment and afraid of being alone may hide their inner feelings from others for fear that others would not be interested or would withdraw. Discontentment may be suppressed. Unfortunately, this style of relating means that those around the patient who may actually be emotionally available are left unaware of the depressed person's internal states and feelings, inadvertently leading to the person's needs not being met by others.

Rationally, one might expect that if someone has experienced loss and abandonment within relationships in the past, they would be drawn to partners who are different to previous figures. However, this depends on the degree to which past losses have been processed and worked through. Freud formulates that what doesn't get remembered gets repeated. Namely, when a troubling past situation has not been worked through, it may get repeated in the present. If abandonment or emotional unavailability has been the defining experience of someone's early relationships, there may be an unconscious draw towards repeating these patterns in adult relationships by virtue of their familiarity and sense of 'normality'. It is remarkable how powerful is the allure of the familiar – partly because it appears unremarkable to the participant (even though it may appear destructive to an outsider). In these circumstances, a person's default 'object choice' may therefore be to form relationships with others who are not in reality available to enter into a reliable bond. Once in this kind of unreliable relationship, the person may feel lonely and unwanted. However, due to yearnings for the other along with an expectation (or resignation) that others will be unavailable, the person may feel they have to tolerate (what can seem to outsiders) careless, unkind, or rejecting treatment by partners, employers, and others.

These inner dynamics can leave someone vulnerable to depressed states. Current disappointments relate to the abandoning/abandoned relationship in the person's inner world and evoke earlier losses that have not been worked through. Symptoms – or rather signals – may then emerge. Through tactful and empathic exploration in therapy, the patient may be supported to identify and understand the processes behind these repeated experiences of loss and abandonment in relationships (see Clinical Example 1).

Clinical Example 1 Mr White

Mr White was a man in his fifties who came for therapy because of low mood, tiredness, and a loss of interest in life.

When he was aged seven, Mr White's sister (then aged five) died from meningitis. By his account, the death was not really spoken about, and it appeared his parents became depressed and withdrawn. When Mr White was growing up, in general, he experienced others as unavailable and as not being interested in him, and in reaction to this he 'just got on with things'.

In his adult life, he was repeatedly drawn to form relationships with married women. Ultimately, none of these women were in a position to commit to him. Once in a relationship, he would stay in it well beyond a point that made sense to his friends, usually ending when the other finally brought it to an end.

Mr White came to therapy able to describe this pattern but did not think it remarkable in any way or as having any bearing on his depression.

Mr White worked with a therapist for six-months of weekly psychodynamic therapy. Supported by the therapist, the successive 'tasks' for Mr White that emerged in therapy were to:

- notice the effects and meanings of this pattern of relationships
- understand what was driving these kinds of attachments
- articulate feelings to do with early loss that had not been fully mourned
- to explore what it would be like to contemplate forming different relationships.

In the middle phase of therapy, this brought Mr White against a question that was unexpectedly fearful for him. The therapist asked him, 'What would it be like to contemplate being with someone who was actually available to commit to you?' The remainder of the course of therapy was spent working this through, as it brought to life his fear of dependence, given past experiences of rejection.

Dynamics of Internal Criticism (an 'Introjective' Dynamic, Number 8 in Box 12.2)

This section discusses a dynamic to do with internal criticism that is commonly observed in depressed states. This has a different character to what has just been described. In internal criticism, there is a relationship between a criticising internal object, which judges or is hostile towards other aspects of the self. In relation to the critical object, the self-representation may feel inadequate, 'bad', guilty, or experience shame. The internal criticising object also functions as a lens through which external others are perceived. The person may therefore expect criticism and disapproval from those around them, including therapists, and distrust others' declarations of concern or approval. So in fact, rather than this clinical picture being summarised as a 'depressed' state, it is also a 'depressing' state in an active sense, as there is an aspect of the person's mind depress*ing* other parts.

Developmentally, this dynamic may be associated with early relational experiences of repeated and prolonged intense criticism, reprimands, and absence of acceptance directed towards the child about themselves and their emotional responses (e.g. 'stop whining').[9] Blatt refers to this clinical picture as 'introjective depression' in reference to the process of 'introjection' of a criticising object,[8] that is, the taking in and adopting of a harsh and critical way of relating to oneself. As a result of feeling bad and inadequate, the self-representation may strive to meet the demands and standards set by the internal object-representation. The individual may experience brief respite when the highest of the high is reached – for example, if they unequivocally excel at something. However, these can be impossible ideals to live up to as any departure from the pinnacle of perfection may provoke a devaluing response from the internal criticising object. This phenomenon may account, in some people, for the brief lifting of depressive symptoms when the criticising aspect of the self (the object-representation) is satisfied, and the return of symptoms when this fragile position cannot be sustained.

Whilst some people with this kind of internal dynamic are preoccupied with striving to be 'good', 'perfect', and are highly driven, others have given up on the struggle for the ideal and are convinced and convincing of their own defectiveness and failure. External signs of depression – such as 'giving up', inactivity, and a refusal to try things out – may serve to provide some protection in response to long-standing unreasonable and unwinnable demands. In more extreme situations, manic defences may emerge to offer an individual more extreme protection from an internal criticising object that can never be satisfied. Manic distortions give the individual feelings of super-human importance, ability, and accomplishment, which mirror in magnitude underlying feelings of inadequacy and defectiveness.

At times, the interpersonal roles reverse with the patient adopting the role that the object-representation plays, and he criticises external others. In this configuration, the patient projects his self-representation on to others, who are subjected to the same treatment and held to the same standards as applied internally. Criticism of others may be done implicitly and denied if the person feels it is not 'good' to show disapproval, or may be done overtly ('Oh, I've waited all this time just to see a *junior* therapist'). The therapist may experience countertransference feelings of a pressure to succeed or impress, and worry about 'failure'. Unfortunately, this devaluing of others may leave the patient feeling that he is repeatedly let down, and angry at the perceived failings of others. This can make it hard for the patient to derive benefit from relationships with therapists and other caring figures, who are experienced as deficient when they inevitably fall short from an ideal.

Someone acting in a highly critical and devaluing style towards themself or others may 'unconsciously and unwittingly elicit criticism and dislike by others' in a way that confirms and repeats his sense of the way of the world (this is an example of projective identification).[2] In this situation, it is important for the therapist to be aware of their countertransference feelings and try and acknowledge and make sense of these in supervision or other reflective spaces. This processing reduces the chance of the therapist outwardly criticising the patient or conveying that the patient is unacceptable.

Depending on the patient's current capacities for reflection, the transference and countertransference situation (i.e. how the dynamics of criticism and devaluing emerge in the patient's relationship with the therapist) can be used as a portal to understanding what goes awry in relationships. This carries the potential to rework old patterns.

Other Feelings in Depressing/Depressed States besides Low Mood and Sadness

As will hopefully be becoming clear, people with the dynamics of depression may experience a range of emotions besides low mood and sadness. This is easier to observe when seeing a person frequently for therapy, or through the actual experience of living with someone (or oneself) who is depressed. A person's emotions are influenced by current interpersonal situations in their life, social adversities, their internal object relationships, and the configuration of the object relationship that is most prominent at any given time (see Chapter 8, Figure 8.2, 'Different ways the same object relationship can manifest'). Emotional states may be associated with an individual's self-representation or their object-representation. For example, a person may feel driven to work harder and be furious at themself for making mistakes (associated with a depressing object-representation), whilst the person may also feel like crying because of a sense of inadequacy and want to give up trying (associated with a depressed self-representation). These self and object experiences may alternate or occur at the same time. For some people, there may be a main affect that links both poles of an inner object relationship.

Anger[6] and anxiety[2] are closely associated with depression. Indeed, as discussed earlier, depression can arise out of overwhelming anxieties or painful experiences. Some patients begin therapy for issues apparently quite different to depression. However, as they develop insight and recognise the role they play in their difficulties or harm they may have caused to others, they become depressed. This can be viewed as part of a journey towards better integration and awareness. Equally, for others during therapy, as feelings of depression wane, new feelings such as anxiety, sadness, or anger may emerge that had previously been warded off.

On occasion, depressed feelings may lift suddenly (see Clinical Example 2). This may not always be because something is worked through, but because other defences are being deployed.[14] In this 'flight into health' (see also section on 'Working with Resistance' in Chapter 7), the underlying situation has not been addressed so depression may reoccur easily.

Clinical Example 2 Ms McLean: flight into health

Ms McLean, an inpatient in a psychiatry ward, had felt intensely depressed for months. She suddenly 'felt better' one day. On exploration, she had taken out a complaint against a former employer the day previously. This had provided her with a temporary feeling of superiority and a place to project her own feelings of fault and inadequacy (i.e. onto the former employer). The underlying depressive dynamics were completely untouched and, in a way, harder to reach. This 'happy' state lasted for some weeks and she was discharged from hospital, although she felt depressed again as soon as the complaint fell through.

Therapeutic Working with People with Depressing/Depressed States

General Principles

The core psychodynamic approach and attitude (see Chapter 7) is well-suited to someone with depressive relational dynamics – in particular, 'an atmosphere of acceptance, respect, and compassionate efforts to understand'.[9] As a very general guide, for people with an 'introjective' presentation, interpretation and insight may be more important for therapeutic progress, whilst for those with an 'anaclitic' presentation, 'the experience of a reliable relationship' appears more central for improvement.[16,17] In the rest of this section we will cover general remarks about therapy with someone with the dynamics of depression, whilst subsequent sections will look at different therapeutic slants depending on the pattern of dynamics present (i.e. introjective or anaclitic).

One of the key activities of therapy can be to try and unpick what function the depressing dynamics and responses were and are serving – that is, what is being depressed and why. As discussed in Chapter 4, exploring feelings is a key way in to understanding the meanings and relationships behind the presenting symptoms. This can bring to light the dynamics and meanings of what might initially seem to someone like a symptom without meaning. Take, for example, a person in the early stages of therapy who is depressed and troubled by feelings of tiredness; they speak about these feelings in a somewhat passive way and do not yet have any idea of what is depressing them. The therapist might enquire: *What are you tired of?* Or perhaps, *I wonder what is tiring you out?* This curiosity and interest in the patient's feelings, and an implicit assumption that symptoms arise out of an active and meaningful dynamic, can lead to understanding the intra- and inter-personal relations out of which the experience of tiredness emerges. For example, it might transpire that the person experiences relentless inner criticism in relation to a worn-out and exhausted self. The therapist may then be able to empathically reflect back an understanding: *No wonder you feel so tired all the time.* The focus might then shift to developing awareness and understanding of the inner critical authority: *Let's look at this criticism that is going on all the time.* In this way, over time, the patient can get to know the various dimensions of a depressive internal object relationship and how it operates.

In therapy, it can be a revelation to a patient to discover that admission to the therapist of so-called 'negative' feelings does not result in damage to either party. The patient may then find out that acknowledging a range of feelings can actually increase a sense of intimacy and contact. As McWilliams explains, an expression of normal feelings such as anger or worry or failure 'interferes with normal dependency only if the person one is depending on has pathological reactions to it – a circumstance that defines the child experience of many depressive clients but not the possibilities for adult relationships'.[9]

Having said this, sometimes the way feelings are avoided and then subsequently forcefully expressed may need to be sensitively but firmly looked at in therapy. Taking the example of anger, which can be very relevant for some adults who present with depression – some people attempt to avoid expressing their anger or dissatisfaction in present-day relationships because of an expectation of being abandoned or criticised.[2] However, because anger is avoided, the person may become increasingly frustrated and depressed inside. Lacking practice at expressing frustrations, when angry feelings do emerge, they may be expressed 'in a passive or overly aggressive manner' that can actually induce others to withdraw from relationships or become aggressive in return.[6] An understanding of anger and how a person relates to this feeling may be a key theme in therapy for some people. As Gabbard puts it within a clinical vignette, a key question to raise with a patient may be, 'Isn't there a middle ground, a vast middle ground between exploding and keeping it all in?'[18]

Issues of limitation and loss may emerge in relation to the therapy and the therapist. With a patient who brings dynamics to do with loss and absence, matters may crystallise around an experience of imperfect care, perhaps precipitated by planned or unplanned breaks in therapy. With a patient who has more criticising and devaluing relational dynamics, a central theme may be around judgment of the therapist's abilities. For either dynamic, the limits of what is possible can provide an opportunity to come to terms with the imperfections or perceived deficiencies in themselves and others.

A proportion of people with depression experience positive changes with shorter-term psychodynamic therapy (such as weekly sessions over six months) and benefits are maintained. For others, therapeutic gains are not sustained. For the latter group, more time may be needed within therapy for initial improvements to be consolidated and to avoid recreating a situation 'in which they make an attachment and then lose it prematurely under circumstances beyond their control'.[9] A longer course of therapy may be needed to allow sufficient time for a patient to 'gradually internalize a psychological capacity to relate to pathogenic personal experiences, memories, feelings, beliefs and relationships in a reflective, yet also more active, manner'.[5] For example, the Tavistock Adults Depression Study[5] used 60 sessions over 18 months. After longer-term psychodynamic therapy, some time may be needed for full effects to manifest (see Chapter 8, section on 'Post-Termination Phase'). Some patients may benefit from open-ended therapy if this is available (for definition of 'open-ended' see Chapter 4).

Therapeutic Working with Dynamics of Loss and Abandonment (an 'Anaclitic' Pattern)

This section follows on from the theory of 'anaclitic' dynamics discussed earlier, and first mentioned in point 7 in Box 12.2.

Many people with an anaclitic pattern of depression who are referred for therapy may consciously be keen for a regular therapy session, perhaps hoping at some level that this may provide what has been felt to be missing. In turn, they may be regarded by therapists as 'good candidates' for therapy.[9] In the early phase of therapy, there may well be symptom relief as a steady and available figure is found in the therapist through the working alliance. However, after initial respite, underlying issues of loss and relational difficulties may come to the fore in the way the patient relates to themself, others, and with the therapist. This presents a therapeutic opportunity.

A central task in therapy may be to articulate losses which have not yet been worked through and to provide conditions where a mourning process can unfold where previously it had become stuck. The dynamics of mourning and how a mourning process can be facilitated in therapy are discussed in Chapter 8. The section here will comment on relevant aspects of the therapeutic relationship related to mourning in someone with a leaning-on/abandoning (anaclitic) dynamic.

The patient's relationship with the therapist may itself be infused by a sense of loss and abandonment – such as a patient feeling that the therapist is going to leave, is not giving enough of themselves, or is disinterested. In this situation, one approach is for the therapist to help the patient attend to the present transference dynamics so they can be understood and put into words rather than played out. For example, '*Your concern that I might leave you without warning keeps coming up – it must be important. I wonder what it is about, where it comes from?*'. Exploration and containment of transference anxieties to do with expectations of withdrawal or loss of the therapist can start a reparative process and leave the patient feeling secure enough to begin to mourn earlier losses.

Some of these themes are explored in Clinical Example 3.

Clinical Example 3 – Part 1 Barbara: early phase of therapy

Barbara was a 40-year-old woman, who was referred for psychotherapy following the unexpected loss of her job a year previously. She saw Dr Marshall for 12 months of weekly therapy. Early in the therapy, in order to accommodate another commitment, Dr Marshall had asked Barbara if it was possible to move her session time. Barbara said she had no issue with this, remarking: 'I have nothing else to do!'

In the beginning phase of therapy, the following account emerged. Barbara had worked as a clerical assistant for 15 years for a large insurance firm. She had disliked the job, finding the organisation large, anonymous, and uncaring, but had tolerated it, never considering any other possibilities. She had fluctuating symptoms of depression over 20 to 30 years. Previous shorter-term therapy had brought initial relief, but she would become depressed again several months after each treatment ended. She had 'collapsed mentally' after losing her job, experiencing feelings of low mood, thoughts of ending her life, and a marked loss of energy and enthusiasm. She had been unemployed since.

Barbara was in a long-term relationship with her partner, Sumeet, who was described as supportive. With Sumeet, she rarely expressed her personal feelings – such as sadness – due to a worry that he would not wish to hear her 'gripes'. Barbara said she '[could] not really fathom why he stays with me', and she had recently said to Sumeet, 'You're probably going to leave me.'

Barbara portrayed a lonely childhood. Her father had worked abroad for long periods whilst her mother had looked after Barbara and her two siblings. Growing up, Barbara recalled her mother as quite a distant figure who was private about her own feelings and difficulties. Barbara felt the family was loving in many ways but that, looking back, there was little opportunity for expression of emotions.

Barbara seemed passively accepting of her present-day situation, including her unemployment, and conveyed an inevitability to her life circumstances. At times, Dr Marshall felt somewhat irritated by Barbara's passivity, and it seemed that Barbara's friends and her partner could also feel frustrated with her about this. Dr Marshall also felt a liking for Barbara – she found her to be considerate and grateful of her time and efforts.

By four months into the therapy, Barbara was becoming neglectful of her appearance, sometimes being malodorous. She occasionally smelled of alcohol, though strongly denied drinking. Barbara worried that her partner, Sumeet, might be thinking about leaving her. By Barbara's account, he was finding her recurrent periods of depression hard to bear. The therapist, from her experience of Barbara, could understand how it might be hard for someone to stay with Barbara as she too experienced an impulse to pull away, connected to Barbara's smell and the countertransference feelings of irritation. With Barbara's worsening condition, Dr Marshall started to feel more anxious. When in the room, Dr Marshall sometimes had a countertransference image of an abyss and a sense of Barbara's distress as bottomless, and Dr Marshall wondered what she had got into.

As described earlier in this chapter, an aspect of the self may have yearnings for another to be caring and close to them, whilst having a representation of others as abandoning or unavailable. Someone with these dynamics may, unconsciously, invite others – the therapist included – to take part in the script of this internal drama. These unconscious, interpersonal 'nudges' can occur verbally (e.g. 'You're probably going to leave me.') and through actions such as becoming off-putting through self-neglect. Others around the person may then come to feel annoyed with the person or experience an urge to withdraw, potentially falling into the abandoning role assigned to them.[2]

Clinical Example 3 – Part 2 Barbara: middle phase of therapy

Through reflective discussions in supervision, Dr Marshall wondered if she was identifying with a rejecting and abandoning aspect of Barbara's internal world. Whilst Barbara could be compliant, grateful, praising, accommodating of changes of session times, Dr Marshall began to wonder, what does Barbara really feel? In supervision, Dr Marshall discussed the image of the abyss, and what projected feelings this might be picking up. Despite Barbara talking a reasonable amount, Dr Marshall realised that Barbara didn't usually express her feelings.

Dr Marshall wondered if a pattern was being repeated by which Barbara was avoiding expressing inner feelings to her for fear of what would happen – perhaps a concern that Dr Marshall would not want to hear her 'gripes' or the depth of her feelings. Back in the therapy sessions, Dr Marshall floated this idea to Barbara – she agreed with this intellectually and tried to talk more about her feelings. Yet whilst intellectually 'agreed', Barbara continued to drink, and her sense of inner disturbance continued which she found hard to articulate.

Eight months into the therapy, Barbara brought a dream about coming to the psychotherapy clinic. *In the dream the clinic was grey, with frightening sculptures on the door. She was left waiting for hours in the waiting room, then a shifty looking person came who turned Barbara away.*

Through discussing the feel of the dream, the themes contained within it, and Barbara's associations to the scenes in the dream, Barbara began to articulate various discontents towards the therapist. For example, Barbara was able to say that she had not wanted to change her session time many months previously, but had gone along with Dr Marshall's request, despite the change meaning she had to miss out on a regular meet-up with former work colleagues. With encouragement from Dr Marshall to continue, Barbara went on to explain that this meet-up with friends the 'one thing in [her] life' she derived some enjoyment from. She had been feeling increasingly neglected and not cared for. With this disclosure, Dr Marshall felt a sense of contact deepening with Barbara – things felt somehow more genuine and direct, and Dr Marshall commented *'It seems like you are risking talking to me directly, about how you really feel.'*

The main theme over a number of sessions that followed was about how it felt to try out 'risking' expressing her inner needs directly – rather than storing things up and, in Barbara's words, 'growing a tumour of resentment'. Barbara was able to articulate her fear that, by being more open, she would drive the therapist away. Dr Marshall and the therapy were offering Barbara a chance to explore this central predicament but with a different outcome – to play with a new way of being within a relationship.

This offer of a stable relationship – and of sticking with it through the insecurities inherent within it – is an example of what is meant by an 'experience of a reliable relationship' mentioned earlier. This was suggested as being important for therapeutic change for someone with these kinds of dynamics.

Clinical Example 3 – Part 3 Barbara: late phase of therapy

There was a temporary increase in Barbara's distress as the ending of therapy approached. The prospect of separation from Dr Marshall brought up feelings of loss and loneliness that had deep roots. Barbara found herself revisiting childhood experiences of losses and exploring feelings of anger and sadness associated with these. For Dr Marshall, this feeling connected with her countertransference association some months previously about 'something being bottomless'. Whilst this phase of therapy was upsetting for Barbara, she felt relief at being able to express something that had not been articulated before. Through this phase of work, Barbara came to be more benignly curious about her parents' situation and motivations, and the intergenerational patterns within her family that rarely got spoken about – including early trauma and loss in both her parents' histories.

Towards the end of therapy, Barbara's relationships outside the therapy began to change. Barbara found she could better express her feelings to her partner. Additionally, being less preoccupied with avoiding abandonment, she began to find space to contemplate questions such as: What do I really want from work? What am I really interested in in my life? The therapy came to an end with noticing these stirrings of curiosity and benign interest. These stirrings may have reflected the beginnings of 'structural change' (see Chapter 6) taking place in Barbara's internal world.

Therapeutic Working with Dynamics of Internal Criticism (an 'Introjective' Pattern)

This final section follows on from the theory of 'introjective' dynamics discussed earlier, and first mentioned in point 8 in Box 12.2. We turn again to the dynamics of internal criticism, focusing on a common clinical situation that arises. This is the process of getting to know the criticising internal object. Here is the opening line from a session with a patient, Ralph, who had been depressed for years:

'I'm afraid I've never been good at anything; I can see why no person would come near me . . . you must think I'm a hopeless case . . . '

(Ralph is the same patient as discussed in Chapter 8. The clinical material in Chapter 8 focuses more on later stages in the therapy and on working in the transference.)

It may take some time and work in therapy for a patient to be able to notice and consciously consider the internal object that is 'doing' the depressing, as the way this aspect operates and undermines may be so long-standing that it is hard to notice. Or if it is noticed, it may appear ordinary and unremarkable ('ego-syntonic'). In the early phase of therapy, the therapist might support the patient to become interested in how they treat themself by listening closely to the patient and enquiring about changes in state of mind that the therapist notices (*e.g. 'Did you notice a moment ago that you suddenly stopped what you were saying, as if you cut yourself off?'*). Or perhaps by enquiring directly about the depressing internal object whose presence is inferred but not yet obvious to the patient: '*I think I have a sense of how downtrodden and depressed you can feel. I wonder . . . what is depressing you?*'

In the session excerpt below from a trainee therapist working with Ralph, the therapist attempts to direct the patient's attention to the depressing internal object.

Clinical Example 4 Ralph: extract from the middle of a session in month 2

[Ralph had been talking about his feelings to do with not having a job.]

RALPH: *Yeah, it's difficult. Being human.* [There seemed to be a moment where Ralph was sympathetic towards himself.]

[Short silence, Ralph shakes his head slightly]

RALPH: *I'm sorry, I'm such an idiot.*

DR THOMAS: *Can we pause a moment; something is happening here. Where is this coming from, this calling yourself an idiot?*

RALPH: *This is with me all the time.*

DR THOMAS: *Can you say more about it?*

RALPH: *. . . Oh God, it's just too pathetic, me droning on.*

DR THOMAS: *It must feel terrible for you to put yourself down like that.*

RALPH: [Looking directly at Dr Thomas, a puzzled, slightly cross look on his face.] *But I deserve it, surely you can see that?*

DR THOMAS: [Takes a little whilst to think.] *An aspect of yourself seems to have a concern with talking about feelings, with just talking, with being . . . imperfect. I wonder what is disturbing this aspect of you about . . . being human?*

RALPH: [Seemed a bit stopped in his tracks.] *hmm . . . I think I've always felt . . . sort of a voice in my head: 'people should be strong and not mess about. You're weak, you're droning on, just stop droning.' It just makes me . . . cringe . . . what is the feeling . . . almost disqust at myself for droning on about my difficulties.*

DR THOMAS: *Ah, ok – this is important to hear about this aspect of you and for us to start to notice this. I think this is something we may need to keep coming back to. How much is this going on inside, this aspect of you saying, sort of, 'stop droning, you're weak'?*

RALPH: *I think pretty much all the time.*

DR THOMAS: *No wonder you can feel depressed and . . . you mentioned almost disgusted . . . can you say more about this?*

[Session continues.]

In this excerpt, when Dr Thomas tried being supportive towards the depressed self-representation ('*It must feel terrible for you to . . .*') the patient reacted as if Dr Thomas was stupid if she couldn't see how inadequate he was. Whilst offering support to depressed parts is a reasonable and humane first step, in some people this may merely provoke the criticising internal object. Instead, the therapy may become more freed-up when the therapist also addresses the criticising object. This is what Dr Thomas attempts when she goes on to speak to the criticising part of Ralph directly about what the concerns and issues are with discussing feelings ('*What is disturbing this aspect of you . . . ?*').

After the end of the excerpt above, the session continued with the therapist trying to raise awareness of the criticising object. This entailed the therapist taking an interest in various aspects to do with this internal object, including what came to Ralph's mind about it, what feelings came with it, and how other aspects of him felt when he chastised himself for 'droning'. Over time, Ralph started to become more aware and interested in his way of relating to himself.

Depending on how entrenched someone's internal structures are, progress may be halted at each step of the therapy by a patient's self-remonstrations. With each new insight or possibility of change, the criticising object can come to the fore along with established defences, leaving related aspects of the self feeling depressed, bad, shamed, and that they should not feel as they do. It can be important to understand and empathise with the criticising object for the function this once served and feels is serving, whilst also attending to the other side of the dynamic – the costs of this way of being, and the anxieties and fears about change (see Chapter 8, section on 'Working Through').

The therapist also listens out for movement or other voices in the patient's narrative and communications, particularly for more moderate or benign object relations that may already exist or be developing. If other more moderate object relations can develop and be allowed to become active alongside the more established 'old ways', this can help ameliorate the intensity of the 'problematic' dynamic.

Concluding Remarks

A psychodynamic approach offers the potential to understand the meanings and the relationships that sit behind symptoms of depressing/depressed states, locating feelings as part of a lively and active internal world. This chapter has taken a broad approach to the subject, drawing on common developmental themes and therapeutic situations in people who present with depression.

References

1. Hoch PH. Psychodynamics and psychotherapy of depressions. Can Psychiatr Assoc J 1959;4(Suppl):24–31.
2. Luyten P, Blatt SJ. Psychodynamic treatment of depression. Psychiatric Clinics of North America 2012;35(1):111–29.
3. Gabbard GO, Bennett T. Psychoanalytic and psychodynamic psychotherapy for depression and dysthymia. In Textbook of Mood Disorders, DJ Stein, DJ Kupfer, AF Schatzberg, eds. Washington, DC: American Psychiatric Publishing; 2006. pp. 389–405.
4. Dowds B. Depression: An Introduction. Phoenix Publishing House; 2021.
5. Fonagy P, Rost F, Carlyle JA et al. Pragmatic randomized controlled trial of long-term psychoanalytic psychotherapy for treatment-resistant depression: the Tavistock Adult Depression Study (TADS). World Psychiatry 2015;14(3):312–21.
6. Busch FN. Anger and depression. Advances in Psychiatric Treatment 2009;15(4):271–8.
7. Pedder JR. Failure to mourn, and melancholia. The British Journal of Psychiatry 1982;141(4):329–37.
8. Blatt SJ. Experiences of Depression: Theoretical, Clinical, and Research Perspectives. Washington, DC, US: American Psychological Association; 2004.
9. McWilliams N. Psychoanalytic Diagnosis, Second Edition: Understanding Personality Structure in the Clinical Process. New York: The Guilford Press; 2011.

10. Fairbairn WRD. Psychoanalytic Studies of the Personality. London: Routledge & Kegan Paul; 1952.
11. Abraham K. Notes on the psycho-analytical investigation and treatment of manic-depressive insanity and allied conditions. In Selected Papers on Psychoanalysis. Hogarth Press; 1927. pp. 137–56.
12. Freud S. Mourning and melancholia. In J. Strachey, ed. & trans. In The Standard Edition of the Complete Psychological Works of Sigmund Freud. London: Hogarth Press (original work published 1917); 1957. pp. 237–58.
13. Arieti S. Psychotherapy of severe depression. AJP 1977;134(8):864–8.
14. Sandler J. From Safety to Superego: Selected papers of Joseph Sandler. New York, NY, US: Guilford Press; 1987.
15. Bowlby J. Loss: Sadness & Depression. Attachment and Loss (vol. 3); (International psycho-analytical library no.109). London: Hogarth Press; 1980.
16. Blatt S. The differential effect of psychotherapy and psychoanalysis with anaclitic and introjective patients: The Menninger psychotherapy research project revisited. J Am Psychoanal Assoc 1992;40 (3):691–724.
17. APA. Psychodynamic Diagnostic Manual (PDM). Silver Spring, MD: Alliance of Psychoanalytic Organizations; 2006.
18. Gabbard GO. Long-term psychodynamic psychotherapy: a basic text. In Long-term Psychodynamic Psychotherapy: A Basic Text. Washington, DC: American Psychiatric Pub.; 2010.

Chapter 13

Dynamics of Borderline States of Mind

Table of Contents

Introduction 200

On the First Encounter 201

Self-Harm 202

The Meaning and Dynamics of Self-Directed Attacks 204

Staff Countertransference Enactments in Relation to Self-Harm 205

Splitting of the Self 205

Relation to the Self and Other 206

The Process of Ending Therapy with Someone with Borderline Difficulties 208

Some Adaptations of Technique 209

Concluding Remarks 210

Introduction

Sometimes the most challenging patients for clinicians are those who evoke strong or uncomfortable feelings in us. These might include feelings of anxiety, irritation, helplessness, fear, or failure. These are feelings that commonly occur in clinicians when working with patients who experience relational difficulties and who may function predominantly at a borderline level of psychological organisation (see Chapter 9 for more detail about the neurotic-borderline-psychotic continuum). It is vital if we are to be able to work effectively with these patients that we recognise and understand where these feelings come from.

In his book 'Becoming Freud', Adam Phillips writes that, 'Freud sees adults as people who cannot recover from their childhoods … '.[1] Phillips goes on to say, 'From a psychoanalytic point of view modern people [are] as much the survivors of their history as they [are] the makers of it. We make histories so as not to perish of the truth.'[1] Phillips is pointing to the importance of our experiences from early life in influencing how we develop and 'survive' in the world as we find it. This chapter links early developmental experiences to present-day dynamics between patients and therapists, with an emphasis on patients with a marked propensity to borderline states of mind.

On the First Encounter

This group of patients will commonly have had experiences of early trauma, and childhood abuse or neglect (estimated 30–90% in a recent review).[2] The quote above from Adam Phillips gives an elegant description of the way in which these patients are continuously influenced by their early traumatic experiences which pervade their lives. At the same time, they find ways in which they can avoid being in contact with the pain of what they have had to survive in order that they can go on surviving.

Furthermore, it is important that we don't simply consider neglect as an absence of appropriate care. Neglect of an infant will evoke primitive annihilatory fears, as an infant left uncared for cannot survive. Therefore it is useful to consider the early experience of neglect as a threat to the life of the infant. If we think about these early experiences, they involve being in a position of helplessness and feeling threatened and in the case of abuse, intruded upon. These patients tend to become disturbed if placed in situations which evoke these feelings in them again; for example, when asked challenging or probing questions, when left in silence in an unfamiliar situation, when they feel that they are not in control of what is happening to them – all of which may occur in an encounter with a therapist. Their reaction will often be one of anger with the unconscious aim being to push the other away, to create space (remove the intruder), and to regain a sense of control. Displays of anger and aggression do this effectively. With this response there is also a projection of the feelings of being scared, out of control, humiliated, and small into the other, in this instance the clinician. The experience of these feelings in the therapist can then evoke the wish to get rid of the patient, to get away from them.

It is interesting to bear in mind a study that examined how people with a borderline developmental organisation rated facial expressions. It was found that the study group overrated neutral faces as expressing 'negative' feelings, such as anger or fear, and as being untrustworthy.[3] This means that a patient with borderline difficulties entering a clinical encounter may well experience a therapist's neutral expression in this way and become suspicious and defensive. This has significant implications for the therapeutic alliance.

Ogden[4] suggested that an encounter with the inner world of another person is always suffused with anxiety – we are considering in this chapter patients with disturbed and disturbing internal worlds. It can be a very unsettling thing for these individuals to experience being taken in and understood, as it is unfamiliar and can feel intrusive and exposing for the patient. Thus, the experience of psychodynamic psychotherapy can stir up complex feelings for these patients. In the absence of an early experience of consistent and considerate care – and frequently the opposite – we can understand how the patient will be suspicious and alert to the anticipated attack or threat when entering a therapy.

Clinical Example Nora: Part 1

Nora was a young woman who arrived for her first session of therapy. Growing up, she experienced her mother as critical and denigrating. The newly qualified therapist was struck by her appearance. She was very attractive and dressed all in black with a T-shirt with a skull image, heavy studded boots, with her hair and nails done immaculately, and multiple facial piercings. She brought her three-year-old daughter with her, explaining that she couldn't get childcare. The therapist explained that it was important the she attend the sessions alone and said that it was not appropriate that she bring her young child to the therapy. Nora immediately became enraged and said that she would not carry on with the session. She left and later contacted the service to say that she would not work with this therapist. She said that it was a disgrace that the therapist did not take into consideration the importance to her of having good childcare to enable her to enter into the therapy, and how difficult this was to find.

On reflection, we might think that coming to start therapy was a very anxiety-provoking experience for Nora, something that she anticipated would feel exposing. We can understand that although there may have been a very real difficulty in arranging childcare, at another level Nora was communicating something to the therapist by bringing her small child to the session. She was at the same time bringing childlike feelings of vulnerability in herself and simultaneously projecting these into her daughter, who was a young child in need of care, thus defending herself against these feelings of vulnerability and need. We can consider Nora's appearance as a kind of armour or carapace, a defence against feeling vulnerable and not in control in this new and unfamiliar situation. The therapist's intention was to establish a secure setting for the therapy and ensure that Nora was able to use the space for herself, and may have felt that her comment about Nora bringing her child not being appropriate was neutral. We can see that Nora felt that the therapist's comment was critical, and she was likely to have felt humiliated, the implication being that she was stupid and didn't even know what was appropriate. The experience for Nora was of an uncaring and critical mother figure who denigrated her, a transference of her experience with her own mother. Her response was to get angry and leave, thus moving her away from these difficult feelings of vulnerability and humiliation, and allowing her to feel she had regained control.

The therapist later admitted that she had been somewhat intimidated by Nora when she first arrived and there may have been an enactment in response to countertransferential feelings of being inadequate and not in charge, and thus an unconscious wish to denigrate Nora and bring her down to size, so that the therapist no longer felt these things.

Self-Harm

One of the most challenging situations clinically is working with patients who self-harm, and those who tell you that they plan to harm or kill themselves. A common situation is that a patient will come to see you, often at the end of the day, last thing on a Friday, or out-of-hours and, at some point in the interaction, disclose that they plan to cut themselves or that they intend to end their life. The clinician is often left feeling very anxious and alone with this, and they feel that they have to do something to keep the patient safe and to make things better. If we think about this in the context of the patient's early experiences, then we can understand what might be happening in this instance. In *Remembering, Repeating and Working Through*, Freud described the compulsion to repeat.[5] This is based on the idea that when feelings and experiences, including traumatic experiences, cannot be borne or contained, thought about, and processed psychically, they are acted out as behaviour. When patients repeatedly self-harm or make suicidal acts, it may be understood as an unconscious repetition of an act of violence that they previously experienced and that could not be made sense of. The patient is spared the painful experience of remembering the trauma and through action is put in a position of being in control, although temporarily, of something that originally was completely out of their control. To give up the option of suicide is to forfeit a crucial sense of agency and control.

We can imagine that as infants our early experiences are confusing, feelings are overwhelming and inexplicable, and seem to come from nowhere or even somewhere external.

As described in Chapter 2, a task of the mother (or other primary caregiver) is to help the infant bear and then make sense of and learn about these emotions. The infant projects the disturbing feeling into the mother who, in a state of reverie, uses her own mind and experience to process and digest this experience. She then gives the infant back the feeling in a digested and manageable form. This is the process of 'containment' described by Bion (see also section on 'Containment' in Chapter 2).[6] An example of this is the infant who wakes in terror in the middle of the night, having had a nightmare. The infant's mother on hearing the scream will go quickly to her child, while experiencing a fear herself that something terrible is happening; then, after taking in the scene, will sit down and hold the child, saying soothingly 'it's okay, it's just a nightmare. I know it's scary but it's over now and I'm here'. This not only comforts and soothes the child through touch and the sound of her voice, but what is communicated to the child is that their mother has experienced the fear and has understood it. It is something bearable and it will pass.

Patients with a borderline difficulty often don't have this kind of early experience, and so they have not developed the capacity to recognise feelings and to know that they are not dangerous, that they are bearable, and will pass. What they are left with is a feeling that they are experiencing something terrible, dangerous, overwhelming, and unbearable. There is no sense that it will ever pass.

Acts of self-harm are frequently a response to manage unbearable feelings. These and the experience of suicidal thoughts can be understood as a wish to get rid of these feelings. If we think about a man who leaves to go to work on a cold morning only to discover that his car doesn't start – this man will perhaps hit his car and say that it is a piece of junk and only fit for the dump. We can understand that he does not want to destroy the car but just its 'not starting-ness'. However, in these patients that I am describing, there is a difficulty in recognising and distinguishing a wish to get rid of an aspect of them that is experienced as problematic (the 'not starting-ness'), from the whole of themselves. The wish is extrapolated to the whole, so they feel that they have to destroy all of themselves to get rid of the aspect that is causing the disturbance.

We can also see that with the disclosure of suicidal intent, there is a projective communication of the unbearableness of what they are experiencing. In response to the communication, the clinician experiences a feeling of anxiety or dread, that there is something that can't be tolerated and so something has to be done to get rid of it. There is an intense pressure to act, which is often responded to either by referring to another service or crisis team, by prescribing medication such as anti-depressants or benzodiazepines, or in some instances by arranging for the patient to be admitted to a psychiatric unit. These patients don't have an experience of thoughtful care or care as an emotional process and, as such, they need concrete acts from the other in order to feel cared for. It is important to note that sometimes we need to act to ensure the patient's safety, but what is essential is that the needs of the patient, the underlying dynamics, and the emotional experience are attended to thoughtfully.

Clinical Example Nora: Part 2

After the initial meeting, Nora's GP contacted the therapist who had seen her. He noted that she had come to see him in a state of despair, feeling overwhelmed, and describing suicidal thoughts. Her family were vocal in insisting that she needed help, that they could not manage her, and that something had to be done. The GP noted that Nora's mother and father were under the care of mental health services as her mother was dependent on alcohol and her father had episodes of psychosis and was dependent on substances, and that they had a difficult relationship with services themselves. They were adamant that she needed to see a psychiatrist and to be prescribed medication.

The therapist met with Nora again and they agreed to start once-weekly therapy. In the sessions, Nora struggled to speak about her feelings and would mostly talk about the practical details of her life, often requesting that the therapist help her with certain tasks around moving to her own flat or with applying for benefits. She would request letters of support or references and referrals to other agencies. Between the sessions, Nora would get drunk and leave telephone messages late at night for her therapist to say that she was thinking of killing herself. On a number of occasions, the therapist was contacted to say that Nora had presented at A&E out-of-hours, having self-harmed and describing suicidal thoughts; however, when she attended the sessions following this, it was very difficult to explore what had happened with her. She would say that there was no point and that she was beyond help. One Monday morning Nora's therapist arrived at work to see a message saying that Nora had contacted the crisis team over the weekend, as she was suicidal and had a plan to take an overdose. They had been very worried about her risk and she had been admitted to one of the psychiatric wards and prescribed medication.

We can see that Nora's experience from early in life was of being with 'objects' who were either disturbed or who had blanked their minds with alcohol and drugs, and so had little capacity to take in or process what she was feeling. As an infant, Nora's normal attempts to communicate her feelings to her mother by projection would have failed, as her mother was not in a state to receive them. We know from Bion's work that if this happens, in order to evoke a response, the child will use increasing force with which to project her feelings into her object. Nora had thus learned that the only way to get through to her objects was to violently project her psychic distress into them. We might also think that what was communicated back to Nora was that difficult or painful feelings could not be tolerated and had to be wiped out with alcohol and drugs. Her family's response to her expression of distress was to try and get away from the feeling of anxiety that it evoked in them by insisting that mental health services act to make her 'better', and by becoming angry that she wasn't being adequately treated, which included being medicated.

The Meaning and Dynamics of Self-Directed Attacks

Through acts of self-harm, the individual enacts both the role of perpetrator and victim of something very damaging. This dual aspect can be identified in acts of self-harm or suicide in that, in one way, the patient is engaging in something lively that is an attempt to reach out to another and communicate distress; but there is also a murderous and angry attack on both the self and the other. The act of self-harm is at the same time both a moving towards and a destructive assault on connection and closeness. All acts have meaning and it is important for us to consider both the apparent and the unconscious meanings of acts of self-harm.

For example, a young woman takes an overdose after she discovers that her friend has not invited her to a night out that she has arranged with others in their group. After taking the tablets she texts her friend to say goodbye. Her friend calls an ambulance and the woman is taken to hospital. Afterwards, the young woman explains that it was because she had an overwhelming feeling of rejection and of being unwanted and worthless. She says that she feels like she is bad and so people don't want to be around her. Her friend feels upset, but also angry that her night out had been spoiled.

We can, however, also consider that there may be a more unconscious feeling of rage at the friend and a wish to hurt her and evoke in her a feeling of guilt and of being the one who is bad or damaging. There may be unconscious feelings of envy at her friend having something she doesn't and a wish to spoil the night out. It is helpful to reflect that the communication within this act is that the young woman feels very hurt by her friend's actions and that she desperately wishes to be included and wanted. Also, just how painful this feeling is for her, that it is not just upsetting, but it feels unbearable. We can see in this example how projective identification has the dual roles of being both evacuative, in which the young woman gets rid of the unacceptable feelings of anger and aggression, but that it also communicates something of her experience in that it is the friend who ends up feeling upset and angry.

Staff Countertransference Enactments in Relation to Self-Harm

When working with patients who self-harm and make attempts to kill themselves it is important to recognise the anger and aggression within these acts. This is something that is often either repressed or disavowed by the patient. It is split off and projected as it is felt to be too dangerous or destructive. It is not uncommon for patients having self-harmed or attempted suicide to describe experiences of feeling treated in a cruel, dismissive, and uncaring way by healthcare professionals. This may be the patient's perception of care based on their projection of something aggressive into the healthcare professional. Alongside this, however, there may be an evocation of these projected aggressive or attacking feelings in the healthcare professional, which are then expressed and enacted via projective identification, in acts such as suturing a wound before the anaesthetic cream has taken time to work, using a harsh or dismissive tone, or speaking to the patient about their self-harm in the A&E reception rather than taking them to a private area. This can then reinforce in the patient an idea that they are bad, toxic, or unwanted.

Splitting of the Self

Splitting of the self is something that is key within the act of suicide. Campbell and Hale described there being a phantasy that the individual will both kill off the problematic aspects of themself and their feelings in the body where these are often located, and at the same time survive in an idealised state where these feelings, experiences, and unwanted aspects no longer exist, 'the surviving self'.[7] This state can be envisioned as a permanent sense of peace. It is interesting to note that the most common drugs taken in overdose are painkillers and anti-depressants, which can be thought of as removing psychic pain. This phantasy is predicated on the patient's experience of their body as a separate, non-self object. There are moving descriptions of patients who have been caught on CCTV as they jump in front of trains, that just as their feet leave the edge of the platform and their course of action cannot be altered, they can be seen to pull back; we can envisage that in this moment reality impinges on this phantasy and these two states come together with a recognition of what the individual has done – that they have taken the final step and killed themself in what can be thought of as self-murder.

Clinical Example Ikraam

Ikraam's mother suffered from post-natal depression after he was born and never really recovered from the depression. His father left them not long after he was born and, although Ikraam made contact with him again in his teens, his father had another family and tended not to return Ikraam's calls or would find reasons he couldn't see him. Ikraam was sexually abused by one of his mother's partners as a child. He felt very low and depressed and he tended to cut himself on his arms and thighs. He was under the care of psychiatric services who referred him for a psychodynamic consultation for assistance with understanding Ikraam and his presentation. His community psychiatric nurse explained that he was a pleasant but troubled young man who could be reflective at times. At consultation Ikraam was pleasant and funny and the therapist warmed to him. He explained to her that he felt that he had, at times, an inner angry voice which would tell him to kill himself. Ikraam said that he wanted to live, but sometimes found it hard not to do as the voice said. From his records, the therapist could see that Ikraam had made numerous suicide attempts and that he frequently used drugs and alcohol. He explained that this was because of the voice and that he had to do something to make it stop.

We can see in Ikraam the split, in which there is one part of him that desperately wants to be taken in and which is pleasant and accommodating, and another more murderous and destructive part reflected in the inner voice. There is a wish to get rid of his body which is seen as damaged and damaging. He attacks his body which is identified with all the unwanted, 'bad' aspects of the self, cutting himself, using drugs and alcohol. There is at some level a phantasy that he could get rid of this 'bad' part of himself and leave a part that is wanted and 'nice'.

Relation to the Self and Other

Individuals with a borderline psychology often enter crisis in response to experiences of rejection or threats of abandonment. Again, we can think of this in the context of early experiences. As discussed, these patients have often had an experience of a lack of a containing other, such that they have not yet developed a solid sense of an internal containing object. Projective identification as a normal developmental phenomenon only works if there is a responsive person to project into. Without this, there is then a feeling that if the external object (who they depend on) leaves, they won't survive. This is separation anxiety which is well-known in infants, but less considered in adults. Fonagy described this as there being a failure in the capacity for mental representation of the other with a resulting impairment in object constancy and an inability to keep the other in mind when they are absent.[8] Without a dependable and containing other, there is a corresponding deficit in the self-representation – the individual lacks a sense of who they are, and may struggle to make sense of their feelings and intentions. As they grow up, the individual may therefore attach themself to another person, who provides a temporary representation for the individual, which becomes their identity. This representation is unlikely to be a reflection of the individual's 'true' feelings and intentions, but more like putting on a set of clothes to wear picked off a shelf. When that other person leaves, the patient's representation or identity is lost with them and they are left with a feeling of falling apart and an associated annihilatory anxiety. For example, a patient was immersed in the world of sport when he was with a girlfriend for whom this was important. However, when the relationship broke down, the patient found that he had no real connection to or interest in sport and felt a profound feeling of emptiness. He quickly got into a relationship with someone else. Her interests in theatre then 'became' his.

The early developmental dynamics become further complicated if a caregiver, on whom the patient was dependent for survival as a child, was either unpredictable and erratic or intrusive and abusive. In this situation, there may be a fear of being close to the caregiver coupled with a fear that if they are separated they will perish. This can lead to the 'claustro-agoraphobic dilemma' described by Henry Rey where some patients seek closeness and contact and then feel overwhelmed and intruded upon (claustrophobic); they push the other person away and then feel terrified of being alone and helpless (agoraphobic), so again they seek closeness.[9] It is helpful to keep this in mind when we consider how patients with a borderline psychology may present in crisis. This can be illustrated if we return to the example of Nora (see also Chapter 14 for a discussion of when projective identification dominates a person's psychological functioning to an even greater extent).

Clinical Example Nora: Part 3

Nora contacted her therapist as she was feeling very distressed. She had received a text message from her partner to say that she wanted to have some more space as things had become quite intense between them lately. Nora felt immediately angry, then devastated, her emotions were all over the place. She was left feeling that there was no point to life and she was thinking of killing herself by taking an overdose of amitriptyline. She didn't feel able to keep herself safe and could see no other way. Her therapist called her and suggested that she work with the crisis team, but she immediately responded that she didn't want to see a lot of different people who she had never met before. The therapist suggested admission to a crisis house, but Nora rejected this suggestion saying that that wasn't going to solve anything. She became angry with the therapist's suggestions and hung up, saying she was going to go and take the overdose.

The therapist discussed the situation with the team psychiatrist and ultimately Nora was detained under the Mental Health Act and admitted to an acute psychiatric ward. While on the psychiatric ward she was withdrawn and didn't discuss her thoughts with the nursing or medical staff. She was found on a number of occasions having cut herself with razor blades that she had hidden. The ward team had a discussion and felt that the admission was not offering any therapeutic benefit and made the decision to discharge Nora. When this was discussed with her, she became very upset and said that she was going to kill herself and she was not safe to go home. She was given an unescorted pass from the ward on the day before the planned discharge, but when she returned to the ward she disclosed to staff that she had taken an overdose of morphine that she had purchased online. Her urine drug screen was positive for morphine. The medical staff felt that they could not then discharge her from the ward as the risk was too high.

We can see here how Nora feels terribly anxious when on her own and reaches out for help and contact, but then when there is an attempt to get closer to her and bring her into either the crisis team or ward, she feels overwhelmed and intruded upon and withdraws, accompanied by an increase in her disturbance. If there is then a move away by the clinicians, she again feels extremely abandoned and scared and through self-harm communicates this, and so the clinicians bring her close again.

Some interesting research has been done examining the experience of rejection and exclusion in individuals with borderline difficulties. The study found that when these patients were placed in simulated situations where they were excluded or rejected, individuals with borderline difficulties experienced greater negative affect than those without. Also, those with borderline difficulties felt rejected, even during situations of inclusion.[10] Thus, we can see that there is an extra sensitivity and increased negative response to rejection in these individuals. One of the key features of someone with borderline difficulties is fear of abandonment and attempts to avoid this experience.

The Process of Ending Therapy with Someone with Borderline Difficulties

Clinical Example Nora: Part 4

Nora had worked with her therapist for nearly a year and a half, and they were approaching the planned end of the therapy. Her therapist had been impressed that she had made moves towards becoming more aware of her experience of others as being uncaring and that they didn't listen to her. Nora was able to make a link between this and her feeling with her mother when she was growing up, and reflected that actually it might not be the case that people in the present day didn't care, but that this was just how she was perceiving them. As the sessions got closer to the end date, Nora's therapist noticed that she was increasingly late for sessions or would not attend, leaving no message. She began receiving calls from Nora's GP, who was worried about her as she had been attending the surgery saying that she was feeling very low and was having more thoughts of suicide. Her self-harming had become worse again, having decreased and stopped over the course of the therapy. Her GP expressed concern, saying that this was not the right time to end the therapy and asked Nora's therapist to extend it until things were more stable again. Nora's therapist wondered what had happened to cause this deterioration after her having done so well, had she said or done something wrong?

As the end of the therapy approaches, Nora begins to anticipate the loss of her therapist and finds this very difficult. It brings up feelings of being abandoned and left on her own without care. This creates huge anxiety in Nora, which she manages by (unconsciously) projecting it into her GP. Her GP then experiences anxiety and a sense of being left on his own with something disturbing and scary, with an accompanying sense of dread. He acts to manage this by trying to prevent the ending. We can also understand Nora's therapist's feeling of having done something wrong as an identification with Nora and her feelings that she must have done something wrong to be gotten rid of by her therapist. This situation reflects how painful loss of the therapy and the therapist is, and that Nora manages this by avoiding it and creating the feeling that the therapy and therapist are no good. If they are no good, then there is nothing to miss.

As discussed in Chapter 8, there are multiple, complex, and difficult feelings that come up with the end to a period of therapy. These may be particularly so in someone with borderline difficulties, and it is therefore essential to be aware of these feelings and to speak to them in the therapy so that they can be thought about and worked through. Loss is always a painful thing, but being able to bear that loss and still hold on to having had something good is an extremely important experience and one that many of these individuals have never had.

Some Adaptations of Technique

If we understand what underpins the relational difficulties that these patients have, we can take them into account in the therapeutic work with them. It is vital to have clear and consistent boundaries so that when there are enactments or acting out by either the patient or the therapist, these can be noticed and brought into the therapy. Because of the tendency to misinterpret neutral expressions as untrustworthy or hostile, it is important to be more expressive than would usually be the case. These patients tend to make assumptions about what the other person is thinking (e.g. 'I am a burden and not worth their time') or feeling (e.g. 'they want to get rid of me'). They can find evidence for this in neutral gestures (e.g. 'the therapist is late which means they really don't want to see me'). It can be helpful to be curious about what their experience of you as therapist is. Therapist-centred interpretations can be problematic. Interpreting 'you feel that I am judging you' is likely to evoke the response 'yes, because you are'. There is an experience for these patients that what they think and feel is undoubtedly what is real. This is what is termed 'concrete thinking' or the lack of an 'as if' quality; so the therapist's interpretation might not be understood as 'you are experiencing me as if I am judging you because this was your experience of your mother', but as a statement of fact. Given this struggle to mentalize, rather than making a classical analytic interpretation, it can be more helpful to take a stance that is curious about and empathic of their experience, rather than knowing or interpreting from a position of certainty. For example, '*I wonder if when I said X you felt that I was judging you. I imagine that would make you feel hurt and angry with me.*' This stance of curiosity and transparency on the part of the therapist can feel more helpful with the patient who has been traumatised in the past, and struggles to reflect on what is in the other's mind in the present.

A patient operating at a borderline level quickly moves to certainty about what the therapist is thinking, often that it is negative or critical, and then takes up a defensive position. The therapist can have an analytic formulation or theory in mind and make use of this to help the therapist understand the dynamics, projections, and transference–countertransference relationship, but this doesn't necessarily need to be interpreted to the patient. It is, however, important to try and work with the patient to understand and articulate their feelings in the room with the therapist, even if these are hatred, contempt, or anger. This should be done in a caring and non-judgmental way, which does not act to accuse, humiliate, or push the feeling back into them. The aim is to help the patient recognise and name their feelings and experiences, so that they can be worked through. As detailed above, it is important to understand where splits occur and it can be helpful to talk to both sides of the split; for example, the feelings of being vulnerable and exposed, and angry and contemptuous. The therapist might say '*It seems that you have more than one feeling about the therapy as we are coming to the end. On the one hand I think you feel that seeing me has been helpful and you will miss the therapy. But on the other hand there are perhaps feelings of anger that it is ending and so you can then go to a place where you feel that it was inadequate and you are left no better.*' It can be helpful when the therapist attempts to integrate these experiences of the patient, bringing the experiences closer together, and accepting the ambivalent feelings that the patient has for their objects: both a love and pining for and anger and hatred (see theory Chapter 2 for further discussion on splitting and the paranoid-schizoid position). This is a painful process as it involves getting in touch both with the disturbing past and also the damage that has been done by the patient to themself and others.

Concluding Remarks

Therapeutic work with people who have experienced complex developmental trauma can pose challenges on a clinical and emotional level. However, if we can understand the meaning behind a person's behaviour, the way it impacts on clinicians and others, and how it is rooted in their early relationships, this can make the work rewarding and useful. A therapeutic space, informed by this understanding, can provide the means for them to get to know themselves better. This involves beginning to unpick how, as Adam Phillips describes, the fear of 'perishing from the "truth"' of their early experiences leads to them creating a history that is unconsciously relived around them and by which they are tormented, and at the same time reassured. This then allows for the possibility of remaking their story.

References

1. Phillips A. Becoming Freud: the making of a psychoanalyst. New Haven and London: Yale University Press. 2014; 5, 7.
2. Cattane N, Rossi R, Lanfredi M et al. Borderline personality disorder and childhood trauma: exploring the affected biological systems and mechanisms. BMC Psychiatry 2017;v17:221.
3. Mitchell AE, Dickens GL, Picchioni MM. Facial emotion processing in borderline personality disorder: a systematic review and meta-analysis. *Neuropsychology Review*, 2014; 24(2): 166–84.
4. Ogden T. The initial analytic meeting. The Primitive Edge of Experience. London: Karnac. 1992.
5. Freud S. Remembering, Repeating and Working-Through (Further recommendations on the technique of psycho-analysis II). In J. Strachey, ed. & trans, *The Standard Edition of the Complete Psychological Works of Sigmund Freud* (Vol. 12, pp. 145–156). (Original work published 1914) London: Hogarth Press. 1958; 12.
6. Bion WR. Learning From Experience. London: Karnac. 1962.
7. Campbell D, Hale R. Working in the Dark: Understanding the Pre-Suicide State of Mind. Oxford and New York: Routledge. 2017.
8. Fonagy P. Thinking about thinking: some clinical and theoretical considerations in the treatment of a borderline patient. *Int. J. Psychoanal.* 1991; 72: 639–56.
9. Rey JH. Schizoid phenomena in the borderline. In Melanie Klein Today. Vol 1: Mainly theory. Spillius, EB, ed. London: Routledge. 1988.
10. Domsalla M, Koppe G, Niedtfeld I et al. Cerebral processing of social rejection in patients with borderline personality disorder. *Social Cognitive and Affective Neuroscience* 2014; 9(11): 1789–97

Chapter 14

Narcissistic Difficulties, a Trans-Diagnostic Presentation Requiring a System-Wide Approach

Table of Contents

Introduction 211
A Psychiatric Perspective 212
Severity 212
Complexity 213
Unwanted Consequences of Admission 213
A Psychodynamic Perspective 214
Narcissistic Defences and Projective Identification 214
Concreteness and Containment: What Admission Means 216
Transference, Countertransference, and Formulation 217
Acquisitive Projective Identification 218
Attributive Projective Identification 220
Acquisition, Attribution, and the Boundary of the Self 222
Using the Relational Affective Formulation (RAF) in Practice 223
Designing a Psychotherapeutic Pathway: A System-Wide Approach 223
Adaptations of Therapeutic Technique in Specialist Psychotherapeutic Teams 224
The RAF and Risk Assessment 225
Concluding Remarks 227

Introduction

In Freud's theory of primary narcissism, he described an inborn hatred of those aspects of bodily and mental life and the external world which, being outside the subject's control, were experienced as alien, disturbing, and demanding.[1] He proposed this hatred was overcome by treating the unpredictable external world as part of the ego so it came to be loved as belonging to the self. Ultimately this egocentric view must be relinquished in favour of recognition of the individual's true state of dependence upon the external world. In this way Freud saw narcissism as a normal stage in psychological and psychosexual development. Confusingly the term narcissism is used in different ways in the contemporary psychoanalytic literature, referring to the phenomenon of lack of interest in others and self-preoccupation; describing an innate tendency within the personality that opposes relationships outside the self; and finally it is used to refer to a specific set of personality dysfunctions called the narcissistic difficulties.[2] This chapter will use the term 'narcissism' in this third sense, referring to problematic patterns of relating that result from narcissistic defences; in particular, two states of mind which arise from projective identification (PI).

This chapter sets out the way in which the persistence of narcissistic defences into adulthood results in a disordered psychosomatic experience of self in relation to other, giving rise to marked interpersonal difficulties across a range of settings, and psychic and somatic symptoms. The more severe the underlying disturbance, the more common the trans-diagnostic presentations and the more physical health, mental health, and social care services these patients attend. This chapter focuses on a psychodynamic understanding of patients with the most severe difficulties who ultimately find their way into inpatient settings and require a system-wide approach. It is written for mental health professionals, having implications for all whose work brings them into contact with these patients. For information, in Box 14.1 we explain the overlap and differences between the focus of this chapter compared with Chapter 13.

In this chapter, a psychodynamic formulation and description of the states of mind arising from narcissistic defences is offered (the Relational Affective Formulation),[3] along with case studies for illustration and some suggestions about using the formulation in everyday practice. For clarity, in this chapter patients are referred to as he/him and 'mother' is used, being less clumsy than the more neutral term 'primary caregiver'.

A Psychiatric Perspective

Severity

A spectrum of severity of interpersonal difficulties is recognised, and described as 'personality disorder' in the ICD 11 classification.[4] Patients at the severe end of the spectrum have more pervasive disturbance in their relations towards themselves and

Box 14.1 Overlap and difference between this chapter on narcissism and Chapter 13 on borderline dynamics

There is some overlap in focus between the present chapter on narcissism and the previous chapter on the dynamics of borderline states of mind. Both chapters are talking about presentations where the defences of splitting, projection, and projective identification are dominant.

The key difference in focus between the two chapters is the degree to which projective identification is used, in terms of how much it is employed, and how intensely. This varies between people.

Chapter 13 discusses people with this constellation of defences who have unstable relationships and may harm themselves. Chapter 13 has an emphasis on clinical examples where projective identification, whilst important, does not preclude a degree of 'real' relating to others. Such people may have periods of crisis, some of which may result in a short inpatient stay but are less likely to get 'stuck' in escalating problems as an inpatient.

The present chapter focuses on clinical presentations where powerful projective identification is used in a more protracted way, such that it dominates almost all psychological functioning. A person needs to be able to relate to the other as a separate person in order to make therapeutic progress. When someone is continuously relating to others in terms of a projected part of themself (the narcissistic presentation), they are always cycling round defensive processes, lurching from one crisis to another; they cannot take in ideas, information, or learning from others and the external world. This can lead to more extreme encounters where staff and patients get stuck in entrenched positions with seemingly no way out. This is the subject of the present chapter where a system-wide approach is required.

others, more profound difficulties in experiencing and expressing emotion and appraising their own and other's feelings, and greater difficulty with impulse control. One of the consequences of this global impairment is an increase in the likelihood of hospitalisation.[5] Whilst most clinicians express the view that people with marked relational difficulties are best cared for in community rather than inpatient settings, the evidence suggests that they account for around 20% of acute mental health bed occupancy.[6,7,8] In some instances, admission is unavoidable as a consequence of persistent para-suicidal behaviour or physical health complications of associated conditions. A common, but not universal, finding is that admission itself appears to escalate the severity of symptoms, especially when patients are detained under the Mental Health Act. 'Severity' in this context refers to the likelihood of hospitalisation as a consequence of risk to self.

Complexity

In this chapter, complexity refers to the associated conditions which become more common as the severity of the underlying relational disturbance increases. These associated conditions include eating disorders,[9] somatisation,[10,11] substance misuse,[12] and neurodevelopmental conditions including autistic spectrum disorder.[13]

Mental health pathways are often organised in symptom specific specialisms such as specialist eating disorder or complex needs services, liaison psychiatry, and health psychology. These services can struggle to manage the trans-diagnostic presentations of patients with marked relational difficulties. Commonly, when one symptom is managed another emerges, so patients can move between services, becoming system-wide frequent attenders across physical health, mental health, and social care. Usually, no one pathway addresses their difficulties as a whole.

These associated conditions increase the likelihood of hospitalisation in either physical or mental health services. For example:

- Increased impulsivity associated with problematic use of alcohol and drugs
- Disordered eating
  - Food restriction leading to rapid weight loss requiring refeeding
  - Physical health consequences of frequent bingeing and purging
- Investigation and surgical interventions for functional physical symptoms.

Unwanted Consequences of Admission

Once admitted, problems commonly arise in management. Professionals observe that patients tend to get worse in inpatient settings and so are concerned about the potential for iatrogenic harm. It is important to say that there is some evidence admission can be beneficial to such patients.[14] However, these fears can be based on a realistic awareness of lack of specialist expertise and direct experience of the powerful transference and countertransference responses in teams working with this patient group.

Many clinicians will be aware that iatrogenic harm can in fact arise. This may result from certain interactions between the patient's inherent difficulties and aspects of inpatient care, or from the clinical team themselves becoming disordered in the way they relate to the patient, as in the examples in the following bullet points.

Factors related to How the Patient May Experience Inpatient Care

- Removing responsibility from the patient, for example, through detention under the Mental Health Act, can exacerbate regressed feelings and behaviour.
- Professionals who have adopted legal responsibility for a patient may be obliged to step in to prevent para-suicidal behaviour. Where the patient's difficulty originates in the need for relational control this can result in escalation.
- Where restraint results from attempts to prevent para-suicidal behaviour, the attempt to provide 'safe holding' can replicate historic abuse.

Professional Factors

- Professionals' attitudes can become split towards patients with marked relational difficulties, resulting in discriminatory exclusion or over-involvement and enactments of relationships which cross the professional/personal divide.
- Professionals can feel under pressure to over investigate and treat functional physical conditions leaving them in doubt about whether they are participating in the patient's self-harm.
- The emotional obstacles to discharge from hospital can result in institutionalisation of the patient.

For health and social care professionals, being clear about the distinction between providing care and doing harm is an important container for anxieties about professional roles.[15] Where this distinction becomes unclear, professionals can become personally anxious in a way which is outside their usual working experience. This is especially so when teams have had little training to work with people with these trans-diagnostic presentations, or are relatively inexperienced.

A Psychodynamic Perspective

To understand such complex patients, it is important to understand both the anxieties and defences which underlie their behaviour. This requires some translation between psychiatric and psychodynamic thinking. 'Personality disorder' is of course a psychiatric term, defined in ICD-11 as 'An enduring disturbance characterized by problems in functioning of aspects of the self . . . and/or interpersonal dysfunction . . . '[4]

This focus on relating between self and others accords with the psychodynamic emphasis on disordered relating. In psychodynamic terms, these patients rely on narcissistic defences to manage their anxieties.

Narcissistic Defences and Projective Identification

The term narcissism is derived from the myth of Narcissus who fell in love with his own reflection, failing to recognise that the beautiful young man he was looking at was, in fact, himself. As stated in the introduction, our psychodynamic concept of narcissism started with Freud.[16,17] Freud's contributions were later developed and described in object relations terms. Henri Rey described the developmental task facing the infant, who comes into the world in a state of complete helplessness and dependence on an 'other' over whom they have no control. The infant, in a state of absolute dependence, must come to terms with the reality that the other is at once needed, good, and separate.[18]

This state would be extremely anxiety-provoking if the baby were not protected from the reality of its position, by 'mother's' attentive responsiveness which allows the baby the illusion of being powerful and in control of her comings and goings.[19] When mothering is 'good enough', the baby's disillusionment takes place at a pace which doesn't exceed the baby's capacity to tolerate anxiety. However, where the baby's anxiety becomes excessive, through excessive hunger or frustration or the mother's inability to respond contingently upon their needs, the baby may no longer be able to avoid being aware that their survival depends upon the presence of a mother who is not under their control. A premature awareness of their true state of helplessness may exceed the baby's limited abilities to tolerate distress. This may arise either in a few episodes of extreme distress or through ongoing relational non-attunement on the part of caregivers.[20]

In this case, the baby must find a way to defend themself against intolerable reality. Two alternatives are available – they can either develop a phantasy that they and mother are not separate at all; or they can develop a phantasy that, although they are separate from mother, they do not need her. Either way the original anxiety-provoking problem is solved, but at the cost of a distortion in the perception of the real relation between self and other. These two defences are the narcissistic defences, so-called because the infantile solution is carried forward into relationships in adulthood, which are coloured by the projection of parts of the self onto the other. In a sense, when the patient is relating to others, he is always looking at his own reflection, a projected aspect of himself, instead of being able to relate to others as separate intentional beings with motivations that might bear little relation to his own.

In psychodynamic terms, narcissistic difficulties differ fundamentally from 'neurotic' difficulties. In neurotic conditions, the psychological defences are intrapsychic, being defences within the psyche of the individual. For example, in repression, psychological conflicts are resolved by rendering problematic mental contents unconscious. In contrast, in narcissistic difficulties the defences are interpersonal, the defence mechanisms being projection and projective identification. A narcissistic defence requires the presence of another person to participate in the defence and to manage anxiety. In some instances, the need for the immediate presence of the other is obvious, in others the 'other' must be available, but kept at a distance because of the projection they carry. Before going further, it is necessary to explain the psychodynamic term Projective Identification (PI) (see also section on 'Projective Identification' in Chapter 2). PI differs from projection. In PI the patient's projection elicits an identification in the other so that the other unconsciously becomes an active participant in the patient's projective world, unwittingly acting out an internal object relationship.

Ron Britton described two forms of PI which he considers of central importance in people with narcissistic difficulties.[21] These two forms correspond to the two narcissistic defences described above. They are acquisitive and attributive projective identification.

In acquisitive PI, the mental and bodily attributes of the other are treated as though they truly belong to the patient – in this state of mind the patient behaves as though 'You are me'. Otherness is denied, two minds and bodies are felt to be one. In the original infantile situation, mother is related to as though she and baby exist inside the same skin and all that represents separateness between them is attacked.

In attributive PI, painful or threatening attributes of the self are disavowed and treated as though they belong to the other – the subjective connection with the disavowed part is denied, one mind/body is felt to have become two. In this state of mind, the patient behaves as though 'I am you'. Dependent parts of the self are projected, the patient behaving as though they need nothing and provide all.

It is important to emphasise that both defences operate at a psychological and somatic, bodily level. Both mind and body of self and other participate in the projective process. The real external world 'other' participates through experiencing a characteristic countertransference in each state which may be somatic, and through the implicit pressure to act in accordance with the patient's phantasy in response to the projective process (see later section on Transference, Countertransference, and Formulation).

Concreteness and Containment: What Admission Means

One more important concept is required to make sense of patients with such complex presentations – that concept is the concreteness of infantile emotional experience and the process of symbolisation required to relate and communicate symbolically and verbally in adulthood. Small babies do not experience themselves or their parents conceptually, they experience them directly through gesture, facial expression, and the timing and vitality of interactions between parent and child.[22,23,24] Containment in the first instance is physical 'holding'. The infant may infer in the course of time that the actions of their parent are motivated by a mind and ultimately may come to feel that they are contained by or held in the mind of others, but this is not their experience in the first instance. From these concrete beginnings it appears the dyadic interaction between mother and infant is essential to the development of the capacity to symbolise.[25]

From birth, infants orient themselves towards the faces of others and spontaneously engage in playful interaction. The developmental importance of this is demonstrated by the still face experiment and the distress evident in infants who are temporarily deprived of the anticipated responsiveness of their mothers.[26] In the first instance, infants see the world from their own egocentric perspective. Dyadic interaction brings about an important developmental shift. Towards the end of the first year of life, a new realisation occurs that their point of view is just one amongst many. Before this change comes about, the baby will look at their parent's hand if they point to an object. Subsequently they will follow the parent's gaze to see what they are looking at.[25] They have taken the first steps from an egocentric to an allocentric perspective, that is, the ability to recognise another's point of view. This allocentric perspective, also referred to as secondary inter-subjectivity,[22] appears to be a critical step in the development of the capacity for abstract thinking, symbolic play, and semantic language during the second year of life.[27]

In short, the capacity for symbolisation is dependent upon the capacity of parents and their babies to engage affectively in dyadic interaction during this critical period.

Patients with narcissistic difficulties may have significantly impaired capacities for symbolisation.[28,29] These may arise because of neurodevelopmental vulnerabilities, relational and mentalizing failures during development, or the capacity to symbolise may be undermined by the projective mechanisms described above.[21,3] The absence of the capacity to symbolise has some important consequences for:

- The perception of their surroundings and relationships. They experience themselves as trapped inside or outside the physical spaces they occupy, and similarly either excluded from others' minds or trapped within others' controlling influence.[18]
- The quality of the objects which populate their internal world.[21,30]
- The way in which patients with these difficulties communicate through body language.

One of the important principles here is that patients with narcissistic defences are often developmentally archaic (sometimes referred to as 'primitive') in psychodynamic terms. This may be because psychological development has been delayed by constitutional or relational deficits or as a result of regression. Regression commonly arises in patients with narcissistic defences following separations from significant others in adulthood, or from the patient's emerging dependence on professionals. In these circumstances, internal objects are concrete, archaic, and persecutory and are projected into the environment. In people with a well-developed capacity for symbolisation, containment of overwhelming feelings can be provided by being understood and held in mind by a dependable other person. For patients with narcissistic defences, this symbolised form of containment is not enough. For those with the most severe difficulties, relief from overwhelming anxiety can only be achieved by being inside a physically containing object such as an inpatient setting. However, because of their primitive concrete relational world, the physical setting tends to be experienced in a claustro-agoraphobic way.[18] This is a paradoxical emotional world in which the solution to the emotional problem for one part of the patient threatens the survival of another part. It has important implications for psychotherapeutic work and psychiatric management of those patients with the most severe and complex relational difficulties.

In these patients, the mode of communication is concrete, predominantly carried out through body language. Emotional feelings are not put into words but communicated directly, for example, through self-harm, disordered eating, or somatic symptoms. These expressions through action evoke emotional responses and disturbed states of mind directly through PI in others.

Transference, Countertransference, and Formulation

For professionals one of the most taxing aspects of work with this patient group is the paradoxical transference and countertransference. This can best be understood by recognising that some patients with marked relational difficulties tend not to experience mixed feelings, their feelings are split, and they commonly experience themselves in parts which are in conflict with one another. The solution to emotional problems with separation for one part of the personality – that is, containment as an inpatient – threatens another part of the personality which feels trapped and controlled.

Clinical Example 1

In the patient's paradoxical internal world, care and harm can feel inseparable. This is perhaps not surprising given that many have had traumatic experiences during childhood. Trauma tends to be relived rather than remembered. When a person with marked relational difficulties in an inpatient setting relives a traumatic experience, they may try to harm themselves. If detained under the Mental Health Act, nursing staff may feel obliged by their position of legal responsibility to intervene to keep the patient safe. This can lead to nurses restraining a patient who is determined to harm himself. In doing so nurses are often aware that they are enacting the original traumatic incident. They may feel that they have become the abuser whilst trying to fulfil their duty of care. If they stay with the patient and observe them one-to-one, they can soon realise that removing responsibility for staying safe can also make the patient more disturbed. Not surprisingly, they may conclude that the admission is not useful or even harmful and the multi-disciplinary team may decide collectively to discharge the patient from their section and from hospital, on the basis that they are not making therapeutic use of the admission. Within a few hours or days, the patient's repeated high-risk suicide attempts and numerous Mental Health Act assessments result in readmission in one setting or another. Teams can feel unable to escape a re-enactment with the patient in which they alternately 'trap' the patient by detaining them in inpatient settings and 'drop' them when the relational consequences become intolerable. The revolving door continues despite the team's best efforts to provide therapeutic care.

Commonly the whole health and social care systems are involved in trying to manage such complex patients and may feel stretched to breaking point. Under such circumstances, finding a way forward for the whole system and the patient requires a clear formulation of the patient's problem, which can be shared with the patient and the agencies involved in their care. The formulation is practically useful, informing co-ordinated system-wide care and identifying what form of psychotherapeutic work is needed. It is also emotionally useful in making sense of the relational world professionals are engaged in when working with the patient.

Psychodynamic formulation aims to account for all the patient's associated symptoms and the relational repetitions taking place with the team. Understanding PI and the concrete emotional world of the patient is an important step in being able to develop a formulation. The Relational Affective Formulation (RAF) is a helpful template for developing formulations for complex narcissistic cases. Its starting point is the claustro-agoraphobic transference and countertransference which commonly arises, as introduced earlier. This transference arises from an internal object world that Henri Rey termed the claustro-agoraphobic dilemma (this concept was introduced in Chapter 13).[18] This can be most easily understood by looking more closely at the two types of projective identification described by Britton.

Acquisitive Projective Identification (PI)

Earlier this was described as a solution to the problem of premature awareness of the absolute dependence on a separate other. To recap, in this solution the separateness of the other person is denied so that two people (self and other) are experienced in phantasy as one person or are felt to exist inside the same skin. In projective identification the other is unconsciously pressed to act in ways which conform with this phantasy, that is, as though the mind and body of the other belong to the self. So long as the other behaves in accordance with this phantasy, then the other is loved. As soon as the other behaves in a way that brings home the reality of their separateness, they are 'hated'. This may take the form of aggressive behaviour, either physically or mentally, until the other person falls back into compliance with the acquisitive phantasy. This not only applies interpersonally between the patient and professionals but also from the patient towards any aspect of his own mental or physical self that reminds him of the reality of his separateness from and dependence upon the outside world. For example, in the physical domain this may include appetite and the need for food, drink, or sex which must be constantly available, leading to bingeing or sexual vulnerability. In the psychological domain, adult functioning may be undermined because it signifies independence and so the patient may become more concrete and childlike in their behaviour.

Acquisitive PI results in a state of mind which has clinical and interpersonal characteristics, which all occur together. It comes about following an event in which the narcissistic patient can no longer remain unaware of their separateness from, or loss of, a person whom they depend upon. Following the loss or separation the patient feels uncontained, dropped, and agoraphobic. The solution to the conscious recognition of separateness is to 'get inside the object'. The 'object' here refers to an internal maternal object in phantasy which is enacted concretely in the act of gaining admission to hospital. This may be brought about by life-threatening para-suicidal behaviour which generates anxiety in others, realistic or otherwise, about the imminent possibility of the patient's death. Where this results in admission, this is experienced by the patient as a form of re-entry to mother's body, the hospital being the 'brick mother'.[18] What psychiatrists call 'risk', psychodynamic psychotherapists call 'projected anxiety'. In acquisitive states, anxieties about imminent abandonment and states of helplessness are projected into the team though the patient's threats to abscond or to make suicide attempts. To manage these risks/anxieties the team may detain the patient so that they can't leave or keep them under constant observation to prevent high-risk suicide attempts. However, this leads to a cascade of consequences. Once 'inside' and receiving one-to-one care, the patient feels themselves to be 'inside mother' in a system that provides all. In this state and environment, they increasingly lose contact with or attack their capacity to function as an adult driving a regression to increasingly archaic and infantile forms of relating. This form of progressive regression was described by Balint as 'malignant regression', contrasting it with therapeutic regression in the service of psychological development, which is characteristic of patients with less severe difficulties. This can be seen to take the form of childlike behaviour such as loss of continence or the reliving and re-enactment of traumatic childhood experiences, as described in the first clinical example. This can extend to loss of the capacity to communicate verbally and psychomotor retardation more usually associated with severe depression. These presentations are commonly mistaken for depression which can also occur commonly as an associated condition. Patients in this state may in fact appear to be overwhelmed with feelings that they are unable to express (feelings without words). Britton called this hyper-subjectivity. As he puts it, in acquisitive states, objectivity is intolerable. This type of projective identification was first described by Rosenfeld who called it thin-skinned narcissism.[31] This 'thin skin' describes the interpersonal and sensory boundary of the self, which can all but disappear with sensitised visual and auditory perception and overwhelming affect.

Clinical Example 2 Predominant state: acquisitive PI

This account is highly condensed, describing an intervention by an experienced psychoanalytic psychotherapist. It is not a recommendation for routine practice.

Miss A developed disordered eating in her late teens as she was thinking about leaving home. She refused to eat her mother's food and developed orthorexia, confining herself to eating one food type at a time. Following an argument with her mother, she tried to storm out but on reaching the front door was physically unable to cross the threshold. She got a holiday job and whilst at work one day came to a stop again. She was unable to move and stopped eating and drinking. No physical abnormality was found and she was admitted to an acute mental health unit. She remained akinetic and mute, was thought to have catatonia, and this was presumed to be a first psychotic episode. She remained unresponsive despite ECT and a long admission during which she was incontinent and required full nursing care, including nasogastric feeding. Following a long admission, her diagnosis was revised to be 'dissociative' rather than psychotic.

She emerged from this state after a therapeutic intervention. During phases when her symptoms improved a little, she could indicate her wishes by eye movements or hand gestures. The psychotherapist visited her on the ward and carefully reviewed her history. Miss A gestured her willingness to be seen so the therapist instructed her to stand and applying gentle pressure to the small of her back propelled her to a seat in the garden whilst commenting as they went 'This is interesting, it is like I am the mind and you the body and we are joined just as though you were my arm or leg'; Miss A nodded. Once seated outdoors the therapist pointed out how Miss A had come to a stop when she was trying to work out how to leave home. Perhaps going to hospital had been the only way she could manage to leave, but now she was stuck inside again. If the therapist could arrange for her to live in supported accommodation and attend psychotherapy as an outpatient, would this solve the problem for her? Miss A signalled her agreement that this was what she wanted. A day or two later she emerged from the akinetic state.

Formulation

Miss A's mother, by her own admission, had significant problems managing loss and separation herself and had not been able to support Miss A to develop an identity as a separate person in her own right during her early years. Because Miss A was not able to tolerate loss and separation, she could not emotionally manage the imminent arrival of adulthood in her teens. She attempted to separate concretely by refusing her mother's food (an attributive dynamic) and attempting to leave the house only to find herself unable to motivate her own action to cross the threshold. Her akinetic state, incontinence, and food refusal requiring 24-hour nursing care represented an unconsciously motivated profound regression to an infantile state to relieve her from the anxieties of separation. She required the nurses to care for her as if she was a baby who could do nothing for herself. The akinesis represented a state of psychosomatic unity between herself and others in which she passively responded to their instructions as though she was a part of their body. The psychotherapist who had come across these presentations before conveyed her to an outdoor space, recognising her to be in a 'trapped inside' acquisitive state, describing to Miss A the state of psychosomatic identity as she did so. The conversation about finding a solution to Miss A's problem in making a separation, by providing her with therapy and an alternative place to live so she didn't return home, appeared to bring her out of the regressed state. It is worth noticing that intervention was as much concrete (conveying her outdoors, providing her with a place to live) as it was verbal.

Attributive Projective Identification (PI)

This is the alternative defensive solution to the problem of premature awareness of the absolute dependence on a separate other. To recap, in this 'solution', painful, threatening, or dependent attributes of the self are disavowed and treated as though they belong to the other. The subjective origin of the disavowed part is denied. In this way one mind is felt to have become two, the boundary of the self being redrawn to exclude the disavowed part. The countertransference in attributive PI differs from acquisitive in that professionals may find the patient difficult to engage, to be remote emotionally, and poor at attending appointments whilst aspects of their behaviour, such as not eating or psychosomatic presentations, may mean they cannot be discharged. The patient appears claustrophobic, being afraid of that disavowed aspect of themselves which would lead to 'admission' to a trap from which they cannot escape. Where these presentations are very risky, professionals may go to increasing lengths to engage the patient. A patient in this state may feel it is the professional who needs them to engage rather than recognising that they themselves need help. It seems the patient needs professionals to continue to be involved, so that others feel left in the state of helpless uncertainty, which the patient cannot allow themself to feel. Whereas patients in acquisitive states direct their aggressive feelings towards anything that threatens to separate them from the care-taking object, patients in an attributive state direct their aggressive feelings towards anything in the internal or external world that makes them aware of their true need for others. Dependence is seen as weakness and is attacked or suppressed (these dynamics are relevant for some people who experience long-term homelessness – see Chapter 20).

In contrast to the regressed presentation of patients in acquisitive states, attributing patients present as pseudo-independent, feeling they need nothing which they cannot provide for themselves. This extends as far as not needing food and drink in which case restricting eating disorders are the presenting symptom. They may however maintain a connection with the disavowed dependent part of themselves by compulsively providing for others. In contrast with the depressed presentation of patients in acquisitive states, their mood may be elevated. They may be over-active, mentally and physically, and are grandiose and omnipotent, feeling they need nothing and are able to provide everything. Patients in this state have difficulty experiencing their emotional feelings as belonging to them. The patient cannot be the subject of his own experience, subjectivity being intolerable. Britton described this as hyper-objectivity. They may talk about themselves as though they are a professional talking about a patient who is not present in the room (words without feeling). This is Rosenfeld's thick-skinned narcissism.[31] This 'thick skin' describes the interpersonal and sensory boundary of the self which can seem impenetrable. This is the case in relation to other people, but also to parts of the body. Parts of the body, which represent the patient's need for the other or which are perceived by the patient to be weak, may be designated as other or not part of the self. In this case the patient may present with dysmorphophobic symptoms, seeking to have the offending part removed.[32]

Clinical Example 3 Predominant state: attributive PI

Miss B, a woman in her late twenties, had been an inpatient since her early teens. She had post-traumatic stress disorder, dissociation, paranoid ideas, and severe self-harm. This was thought to result from sexual abuse within the family. Her mother had mental health problems and hospital admissions when Miss B was growing up. When discharged home from inpatient care, Miss B persisted in severe self-harm and suicide attempts. She self-harmed when her mother and she disagreed. Her agoraphobia prevented her from leaving home unaccompanied, but when talking to professionals she felt claustrophobic and had to walk out. Her moods fluctuated – when 'high' she felt invincible, when low she would stay in bed. She started psychotherapy in a day programme and was observed to be in a constant state of physical activity. She was insightful about other patients but kept a physical and emotional distance. She wanted to leave home where she lived with her mother. She said her mother behaved as though Miss B's mind or body belonged to her. Arrangements were made for her to move into supported accommodation. Once the arrangements were made, she stopped self-harming but also stopped eating and started to exercise compulsively. She rapidly lost weight and was admitted to an eating disorder unit. When she had no option but to eat in this setting, she became acutely disturbed, feeling she had permitted the devil to enter her body and began to cut herself to 'let the evil out'.

Formulation

This case example illustrates how the two forms of PI can be employed at different times by the same patient. Miss B recognised that she and her mother were in a state of identity, or acquisitive projective identification. She tried to use the day therapy programme to support her to separate from her mother and leave home. Being unable to manage a true psychological separation from her family, that is, acknowledging and grieving for the loss, she resorted to the alternative form of projective identification, attributive PI, to deny her need for her mother as a way to escape her trapped state of mind. This attributive state took the form of restricting her food intake. In this state Miss B described her mother tightening the apron strings when she tried to leave home. Whilst there might be some truth in this, she saw professionals in the same light, perceiving their concern about her weight loss as unnecessarily controlling. She had disavowed her own needy self, projecting it into her mother/staff whom she then distanced herself from. When her food restriction became life-threatening and she was admitted to an eating disorder unit where she had to start eating, she experienced eating as allowing a poison inside herself which she then had to cut out of her body, so her self-harm returned.

Acquisition, Attribution, and the Boundary of the Self

In both acquisitive and attributive states, there is a change of location of the boundary of the psychosomatic self (Figure 14.1). In both, the presence of another, for example the professional, is required to manage claustro-agoraphobic anxieties. The 'other' is both the source of the anxiety and the means of managing it. In acquisition, two minds/bodies become one. In attribution, one mind/body becomes two. Acquisitive states are characterised by psychosomatic identity with the other. In attributive states, the boundary of the psychosomatic self contracts, excluding unwanted parts of the self which are projected simultaneously into others (including professionals) and into parts of the body which signify weakness or dependence. These body parts are then disavowed and felt to be 'other'.

These two states account for the transference/countertransference relationship between the patient, professionals, and the settings in which they work, as well as the psychic and somatic symptoms patients present with. They are the basis of the formulation in Table 14.1 which summarises the states of mind arising from Acquisitive and Attributive PI, which we refer to as the 'Relational Affective Formulation' (RAF). The RAF can be a useful tool for consultation and therapeutic work in teams working with highly complex patients.[3] The

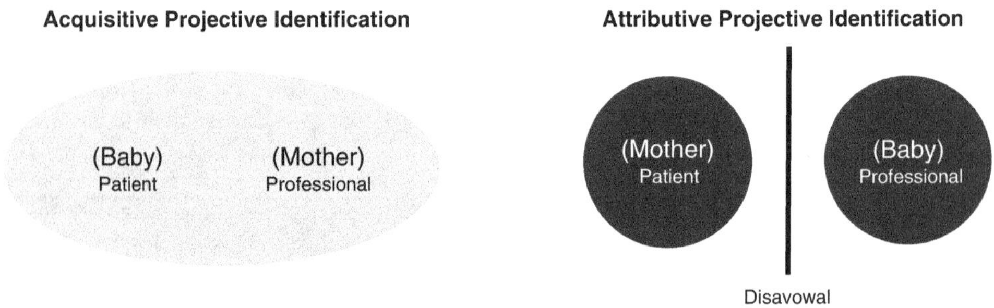

Figure 14.1 Depiction of self-other relations in acquisitive and attributive states. This figure depicts a patient in relation to a health professional. The words in brackets represent the role (baby or mother) the patient and professional are inhabiting, in the patient's phantasy.

Table 14.1 The Relational Affective Formulation (RAF)

Agoraphobic state (acquisitive PI)	Claustrophobic state (attributive PI)
'Only love' (split off hate)	'Hatred of love' (split off love)
'I only want to be with you'	'Only want to be apart from you'
'I want to be inside the object'	'I want to be outside the object'
'I hate the possibility of separation from you'	I hate the possibility of feeling attached to you'
'I have feelings without words'	'I have words without feelings'
'I am the baby, you are the adult' (malignant regression)	'I am the adult, you are the baby' (pseudo-independence)
Thin-skinned	Thick-skinned
Depressed mood	Elevated mood
Ultimately feel trapped	Ultimately feel dropped

claustro-agoraphobic internal state drives the pattern of revolving door admissions. The two states of mind, being a consequence of splitting, are more or less mirror images of each other. Patients may either remain relatively stable in one of these states or the other, or they may alternate rapidly between states producing affective instability. The paradox described earlier is clear – each state is oblivious to the existence of the other. The fulfilment of the needs of one state is the realisation of the greatest terror of the other. So the relationship between these two states of mind within the individual is highly conflicted and in a state of mutually assured destruction. This is termed a narcissistic conflict.

Using the Relational Affective Formulation (RAF) in Practice

The RAF is part of the Relational Affective Model, an adaptation of established psychodynamic therapeutic community practice designed for patients with marked relational difficulties who are detained under the Mental Health Act or have associated conditions which would otherwise exclude them from therapy.[2,33,34] The model defines the overall service design most likely to be effective with such patients when in hospital and the adaptations of therapeutic technique required of the specialist psychotherapeutic team.

Designing a Psychotherapeutic Pathway: A System-Wide Approach

Too often, services are configured in ways that inadvertently replicate the claustro-agoraphobic anxieties of patients with relational difficulties. The case studies illustrate the tendency of services to admit patients to hospital, sometimes detained in locked settings, and then to discharge them to outpatient services where therapeutic help may not be available. Psychotherapy of any model is likely to be less effective when provided in a setting that replicates internal world anxieties. The RAF can inform the design of a therapeutic pathway for patients with relational complexities, which requires a graduated transition from inpatient to day patient to outpatient care whilst therapy is in progress, so that the anxieties about separation can be worked on as concrete care is reduced.[35] To be effective at containing patients outside hospital, therapeutic work must be intensive. For example, a day programme offering three or four full days a week of group and individual psychotherapy and psychodynamic psychosocial practice for patients leaving hospital and a step-down outpatient programme offering at least twice weekly therapy. The duration of therapy should be a minimum of three years. A small number of the most complex and risky patients will need specialist psychotherapeutic care in inpatient settings. The majority can make the transition to a specialist non-residential therapeutic day and outpatient service if it is commissioned alongside supported housing which includes some 24-hour support. This provides a route out of inpatient care. The process of engaging such complex patients and working with the many agencies who are involved is time-consuming and requires a well-staffed specialist outreach team with expertise in personality functioning. The psychotherapeutic and housing support teams must develop a close working relationship. This can be facilitated by training the housing team to provide a psychologically informed environment for patients attending the therapeutic programme (see also Chapter 17 for some discussion about psychologically informed services).[36]

The therapeutic community approach (see R. Haigh's 'The quintessence of a therapeutic environment'[37] for further reading on this approach) in both day and outpatient settings, provides the relational containment required for patients to progress from reliance on concrete containment and inpatient care. The RAF provides a framework for staff to understand patients' states of mind and adapt their therapeutic technique accordingly. The formulation informs how individual practitioners practice, how the team understands the patient, and the relationships between patients attending the service. It is also used for the assessment and management of risks and acts as a container for professionals' anxieties. The risk management and allocation of support is done in multi-agency meetings, when the formulation is shared with all professionals and the patient to plan the management of the crises, which commonly arise when patients with such complex problems are in psychotherapy (see section on Risk Assessment, below). Contingency plans are agreed with the patient and other agencies as a therapeutic contract before therapeutic work starts. For patients who are not able to use therapy or who do not want it, the RAF can be used as a consultation tool for teams responsible for their ongoing care.

Adaptations of Therapeutic Technique in Specialist Psychotherapeutic Teams

Psychotherapeutic technique is different in acquisitive and attributive states. The RAF helps the team to identify the state which the patient is in. They can then think about how to manage that state therapeutically using both therapeutic relationships and internal and external spaces of the building itself.

An important therapeutic community principle used in managing these states is that the patients project their internal states into the team whose feelings become split about how best to work with the patient(s). Through reflective practice, the team think about this split and put together a picture of the patient's internal world (see also Chapter 18 on Reflective Practice). This thinking together is conveyed to the patient(s) through the team's relational behaviour, providing the patient with a coherent understanding of themself as a whole. The quality of the splitting is particularly powerful working with the most complex patients and can take the form of irreconcilable differences within the team. The formulation can help in identifying this along with paying close attention to the emotional pressures against

Table 14.2 Mutative factors in the Relational Affective Model

1. Containment	From concrete to relational containment – relational containment is defined in psychodynamic terms. The team is contained if the wider system of managers and clinicians understands its purpose and supports it to undertake the task.
2. Holding regression and flight	When patients first engage in therapy, they go through claustro-agoraphobic crises. They may regress profoundly in individual therapy or try to prevent this through disengaging or, for example, restricting food intake or taking non-prescribed drugs. Risk assessment and the way the team manages these crises supports the patient to stay in therapy and avoid readmission.
3. Triangulation	Regular reflective practice – staff get together to think for the patient's benefit, modelling the parental couple, and thoughtful mentalization.
4. Splitting and integration	Therapeutic community with individual therapy allows multiple transference to team members and patients which allows splitting to emerge. This is then integrated through supervision and reflective practice.
5. Linking	Meetings between agencies, between the team, and intrapsychically are prioritised.
6. Translating concrete modes of relating to symbolic	Body language is translated into words by 'doing with' alongside the patient in psychosocial practice.
7. Working with body language and the body as other	Using weight charts and blood results in community meetings and reflective practice to understand what the patient is communicating through eating behaviour or physical health presentations. Therapists understanding the link between the transference and the pattern of relating to the body which generates the physical health presentation.
8. Therapeutic use of space	Using inside and outside spaces to help manage claustro-agoraphobic anxieties.
9. Working with transitions and endings	Attending at all times to the realities of separation and loss.

meeting, talking, and thinking. When reflective practice is lost the team lose the 'triangular space' – that is, the ability to take a more objective, 'third position' – which is crucial in promoting symbolisation. The adaptations of technique specified in the Relational Affective Model are summarised below (see Table 14.2).

For psychotherapists working outside the setting of a fully funded specialist pathway, the adaptations of technique can be applied in individual, group, or family therapy.

The RAF and Risk Assessment

One of the main challenges facing teams working with patients with complex relational difficulties is managing risk. Understanding risk as projected anxiety makes it possible to understand it in interpersonal terms, which can lead to a more therapeutic and containing approach. Patients may feel bewildered by their shifting states of mind and feel they are 'too much' for the teams working with them. This adds to their sense of themselves as poisonous and destructive, and to feelings of hopelessness and suicidality. Using the RAF to draw up a psychodynamic risk assessment is an important therapeutic process in itself, setting out the patient's and team's understanding of the relational drivers for the patient's symptoms and making clear that the team are prepared for their most difficult presentations from the outset. It is an important container of anxiety for professionals and patients alike.

The first step in drawing up a RAF is a psychodynamic psychotherapy assessment. The RAF is based on this and the discussion with the patient in the multidisciplinary team. It is drawn up in a similar way to any other psychodynamic formulation, linking early object relationships with current transference and presenting symptoms (see also Figure 7.1 on 'Malan's Triangles' in Chapter 7).[38] This can be organised in the following three areas:

Early Attachment History and Object Relations

A detailed history of early development is obtained from the patient during the psychotherapy assessment and from relatives, where appropriate. This focuses on:

- The quality of relationship between the patient and parental figures
- The perceived relationship between parental figures
- Relationships with siblings, extended family, and other adults
- Childhood adverse experiences
- Response to separations, for example, first attending school

Current Relational Patterns with Professionals

- Explored with the patient and professionals in multi-agency meetings, discussing the pattern of professionals' responses to symptoms and risky behaviour
- Time for professionals alone allows an opportunity to speak freely about splits in the team

Symptoms

- A detailed account and psychodynamic understanding of the crises leading to admission, recognising that this may recur during therapy
- Listing all associated symptoms including psychotic symptoms

Pulling Together the Formulation

The RAF is drawn up with the patient and the multi-agency team, by drawing a table with two columns, one for Acquisitive presentations and one for Attributive. Then:

- Show the patient and the team the generic RAF (Table 14.1) and describe the two states of mind and the conflict between them
- Invite the patient to work with the team to allocate each of their symptoms to the acquisitive or attributive side of the table, and to describe the objects relations and relational repetitions associated with that symptom. This is led by the patient who, along with the team, puts into words in as much detail as possible what they feel when the symptom occurs and describes the relational context

- Ask the patient and team to think how they would interact if they functioned as a whole instead of as a split self. The aim is to be specific about how change can happen. This is put in a merged cell for each symptom on the table, implying integration of the split

This leads into thinking about how to manage the risks associated with the symptom in a way that is going to promote development, that is, this becomes the risk management plan.

Concluding Remarks

This chapter outlines how understanding projective processes can inform psychiatric and psychotherapeutic management and treatment of patients with complex relational difficulties. A formulation-based therapeutic approach like the Relational Affective Model can provide a way forward for patients and teams where symptom-specific treatment pathways have not worked.

References

1. Freud S. The Ego and the Id, Standard Edition of the Complete Psychological Works of Sigmund Freud, Vol. 19. London: Hogarth Press and the Institute of Psycho-Analysis; 1923.
2. Britton R. Narcissism and narcissistic disorders. Sex, Death, and the Superego. Experiences in Psychoanalysis. London: Routledge; 2003.
3. Mizen CS. Neuroscience, mind and meaning: an attempt at synthesis in a Relational Affective Hypothesis. Psychoanalytic Psychotherapy. 2015 Oct 2;29(4):363–81.
4. International Classification of Diseases 11th ed.; ICD-11; World Health Organization, 2019
5. Zanarini MC, Frankenburg FR, Khera GS et al.. Treatment histories of borderline inpatients. Comprehensive Psychiatry. 2001 Mar 1;42(2):144–50.
6. National Institute for Clinical Excellence. Borderline personality disorder: recognition and management. Clinical guideline. Published 28 January 2009
7. Lewis KL, Fanaian M, Kotze B et al. Mental health presentations to acute psychiatric services: 3-year study of prevalence and readmission risk for personality disorders compared with psychotic, affective, substance or other disorders. BJPsych Open. 2019 Jan;5(1).
8. Skodol A, Stein M, Hermann R. Borderline Personality Disorder: Epidemiology, Pathogenesis, Clinical Features, Course, Assessment, and Diagnosis. UpToDate. Waltham, MA: UpToDate. 2019.
9. Cassin SE, von Ranson KM. Personality and eating disorders: a decade in review. Clinical psychology review. 2005 Nov 1;25 (7):895–916.
10. Sansone RA, Farukhi S, Wiederman MW. Utilization of primary care physicians in borderline personality. General Hospital Psychiatry. 2011 Jul 1;33(4):343–6.
11. Crimlisk HL, Bhatia K, Cope H et al. Slater revisited: 6 year follow up study of patients with medically unexplained motor symptoms. BMJ. 1998 Feb 14;316 (7131):582–6.
12. Bowden-Jones O, Iqbal MZ, Tyrer P et al. Cosmic Study Team. Prevalence of personality disorder in alcohol and drug services and associated comorbidity. Addiction. 2004 Oct;99 (10):1306–14.
13. Dudas RB, Lovejoy C, Cassidy S et al. The overlap between autistic spectrum conditions and borderline personality disorder. *PLoS ONE*, 2017[Sep][8], Vol 12 [9][e0184447].
14. Fowler JC, Clapp JD, Madan A et al. A naturalistic longitudinal study of extended inpatient treatment for adults with borderline personality disorder: an examination of treatment response, remission and deterioration. Journal of Affective Disorders. 2018 Aug 1;235:323–3.

15. Menzies IE. A case-study in the functioning of social systems as a defence against anxiety: a report on a study of the nursing service of a general hospital. Human Relations. 1960 May;13(2):95–121.
16. Freud S. The Ego and the Id, Standard Edition of the Complete Psychological Works of Sigmund Freud, Vol. 19. London: Hogarth Press and the Institute of Psycho-Analysis; 1923.
17. Freud S. On narcissism: an introduction. Standard Edition of the Complete Psychological Works of Sigmund Freud, Vol. 19. London: Hogarth Press; 1957.
18. Rey H. Universals of Psychoanalysis in the Treatment of Psychotic and Borderline States. Free Association Books; 1994.
19. Winnicott DW. The theory of the parent-infant relationship. International Journal of Psychoanalysis 196041:585–95.
20. Fonagy P, Gergely G, Target M. The parent–infant dyad and the construction of the subjective self. Journal of Child Psychology and Psychiatry. 2007 Mar;48 (3–4):288–328.
21. Britton R. Narcissistic problems in sharing space. In Sex, Death and the Superego. Experiences in psychoanalysis. Karnac; 2003.
22. Trevarthen C, Hubley P. Secondary intersubjectivity: confidence, confiding and acts of meaning in the first year. In A Lock, ed. Action Gesture and Symbol: The Emergence of Language. London Academic Press; 1978. pp. 183–229.
23. Tronick EZ. Emotions and emotional communication in infants. Parent-Infant Psychodynamics. 2018 Nov 9:35–53.
24. Stern DN. The Interpersonal World of the Infant: A View from Psychoanalysis and Developmental Psychology. Routledge; 2018 Apr 19.
25. Hobson P. The Cradle of Thought: Exploring the Origins of Thinking, Pan Books; 2004.
26. Brazelton TB, Tronick E, Adamson L et al. Early mother-infant reciprocity. Parent-infant Interaction. 1975;33(137–154): 122.
27. Hobson JA, Hobson RP. Identification: The missing link between joint attention and imitation? Development and Psychopathology. 2007 Apr;19(2):411–31.
28. Ruocco AC. The neuropsychology of borderline personality disorder: a meta-analysis and review. Psychiatry Research. 2005 Dec 15;137(3):191–202.
29. Derks YP, Westerhof GJ, Bohlmeijer ET. A meta-analysis on the association between emotional awareness and borderline personality pathology. Journal of Personality Disorders. 2017 Jun;31 (3):362–84.
30. Segal, H. Notes on symbol formation. International Journal of Psychoanalysis 1957 38:391–397.
31. Rosenfeld, H. Impasse and Interpretation – Therapeutic and Anti-Therapeutic Factors in the Psychoanalytic Treatment of Psychotic, Borderline, and Neurotic Patients. London: Routledge; 1987
32. Mizen CS. The self and alien selves in psyche and soma. *Journal of Analytical Psychology* (in press).
33. Mizen CS. Narcissistic disorder and the failure of symbolisation: a Relational Affective Hypothesis. Medical Hypotheses. 2014 Sep 1;83(3):254–62.
34. Mizen CS. Towards a Relational Affective Theory of personality disorder. Psychoanalytic Psychotherapy. 2014 Oct 2;28(4):357–78.
35. Mizen CS. (2019) Business Case for Devon Partnership NHS Trust Personality Disorder Service.
36. Haigh R, Harrison T, Johnson R et al. Psychologically informed environments and the "Enabling Environments" initiative. Housing, Care and Support. 2012 Mar 9.
37. Haigh R. The quintessence of a therapeutic environment. Therapeutic Communities: The International Journal of Therapeutic Communities. 2013 34(1):6–15.
38. Hinshelwood RD. Psychodynamic formulation in assessment for psychotherapy. British Journal of Psychotherapy. 1991 Dec;8(2):166–74.

Part 4:

Application of Psychodynamic Psychotherapy in Different Populations and in Different Settings

Chapter 15

Applications of Psychodynamic Theory and Principles outside of Specialist Psychotherapy Settings

Table of Contents

Introduction 231
The Invisible Relationship 234
Staff Responses to Patients who have Complicated Relationships with Care 235
Thinking about 'Engagement' 237
Tolerating Slow or No Change 237
Relational Health and the Inverse Care Law 238
Potential for Therapeutic Change 239
Splitting within a Clinical Team 239
System Dynamics 241
Concluding Remarks 241

Introduction

This chapter provides an introduction to psychodynamic theory as applied to settings outwith the specialist psychotherapy clinic and paves the way for the chapters that follow in Part 4 of this book.

Human life is fundamentally relational. We all start in an utterly dependent situation: the foetus in the uterine environment, connected to the mother for survival and development. Expectant parents begin to form a psychological relationship with the child-to-be during pregnancy or earlier, in their ideas, anxieties, and fantasies about having a child and becoming a parent. This relationship is influenced by the parents' own inner worlds and experiences of being a child and being parented; it evolves as the pregnancy develops, the baby is born, and grows up.[1]

Long after the umbilical cord is cut, our psychological and physical existence remains dependent upon the presence and quality of the relationships we form with others. This dependency on relationships continues throughout the lifespan. There are myriad ways these early relationships can play out – some are more conducive to the infant forming trust

Box 15.1 If we can form trusting relationships with others, this makes it possible to:

- Make sense of our feelings and intentions (this links to mentalization, see Chapter 2)
- Get help with things we can't do ourselves
- Learn new things

with others, others are less so. The capacity to trust others enough to communicate our needs and take in what others have to offer plays a large part in influencing our mental and physical health and wellbeing (see Box 15.1, and also Chapter 2).

The implications of this are broad. Any situation where people need to come into contact with each other will involve a relational dynamic that may go some way in influencing the outcome of the interaction. This is true in healthcare settings, but also at dinner parties, the supermarket, educational settings, the housing department, at music lessons, and so on. This relational foundation could be thought of as occurring in all settings where human beings come into contact with other human beings.

In addition, from a psychodynamic point of view, we might be interested in the relationship a person may have with food, pets, the running they do for exercise, or the record collection they own. For example, we might view 'substance misuse' as a relationship between someone and the alcohol they drink or the heroin they inject. In fact, there are times when the human capacity for attachment seems to have no bounds and no discretion about its target. We appear to have an ability to develop relationships with everything from our favourite mug to a T-shirt we bought thirty years ago. Famously, in the Robert Zemeckis (2000) film 'Cast Away', we are treated to Tom Hanks's character forming a deep and loving relationship with a volleyball, and few blink an eye. Winnicott's thinking about 'transitional objects' is relevant here, in considering how objects can be invested with special value and 'made use of' in various ways.[2]

In this chapter, we aim to convey the breadth of settings where relational dynamics can be central to their operation. Hence, we give examples from a range of settings. The examples move from the broad and everyday with piano lessons (see Example 1) and a visit to the hardware store (Example 2), to the benefits office (Example 3), and then to the more explicit caring settings of healthcare (Clinical Examples 4 and 5).

Example 1 Piano lessons

Take for example, a piano lesson involving two people, a student and a teacher. For piano-playing to be learnt, a relationship needs to develop between these two people; a vehicle of interpersonal connectivity that will allow technique to be acquired and music to be played.

The piano teacher may believe that the pupil who has sought their services will be able to trust and connect with them in a relatively uncomplicated manner, and the person seeking tuition may similarly believe that they can trust the tutor enough to take on board most of what is suggested. The pupil may also have the capacity to show vulnerability and make mistakes. Neither may be aware of, or ever articulate these assumptions to each other or even to themselves, but they will be a rate-limiting step as to how much piano-playing is actually learnt. If both parties can be open to each other, and develop a trust and connection, the skill of piano-playing might be acquired, and personal growth might occur.

Now, we imagine a situation where either party is unable to trust the other, and suspects that the other's motives are disingenuous or malevolent. Communication may be heard as deception. Not much music will be learnt – or at least, it may take a lot more work from both sides.

To be open to each other takes trust, trust that has typically been learnt in situations that arose prior to seeking out piano lessons. It may seem strange to think of trust as underpinning something so mundane, but one could think of trust us underpinning a very great deal of things that many of us take for granted.

The infantile care relationship is the first relationship we ever enter into. It is primitive and necessary and, perhaps because of that, one in which there is a great potential for anxieties to emerge. There are countless possible beginnings to a life – from a teenager who became pregnant by accident; to a couple who felt ready to have a child; to a woman who took drugs during pregnancy as a long-standing attempt to block out feelings. There may be 'ghosts in the nursery'[3] – unresolved conflicts 'in the family's past or within a parent that cast a shadow over their perception and experience of their child'.[1] Linked to these inner dynamics, there is huge variation in the outer environment in terms of stability of a place to live, poverty or economic security, and the nature of the wider family and bonds – ranging from a supportive network of people to dangerous situations.

The experiences we have in relationships, particularly through our early years (in interaction with biological and social influences), influence the development of templates of connection. These templates of self and other affect how our internal world becomes organised and colour our external experiences (see also section 'Development of the Internal Relational World' in Chapter 2). In circumstances where developmental relational experiences have carried high levels of adversity, such as trauma, neglect, and other mistreatment, without the buffering of other more nurturing relationships, future relations can be affected (see Example 2).

Example 2 Hardware shop

Version 1. Mr Green, a man in his forties, goes to a hardware shop looking for something he does not know the name of. He seeks out the shop owner and simply asks him for some help: 'I'm looking to fix this thing in the shower – the wheel-thing the shower door slides on is stuck.'

To have got to this point successfully, quite a lot has gone on. Mr Green is comfortable enough with his own vulnerability to admit to the shop owner that he has no idea what he is looking for – that he is ignorant about the name or even existence of the fitting that he is after. He trusts that the shop owner will probably respond to his lack of knowledge with reasonable sensitivity and the correct information, and be unlikely to humiliate him, mock him, or in some other way shame his request. Mr Green has a secure-enough internal world that he feels he could manage in the event that the shop keeper mocked him for his ignorance.

Version 2. Mr Blue, a man in his fifties, experienced regular and repeated shaming and humiliation when asking for help as a child. Mr Blue manages to get into the hardware shop and is asked by the shop owner if he needs any help. Because of the anxiety that this potentially helpful relationship evokes in him, a part of Mr Blue says, 'No, I'm absolutely fine', and then he proceeds to wander around the shop looking for something that he has no idea about. Mr Blue then buys something in the hope that it is correct, to avoid an anxiety that he would be humiliated for buying nothing, only to get home and find it is completely the wrong thing.

This might seem at some level a trivial consequence for Mr Blue, but when played out over many situations, a difficulty in trusting others can have extremely life-limiting consequences in terms of not being able to get one's needs met. As discussed in Chapter 2, an individual's internal world unconsciously affects how they relate to others. Others may be unconsciously invited into playing old roles that are familiar to the individual (such as rejecting, not listening, criticising), even though these roles bring difficulty and distress to both sides.

In circumstances where services and professionals are able to sustain a good-enough therapeutic environment in the face of these unconscious invitations to repeat the problematic relationship, trust may develop between service user and service, and many people are able to discover new ways of forming relationships. This depends partly on the capacities and current state of the person using a service but also, crucially, on the capacity of the professionals and services to observe and be reflective about *both* sides of the relationship. The essence of a therapeutic frame (see Chapter 5) and processes of change (see Chapter 8) apply to relationships with all caring figures as well as to specialist psychotherapists.

This chapter explores how these interpersonal dynamics may play out between service users and staff in settings where the human relationship is at the fore (such as schools, social service agencies, and hospitals). We look at the potential for positive relational change and practices that can support helpful interactions, as well as common pitfalls that may arise and the theory of how to mitigate these.

The Invisible Relationship

Given the central part that relationships play in the outcomes of human activity, it is interesting how little they may be noticed and considered from both users and providers of human services. One potential reason for this is the relative invisibility of relationships. For example, when coming to design a service, such as a school, it can be easy to think about where the desks will go, what sort of lessons will occur, and what equipment will be required. It may even be relatively straightforward to determine how many staff will be needed, how many pupils will be attending, and what people's roles and tasks should be. But it might be far harder to imagine, much less plan for, all the relationships that will go on between all the human beings involved, even though, as anyone who has worked in a school will testify, it is often those very elements that begin to define the relative success or failure of the venture. Even after the school has opened, relationships can be hard to 'see' and measure, far harder than the desks, lesson plans, and whiteboards. (Box 2.4 in Chapter 2 discusses further about the unconscious nature of much of human functioning.)

There may be a number of additional pressures and dynamics that add to a difficulty in tuning in to the relational undercurrents that underlie outward features. What follows is not an exhaustive list, but rather some general observations. Firstly, some people have a template of others as neglecting and see themselves as unworthy of care; they may project into others a lack of care and concern, which professionals may identify with without necessarily realising (see section on 'Relational Dynamics' in Chapter 2). Hence, at times, we as clinicians may fall into paying little attention to someone who may be in marked need of help (see also Clinical Example 5 in Chapter 7). Secondly, related to structural and financial limitations, if staff are trying to care for too many people than they can realistically attend to, they may develop defences against what might otherwise be an overwhelming anxiety to do with the scale of the needs of service users that cannot be met. We as staff may become more detached and, without realising it, minimise or deny the extent of service users' needs. Finally, and practically, the concepts of internal worlds and interpersonal dynamics may not be taught in depth during professional trainings.

Due to the relative invisibility of relationships, the more visible consequences of the patient or service user's relational difficulties may be noticed and attended to (such as violence or drug use) whilst the dynamics underpinning these symptoms can continue unnoticed. Furthermore, some clinicians believe (erroneously) that having emotions in response to work situations is somehow unprofessional or 'weak'; this can lead to staff becoming anxious when they do experience feelings, and to feel that they are somehow failing, which can lead to attempts to avoid feelings.[4]

As explained in Chapter 2, underlying feelings and dynamics may be initially out of our conscious awareness. This applies to service providers and users alike. However, when these dynamics are acknowledged within a service culture and when time is made for staff to stop and reflect, we as clinicians and providers can notice and tune in to underlying relational issues and feelings (see Chapter 18 on Reflective Practice).

Staff Responses to Patients who have Complicated Relationships with Care

From the perspective of a staff member, they may experience a range of emotions when working with a service user who has an ambivalent or complicated relationship with care.[5] For example, the staff member might feel anxiety, a lack of desire to care for the patient, frustration, helpless to make a positive change, or worry about provoking the person. Such feelings and responses in staff are expected and usual and are to do with both the staff member's own internal world and the relationship dynamics involving the service user (see Chapter 2, section on Countertransference). If reflected on, the staff member's feelings can provide very useful information about the relational dynamics the service user carries with them and how the staff member is responding to these.[6,7]

However, unless staff emotional responses to work situations can be named, thought about, and 'digested', these can place a strain on practitioners and teams, potentially reducing interest and satisfaction from the work and increasing stress.[7,8] Furthermore, if staff do not have the time, opportunity, or capacity to reflect on the relational dynamics they are a part of, sometimes these feelings can lead to unreflective actions, such as inadvertently assuming restrictive or rejecting ways of working. These are referred to as staff 'enactments' – the acting out of a relational dynamic rather than reflecting on it. These may hinder attempts to form consistent and long-term relationships with the people they are working with.[9] All professionals have the potential to act on countertransference feelings in this way; this is not restricted to the 'formal' therapy situation. Via this interpersonal 'nudging',[10] which may occur without either party realising what is happening, there is the potential for aspects of the patient's expectations about (dysfunctional) relationships to be repeated in some form in their relationships with staff and services.[11] As discussed in more length in Chapter 2, small 'countertransference enactments' by professionals are inevitable, and may be put to good therapeutic use if the clinician can recognise what is happening, and repair the relationship if there has been a rupture. However, when staff enactments are larger or not recognised, these can be fundamental to the maintenance of patients' difficulties.

Take for example, an emotionally intense encounter, such as a doctor working with a patient who has come to A&E for help with a leg wound that he has inflicted on himself, but the patient is now shouting at the doctor to 'get your hands off me'. At an underlying level, the patient might perhaps feel fear, anger, and dislike towards previous needed figures in his life who he experienced as neglectful and abusive, with this situation now being transferred on to staff in caring roles. Unless the doctor can register and process feelings of anxiety or perhaps a feeling of loss of competence that may be experienced in such a situation, they may without realising it act on those feelings and assume a judgmental and overly harsh stance towards the patient. This may result in the patient feeling worse and shouting louder, and potentially not getting treatment for his leg wound nor receiving attention for the problem that had led to him harming himself in this way.

Someone's outward presentation (in this case, the man's shouting at the doctor) can dominate the scene to the point where this is the only thing that is talked about or attended to. Such symptoms can be loud, visible, and distressing, and draw attention to themselves in ways that the relational dynamics behind them may not. When the invisible relationship is not taken seriously, a service may be more likely to struggle with both staff well-being and with caring for people who have ambivalent relationships with care. Those who express their own histories of distress in distressing ways are always at risk of having those very histories re-enacted in the present (see Example 3).[11,12]

Example 3 Benefits office

Mr Black has marked difficulties in relation to those who may be able to meet some of his needs, and he has eventually ended up needing to seek help from the state benefits office. This is a somewhat more complicated version of the hardware shop situation because this person knows that he cannot afford to leave the office without communicating his need. In Mr Black's internal world, experiences of need and vulnerability are closely connected to rejection and mistreatment. The battle within this person's mind is pretty furious as he approaches the benefit office. He is scared and anxious about an impending humiliation that his early experiences of seeking help have left him with. Imagined scenarios drawn from previous experiences come to the fore.

Mr Black arrives at the office sweating and talking loudly. His demeanour is experienced as somewhat intimidating by Ms Smith, the benefits clerk who he meets first. There are various ways this fictionalised scenario could go at this point. We will illustrate two possibilities.

Version 1. Ms Smith tells Mr Black that 'You don't need to shout, can you just wait a moment?' This is experienced by Mr Black as rejection, turning up the volume on his anxiety and his voice, leading to further anxiety in Ms Smith who calls security. Before the security staff arrive, Mr Black leaves, not having had his needs heard, still less been met, and with his expectations of caring relationships having been reinforced. Ms Smith is left feeling rejected and somewhat abused, in ways that are not so familiar to her. Both are left with a mutual dislike and misunderstanding of one another. Several more encounters like this one might even lead to Mr Black being excluded or barred from this service, meaning that his needs remain unattended to and likely intensifying as a result.

Version 2. Ms Smith and her colleagues have had training in interpersonal dynamics, and a regular reflective practice session is embedded into their service. Ms Smith is able to register that she feels anxious and somewhat intimidated. She greets Mr Black and asks him to take a seat for a moment, explaining that she will gather his details, and be with him shortly. Ms Smith takes a few minutes to discuss the situation with her senior colleague, including her responses to meeting Mr Black. They agree that he is not making any threats, and whilst he is talking loudly, he is not acting aggressively. They look up his old notes and see a history of anxiety and past trauma, as well as a pattern of presenting to services in a similar style to today, and that he tends to settle with a bit of time. They think it is possible that Mr Black himself is feeling extremely anxious, which is being communicated to Ms Smith through his external presentation and projection of strong feelings. They consider where on a spectrum this situation is in terms of 'feeling difficult' as opposed to being dangerous;[13] they feel that at present things point to the former. Ms Smith goes back to see Mr Black, with the senior colleague around if needed. Mr Black is looking a little less anxious. Some time, reflection, and containment had helped Mr Black's anxiety to settle to a tolerable level. The session goes fine, and they work out what they needed to about his benefits.

Thinking about 'Engagement'

A patient may be described as 'engaging well' when they turn up to appointments, listen to what the clinician is saying, and take the treatment as it is prescribed and indicated. This sort of engagement does not tend to take up too much time in clinical or case discussion meetings, just a passing note that the patient is 'engaging well'. In this scenario, clinicians often implicitly acknowledge that a relationship is occurring between provider and recipient.

However, much more discussion tends to happen when someone is felt to be 'not engaging'. What is interesting at these times is that the term 'not engaging' seems to imply that there isn't a relationship going on between the person and the service, perhaps because they haven't turned up for an appointment, or they are not taking their treatment as prescribed. A discussion can ensue about how to get the person to engage, or engage 'properly'. Despite the idea that the person is 'not engaging', there may be up to eight qualified health professionals sitting around a table (or on a video call) discussing their 'non-engagement'. On reflection then, the patient really is engaging – after all, they seem to have managed to get eight people to discuss them for a period of time. This reframing of engagement can free things up, moving away from a sense of winning or losing a battle to get someone to 'engage', to becoming interested *in the way the person is engaging.*

Freud hypothesises that what doesn't get remembered, gets repeated. Perhaps the person, through actions such as missing appointments, is unconsciously communicating something to us through this engagement-by-absence that they don't yet have the words for; perhaps something of their own experience of feeling neglected and abandoned is being projected so the healthcare worker feels neglected and unimportant. This shift of frame can be important clinically. Without it, the patient may be blamed for 'non-engagement', and unprocessed feelings may be expressed by us back towards the patient for 'choosing' not to make use of the good resources being offered. Over time, this brings the risk of abrupt discharge from the service or some other form of disconnection.

Tolerating Slow or No Change

We now consider staff-patient dynamics where clinical improvement occurs very slowly or seems not to occur at all. It is well-described in the literature that caring for people with chronic conditions can be difficult to tolerate for those of us in the caring professions, as this may conflict with personal, unrealistic aspirations and expectations about patients getting better.[14] The resultant anxieties and frustrations about patients not getting better, if unacknowledged and unprocessed, can lead clinicians to inadvertently assuming unhelpful or harmful responses towards patients. These include inappropriate use of treatments connected to a denial of the limitations of treatment;[15] unprocessed anger or frustration in clinicians at not being able to find the means of helping the patient;[16] or to withdrawing (see Clinical Example 4). These difficulties can be compounded in mental health where the dynamics of the clinician-patient relationship are arguably even more central to outcomes (whether this is acknowledged by the clinician or not).

Clinical Example 4 Within a day service

Mr Gray, a man in his fifties, has been coming to a day service for ten years. Mr Gray avoids staff and is distant, not taking part in conversation with staff. He has experienced violence and neglect in relationships growing up and has great difficulty in trusting others. If the clinical team do not have a regular opportunity to reflect together on these underlying dynamics, over time some of the staff may experience a decrease in interest in Mr Gray and, without fully realising it, act on an impulse to avoid him or 'give up', potentially fulfilling his expectations of others.

The skills, internal workings, and stance that go into mental health work can feel less tangible to clinicians than treatments in some other parts of medicine and surgery, where the means of treatment may be simpler to separate from the self. Hence, 'the psychiatric carer is [particularly] prone to confuse professional capacity to heal with a sense of self-worth'[17] – that is, to feel that 'when my patient doesn't get better, I am rubbish'.

Relational Health and the Inverse Care Law

To discuss further the relationship between someone's needs and their ability to access care, we outline one final example (Clinical Example 5).

Clinical Example 5 Referral to the breast clinic

Over several years, a young woman, Ms Jones, has developed just enough trust in Dr McNeil, her GP, to talk to her about physical health issues. This has been made possible by Dr McNeil remaining consistent and available over time to Ms Jones. Dr McNeil recognises that Ms Jones's early developmental experiences have made it difficult for her to trust those in authority and in caring roles. Ms Jones rarely leaves the house due to intense anxiety.

Ms Jones notices several painless lumps in her breast and after several weeks just manages to tell Dr McNeil about this. Following this disclosure, she is then referred to the breast clinic. The breast clinic is some distance away. The GP explains that the appointment would entail a further examination and some scans. From the moment Ms Jones is told this, and even though she nods her head in understanding, there are parts of her that are already saying that there is absolutely no way she would ever go to such an appointment. Ms Jones experiences increasing thoughts telling her not to go and that nothing good will come from having somebody who says they care for her put their hands on her body. As the day comes closer, this inner dialogue becomes louder from those aspects of her which are alert to maltreatment in relation to caring figures. The thoughts from the small part of her that might go are outweighed.

The staff at the clinic are waiting for her to arrive on the appointed day and are a little surprised when she does not attend. One letter is written to the patient to offer a further appointment before Ms Jones is discharged after not attending.

The relational bridge between Ms Jones and the breast clinic was too large to cross. Ms Jones's actions might be described as 'self-sabotaging', but from her experience, she was self-protecting. The fact that she was willing to miss an appointment intended to explore something that may be life-threatening, communicates a great deal about the severity of the anxiety she had about having people touch her body.

We are back to the invisibility of the relational element of care. If someone who uses a wheelchair was trying to access care, and that care was placed at the top of three flights of stairs with no lift access, the problem might be clear (if not necessarily addressed). For people who have severe and enduring difficulties with issues such as trust or attachment we may, without realising it, be metaphorically at the top of three flights of stairs with no lift access. Chapter 17 provides some thoughts about how a service might configure itself to mitigate such a situation.

This invisible element of health and social care might be understood as one factor underpinning the 'inverse care law', where the delivery of care varies inversely with need.[18] On a population level, those who struggle to trust, believe in, or connect with care may miss appointments, find the relational hurdles too high to jump, and avoid situations that raise huge anxieties for them. Care can begin to drift towards those who can make the best use of it.

Potential for Therapeutic Change

This section has summarised common complications that may arise in relationships between service users and staff. The converse of this is the potential for staff and services to offer a steady, containing, and thoughtful relationship in the face of these pressures (see Box 15.2 for a summary). When services are set up with training in interpersonal dynamics and reflective spaces embedded into the culture, one would expect better outcomes for staff and patients.[19,20]

Box 15.2 To create a safe and well-functioning clinical team, it is essential that staff are:

- *aware* of emotional responses to the work
- recognise that these *are usual and expected*
- able to *reflect on and process* these responses within appropriate settings[21,22]

Splitting within a Clinical Team

We now move on to team dynamics and the phenomenon of splitting within a clinical team. As described in Chapter 2 (section 'Movement between Defensive "Splitting" and a More Integrated Position'), some people inhabit a state of mind where 'good' (idealised) and 'bad' experiences of self-and-other in relationships are unconsciously separated from each other – this is known as splitting.

Where splitting is in operation, this may affect how a patient relates to different members of staff within their treating team. A patient may unconsciously present one 'self-representation to one group of treaters and another self-representation to another group of treaters'.[23] In each presentation, different aspects of the patient may be communicated (projected) to others, potentially evoking corresponding countertransference feelings in different clinicians. For example, with some staff, a male patient in an inpatient setting presented as suspicious about others, acting aggressively, and projecting fear and a sense of dislike into the clinical team – this was identified with by these clinicians who felt afraid and a sense of dislike towards the patient. Whereas with other clinicians, the same patient came across as vulnerable and projected a need for care – these projections were identified with by the latter clinicians who felt a sense of caring towards the patient and felt sorry for his adversities. As Gabbard observes, splitting and projection do not occur in a vacuum. A patient may unconsciously inhabit one or other side of the split when there is a closer 'fit' between the external 'real' figure of the staff member and one of the patient's internal representation of others.[23]

If the patient's projections are particularly intense, and if these projections are not processed by the staff members, their countertransference feelings can affect how they act towards to the patient and towards each other. In full-blown team splitting, dynamics within the staff team can come to resemble the dynamics of the inner world of the patient. Staff members may 'find themselves assuming polarised positions and defending those positions strongly against one another'.[23] For example, one subgroup of staff may accuse the other of being punitive and overly focused on seeing the 'negative'; the other subgroup may feel they are the only ones recognising the risks posed by the patient and that the first subgroup have been 'taken in'. When teams have reached this point, often the patient is blamed for the whole situation.[24] In the heat of the moment, it easy to forget that these are unconscious interpersonal processes involving both patients and staff. Team splitting brings stress and conflict within the staff team. Furthermore, a vicious cycle can emerge of inconsistent approaches towards the patient which can unsettle the patient and lead to further splitting and projection. A similar process can also occur between staff teams (e.g. between the day shift and the night shift on a ward) and between different services (e.g. between an accident and emergency department and a mental health service), with each team identifying with different projected aspects of the patient.

A facilitated reflective space, such as a regular reflective practice group (Chapter 18) or potentially a shorter-term consultation approach (Chapter 19), can allow a working through of this situation. Facilitated by an external therapist, these activities explicitly explain that for any individual staff member working with a patient, where splitting and projection are prominent, it is often hard to get an overview of all aspects of the patient – an individual clinician may tune in more to one aspect or another. A facilitated reflective space can validate both sides of the team's impressions, but then bring the experiences together to form a fuller picture of the patient. This can shift the team dynamic away from a debate within the team about who is 'wrong' or 'right'. When the various members of a team can agree a consensus understanding of the patient that demonstrates a capacity to hold disparate aspects of him in mind, this is likely to be containing for the patient in the long run and provide conditions where the patient's own inner splitting might moderate. Practically, part of the management of team splitting is agreeing a compromise amongst the team on different views on clinical management, in order to achieve consistency of approach.

Not all intra-team conflicts are linked to splitting. Staff members in a team may have a variety of pre-existing differences in treatment approaches, including on matters such as 'use of structure, limit setting, gratification versus frustration of transference wishes, optimum level of staff control versus patient autonomy.'[23] As such, 'there are many instances in which staff members simply disagree because of different philosophies'.[23] Commonly, team splitting (in relation to a patient) may occur along an existing fault-line (i.e. an existing area of difference, tension, or fragility within the team).

System Dynamics

Those not immediately involved with patients (e.g. managers) can also experience important reactions, as the core staff-patient relationship dynamics tend to be mirrored in all relationships within a system.[25] At a systems level, it is recognised that an institution can pick up difficulties and defences of their particular client group.[26] For example, a general ethos within staff in a forensic institution might be somewhat suspicious. Or a service working with people in crisis may itself lurch from crisis to crisis and feel on high alert the whole time. This can be understood as the cumulative effect on the service as a whole of the interpersonal processes described earlier – that is, the effect of working with a client group over a long period of time who have similar relational difficulties and projections, with repeated unconscious invitations for the service to mirror some of the service users' early developmental experiences. These processes may happen subtly and imperceptibly, but over time it may get to the point where something of the operation of the organisation begins to reflect the very dynamics it has been established to address.

Menzies-Lyth (1960) introduces the concept of social systems as defences against anxiety.[27] This refers to certain patterns that emerge within a service as a result of the service attempting to unconsciously avoid troubling experiences such as anxiety, guilt, and uncertainty. Writing about nurses in a general medical hospital, Menzies-Lyth contends that the realities of caring for patients – life-and-death concerns, dynamics to do with dependency – 'stimulate afresh [. . .] early situations and their accompanying emotions'.[27] In response to these intense 'archaic' anxieties, Menzies-Lyth observes a pattern whereby responsibility and a sense of competence may be passed 'up the hierarchy' ('I can't manage this, I'm going to hand this over to my boss'), with a reciprocal projection of irresponsibility and incompetence down in the hierarchy ('I have to take this on myself, I can't leave this with the staff I manage'). Menzies-Lyth describes how what starts as projection can become reality as people act according to the roles assigned to them. As a consequence, some staff can be left undertaking a low level of task compared to their abilities and skills, whilst simultaneously feeling controlled from above and excluded from decisions; and senior staff can feel overwhelmed and untrusting of the abilities of junior staff. Menzies-Lyth describes other relevant phenomena – how change may be avoided until the point of crisis as we cling to the familiar in the face of anxieties; and how there can be an obscurity in formal distribution of responsibilities. However, all is not lost as we are not compelled to play out these patterns. Through observing and discussing these patterns, 'staff are more likely to be aware of when this is happening and to use feelings to tackle the problem in a direct and appropriate way'.[26]

Menzies-Lyth's model has proved useful in the understanding of other human service organisations, beyond the general medical hospital.[28] Whilst certainly not every defence she observed applies everywhere (and each service will develop its own flavour of systemic defences), we have found that many of her observations ring true and are helpful in understanding systemic dynamics within healthcare services.

Concluding Remarks

A psychodynamic approach views symptoms as arising out of interpersonal and intrapersonal relationships, and aims to shine a light on these less visible underpinnings as a way of understanding and, on occasion, alleviating their more visible manifestations. The implications of this are to notice and think about our responses (i.e. emotions) to working with patients and service users as part of the everyday process of caring.[11] This kind of work is not a luxury or an accessory to treatment but an essential part of treatment itself. Indeed, there are signs that this culture is developing in a positive direction through initiatives such as Enabling Environments, increased provision of Balint groups for medical students, and through 'psychologically informed' services.

From a psychodynamic point of view, anyone who is considering working in a field where they will be in regular contact with people who may not have had the most straightforward of developmental relationship experiences, should receive training around these issues. This training can hopefully lead on to a more regular space for staff to reflect about the part that they play in something as primal and important as a caring or helping relationship.

The following chapters expand on how to observe and work with the dynamics described in the present chapter. Chapter 16 is a predominantly theory chapter that looks in more detail at the dynamics of anger, aggression, and violence. Chapter 17 outlines the principles of a 'psychologically informed' service – that is, how practically to organise and structure a service to offer a good relational experience for patients, particularly those with more complicated relationships with care. A psychologically informed approach is underpinned by spaces for reflective practice for staff – this forms the subject of Chapter 18. Chapter 19 draws on many of the themes discussed in Chapters 15 to 18, outlining a process of psychodynamic consultation for a clinical team.

References

1. Seglow R, Canham H. Intra-uterine life and the experience of birth. In Personality Development. London: Routledge; 1999. p. 13–32.
2. Winnicott DW. Playing and Reality. Oxford, England: Penguin; 1971.
3. Fraiberg S, Adelson E, Shapiro V. Ghosts in the nursery: a psychoanalytic approach to the problems of impaired infant-mother relationships. Journal of the American Academy of Child Psychiatry 1975;14 (3):387–421.
4. McWilliams N. Psychoanalytic Diagnosis, Second Edition: Understanding Personality Structure in the Clinical Process. 2nd edition. New York: The Guilford Press; 2011.
5. Craissati J, Minoudis P, Shaw J et al. Working with offenders with personality disorder, A practitioner's guide. Ministry of Justice, National Offender Management Service; 2015.
6. Adshead G, Sarkar J. The nature of personality disorder. Advances in Psychiatric Treatment 2012;18(3):162–72.
7. Moore E. Personality disorder: its impact on staff and the role of supervision. Advances in Psychiatric Treatment 2012;18 (1):44–55.
8. Melchior ME, Bours GJ, Schmitz P et al. Burnout in psychiatric nursing: a meta-analysis of related variables. J Psychiatr Ment Health Nurs 1997;4(3):193–201.
9. Patrick J, Kirkland J, Maclean C et al. Reflective practice paper and competency guidelines framework. Forensic Network Matrix Group; 2018.
10. Gabbard GO. Long-term psychodynamic psychotherapy: a basic text. In Long-term Psychodynamic Psychotherapy: A Basic Text. Washington, DC: American Psychiatric Pub.; 2010.
11. Hinshelwood RD. Abusive help – helping abuse: the psychodynamic impact of severe personality disorder on caring institutions. Crim Behav Ment Health 2002;12(2 Suppl): S20-30.
12. Evans M. *Making Room for Madness in Mental Health: The Psychoanalytic Understanding of Psychotic Communication*. Karnac Books; 2016.
13. Boag I. Elastic tolerance. In Psychologically Informed Environment Principles in Adult Residential Care. Routledge; 2020.

14. Main TF. The ailment. British Journal of Medical Psychology 1957;30(3):129–45.
15. O'Connor S. An analytic approach in a psychiatric intensive care unit. Psychoanalytic Psychotherapy 1998;12 (1):3–15.
16. Colson DB, Allen JG, Coyne L et al. An anatomy of countertransference: staff reactions to difficult psychiatric hospital patients. Hosp Community Psychiatry 1986;37(9):923–8.
17. Watts D, Morgan G. Malignant alienation: dangers for patients who are hard to like. The British Journal of Psychiatry 1994;164 (1):11–15.
18. Hart JT. The inverse care law. The Lancet 1971;297(7696):405–12.
19. Haigh R, Harrison T, Johnson R et al. Psychologically informed environments and the 'Enabling Environments' initiative. Housing, Care and Support 2012;15 (1):34–42.
20. Johnson R, Haigh R. Social psychiatry and social policy for the 21st century - new concepts for new needs: the 'psychologically-informed environment'. *Mental Health and Social Inclusion* 2010;14 (4):30–5.
21. Thorndycraft B, McCabe J. The challenge of working with staff groups in the caring professions: the importance of the 'team development and reflective practice group'. British Journal of Psychotherapy 2008;24 (2):167–83.
22. Johnston J, Paley G. Mirror mirror on the ward: who is the unfairest of them all? Reflections on reflective practice groups in acute psychiatric settings. Psychoanalytic Psychotherapy 2013;27(2):170–86.
23. Gabbard GO. Splitting in hospital treatment. Am J Psychiatry 1989;146 (4):444–51.
24. Rinsley DB. Treatment of the Severely Disturbed Adolescent. Northvale; London: J. Aronson; 1994.
25. Skynner ACR. Institutes and How to Survive Them: Mental Health Training and Consultation. London: Routledge; 1989.
26. Moylan D. The dangers of contagion: projective identification processes in institutions. In The Unconscious at Work: Individual and Organizational Stress in the Human Services by Obholzer A & Roberts V. London: Routledge; 1994.
27. Menzies IEP. A case-study in the functioning of social systems as a defence against anxiety: a report on a study of the nursing service of a general hospital. Human Relations 1960;13(2):95–121.
28. Whittaker A. Social defences and organisational culture in a local authority child protection setting: challenges for the Munro Review? Journal of Social Work Practice 2011;25(4):481–95.

Chapter 16

An Introduction to the Dynamics of Anger, Aggression, and Violence

Table of Contents

Introduction 244
Dynamics of Anger 245
Expressions of Anger to Others 246
Anger When Communication to the Other Is Unacknowledged 247
Ways of Understanding Aggression and Violence 249
Shame and Humiliation 250
Expelling Feelings 251
'Self-Preservative' Violence 251
Attempts at Communication 252
Staff Countertransference Dynamics in Relation to Aggression and Violence 252
Appropriate Boundaries 253
Societal Responses to Violence 254
Concluding Remarks 255

Introduction

In this chapter we aim to provide an introduction to understanding the dynamics of anger, aggression, and violence. These dynamics are not necessarily straightforward to make sense of, and it is easy for any of us to inadvertently become drawn into responses that may make a situation worse. Conversely, with an awareness of key dynamics and time to reflect on these, professionals and teams can find an understanding of angry, aggressive, or violent encounters, which is a prerequisite for safe practice, working matters through, and resisting harms. In our view, there is not a single theory or concept that can be used to understand the interlinked areas of anger, aggression, and violence. Rather, there are a number of overlapping concepts, more than one of which may be relevant to a particular situation.

Anger is a basic (i.e. fundamental) emotion.[1] There are various ways of defining aggression and violence. We find the etymology of 'aggression' to be helpful (*ad-gradior*: I move towards)[2] in capturing a working understanding and differentiating aggression from violence. We use the word 'aggression' to refer to moves towards another person, to 'get something through' to the other, with various possible conscious and unconscious intentions – including an attempt to be heard, to defend or assert oneself, or to intimidate. The intensity of aggression may increase in a continuum; above a certain point the 'move towards' another becomes an action involving an intrusion ('ingression') of the other's body. Following Glasser[3] and Yakeley, we take a definition of violence as starting at this point, as being to do with 'actual bodily harm inflicted by one person on another person, in which the body boundary is breached and physical injury may occur'.[4] We recognise, in the interest of clarity as well as the scope of the chapter, that these working definitions are simplified and neglect certain nuance and dimensions, including the violence of words and violence towards inanimate objects. We also note that aggression may also be expressed 'passively' – non-responsiveness or moving away from someone can, in certain circumstances, communicate aggression.

Because of constraints of space, this chapter does not cover aggression in groups or in the context of war. We are also not attempting to cover specific 'treatment' or 'management', although some direction about clinical approach will follow on from an understanding of the underlying dynamics.

This chapter starts with examining the dynamics of anger. Then, several ideas for understanding aggression and violence are discussed. The chapter closes with a brief introduction to thinking about societal responses to violence.

Dynamics of Anger

Who or what is a person angry with? Out of what situations does anger arise? What was someone experiencing before they felt anger? In our view, there are many routes to the feeling of anger.

A number of ideas are linked with the concept of anger as a basic emotion. In the early years of life, expressions of anger can be part of the process of developing autonomy and a sense of mastery ('I can do this by *myself!*'). Secondly, anger as a response to frustration can lead both the child and adult to assertive actions, functioning as 'an inwardly directed signal concerning a pressure to overcome an obstacle or an aversive situation'.[1] For example, when an adult feels unfairly treated at work, anger may serve as a motivator to put in a complaint, or not put up with something inappropriate. Thirdly, any situation that gives rise to fear can also cause anger.[3] This might include when one is experiencing bodily pain, or when one feels under attack by another.

In relationships, a person may become angry when they feel, for example, encroached on by the other; badly treated or hurt by another; shamed in relation to another; rejected, criticised, abandoned; or that one's communication is ignored by the other. As such, anger works as an outwardly directed signal aimed at communicating something important to the other. If these kinds of interpersonal experiences are prolonged or repeated in a person's developmental years, a person can end up internalising them (see Chapter 2), in which case, anger may become associated with a particular pattern of internal object relations, for example, rejecting, criticising, etc. Anger may then be 'turned inwards' – where one aspect of the self is angry towards another aspect – (see also Chapter 12 on depression) as well as directed outwards towards others.[5] In the context of overwhelming relational trauma, a person may dissociate (i.e. unconsciously cut off) from their feelings as way of psychologically surviving in the moment. These dissociated feelings may include intense anger (rage) amongst other feelings. When anger is dissociated in this way and not processed, it is prone to return later in a person's life when circumstances in the present resemble the original trauma.[6]

A person may feel anger as part of a response to loss – this may arise when someone close has died, but what is lost can take many forms (see Chapter 8, section on 'Mourning').

Feelings of anger may be experienced in the dynamics of borderline states of mind. When splitting occurs, others and the self may be experienced as 'all good' (associated with intense loving feelings). But at other times, the person may feel surrounded by persecutors. This 'all bad' state may be associated with feelings of fear, anger, and hate (see Chapter 13).

In understanding someone's anger in the present day, anger might be predominantly internally driven (from the disturbance and confusion within one's mind) or externally driven (e.g. from an outsider provoking), or arise from an interaction between internal and external worlds.

Anger may be combined with other feelings. For example, anger can be mixed with sadness, or combined with grief or anxiety. For some, anger may be a more acceptable feeling than other feelings – indeed, during therapy, anger may 'give way' to more vulnerable experiences. As with any feeling, there are varying intensities of anger, from irritation through to rage. Some people feel anger rarely, and others feel angry much of the time. Anger may be displaced from the object of the anger onto another person or thing, or defended against in other ways, if it feels unacceptable to the individual to recognise who they are actually angry with. This is the defence of displacement (see Chapter 2, section on 'Defence Mechanisms'). For example, it might arouse problematic conflicting feelings for a child, who will necessarily be dependent on others, to recognise intense anger towards someone who is depended on. The anger may, instead, be expressed at school or taken out on a friend.

Expressions of Anger to Others

Anger may be expressed by one person to another in a relatively open and straightforward manner before it builds up excessively. This tends to diffuse the anger, especially if the communication is heard by the other, who does not react defensively. The ability to express anger in a relatively uncomplicated way may be more likely to arise in the context of good-enough developmental experiences – that is, growing up in a family culture where anger could generally be expressed and acknowledged, and issues acted upon without excessive problems arising.

Other people have complications with expressing anger. Developmental influences to this may include: if anger was repeatedly not acknowledged growing up (see section on 'When Anger Communication to the Other is Unacknowledged', below); if expressions of anger led to violent actions by others or oneself, leaving a person afraid of anger and its consequences; if expressions of anger frequently elicited aversive responses such as rejection or criticism by the other. In these circumstances, a person may then learn to suppress or repress feelings of anger (or displace, project, sublimate, etc.). The resulting avoidance of acknowledging and processing anger – as with any feeling – can lead to anger intensifying. Furthermore, if a person attempts to manage a difficult feeling by themself, secondary issues may become attached to the feeling. For example, guilt or shame, associated with a thought that it is somehow 'bad' to have angry feelings. As explained in more length in Chapter 12 on depression, this can then contribute to difficulties in future relationships. When anger is not communicated by an individual to the other, the other person may not know something is amiss and so the issue giving rise to the anger cannot be properly addressed. A common situation is that the individual then grows angrier and more resentful, with eventually their anger being expressed in an actively or passively aggressive way that may evoke a negative response from the other.[5]

Anger When Communication to the Other Is Unacknowledged

As mentioned above, one route to anger is to do with a perception that one's communications are not acknowledged by another person. This dynamic has relevance for everyday communications in 'healthy' functioning and also in the dynamics of more distressed presentations. One approach to understanding this route to anger is through the 'still-face' experiment[7] (see Box 16.1), which was mentioned in Chapter 14. Other routes to anger are important too, but it is not possible within the scope of this chapter to expand in detail on them all.

The still-face experiment can be thought of as showing a great many things that are relevant to human relations, not least of which is how anger may arise when an individual feels that their communication to the other is unacknowledged. The other may not acknowledge the communication for various reasons – for example, they may not be in a position to receive and acknowledge the communication due to their own preoccupations, internal world, and defences. If an important relationship is disrupted in a way that leaves one party in a state of disconnection, the initial experience for that person may be one of anxiety and attempts to gain reconnection. If these attempts to reconnect with the other go unheard, then disconnection piles upon disconnection and there can be a build-up both of the experience that needs to be understood, and of the experience of being unheard. As this accumulation of anxiety develops, anger may start to make an appearance associated with the anxiety that gave rise to it. Suttie summarises this premise as, 'at the root of anger is induction to love. It is the maximal effort to attract attention and as such must be regarded as a protest against unloving . . .'.[8] Thus anger may become part of a forceful attempt to re-establish connection with the other and have the original communication heard. If this situation carries on, then anger may ultimately lead to aggression, as a final desperate attempt to have the communication received by the other (see also discussion of 'protest' in Chapter 12). As a result of the intense emotional pressures in encounters such as these, our experiences of ourselves and others may become 'split' into either 'all good' or 'all bad' aspects – hence, feelings of hate may also arise towards to the other, expressed as anger (see also Chapter 13).

Episodes of infant-parent mismatch and disconnection that are repaired are thought to offer healthy and adaptive mechanisms for an individual's maturation and development.[9] However, some people's developmental experiences are characterised by a chronic sense of

Box 16.1 The 'still-face' experiment, Tronick 1978

A two-minute video of this experiment shows a girl of preverbal age interacting with her mother in a playful and joyous way. All of a sudden, the mother (on request of the researcher conducting the experiment) looks down and when she looks up again a short time later, she is holding her face in a still manner with no expression or movement. Her little girl initially looks confused and makes a range of attempts to bring her mother's face back to life. When these attempts at reconnecting with her mother continually fail to elicit a response, the little girl's emotional state appears to move from confusion to distress. She screams, her face is furrowed, and she appears angry. Towards the end the video the girl is flailing around in her high chair, violently clawing the air, and twisting her body in protest at the experience of being ignored. The girl's anger and upset are soon assuaged by her mother dropping her still face and becoming animated and responsive again.

feeling disconnected and unheard in the relationships available to them, in which case, trying to get communication across can come to be felt as a pointless and frustrating experience. Such experiences do not necessarily remove the fundamental need to connect with others, but can leave a person having to manage such desires and defend against them by regarding a desire to connect as an unhelpful or even dangerous impulse. Chronic early experiences of feeling unheard can leave an adult with an internal conflict, where a part of them has increasing amounts of unheard communication, whilst another part maintains that to try and communicate is pointless and to be avoided. This can mean that all those intermediate stages of communication (i.e. the infant reaching out, the cries for help, etc.) are left unused and unpractised; the individual may have a sense that the extremes of silence or explosive anger are the only ways in which to express themself.

Such an internal tussle can become manifest in present-day external relationships when the adult experiences something that resembles being ignored or unheard. Instead of anger being the *final* attempt at making a connection, it can become the first option. Unfortunately, these angry attempts at connection can typically lead to the recipient of the anger feeling threatened and frightened and so less likely to receive any communication (or actually become someone who doesn't want to listen) – see Clinical Example, Mr Black. The anger may come to overshadow the original feelings such as anxiety, loss, or sadness, which can be lost in the heat of an angry argument.

Clinical Example Mr Black

Mr Black is the same person we discussed in Example 3 in Chapter 15. Here, we go into more detail about his background and then pick up his story several years further down the line from where we were in Chapter 15.

Early Years and Development

Mr Black, a man in his forties, experienced significant adversity during his early development. He experienced his father as a frightening man, who swung between silence and anger and violence depending upon his levels of intoxication. From an early age, Mr Black learnt that expressions of need, want, or vulnerability (such as crying or asking for help) would be unacknowledged, and that to communicate these was dangerous as it drew the angry, intrusive, and frightening attentions of his father. Through his childhood years he learnt to silence himself, keep vulnerability to himself, and deny his own needs as a way of protecting himself from the pain of them being unheard. In addition, he had the pain of needs not being met (and his needs being attacked).

As these dynamics played out through his late teens and twenties, the denial of his needs and of his need for connection with others gave rise to a chronic sense of anxiety, depression, and seemingly unpredictable outbursts of anger.

Current Difficulties

In recent years, for Mr Black, the seeking of care with the associated threat of vulnerability was extremely anxiety-provoking. It could take him days to mentally prepare to try and arrange an appointment with a healthcare service, which would only happen at times when his distress had become unbearable. Often, he was unable to get along on the day due to the fear of expressing need.

On the times when he did manage to get to an appointment, he arrived in a state of extreme anxiety as the defences built up over years would urge him to fight or flee.

Episode of Anger and Misunderstanding

On one occasion, Mr Black arrived at the reception area of his general practice clinic and was asked in a slightly disinterested way by the reception staff what he was there for. Mr Black went straight to an angry response, saying, 'What do they f**king well think I am here for!?'

The reception staff told Mr Black that if he was going to behave in this way then he was most definitely not going to be seen, and that he needed to calm down and lower his voice. In turn, Mr Black experienced these words as more evidence of being rejected, threatened, and silenced and as such became increasingly angry.

The situation escalated to the point where Mr Black was removed from the building and given a final warning that his behaviour would not be tolerated in the future. Mr Black, fuming with anger, retreated back to his home. He did not, ultimately, receive any care. The repetition in the central dynamic between this encounter and the one in the benefits office from Chapter 15 is clear.

One might consider that Mr Black's experience of the seeming disinterest of the reception staff resonated with a deep historic sense of having his fear and vulnerability ignored or even used against him. He responded in the moment as if it were actually all those past experiences reoccurring. Unable to communicate that he found the interaction with the reception staff anxiety-provoking, he moved straight to anger.

Ways of Understanding Aggression and Violence

An old psychoanalytic debate regarding aggression was between conceptualising it either as an instinct or as a reaction to particular circumstances. A contemporary perspective is to embrace 'both biology and psychology, recognising that although the capacity for aggression is innate and universal, aggressive behaviour occurs in response to threats that the self perceives in relation to internal or external objects'.[10]

Glasser, referencing Freud's Inhibitions, Symptoms and Anxiety,[11] observes that any condition that gives rise to anxiety may also give rise to anger, aggression, or violence. Glasser explains that, 'It is not infrequent to see violence erupt when fear is in operation.'[3] As such, the understanding of aggression taps into almost all areas of human relations – the sections on the dynamics of anxiety and depression (Chapters 11 and 12) in this volume may provide useful context.

We all have the capacity for violence in certain circumstances. But why is aggression sometimes contained within thought or words, at other times manifest in outward aggression, and on occasions enacted in violence? Addressing this question requires, as Glasser puts it, the consideration of an individual's 'total psychodynamic repertoire'.[3]

In adults who act violently, disruptions in their early development are common, including disconnection within relationships, and experiences of violence or abuse.[12] In making sense of what can seem like incomprehensible actions carried out by an adult – such as violence towards family members – an understanding of that person's own attachment history as a child can provide a detailed understanding of how and why they can get into 'hostile and helpless states of mind'.[13] Psychodynamic writings on violence explore the role of absent, unpredictable, or abusive parental figures,[14] and the potential impact of an overly-close early relationship with a parent and the subsequent need to defend against this.[15]

A person's early relationships with caregivers, interacting with social and biological factors, are central for the development of a capacity for reflecting on one's own and others' mental states, symbolic thinking, and regulating feelings ('reflective capacity' or 'mentalizing' – see Chapter 2). When someone has limitations in this capacity, it is hypothesised that the crossover point from tolerating distressing feelings into discharging them through actions might come earlier.[16] Violence can be understood as a communication of some sort. However, it may take some time to work out what the communication is and for the person who has been violent to form a narrative that makes sense to themselves and others. Adshead writes that people who have been violent may initially have 'cover stories', which only tell an incomplete picture.[17] Adshead explains, 'It is not that the "cover" story is not true, but rather it represents only that part of the narrative identity of the self that the speaker is conscious of – or can bear to articulate.' Through dialogue in therapeutic settings, these narratives can evolve 'into something richer and more self-reflective'.[17]

Yakeley and Adshead use the analogy of a bicycle combination lock in thinking about how several conditions may need to align to psychologically 'unlock' the potential for violence.[13] The first factor in the 'combination lock' is a person's characteristic ways of relating to themselves and others – this comprises the background to how current life circumstances will be experienced and managed. Other factors in the 'combination lock' might include the use of drugs which magnify or distort feelings or disinhibit actions; being socially isolated; and wider societal adversities including the influences of poverty and unemployment.[18] Out of these circumstances, a specific relational encounter or situation may engender a state of mind in an individual which 'can unlock or disable the inhibitory mechanisms that prevent the violent feelings that are held internally from exploding into the external world'.[13]

This chapter focuses on aggression and violence in the context of high-affect interpersonal situations, as these are perhaps more common and relevant for staff working in the caring professions. Yakeley and Meloy summarise research about a different situation, where violence may be less to do with reacting to and managing an emotionally charged encounter in the heat of the moment, but is more about the use of violence planned over a longer period in pursuit of a sense of power, control, or dominance.[4] This may or may not be associated with 'instrumental' motivations to do with obtaining territorial dominance or material gain. There may be complex interpersonal and neurobiological factors involved, which are beyond the scope of this chapter. For some people, the pursuit of power and control might be a way of gaining a sense of control over one's environment when this has been felt as lacking (linked with early adversity). The interested reader is directed to Yakeley et al. for further discussion about this form of violence.[4]

The following sections are intended as brief introductions to states of mind out of which violence may arise, with a focus on high-affect interpersonal situations.

Shame and Humiliation

At times, all of us feel shame. However, when a person has significant developmental experiences of being unloved, rejected, or denigrated, they may carry a sensitivity to insults and develop a defensive way of being that is centred around the need to avoid feeling shame or humiliation again. In this situation, experiences that give rise to feelings of shame and humiliation can be difficult to bear, and may predispose to violence if a person has not as yet been able to learn non-violent means of gaining self-respect.[19] A present-day incident can evoke distressing early experiences, which then amplify the intensity of the current feelings of shame and humiliation. Such incidents may include perceived 'loss of face', or perceptions of being denigrated by another. The emotion of shame is closely tied to a sense of being seen to be in the wrong by a judging other; one's usual response to shame is to want to turn away or hide to 'escape the painful gaze of others'.[20] If concealment from others is not possible – as may be the case when one's state of shame is witnessed by a group of people – feelings of shame may heighten along with the need to defend against it. If a person lacks the reflective capacity to manage and contain the distressing feelings, they may unconsciously find a way to manage the overwhelming feelings 'by getting another person (the victim) to experience them, by dissociating from them, or by acting out vengefully'.[13]

Expelling Feelings

As in the above discussion about shame and humiliation, violence may occur as part of a process of an individual projecting unwanted, intolerable, or overwhelming feelings into another person, allowing the individual to (temporarily) assume a position that is removed from the unwanted feelings (see Chapter 2 for a full description of projection and projective identification). A forceful induction of feelings in the other, involving violence (as opposed to more benign interpersonal nudging), may arise when an individual lacks other defences or processes to deal with their feelings, in combination with a particularly distressing or disturbing emotional situation. For example, a man in a pub had his advances towards a woman rejected. He experienced overwhelming feelings of inadequacy. A few minutes later, in response to a minor insult from an acquaintance, the man pinned the acquaintance to the ground and felt some sense of relief (perhaps even pleasure) in making his acquaintance feel weak and afraid. This served to provide temporary respite for the man from his own feelings which had been momentarily located (forcibly) in the person on the ground. Such incidents may represent unprocessed earlier experiences that are being repeated in the present, often with the individual assuming the opposite role they felt in originally.

These examples of the acting out of distress are distressing and dangerous for the recipient of the projections and the violence. They are also ineffective for the projector. Their attempts to expel unwanted persecutory anxieties into the other may result in the recipient becoming aggressive themselves, leading to an escalation of violence, and further trauma for the individual.[21] Furthermore, it does nothing to process the underlying difficulties.

'Self-Preservative' Violence

Glasser describes how an individual may engage in 'self-preservative' violence in response to a situation where the self feels under a threat of such severity that they fear they may not physically or psychologically survive.[3] This is a 'primitive' response associated with physiological changes in the body that prepare it to either fight the perceived danger or flee from it (the fight/flight response). In 'pure' self-preservative violence, influencing the other person's feelings is not the aim of the attack. The individual engaging in this form of violence does not necessarily want the other person to suffer – the individual just wants the source of the perceived danger to abate. As Glasser summarises, the violence is focused 'on the dangerousness of the object rather than the object itself'. An example of self-preservative violence might be when an individual lashes out when they are grabbed from behind by a stranger, out of fear of an imminent serious physical threat. Glasser contrasts self-preservative violence with a different situation (which Glasser refers to as 'sado-masochistic violence') where the visible evocation of feelings and responses in the person who is the object of the violence, in particular their suffering, are important to the individual engaging in violence (often serving to distance that individual from feelings of inferiority, vulnerability, and a sense of lack of control, which are instead evoked in the object of the violence).[3] In practice, a continuum between a self-preservative dimension and other routes to violence is common, as opposed to there being completely distinct forms.

The nature of the danger in self-preservative violence can be psychological as well as physical. Glasser gives examples of possible psychological threats as including perceived attacks on one's gender identity, the infliction of a severe blow to self-esteem, an insult to one's self or an ideal to which one is attached, or a feeling of disintegration. Of course, most people who experience such psychological pressures will not respond with violence – it depends on the other dynamics and influences that lie behind how something is perceived and how one reacts (i.e. the other aspects of the 'combination lock').

Attempts at Communication

Winnicott posits that a young person's 'antisocial tendencies', which may include violent acts, can be unconscious attempts to regain a parental figure felt to be lost. Through acts, which may outwardly appear bent on destruction only, Winnicott argues that 'the child is seeking that amount of environmental stability which will stand the strain resulting from impulsive behaviour'.[22]

A related perspective is to consider aggression (which may move into violence) as a continuum of the dynamic described earlier, to do with having an intense need but experiencing others as not acknowledging this. The child at the end of the still-face scenario ends up using physical means to try and get through to her mother – writhing around, hitting out at the air. Similarly, when an adult feels not heard or understood, there may be an escalation in tone of voice, body posture, and physical action. As discussed earlier, someone's internal world influences whether they feel heard by the other in quite a complex way – when a person has an internal representation of others as un-listening, they may interact with others in such a way that makes it more likely that the other will not be in a receptive state.

Staff Countertransference Dynamics in Relation to Aggression and Violence

As discussed in Chapter 2, staff countertransference can be a useful instrument for understanding the internal worlds of the people they work with; however, if not acknowledged or processed, this can lead to difficulties for both parties.

When someone has resorted to acting out something violent, it is usually the case that he has difficulties putting his distress into words and talking to another about it. Therefore, staff observations of how the patient operates, as well as observing their own countertransferences, may be key to understanding the dynamics behind a patient's violence and what he needs help with.[23] (We are using the term 'patient' here but this discussion would also apply to other situations such as the relationships between prison officers and prison residents, or in a community setting caring for people who have acted out violently.) To take the example of staff anxiety, this may be the only clue to the patient's own terror, which may be 'successfully' defended against by the patient's aggressive exterior.

Here it may help to distinguish between two situations: working with patients who have done violent things to others in the past but have not been violent towards the clinicians currently caring for them; and patients who have been violent towards the current staff team looking after them. Both situations have their own challenges, but when working with the latter group, it can be especially difficult work for the staff team to contain and process the feelings evoked within the team when a member of staff has been physically attacked by a patient in their ongoing care. Countertransference feelings to patients acting in violent ways are varied and may be unsettling for the clinician – these feelings are an expected and understandable response to being part of a disturbing encounter, where the staff are in a position of physical risk. These include feeling anxious, afraid, excited, controlled, disgusted, denial of there being a problem, or a therapeutic nihilism[10] (see also Reiss and Kirtchuk's structured approach to assessing staff-patient dynamics, discussed in Chapter 19).[24] When working with a person who acts in a threatening or violent way towards clinicians, through the responses evoked in clinicians, there may be a draw for clinicians to respond in ways that may inadvertently escalate the situation – potentially through overly punitive or placatory responses.

Splitting in staff responses is common when working with both situations – that is, when working with patients who have been violent in the past, and those who are currently displaying violence. For example, a service user who has hurt people may be held by some staff to be 'pure evil'; alternatively, other staff may deny or minimise the service user's past or present violence and tune in only to his vulnerability. Both of these polar opposite positions have their risks and limitations in perspective, whilst each, with reflection and processing, may provide a way in to understanding important elements of the interpersonal dynamics in operation. If the team can work together, the various projections can be brought together to form a more complete and nuanced picture of the person they are working with (see Chapter 18 on reflective practice).

It is important to acknowledge that working in settings that care for people who may be aggressive is in some ways an unusual situation. The nature of work in some caring settings entails staff returning to aggressive or violence situations, sometimes over years or decades, rather than being able to walk away from such incidents. Over time, the experiences of staff may come to resemble something of the adversity experienced by the patients they are caring for (this process is described more fully in the section on 'System Dynamics' in Chapter 15). Considerable efforts may be required by the leaders of such services and the practitioners themselves to acknowledge the existence of these unsettling dynamics and to pay attention to these. Reflective practice groups, in the context of important structural and practical elements of a service, can offer a degree of protection for staff and patients by providing opportunities for staff to process the intense projections (see Chapter 18).[25] The aim of reflective practice is to provide support for clinicians and reduce work-related stresses, and mitigate the potential for staff to enact retaliatory violence towards the patients in their care.

Appropriate Boundaries

A common critique raised in reflective practice groups or similar discussions is that the process of trying to understand why a person did what they did, or taking an interest in their upbringing, can feel to some like excusing or absolving a person of their harmful actions. Countertransference factors (including a dislike for the patient) may be relevant here, but alongside this it may be helpful to clarify that seeking understanding is about getting to the root of matters to help a person and the system around them to understand the person better, including what has contributed to their violence and thus helping to prevent future violence. Understanding is not intended to be absolution.

A process of trying to understanding someone's aggression or violence comes alongside setting or keeping boundaries around harmful actions or behaviour – it is not one or the other.[26] Furthermore, one needs appropriate boundaries in order to come to an understanding of a person's interpersonal dynamics. It is not containing to someone who hurts people to not have appropriate boundaries. In a way, it is depriving to them, and they may keep looking for the boundaries until they are found.

Hinshelwood describes the pull towards 'one-dimensional cultures' with regard to attitudes and approaches towards people who commit violence, and advocates for an integration: 'It is true that the patients might deserve sympathy for their appalling experiences in life (usually in early life), but equally they require determined confrontation' of entrenched ways of relating and harm caused to others.[23] With appropriate timing, staff can raise with the patient aspects of his behaviour which he may be consciously aware of, but is avoiding (see Chapter 7, section on therapeutic 'Confrontation').

Societal Responses to Violence

Emotional reactions also occur on a wider societal stage in response to people who relate in ways that cause serious harm to others. There is often, understandably, a great deal of anger directed towards those who have carried out serious violence towards others. The experiences of sadness, hurt, and tragedy on hearing about the serious injuries, or even death, of the other person may be felt to be futile and unheeded because the event has already occurred – this may add to the strength of anger.

The strength of feeling may be particularly marked in situations where a collective conscious desire to protect the most vulnerable members of society is seemingly ignored by people who have harmed or even killed others. Anger and outrage may be expressed about the apparent mindlessness and meaninglessness of violent crimes. From a psychodynamic perspective, as discussed earlier, violent actions are not mindless or meaningless. Undoubtedly, the reasons behind such crimes are complex, with deep psychological, biological, social, and political influences. In a psychodynamic way of thinking, it is important to try to understand the actions of people who commit violence in order to reduce the risk of harming others again.

There may be something about the nature of a violent crime and the anger that it evokes, that can get in the way of thinking about what might have been going on. We acknowledge that this is a complex and potentially divisive area that can generate strong feelings, and we are limiting our discussion to a psychodynamic perspective. Our societal responses can resemble the dynamics of staff involved more closely in the care of people who have been violent, in that we can all experience a draw towards 'one-dimensional cultures'. For example, one may experience the violent person as 'pure evil' and they may be ostracised in parts of society and the media, with calls for retaliatory punishment. As Adshead contends, one can comprehend why some feel the need to condemn those who have carried out violence, as ' . . . revenge is a basic human impulse, a kind of wild justice that keeps us stuck in our fear and anger, mirroring the very cruelty we claim to abhor'.[27] Furthermore, these situations evoke a splitting apart of a complex situation into 'good' and 'bad' – all of our own propensity for violence and hate may be projected into the perpetrator and then attacked, leaving us with the 'good' aspects.

The reason this matters is that a one-dimensional assessment of a complex situation might ignore the various dimensions and influences behind an act of violence. The strong feelings and the ensuing dynamics of revenge, splitting, and projection within aspects of society may cloud a process of understanding and learning lessons from what has gone wrong. A lack of understanding can hinder attempts to reduce the chances of future occurrences of violence for that person, and for preventing others ending up in the same situation. For example, in the situation of violence against a child, we may split off and project our own feelings of inadequacy and responsibility into one particular professional, or a professional group, involved in the child's care whose 'failings' are held to be responsible for them 'slipping through the net'. This avoids considering what the wider net was like or if, indeed, there was a net – that is, our defences may avoid a more discomforting but potentially deeper appreciation of a complex problem.

Furthermore, stigmatising or shaming practices towards someone who has been violent are expected to have detrimental effects on that person's future risk of violence. Tangney et al. summarise the research evidence in this area, concluding that such practices are 'associated with outcomes directly contrary to the public interest – denial of responsibility, substance abuse, psychological symptoms, predictors of recidivism and recidivism itself'.[28] This might be understood with reference to the discussion earlier in this chapter about how, when thinking about violence, shame is often central to its aetiology. Tauber et al. explain that ostracising and excessively punitive responses by society are expected to increase a person's shame and may engender defensive reactions that reduce the protagonist's feelings of guilt and remorse. (Guilt may be protective against future violence as it is associated with awareness of harms caused to others.)[28] As well as increasing shame, Tauber et al. contend that such societal responses are expected to reduce that person's 'cultural and personal social investment, weakening bonds . . . and, in most instances, likely serve to facilitate violence instead of preventing it'.[29]

Concluding Remarks

This chapter started with considering anger and the various routes to this feeling. We considered how anger can be a desperate call to be attended to and a powerful invitation to neglect. The chapter then introduced psychodynamic thinking on aggression and violence. We took an inclusive approach to contemporary theory, noting that more than one approach may be useful when trying to understand a person's actions. We discussed how, in the face of powerful dynamics associated with violence, the caring capacity of staff can be eroded in ways that can perpetuate problems; reflective practices can help provide some protection against these difficulties and maintain interest and safe working. Finally, we have touched on wider societal responses to violence, acknowledging that this is a potentially divisive area associated with strong feelings.

References

1. Williams R. Anger as a basic emotion and its role in personality building and pathological growth: the neuroscientific, developmental and clinical perspectives. Frontiers in Psychology 2017;8:1950.
2. Rycroft C. A Critical Dictionary of Psychoanalysis. Harmondsworth, London: Penguin; 1968.
3. Glasser M. On violence. A preliminary communication. Int J Psychoanal 1998;79:887–902.

4. Yakeley J, Meloy JR. Understanding violence: does psychoanalytic thinking matter? Aggression and Violent Behavior 2012;17(3):229–39.
5. Busch FN. Anger and depression. Advances in Psychiatric Treatment 2009;15 (4):271–8.
6. de Zulueta F. Theories of aggression and violence. In Forensic Psychotherapy: Crime, Psychodynamics and the Offender Patient, Vol. 1: Mainly theory. London: Jessica Kingsley Publishers; 1996. pp. 175–86.
7. Tronick E, Als H, Adamson L et al. The infant's response to entrapment between contradictory messages in face-to-face interaction. Journal of the American Academy of Child Psychiatry 1978;17 (1):1–13.
8. Suttie I. The Origins of Love and Hate. Harmondsworth, London: Peregrine Books; 1963.
9. Tronick E, Beeghly M. Infants' meaning-making and the development of mental health problems. American Psychologist 2011;66(2):107–19.
10. Yakeley J. Psychodynamic approaches to violence. BJPsych Advances 2018;24 (2):83–92.
11. Freud S. Inhibitions, symptoms and anxiety in J Strachey, ed. & trans. In The Standard Edition of the Complete Psychological Works of Sigmund Freud, Volume 20. London: Hogarth Press; 1926. pp. 75–176.
12. Fonagy P, Gergely G, Jurist EL et al. Affect Regulation, Mentalization, and the Development of the Self. London: Routledge; 2019.
13. Yakeley J, Adshead G. Locks, keys, and security of mind: psychodynamic approaches to forensic psychiatry. J Am Acad Psychiatry Law 2013;41(1):38–45.
14. Perelberg RJ. Murdered Father, Dead Father: Revisiting the Oedipus Complex. New York, NY: Routledge/Taylor & Francis Group; 2015.
15. Glasser M. Aggression and sadism in the perversions. In I Rosen, ed. Sexual Deviation. Oxford: Oxford University Press; 1979.
16. Adshead G, Moore E, Humphrey M et al. The role of mentalising in the management of violence. Advances in Psychiatric Treatment 2013;19(1):67–76.
17. Adshead G. The life sentence: using a narrative approach in group psychotherapy with offenders. Group Analysis 2011;44(2):175–95.
18. World Health Organization. Preventing violence : a guide to implementing the recommendations of the World Report on Violence and Health. 2004.
19. Gilligan J. Violence: Reflections on Our Deadliest Epidemic. London: Jessica Kingsley; 1999.
20. Lewis M. Shame: The Exposed Self. Illustrated edition. New York: Simon and Schuster; 1995.
21. Hyatt-Williams A. Cruelty, Violence, and Murder: Understanding the Criminal Mind. Northvale, N.J: Jason Aronson, Inc.; 1998.
22. Winnicott DW. The anti-social tendency. In DW Winnicott, ed. Through Paediatrics to Psychoanalysis. London: The International Psycho-Analytic Library; 1956. pp. 306–15.
23. Hinshelwood RD. Abusive help – helping abuse: the psychodynamic impact of severe personality disorder on caring institutions. Crim Behav Ment Health 2002;12(2 Suppl): S20–30.
24. Reiss D, Kirtchuk G. Interpersonal dynamics and multidisciplinary teamwork. Advances in Psychiatric Treatment 2009;15 (6):462–9.
25. RCPsych CCQI. Standards for Medium Secure Services. Royal College of Psychiatrists Centre for Quality Improvement; 2014.
26. Craissati J, Minoudis P, Shaw J et al. Working with offenders with personality disorder, A practitioner's guide. Ministry of Justice, National Offender Management Service; 2015.
27. Adshead G, Horne E. The Devil You Know: Stories of Human Cruelty and

Compassion. Main edition. London: Faber & Faber; 2021.

28. Tangney JP, Stuewig J, Hafez L. Shame, guilt and remorse: implications for offender populations. J Forens Psychiatry Psychol 2011;22(5):706–23.

29. Taubner S, Rabung S, Bateman A et al. Psychoanalytic concepts of violence and aggression. In Sturmey, P., ed. The Wiley Handbook of Violence and Aggression. London, UK: Wiley-Blackwell; 2017.

Chapter 17 Psychologically Informed Organisations and Services

Table of Contents

Introduction 258
Enquiry 259
The Importance of Language 260
Beginnings 261
Time 262
Ambivalence 263
Treatment 265
Endings 266
Concluding Remarks 267

Introduction

The need for the concept of a 'psychologically informed' service arises from a recognition that a proportion of people have psychological and emotional needs that may not be appropriately provided for within standard health and social care designs and delivery. As previously discussed (Chapter 15), care-seeking is one of the most primitive and early relational dynamics we engage in. Experiences such as developmental trauma, neglect, and other mistreatment occur in relationships, and often within relationships that would be expected to provide safety, security, and comfort. In many cases, one of the longest legacies of early relational adversity is the loss of trust in others, something that can subsequently give rise to complicated relationships with caring figures and services. In this regard, making a service psychologically informed can be understood as a necessary provision for those who have the highest levels of psychological need.

Health, social, and educational services – amongst others – can play a key part in enabling trust to develop in caring relationships through providing a steady and containing relational experience and resisting the draw to repeat old patterns (see Chapter 15 section 'Staff Responses to Patients with Complicated Relationships with Care'). However, there are circumstances where the actual environment in which staff are trying to provide a service – including its structures and policies – does not facilitate that provision or, at worst, prohibits it from occurring.

The concept of a psychologically informed service might be most broadly understood as a situation where the design, practice, and principles of any given service are informed by the best understandings of the psychological and emotional needs of the people for whom the service is intended, taking particular care to consider those people who struggle to use the service in an uncomplicated way. Johnson and Haigh suggest that a marker of a psychologically informed service is that 'if asked why the unit is run in such and such a way, the staff would give an answer in terms of the emotional and psychological needs of service users, rather than giving some more logistical or practical rationale'.[1] This chapter draws on the principles of a psychodynamic frame (Chapter 5) and extends this to make it relevant outwith the 1:1 therapy or group room. Attention is paid to the ways in which a service is run, interrogating policies and procedures against a psychological understanding of those for whom care is being provided. A new service could be designed from the outset to be psychologically informed, or an existing service could be adapted or more radically redesigned. We do not mean to imply that separate services always need to be set up to provide for those with the most complicated relationships with care. Although specialist services are sometimes required, we are also referring to adaptation or redesign of the running of mainstream services.

Prisons, secure hospitals, and children's homes are obvious specialist settings where a psychologically informed approach will be essential for things to run well, as most, if not all, people served in these settings will have extraordinary needs and complications in their relationships with care. More general settings, such as general practice, community psychiatric services, and schools, would require a psychologically informed approach in order to meet the needs of some users and to prevent inadvertently making matters worse for them. Depending on the nature of the service, the proportion of people who struggle to easily make use of the facility varies. But even when it is a minority, this minority will likely contain those with the highest needs for the service – therefore it is important to take these into consideration (see Chapter 15, section on 'The Inverse Care Law').

To clarify some terminology, the term 'Psychologically Informed Environment' is sometimes used to refer more specifically to a therapeutic and relationally focused approach to the operation of residential services for people experiencing homelessness, such as hostels and refuges;[2] and the term 'Psychologically Informed Planned Environment' to refer to a therapeutic approach in prisons.[3] However, these ideas have wider applicability for any service attempting to work with people with complicated relationships with caring services, not just in a residential setting,[1] and it is this broad approach that this chapter takes.

A psychologically informed approach is underpinned by staff training in relational aspects of care and regular, well-attended reflective practice groups that are embedded into the service (see Chapter 18). While some of the ideas in this chapter may look straightforward on paper, they are not necessarily easy to apply in practice due to the relational dynamics involved. Taking part in a reflective practice group is essential for staff members to process and reflect on the relational dynamics they are a part of, and to support an understanding of what the key issues and stuck points are for a service. A psychologically informed consideration of the service's environment addresses practical areas that may be thought about in reflective practice groups but are hard to influence directly within such groups alone, with their necessary boundaries and limits.

Enquiry

One of the most important aspects in designing a psychologically informed service is an enquiry as to what the needs might be that require accommodation. A central part of this entails discussions with those for whom the service is aimed to discover what might be helpful and unhelpful in terms of facilitating provision of the service. It is important that these enquiries include service users from a range of backgrounds, not just those that speak up first or are the most ‘able’ – as otherwise this would miss the voices of those who believe that their opinions are irrelevant or who mistrust others and so do not readily volunteer. This focus on inclusion is not lip service, but stems from recognising that those of us who lead and design healthcare services are typically relatively ‘healthy’ people, who do not always have the psychological or emotional needs that might allow us to recognise what elements of a psychologically informed service might be required. Without real emotional engagement with those people who have complicated relationships with care, there is a risk that we inadvertently form a service in our own image, based largely on what we ourselves would want to see in a health service, or what is felt a typical person might require.

This enquiry could be supported by a psychotherapist or consultant external to the organisation, or potentially led from within the service – this would depend on the complexity of the situation under consideration and the training and experience of staff. Through a detailed and collaborative relational analysis, the service should aim to build up an approach to running the service that considers the various emotional and psychological needs of its constituency. This process of enquiry and analysis is often supported by reflective practice sessions, with a psychologically informed service evolving through ‘reflective practice and shared action learning within a staff team, as they come to grips with the emotional demands of their work’.[4]

There are many aspects of service design and delivery that can be analysed and changed through the psychologically informed prism. The following sections look at common themes that arise in terms of service principles and design, along with thoughts on how to apply the psychologically informed ideas in everyday practice (these latter ideas are highlighted in the subsections titled ‘Into Practice’). The chapter aims to take a practical and straightforward approach that we hope will be useful to non-psychotherapy staff across a range of services, as well as psychotherapists who are invited to support a service’s work.

The Importance of Language

Language is central to thought and understanding. Within a psychologically informed service, all language used is open to scrutiny and challenge to see if it makes sense, describes the situation as accurately as possible, and is helpful in terms of effectively providing what the service was established to do.

Elements of service users’ adverse relational experiences and inner worlds can creep unwittingly into the language used by staff (see Chapter 2 for discussion on projective identification) – for example, in terms like ‘manipulative’, ‘attention-seeking’, ‘it’s just behavioural’, ‘heartsink’, or ‘time wasters’. With automatic adoption of terms like these, our thinking can become informed by unprocessed emotional responses we have through being in relationships with some patients. These terms may take on an unquestioned currency for some staff, which is at odds with providing care for those who experience difficulties being in relationships.

For example, a circular situation might emerge where a person’s behaviour is constantly attributed to their ‘personality disorder’ and ‘manipulation’, while it is considered that they have this ‘personality disorder’ because they behave in particular ways. Such circles of ‘complete understanding’ run the risk of limiting thought and exploration of other possible meanings and function of the behaviour, and can lead us to forget that we are also playing a part in the relationship in a way that might benefit from analysis and reflection.

Into Practice

If reflected upon, the draw to use terms like these may be informative. What does it say about the kinds of relationships being played out, if a service has been drawn into using certain language? Such language might be an understandable phenomenon to emerge in present-day relationships, where historic versions of such language have been prevalent in a patient's life experiences – that is, the staff's use of such terms may be part of a process of identifying with a service user's internal sense of others. If registered, this can provide insight into the service user's experiences in relationships. This kind of reflective work can help staff to gain perspective on the relational dynamic that they are a part of, reducing the draw to act the dynamic out through the unprocessed use of such terms.

It might be appropriate to describe someone seeking care as 'manipulative' if that is then followed up by a serious questioning of what or who is being manipulated, what function does the manipulation serve, how are we left feeling by the manipulation, and what problem does the manipulation solve for the person. In summary, in a psychologically informed approach, 'behaviour, even when potentially disruptive, is seen as meaningful, as a communication to be understood'.[4]

Beginnings

We now turn to the issue of access to a service for the range of people whom it aims to serve. Access is a key aspect of any service, because if someone or a group of people are unable to attend, then for those individuals the quality and efficacy of the treatments within are as nought.

Often a whole range of steps must be negotiated prior to actually getting into a relationship that might assist in what has brought a person to seek help in the first place. These might include such things as telephone menus and holding queues. There may be appointment letters to read, unfamiliar buildings to arrive at within set time windows, and a range of rooms and clinics to enter, often with doors closed behind. But perhaps most importantly, there is often a wide range of new people to meet and communicate with, many of whom have job titles that can be bewildering to some, and bring with them power imbalances in terms of authority, knowledge, and status.

For many, and maybe even for the majority of us, such steps are not even noticed, or are perhaps experienced as an inconvenience but nothing more. However, a psychologically informed approach is primarily necessary because there are individuals for whom these steps are felt as significant hurdles or potentially experienced so strongly that they are like brick walls.

Take for example those phone calls with their classical music interludes, computer generated voices, and various submenus. For the person who has taken two to three hours to build up the courage to make a call to the doctor, the various and speedily recounted options can overwhelm and increase the anxiety of the already anxious. The wait to speak to somebody, and the occasionally impersonal response once the call does get through, can be more than enough to lead the person to disconnect and end the call. Or perhaps worse than this, the individual's anxiety can be communicated through anger and aggression once contact is made, leading to relational breakdown and an increased anxiety for the care seeker and provider in relation to future attempts.

Into Practice

The issue is about how to develop access provision for those with emotional and psychological needs, where access limitations exist within the arena of relational anxiety, or other anxieties that relate to placing oneself in the vulnerable position of seeking help. Such provision can involve providing adapted means of accessing the service to make it developmentally and relationally achievable for a broader range of people.

We are thinking here about some of the bedrocks of providing a useful service for those with significant relational difficulties: continuity of staff who work with an individual and a consistent approach to allow trust to develop; coherence and transparency in communications;[5] removing unnecessary barriers to contact to allow someone to 'get through' without the individual resorting to escalation of actions; and a willingness from staff to be flexible within appropriate limits and boundaries about how to meet someone requesting care.[6] To do all this is not at all easy due to relational pressures – for example, to become either overly punitive or overly permissive – and so requires reflective practice spaces to underpin the psychologically informed ethos. Financial limitations, staffing levels, and time constraints add to the challenges involved.

Time

Time is a variable that is involved in many elements of care, from the time of day that appointments are available, to the length of time of those appointments, to the length of time those appointments will be available for. Typically, these time arrangements are not decided upon through discussion between the care provider and those seeking care, but more often through practical considerations such as resource availability, waiting list size, and length of time determined to be necessary on average to complete the particular process. Allotted time is therefore a balancing act between these practical elements on one side, and the needs of those seeking help on the other.

But time is relative and experienced differently by different people.[7] For those people who experience high levels of anxiety in situations where need, vulnerability, and asking for help are at the fore, time can become elastic. Perception of time can slow down, or alternatively an hour may pass by quickly. High levels of anxiety can mean a person may struggle to attend to what is going on, what is being said, or what is being asked of them. For those with previous experience of trauma for example, it may take considerable time to get to a point of psychological regulation where much can be taken in from the surroundings, and this time may be longer than the time that has been allocated for their appointment. This can mean that even if someone with such psychological need can actually attend an appointment, they may not recall much at all about what went on within it, even if they have spoken, taken part, and made assenting noises throughout. This may be played out over several appointments, where the time constraints of each appointment mean a person never manages to get to a psychological state where they can make use of the treatment being offered. This can lead to complications down the line if the practitioner (be that in housing, health, or education) is expecting results back from the range of activities they thought they had agreed the person would go off and do. As discussed in the section on 'Ambivalence' below, there is a risk of the service reacting with a script of 'non-engagement', when in fact it may be the case that the person did not retain what was being asked of them due to their psychological state at consultation.

For treatments where a number of sessions might be required – for example, psychological therapies – time needed can vary significantly between people. Many psychotherapies assume that a person seeking such help can develop enough epistemic trust within the time frame given to make use of the material and discussions that occur within that period (epistemic trust refers to an individual's ability 'to consider new knowledge from another person as trustworthy and relevant, and therefore worth integrating into their lives'[8]). While this may be true for many, there will be some who may not be able to develop such trust within the weeks or months provided and may require years to discover any such ability with another person.

Into Practice

It may not always be possible to accommodate time requirements within a healthcare setting, even when both parties agree that more time is required either for appointments or for length of treatment. But it should at least be possible to recognise that time is not a constant for all people. As the American lawyer and human rights activist Kimberlé Crenshaw asserts, 'Treating different things the same can generate as much inequality as treating the same things differently.'[9]

Ambivalence

The psychodynamic lens tunes into the deep ambivalence about seeking care that might exist when someone has a template in their mind of caring relationships as bringing mistreatment, neglect, criticism, or rejection. For example, for a person with early experiences of mistreatment within relationships, in the present day, a part of them may be desperate for help for the consequences of that mistreatment; while another part has a conviction that to ask for help is dangerous because being vulnerable is strongly associated with being maltreated.

Looked at through this lens, some of the situations that we invite people into to get help can end up resembling, to those who have experienced early mistreatment, the circumstances that gave rise to the distress in the first place. The care relationship with professionals often happens in private rooms with one other person who has relatively more power and control, where the door is closed, and where people are asked to reveal some of their most vulnerable aspects. These conditions can recall the sorts of environments and demands where trauma has taken place, and so unwittingly may evoke feelings and responses associated with earlier settings of distress and mistreatment. People may then not turn up or, if they do, arrive in a state of stress and anxiety and might decline the care being offered.

On the other side of the encounter, it is not unusual for healthcare staff themselves to feel ignored or mistreated when they have gone to some lengths to make time for someone, only for that person not to attend without even letting the staff member know they were not coming. As introduced in Chapter 15, if these feelings are not processed or reflected on by the staff and service, they may be relieved through discharging the person felt to be 'not engaging' or not offering any follow-up enquiry (see Figure 17.1).

Figure 17.1: Ambivalence from the service user may be mirrored concretely by ambivalence by the professional. In this figure, the request for help by the service user is received warmly by the professional. But when the service user's conscious or unconscious communication changes to 'go away', the professional feels the patient is 'not engaging'. Both parties struggle to see that the service user both wants help and is afraid of it.
Illustration by Robert Bangham.

Into Practice

A psychologically informed approach might show interest in the why of the missed appointment and put some time and reflection into trying to understand what problem it might solve for someone to go through the lengthy process of seeking a referral only to then not attend the offered appointment. Chapter 20 goes into this area in detail when considering homelessness services, but here we focus on general services. For example, when someone does not turn up to their appointment at a cancer clinic, or a physiotherapy centre, or with an educational psychologist, one might enquire as to whether there was something within the offer being made that might be unmanageable in terms of the psychological and emotional needs of the individual concerned. One could reflect on whether the 'not-turning-upness' carries within it a communication about the person's conflicts and difficulties. Perhaps it is a communication about a feeling of abandonment, disappointment, or some other anxiety? Through not discharging someone after two or three missed appointments, but instead reflecting on the nature of what has happened, new information and understandings might emerge that could have profoundly beneficial impacts on the health and well-being of the person seeking care (see Figure 17.2).

By recognising that the development of connection and some trust is an essential component in the seeking of healthcare for everyone – but that some people cannot readily manage closeness and trust – then we might organise some aspects of new appointments and meetings to recognise and attend to these difficulties. Perhaps open access, or the opportunity for people just to come to see the building without also having to deal with whatever the building is purposed for. It might be possible to arrange initial meetings at a place that might feel safer or more accessible for the person seeking care.

Figure 17.2 In a psychologically informed service, the organisation of the service supports professionals to reflect on the service user's communication. In this figure, the professional wonders if the service user has an internal split between an aspect that wants help and an aspect that is afraid of caring relationships and wants the other to 'go away'. Illustration by Robert Bangham.

Treatment

Thinking about the evidence base that is used to inform treatments, many people are excluded from clinical trials. The randomised controlled trial (RCT) methodology often has strict inclusion and exclusion criteria – this is to keep trial arms similar to aid clear comparison, reducing bias and confounding. What this means, though, is that the internal validity of a trial 'is often achieved at the expense of external validity (generalizability), since the populations enrolled in RCTs may differ significantly from those found in everyday practice'.[10] In trials of 1:1 psychological therapy for example, exclusion criteria may cover those who have a wide range of symptoms, use a large amount of addictive substances, or who are unable to maintain the regularity of treatment sessions required in most trials. This gap between clinical trial evidence and real-world practice would therefore be expected to be large for people with the most complicated relationships with care. As such, treatments for this group may not work as they are 'meant to'. However, an exclusion at the point of development does not always prevent an erroneous assumption that those not represented in clinical trials should then be able to make use of that treatment once it is implemented across health services. Minne quotes a patient with long-standing difficulties, who had been sent for an intervention focused on recovery, who protested: 'How the hell can I recover when I never had cover in the first place?'[11]

Additionally, when practitioners are expected to deliver a treatment that does not fit the person's needs, the practitioners themselves may be left with a variety of feelings, including a sense of inadequacy and frustration. If not reflected on, this can lead on to the practitioners and teams proffering increasingly intrusive but inappropriate interventions as a way of attempting to avoid a sense of inadequacy or therapeutic 'failure' – these new interventions may or may not fit either.[12] At other times, the difficult feelings arising in a practitioner in this kind of encounter may be projected on to the patient who may end up being labelled as 'treatment resistant' or non-engaging; rather than the staff member acknowledging that the client might be being invited to make use of something that has not been subject to evaluation for someone with their specific needs and difficulties.

In Practice

Taking all this into account, a psychologically informed approach to working with people with the most complicated relationships with care would include a degree of flexibility in the treatment approach offered by the practitioner. Furthermore, there would be encouragement from the leaders and managers within their service for practitioners to draw on core skills and develop an individual formulation with each patient. Within the research community there is movement to recognise the need for studies with broader inclusion criteria that reflect the real world, to complement the kind of accuracy that can be obtained with narrower inclusion criteria.

Endings

Like the phases of therapy (see Chapter 8), other kinds of relationships have beginnings, middles, and ends. Endings in relationships with professionals are a time where large therapeutic gain can be achieved. Again, for many, this transition occurs without complication, especially if the healthcare provider communicates in advance their upcoming departure. However, endings are also times where, if handled in a way that does not take account of the psychological and emotional needs of those being ended with, harm can be caused.

Unplanned, unforeseen, and unwanted endings and separations are common in the early lives of people who have complicated relationships with care. Despite this, it is not uncommon for the endings of often quite long-term relationships in healthcare to be unannounced or delivered at short notice in a way that does not allow for discussion, processing, or working through of what the ending might mean for the individual being left. Such situations might go unnoticed for the care provider; but they may be keenly felt by those who have located trust within this relationship, only to find that it ends in ways that are reminiscent of some of the early experiences that gave rise to the distress that brought them to the practitioner.

Take for example, Michael, who had the same clinician Mr X for eight years, and through this time (perhaps unknown to Mr X) came to trust his opinion and recommendations for care, and came to trust Mr X as a person who cared for him. Michael had had a number of traumatic experiences in his past, and developmental experiences of relational unreliability. Michael was not demonstrative in showing that the relationship with Mr X mattered to him – as is common in some people who are insecure in their relationships (see Chapter 2, Box 2.5 on Bowlby and Attachment Theory). After eight years, a letter arrived from the clinic's administration team letting Michael know that his next appointment would not be with Mr X anymore as he had retired, and would instead be with Ms Y. Unwittingly, and through not realising the importance of the relationship, this transition unfortunately provided a re-enactment of relational uncertainty.

This kind of sudden experience of ending may not only bring immediate distress to a patient with this sort of background, but have an impact on the likelihood of them trusting someone else in the future. How long would Ms Y need to be stable and available for Michael to consider trusting her?

In Practice

A psychologically informed approach does not in any way deny that all relationships have limits, boundaries, and endings. It does recognise that for some, and typically those with the greatest psychological and emotional need, transitions in care, including the departure of a key person, require attention, thought, and reflection.

Concluding Remarks

A psychologically informed approach is where a service makes a considered effort to reflect on what it may otherwise take for granted, and then take practical steps so that the service operates in a way that is suited to those who may need it most but find it hardest to use. Through this, the staff might consider how the service may have inadvertently set itself up in relationship to some it seeks to help in a way that has hindered its success. When a service does not operate in a psychologically informed way, this is usually not born out of any conscious or deliberate plan of neglect, but rather because of the imperceptibility of human relationships and the power they can have over us all (see 'The Invisible Relationship' in Chapter 15).

Not discharging people in a reactive way; letting them know that they can remain in contact and seek another appointment at a future time; and acknowledging that they might find attending difficult – these are examples of approaches that can sidestep the possibility of exacerbating the difficulties some people are seeking help for. Continuing contact with a person through discussion of what might work for them, given that the standard approach did not seem to, may form the beginning of a productive connection between the service user and the professional. The hypothesis is that when such psychological aspects are catered for, over time some people who ordinarily miss appointments and engage through not turning up, will become better able to access and make use of the service – in both traditional clinic-based care and specialist services.

References

1. Johnson R, Haigh R. Social psychiatry and social policy for the 21st century – new concepts for new needs: the 'psychologically-informed environment'. Mental Health and Social Inclusion 2010;14 (4):30–5.
2. Phipps C, Seager M, Murphy L et al. Psychologically informed environments for homeless people: resident and staff experiences. Housing, Care and Support 2017;20(1):29–42.
3. Turley C, Payne C, Webster S. Enabling Features of Psychologically Informed Planned Environments. London: Ministry of Justice, National Offender Management Service; 2013.
4. Haigh R, Harrison T, Johnson R et al. Psychologically informed environments and the 'Enabling Environments' initiative. Housing, Care and Support 2012;15 (1):34–42.
5. Bateman A, Campbell C, Luyten P et al. A mentalization-based approach to common factors in the treatment of borderline personality disorder. Curr Opin Psychol 2018;21:44–9.
6. Boag I. Elastic tolerance. In Psychologically Informed Environment Principles in Adult Residential Care. Routledge; 2020.
7. Yoo JY, Lee JH. The effects of valence and arousal on time perception in individuals

with social anxiety. Front Psychol 2015;6:1208.

8. Fonagy P. Epistemic trust in adolescents [Internet]. 2016; www.hra.nhs.uk/planning-and-improving-research/application-summaries/research-summaries/epistemic-trust-in-adolescents/
9. Crenshaw K. Color blindness, history, and the law. In The House That Race Built. Wahneema Lubiano, ed. New York: Pantheon; 1997. pp. 280–8.
10. Blonde L, Khunti K, Harris SB et al. Interpretation and impact of real-world clinical data for the practicing clinician. Adv Ther 2018;35(11):1763–74.
11. Minne C, Collier J. Editorial. The International Journal of Forensic Psychotherapy 2019;1(1):vii–xi.
12. Main TF. The ailment. British Journal of Medical Psychology 1957;30(3):129–45.

Chapter 18

Psychodynamic Reflective Practice Groups

Table of Contents

Introduction 269

What Is a Reflective Practice Group and Who Is It For? 270

The Frame 271

Setting Up a New Reflective Practice Group 273

How Does the Facilitator Enable the Group Process? 274

Concluding Remarks 276

Introduction

Staff in the caring professions often have to contain troubling and unpredictable communications (projections) from those they work with. As discussed in some detail in Chapter 15, it is usual and expected for staff to have feelings in response to these communications – this is part of the process of emotional containment. If reflected on, the professional's feelings and inner responses (countertransference) can be a vital source of information about the relational dynamics the service user carries with them and how the staff member is responding to these.[1,2] However, if staff members do not reflect on and process their countertransference, there is the potential for increased stress for the staff member, and to inadvertently re-enact the patient's relational difficulties rather than provide containment for them.[2,3]

There are examples in the literature of harm coming to both staff and patients through relational pressures being unconsciously acted on by staff rather than spoken about and reflected upon. These include: unprocessed feeling of hopelessness leading to over-intrusive treatment;[4] not taking in key clinical information;[5] and boundary violations in institutions.[6] Furthermore, coupled with anxieties about being blamed for mistakes, over time professionals can withdraw into 'mechanistic and detached ways of thinking and relating to their patients'.[7] Whilst this position may relieve a practitioner's anxieties in the short term, over time this leaves their patients 'feeling isolated, while the practitioner feels demoralised or detached'.[7]

An ongoing and regular reflective process can throw light upon such dynamics, and provide extended time for a deep knowledge of context, function, and history of the service to develop. A regular staff group can be one way to provide a space and opportunity for the constituent members of a service to try and reflect upon the sorts of internal and external relationships they are involved with. Such groups may be named in various ways by different services, but for the purpose of this chapter we will call them reflective practice groups. For a review of the evidence on reflective practice groups, see Patrick et al.[8] By explicitly talking with staff in an reflective practice group about their countertransference feelings and the resulting pull towards certain actions, it is more likely that these dynamics can be understood rather than concretely played out.

Reflective practice groups were discussed in Chapter 17 as underpinning the successful operation of a psychologically informed service. In this light, the reflective practice group should not be viewed as a luxury, but part of the firm foundation of healthcare provision and other settings such as prisons and children's homes. Indeed, in any service where relationships are central to its operation, it could be argued that a facilitated space for reflecting on practice should be an essential part of how the service operates (such as in education,[9] social work, and other human services).

In this chapter we offer a brief introduction to psychodynamic reflective practice groups. The chapter has a focus on the healthcare setting, although the core principles of reflective practice groups apply in settings beyond healthcare. This chapter is aimed at professionals who want to know more about the process, both as participants and as potential group facilitators.

What Is a Reflective Practice Group and Who Is It For?

A reflective practice group brings a whole clinical team together with the primary task being to reflect on and process staff-patient, team, and organisational dynamics, in order to sustain caring relationships with patients and to reduce the stresses of the work for staff. In terms of the constituents of a reflective practice group, it is for everybody within the team seeking reflective practice – for staff from all professions and from all levels of 'seniority'. The facilitator models a supportive, non-judgmental, and empathic approach, whereby clinical situations, encounters with patients, and systemic issues are explored, with a 'constructively challenging and non-collusive position from the facilitator where needed'.[10] The group can help with the improvement of intra-team functioning and help to metabolise some of the projections that can lead to stress and burnout of the individual as well as impacting negatively on team operation. For clinicians who have become inured and detached from clinical work, reflective practice groups may help to sustain interest and awareness in emotional aspects of care.[7] Bringing different perspectives together from the whole team can help piece together a more integrated picture of a patient's interpersonal dynamics, and prevent or minimise splitting within a team. ('Team splitting' refers to the process whereby a patient's inner psychological splitting ends up becoming played out in conflict between different parts of the team; for more detail see Chapter 15, section 'Splitting Within a Clinical Team.') Figure 18.1 summarises key activities of an reflective practice group.

In our view, a psychodynamic reflective practice group is best facilitated by someone who is not a member of the team seeking reflective practice. This 'outsider' position means the facilitator can 'hold a democratic, neutral stance in relation to the teams they work with and [. . .] prevents them becoming part of the problems they are trying to assist with'.[10]

Psychodynamic reflective practice groups have evolved from the Balint group tradition, associated with Michael and Enid Balint.[15] In a classic Balint group, participants – usually from a single professional background – come together from various services to reflect on clinician-patient relationships. Much of the theory (e.g. Rüth[16]) and practice of Balint groups applies to reflective practice groups. This includes harnessing the therapeutic potential of the group to process and contain aspects of the situation under discussion. With a multi-disciplinary reflective practice group, it is a clinical team or service that has requested assistance so all participants are usually from the same team, in contrast to a Balint group where participants are from various services. This difference affects the operation and 'feel' of the group quite substantially. In a reflective practice group, issues may feel more immediate and closer to home as all members work in the same service and most, if not all, members have a connection to the clinical or systemic situations that are raised.

The Frame

Many of the principles of framing a psychodynamic space as described in Chapter 5 apply for a reflective practice group. The essence is the facilitator paying close attention to creating a safe and reliable setting and boundary for the group. This frames a secure and creative space for staff members to undertake the primary tasks of the group as outlined in Figure 18.1. The group needs to be aware of the confidentiality of the space (with appropriate limits to confidentiality). No explicit goals are set for meetings, no agendas written, and no minutes taken. It is a space for open reflection about work matters, free from the administrative constraints of most work meetings.

A reflective practice group is different to a management meeting, ward round, or a supervision. The reflective practice group is not a place for staff to be monitored in terms of their performance or abilities, rather it is a place to reflect on the work of the organisation and their part in it. In a reflective practice group, participants keep responsibility for their own work.[17] The distinction from formal patient management meetings allows staff to explore their responses with less pressure to try and 'solve' problems too soon, which could foreclose the discussion.

For reflective practice groups running in settings where there are shift patterns, it is quite common for the people attending each session to vary from week to week. Furthermore, there may well be disruptions to sessions as the realities of the team's everyday work come into the reflective practice group itself (e.g. alarms going off, incidents occurring nearby). To manage these kinds of situations the facilitator needs to be able to be sympathetic to the disruptions, whilst trying to respect and carve out a space that feels safe-enough for participants to stop and reflect. The facilitator will need to draw on experience in holding an 'internal frame' (see Chapter 5) despite some unsteadiness in the external features of the group.

Discussing the feelings that relational work can bring up can, at least on paper, start to sound something like a personal or group therapy; clarifying the difference between the two is important. Any member of a reflective practice group can expect to be asked about their internal states (feelings, thoughts, etc.) in relation to work matters and to discuss the relationships that are occurring within the sphere of occupation, and it is important to be very clear about this at the outset. However, the task of a reflective practice group is not to relate participants' internal states to their personal history or private life, as would be expected in personal or group therapy. An important boundary limits the exploration to work relationships, with the exclusion of personal relationships (even if there is resonance

Awareness of dynamics

Provide a safe space for participants to:
- reflect on and process staff-patient and systemic dynamics
- register, name and discuss their responses (emotional and otherwise) to work situations

Understanding

Recognise that countertransference feelings are a usual and expected aspect of clinical practice, and not unprofessional.

Explore meanings

Explore the meanings of feelings in terms of the internal and external relationships the team is involved with.

Sustain caring relationships

- Recognise existing therapeutic approaches
- Notice unhelpful actions that might emerge from interpersonal dynamics. Contain and process these to reduce the chance of acting these out. Explore alternatives i.e. what a therapeutic response might look like.

Bring team together

Bring together the various parts of a team to piece together an overall picture of a situation, to reduce team splitting, promote team cohesion and encourage consistency of approach.

Support

Allow staff members to feel supported, understood and valued by other members of the team, providing some protection from the stresses inherent in clinical work.

Improve communication

In relation to work matters, provide an opportunity to get to know other team members' intentions and inner states. This can reduce misunderstandings and assumptions about each other.

Figure 18.1 Key activities of reflective practice groups, drawing on various sources[10–14].

between the two), and the facilitator will step in when needed to keep this boundary. For example, it might be important to ask a staff member how they feel about a particular relationship they are involved in with a patient, but it would not be appropriate to then ask whether this feeling reminds them of how they felt in relation to their father.

It perhaps goes without saying that there may be many circumstances where the particular dynamics of a work situation will resonate with a staff member's historic and/or developmental relationships. Indeed, many of us who work in health and social care may, at least in part, have entered our respective profession due to unconscious desires and motives originating in our earliest relationships. For example, a daughter who was never able to persuade her father to stop drinking finds herself studying medicine and becoming drawn to those with seemingly intractable problems. The feelings of impotence and powerlessness evoked in her by her patients may stir up deep and powerful feelings from her history that may impact on her mental health, as well as how she operates at work.

From a safeguarding point of view, it is therefore important to describe such possibilities and make provision for those who might be unsettled by the process. This might involve making it clear that any member can speak with the facilitator outside the group setting, and that as a facilitator you would be able talk through what might be helpful, with the possibility of direction to find personal support if needed.

Setting Up a New Reflective Practice Group

So how might we go about establishing a reflective practice group within a service? As with any potentially helpful intervention, a reflective practice group is not an inert process, and so requires careful consideration in the setting up phase to create conditions conducive to the group 'working'. The first step in establishing a reflective practice group is to take time to undertake in-depth training and discussion with all concerned as to what the process is, including explanation about why it might be useful (covering relational dynamics as in Chapter 15), and what the boundaries and limits of a reflective practice group are (see Benson[18] for a more detailed account of setting up a reflective practice group). When setting up a new reflective practice group, we have found that the groups are more likely to 'work' when we take time to consider matters carefully with the whole clinical team and not just the referrer – this is analogous to listening to all parts of a person, not just the first part to speak (see also Clinical Example 2 in Chapter 7).

There may be times when considerable explanation of reflective practice is needed, as staff may have had previous experiences of supervision or other staff groups that have been less than useful; staff may also have concerns about attending a group where they are being expected to speak about their work in front of others. There may be many staff who have never had an experience of being in a group where they are being encouraged to talk openly about how they feel about their work, or about parts of their work that they find difficult. For example, in organisations where the overtly stated aim is to care for people, it might feel unusual to then be invited to discuss feelings that – on the surface – appear to run contrary to this ideal.

The facilitator discusses with the team the importance of involvement of clinicians from across the whole multi-disciplinary team. When all parties come to an reflective practice group, this confers the potential for the process to minimise splits and tensions within a team. Conversely, when a particular discipline or certain members are consistently missing from an reflective practice group, this reduces the ability to work through team splits. A regular absence may exacerbate existing tensions as the group members present may project into the absent figure, but with reduced potential for reflection and understanding about the absent member's internal states and intentions – for example, 'they just don't care – if they did, they would be here to listen to us'. (When this situation emerges during the running of a reflective practice group, the facilitator needs to be active in managing the in-session process and consider arranging a review of the sessions if difficulties continue.) In practice, when team leaders are actively involved in the reflective practice group, this models the importance of the process. Staff who look up to the leaders will then be more likely to make it a priority to take part. There may be times when an organisation wants to compel staff to attend a group, but compulsion is not a dynamic that lends itself well to honest and open reflection. We feel that coming to an reflective practice group is something that should be encouraged, expected, and supported, but not mandated.

This initial introduction should be viewed as a central component of the process and as much time as is necessary should be taken in its preparation and delivery. After these initial meetings, teams can then make an informed decision about whether they are in a position to commit to an reflective practice group. To proceed, perhaps as a minimum there should be buy-in from most constituents that the work they are involved in is at least at some level relational in nature, and that the quality, nature, and dynamics of these relationships have a part to play in the relative success or otherwise of the work they are involved with.

The facilitator has a role in deciding with the team as to what might be the best set up of the group in terms of the numbers attending, the frequency of the group, and whether it is a fixed or open membership. Other key questions include how long the group is going to run for, and whether a trial period followed by an evaluation might be helpful. During the setting up process, it is the facilitator's task to ensure that there is clarity about who is responsible for what. The reflective practice facilitator may be dependent upon the host organisation to provide most of the infrastructure, including arranging a suitable room. Furthermore, as the reflective practice facilitator does not directly manage the team, the team leaders need to organise staffing and timetabling that facilitates attendance from anyone who desires it.

How Does the Facilitator Enable the Group Process?

Perhaps the most important functions of the facilitator are to attend to the frame of the reflective practice group and to conduct an open discussion and exploration by the group to support understanding and processing of the relational dynamics present in the subject matter being raised. This openness should be reflected in the facilitator's use of their own emotional responses to inform an understanding of what might be going on within the meeting.

In the author's experience, the 'live' dynamics of a reflective practice group frequently require a warm, 'active', and adaptable approach by the facilitator. Facilitators draw on their training in individual psychotherapy, group psychotherapy (see Chapter 22), Balint group practice, systemic and family work, and teaching skills – and apply and integrate these to the task of setting up and facilitating a reflective practice group.[19] For novice psychodynamic therapists, or for therapists from a related kind of therapy, a suggested competency framework for reflective practice facilitators has been developed which can be used to inform appropriate training for facilitators.[10]

Without being overly didactic, the facilitator attends to keeping the group on task. Some group orchestration might be required, such as gentle encouragement of the quieter members, and a sensitive quietening of those who find it easier to talk a lot. The facilitator helps the group to triage what topics are for the group and what might be for other groups or parts of the organisation to deal with. For example, primarily 'personal' or 'performance' issues would be for other settings. A session typically starts by members bringing for discussion one or more emotionally salient clinical encounters, often involving psychological conflicts, distress, or threats to competence for the clinicians.[12]

The facilitator aims to stimulate and facilitate the group to process and 'digest' what members bring for discussion. Much of what is contained in earlier chapters on the basic psychodynamic approach is relevant here, as is Chapter 22 on group psychotherapy. The facilitator seeks to 'elaborate, reflect and clarify' the participants' feelings and thoughts in relation to clinical encounters, including drawing attention to aspects that are being avoided. An aim is to foster a climate of 'safety, acceptance, and trust'.[20] Within this climate, participants can feel that their emotional responses to clinical work are important and have meaning. This is supportive in and of itself, but is also a prerequisite for the group process to deepen.

It is the role of the facilitator to manage the level of affect within the room, addressing any interpersonal issues that emerge. Linked to this consideration, the facilitator has to hold in mind that, for some teams, staff will have to resume their everyday work immediately after the reflective practice session finishes. The reflective practice group members will also usually hold this in mind and manage their level of exposure accordingly.[12]

On occasion, the dynamics within the group can parallel the staff-patient interaction under discussion. Namely, one person can become aligned with the patient's position and another with the staff member's position, leading to increased affect within the group. When the parallel process can be seen and felt clearly, if the group is experienced and secure enough, an experienced reflective practice group leader can sensitively use this as a vehicle for understanding the clinical encounter.[19,20] If it is not likely to be appropriate or useful to work with the parallel process, then the facilitator would manage the level of affect and steer the group onto less emotionally charged ways of exploring the dynamics under discussion.

As a session goes on, the group may question and re-evaluate initial perspectives on the relational dynamics being discussed, and bring in new perspectives 'that could not be seen before'[16] (see Clinical Example, below, and also Clinical Example 4 in Chapter 22).

Clinical Example Session from an established multi-disciplinary reflective practice group in a 3rd sector-run residential service

The subject of this session was a man in his fifties, Anthony, who had been in the residential service for over two years. Anthony presented as withdrawn and inaccessible, troubled by hearing voices and other experiences that he would not speak about. Members of the group spoke about feelings of hopelessness and confusion when working with him. His keyworker and others felt bad that they were unable to 'successfully treat him' and some people spoke of an impulse to 'try anything'.

There was a turning point in the group discussion in the middle phase. An idea was raised by the facilitator that these feelings (i.e. hopelessness, confusion) may be picking up useful clinical information about the dynamics of working with this man; the facilitator also acknowledged there may be a strong pull to 'try anything' to dampen these difficult experiences. The group members picked this up – perhaps these feelings reflected something of the patient's own state of mind? With a space to process these feelings, as the session went on, staff became less blaming of themselves for somehow not being effective enough, less phobic about feelings of hopelessness and confusion, and less inclined to commence treatments in a desperate way.

Towards the end of the session, the group began to become interested in Anthony's background and how he came to be at this point in his life. One participant realised that they knew little about Anthony, despite working with him for many months. Questions were raised by the group members – might it be possible to find out more about him, or at least be interested in why this was so difficult? A man seemingly without history, was he blocking something out? One member linked the current discussion to a long-standing theme in the reflective practice group – that feelings such as hopelessness might be expected to arise within staff working in a service aimed at recovery, when someone does not seem to be recovering. Some staff took away from the session a new sense of interest in the dynamics of hopelessness, confusion, and inaccessibility that seemed to surround this man.

The facilitator supports group movement in a number of ways. The facilitator aims to 'sit comfortably with uncertainties' and stimulate expression of multiple views and experiences – this harnesses the potential of reflective practice group members to piece together a clinical encounter from the fragments that any one group member may hold.[20]

The facilitator listens carefully – both intellectually to the material but also inwardly to themselves – and offers reflections and questions (but not all-knowing verdicts) embedded within a psychodynamic framework. By the facilitator not purporting to have all the answers, and resisting taking credit for the group's discoveries, the group's own sense of its abilities is maintained: 'It is not the leader's individual brilliance that illuminates the case but the richness and diversity of group participation and interactions he/she facilitates.'[20] At the end of the group, the facilitator offers a summing up of proceedings, resisting the urge to force a 'neat' conclusion if none has been reached.

Concluding Remarks

This chapter has described the essential role of reflective practice groups in sustaining caring relationships between staff and patients. We have highlighted the importance of initial discussions and training involving the whole service, before decisions can be made about proceeding with a reflective practice group. We have given an overview of how the facilitator applies and adapts their psychodynamic training and skills to the task of facilitating staff groups. Effective reflective practice groups can lead a service and its members to become increasingly interested in how they relate to people who use their service. A regular reflective practice group that is embedded into the service culture is at the heart of a psychologically informed service.

References

1. Adshead G, Sarkar J. The nature of personality disorder. Advances in Psychiatric Treatment 2012;18(3):162–72.
2. Moore E. Personality disorder: its impact on staff and the role of supervision. Advances in Psychiatric Treatment 2012;18 (1):44–55.
3. Melchior ME, Bours GJ, Schmitz P et al. Burnout in psychiatric nursing: a meta-analysis of related variables. J Psychiatr Ment Health Nurs 1997;4 (3):193–201.
4. O'Connor S. An analytic approach in a psychiatric intensive care unit. Psychoanalytic Psychotherapy 1998;12 (1):3–15.
5. Mental Welfare Commision. Too Close To See – Mr F. 2009.
6. Fallon P, Bluglass R, Edwards B. Report of the committee into the personality disorder unit at Ashworth Special Hospital. 1999.
7. Evans M. Making Room for Madness in Mental Health: The Psychoanalytic Understanding of Psychotic Communication. Karnac Books; 2016.
8. Patrick J, Russell K, Polnay A. Traditional approaches to reflective practice – history, aetiology, evidence and approaches. In Reflective Practice in Forensic Settings: A Cognitive Analytic Approach to Developing Shared Thinking. S.l.: Pavilion Publishing and Media Ltd; 2021. pp. 21–34.
9. Banardo's Scotland. Supporting the mental health and wellbeing of education staff through professional supervision structures [Internet]. 2019; www.barnardos.org.uk/sites/default/files/uploads/supporting-mental-health-wellbeing-education-staff-through-professional-supervision-structures.pdf
10. Patrick J, Kirkland J, Maclean C et al. Reflective practice paper and competency guidelines framework. Forensic Network Matrix Group; 2018.

11. Johnston J, Paley G. Mirror mirror on the ward: who is the unfairest of them all? Reflections on reflective practice groups in acute psychiatric settings. Psychoanalytic Psychotherapy 2013;27(2):170–86.
12. McAvoy P. Significant events in ward-based reflective practice groups. 2012.
13. Thorndycraft B, McCabe J. The challenge of working with staff groups in the caring professions: the importance of the 'team development and reflective practice group'. British Journal of Psychotherapy 2008;24 (2):167–83.
14. Adlam J. 'Not keeping it in the family.' A mentalisation-based approach to facilitating reflective practice Groups for multi-disciplinary staff teams in forensic settings. 2016.
15. Balint M. The Doctor, His Patient and the Illness. London: Pitman; 1957.
16. Rüth U. Classic Balint group work and the thinking of W.R. Bion: how Balint work increases the ability to think one's own thoughts. Group Analysis 2009;42 (4):380–91.
17. Hawkins P, Shohet R. Supervision in the Helping Professions. 3rd ed. Blacklick: Open University Press; 2007.
18. Benson J. Working More Creatively with Groups. 4th ed. London: Routledge; 2018.
19. Scanlon C. The traumatised-organisation-in-the-mind: opening up space for difficult conversations in difficult places. In The Therapeutic Milieu Under Fire: Security and Insecurity in Forensic Mental Health. Jessica Kingsley Publishers; 2012.
20. Johnson AH, Nease DE Jr, Milberg LC et al. Essential characteristics of effective Balint group leadership. Fam Med 2004;36 (4):253–9.

Chapter 19

Psychodynamic Consultation to Clinical Teams

Table of Contents

Introduction 278
Initial Discussions 280
Meetings with the Team 281
Interest in the Service 282
Relationships between Staff Members 283
Important Past Events in the Service 283
Relationships with the Patient 284
Drawing the Various Strands Together 287
Reflections on Future Functioning 288
Concluding Remarks 288

Introduction

Many people with significant mental health difficulties have regular and, at times, ongoing encounters with various parts of the health and welfare system, be that through their general practitioner, local authority services, or some other part of the public or third sector. Within these relationships there is often significant potential for positive change to take place, sometimes over many years. However, as discussed in previous chapters, some people struggle to make use of offered care, or evoke various anxieties in the team or service providing the care. As such, preserving these important relationships over the longer term can prove challenging for both sides.

A psychodynamic consultation for *clinicians* can help preserve and support these existing therapeutic relationships with patients. A team might ask for some assistance in trying to understand a particular patient they are involved with, where interactions are experienced as stressful, challenging, or difficult in some way (see Box 19.1).

A psychodynamic consultation comprises one or more meetings between a psychotherapist and a clinical team to think about the dynamics surrounding working with a patient. A central premise is that the clinical team are the experts about their patient and the treatment they offer. What the psychotherapist brings is expertise in the dynamics of relationships and in staff countertransference, and the offer to facilitate a containing space for the team to understand and process the dynamics of a clinical interaction.

Box 19.1 Examples of reasons why staff may request a psychodynamic consultation

- To help make sense of encounters with a patient that give rise to strong feelings in staff (e.g. confusion, anxiety, dislike, guilt, hopelessness, rescue fantasies, urge to withdraw care)
- To prevent clinicians becoming 'stuck' in counterproductive situations in relation to a patient
- To support teams in reflecting about difficult clinical decisions and promotion of safe working in high-risk/anxiety-provoking situations
- To support teams with understanding and decision-making for a proportion of patients with relational difficulties whose situation worsens with increasing intensity of contact with services (see also Chapter 14 for discussion of this particular dynamic)

There is overlap in approach between a psychodynamic consultation and reflective practice groups (Chapter 18), but with some differences in emphasis. A consultation process tends to be briefer (e.g. over one to three sessions), more focused, and more explicit in its approach, compared to reflective practice groups which are longer term and so can develop more organically. However, both consultation and reflective practice groups draw on core psychodynamic principles of drawing attention to underlying dynamics and framing a space for containment and processing of projections. Similarly, both approaches may facilitate a service to become more 'psychologically informed' in its overall operation (see Chapter 17). An in-depth exploration of an organisational consultancy approach is beyond the scope of this chapter (the reader is directed to Hinshelwood[1] and Menzies Lyth[2]).

To facilitate a psychodynamic consultation with a team, the psychodynamic therapist requires well-developed skills in group working (see Chapter 22) and systemic approaches, and significant prior experience of supervising clinicians in a group. This chapter is addressed primarily for psychodynamic therapists starting out in consultation work, to provide some orientation. This chapter may also be of interest to professionals and teams who are consulting a psychotherapist about their clinical work or are contemplating requesting a consultation. Chapters 15 to 18 discuss indirect psychodynamic work from various angles – these comprise important background concepts to understanding the present chapter.

In consultation work with a team, the psychotherapist is interested and curious about various dimensions of the system at play in order to understand as fully as possible the clinical interactions the team is struggling with. By 'system' we are referring to the service and the staff in it, the service culture, and the relationship between the patient and staff. A process of non-judgmental and 'neutral' enquiry brings to light the context within which the presenting problem has developed and cultivates the clinical team's interest in this.

For example, in a mental health team, concerns about ongoing funding brought a sense of urgency to demonstrate usefulness. This had a knock-on effect, such that clinicians felt anxious when anything 'went wrong' with patients, leading to more risk-averse treatment. This was experienced as un-containing by patients and 'adverse events' actually increased. If this team were to request psychodynamic consultation about a particular patient, the potential impact of the consultation would be enhanced if this systemic dimension were taken into account. In some situations, as will unfold in the clinical example in this chapter, it is an interaction between a particular clinical situation and the service's history and functioning that culminates in the presenting team's distress, confusion, or a struggle to care.

In this chapter, 'we' or 'our' refers to psychotherapists providing consultation, and 'they' or 'their' refers to clinicians or teams seeking consultation.

Initial Discussions

If a team has been moved to make a request for assistance with a particularly difficult clinical relationship, then they are often putting themselves in a position of some vulnerability. A consultation to a team requires the establishment of a relationship and a secure frame just as in more traditional psychotherapeutic work with a patient. Our task here is to agree from the outset what is available and what the parameters of engagement are, and then, as with all boundaries, to work to keep to that commitment. This helps the team develop trust in the facilitator and a sense of security.

Substance use team and Ms A – Part 1 Initial phone call with the referrer: 'Ms A just won't accept help'

Mr Nichols, a nurse in a team working with people who use drugs, contacted their local psychotherapy service on behalf of the team for some assistance. Mr Nichols spoke by phone with a psychotherapist, Dr Richards. Mr Nichols explained that the team felt frustrated at not being able to get a patient, Ms A, to accept help. Ms A was a woman in her forties, who was dependent on opiates. Ms A's use of opiates was associated with increasing physical and mental health concerns. The nurse was aware that Ms A had a number of difficult early experiences, including a history of being force-fed during childhood, and of being physically restrained several times during her adolescence and early twenties during admissions to psychiatric hospital. Mr Nichols wondered if there was something different that they could do 'to make the patient listen and accept the help she clearly needs'.

The initial contact offers the opportunity for a preliminary discussion about the interpersonal dynamics that the referrer and their team are struggling with. In some initial discussions, it is possible to get to the nub of things fairly quickly – for other teams, it may take years for a team to be in a position to examine their responses to a patient. Towards the end of the initial contact, the psychotherapist can ask the clinician how they have found this kind of discussion, and explore how they would like to proceed. For some, this brief discussion may provide the containment, support, or perspective the referrer was looking for, and the contact may end at this point. For others, it may lead on to a consultation with the whole team. In the latter situation, the referring clinician may need to go away and discuss with their team about next steps before confirming with the psychotherapist.

We note that some teams may request a psychodynamic consultation when, in fact, the primary difficulty lies in leadership or management difficulties, a lack of resources, or unmet general training needs. In these circumstances, a psychodynamic consultation is unlikely to be of benefit; at least, not until these other issues begin to be acknowledged and addressed.

Many staff members working in the health and social care sector, whilst they have years of experience of caring relationships ranging from the straightforward to the seemingly impossible, may not have had substantial training in human development, relational dynamics, or how the nature of relationships influences mental health and well-being. Therefore, some background of what the consultation approach entails may be helpful. This might take the form of written information, a teaching session, or informal discussions with staff, covering what a psychodynamic consultation for clinicians means in real-world terms, and what topics might be up for investigation and discussion.

Depending on the situation, we might ask to come to a handover or team meeting to introduce ourself and 'sit-in' in the background to learn about the team. This may be useful if the therapist and the team are unfamiliar with each other, or if there are misgivings or scepticism about the endeavour from parts of the team. Joining their clinical meetings communicates respect for and interest in what they do, and also helps us learn from direct observation about the service and the patients they work with.

Meetings with the Team

If the psychotherapist and the clinical team agree that a consultation session is likely to be useful, the next step is to organise a meeting. It is preferable for all members of staff who have direct or indirect contact with the patient to be included. This might involve several teams taking part if the patient has significant contact across various services.

The opening of the session involves the therapist putting the team(s) at ease, introductions, summarising the background to the consultation, and setting a frame – including clarifying the duration of the meeting and its purpose. The therapist is respectful towards the abilities and skills of the clinical team, and values the differences between the work of the team and the therapist's own area of expertise. This facilitative and supportive attitude helps the team to retain their sense of value at a time when they may be struggling, and it creates conditions conducive to the team being open to new ideas that may emerge through the consultation process (see Box 19.2).

As an overall sequence for a consultation, usually we would start by taking an interest in the service, then move on to the relationships with the patient in question. Towards the end of the process there is typically a phase of synthesis and drawing things together. In our practice, a consultation would typically unfold over two or three sessions, each lasting one to one and a half hours. In some situations, a leading edge of anxiety emerges straightaway and the team clearly wants to start with a certain topic. The therapist would probably decide to go with that rather than impose a sequence on the session that does not fit.

Box 19.2 A note on therapist countertransference during consultation for a team

Teams may come for help when they feel desperate and doubting of their abilities. Therapists may pick up these feelings, and it can be easy to fall into an overcompensating, all-knowing 'guru' position and try to provide all the answers. Taking up an all-knowing position is uncomfortable for the therapist and may feel persecutory for the team, which may be left holding the feelings of inferiority that they came to consultation for help with.

A consultation 'works' when the therapist works *with* the team and creates a frame within which the team can think, articulate their experiences, and process what is happening. Rather than act on the countertransference feelings of inadequacy and try and enact idealised solutions, the task for therapists is to register and process these feelings, and find ways to put these experiences into words so sense can be made of them.

Box 19.3 Possible areas of enquiry into the service, depending on what emerges:

- What are the service's conscious (and less conscious) aims and objectives, and how do these fit in with those of the wider organisation of which it is part?
- Who is it staffed by, and what do the staff think that they are doing there?
- What is the history of the service and organisation? Where, when, and how was it 'born'?
- What makes it feel good or bad about itself, or makes it feel like it is failing in its function?

The following content is intended to illustrate areas of interest to be held in mind and explored according to what is possible in each consultation. Covering every detail of every element that follows in the rest of this chapter is, of course, an impossible task and not clinically desirable or efficient.

Interest in the Service

Every service has a history, and these histories can often say a great deal about how the service functions in the present, what values it holds dear, and why certain behaviours from service users are experienced as particularly challenging or complicated. A way in to exploring the life of the service and organisation could be to simply say, '*Before we talk about the work with Ms A, can you tell me about your service?*' and then follow up the response with interest (see Box 19.3).

With regard to the aims, a service may have both conscious and unconscious aims. Chapter 15 discusses more fully the topic of unconscious aims and fantasies in caring professionals and services, and how some aims can conflict with the realities of clinical work. In circumstances when it would help with understanding the presenting situation, and if there is sufficient rapport, the psychotherapist may through observation and enquiry support the team to articulate unconscious aims of the service (see Ms A – Part 2). It can be helpful for the psychotherapist to tune in to these undercurrents, but they must ensure that this sort of work does not drift into personal analysis of any individual team member. The latter is not the remit of a consultation and being aware of this means that the therapist will be prepared to intervene to ensure no one person is overly in the spotlight.

Substance use team and Ms A – Part 2 Meeting the team in person: taking an interest in the service itself

Dr Richards met the substance use team for the first 1.5-hour consultation session. The team were happy to talk and explained the following:

- Service – this was a small, third-sector team. Some staff members had lived experience of alcohol problems.
- Service history – this charity was committed to an abstinence model of addressing drug use. Those involved in the development of the service had found this model to be useful in their own lives. The origins of the charity were born in the personal experience of the chief executive, and their mission statement, values, and personnel selection were influenced by the views of the founder.

It was possible to discuss the tension that could arise between the employees' commitment to stopping people from taking drugs, and when a person sought help from the service but refused to work towards becoming abstinent. When this situation arose, it could evoke anxiety and frustration in some employees trying to help. There was an acknowledgement that this in turn could an impact on the care relationship between the clinician and the patient. This background was relevant to the difficulties they were having in caring for Ms A.

Such founders' effects can provide limits to what an organisation and its constituent members can think about or tolerate in their everyday work. Without such an understanding, the consultation may hit brick walls that are hard to understand. Such limits are likely to be present within every organisation, and indeed are present within every psychotherapy service that aims to provide consultation.

Relationships between Staff Members

The personnel, the relational dynamics between them, as well as the protocols of a service all influence how a system functions as a whole (see Box 19.4). This territory overlaps with 'organisational consultancy' and we can only mention this briefly within the scope of this chapter. Whilst of interest, much of the areas for enquiry in Box 19.4 will not be possible within a consultation. However, even within a one-off contact, it might be possible to gain a cursory understanding of some of the dynamics in Box 19.4 that may be impacting upon the presenting problem. Some of these issues are touched on further in Chapter 17 on 'Psychologically Informed Organisations'.

Box 19.4 Possible areas of enquiry into the team personnel, intra-team dynamics, and protocols

- Who are the employees?
- Is there a hierarchy and, if so, who is in charge and how do they run things?
- How do its constituent parts relate to each other and, perhaps just as importantly, how they do not?
- What protocols exist and how do these work in practice?
- Do protocols serve another function beside their manifest (conscious) purpose?

Protocols may function well – such as when used to bring attention to detail when working with high-risk patients – and can help to contain staff anxieties and make it easier to think and reflect. However, at other times, bureaucracy may proliferate and be used defensively to postpone making difficult decisions, and so end up increasing anxiety through avoidance and displacement.[3]

Important Past Events in the Service

There may be past significant experiences within the service, including successes as well as traumas such as the death or untimely departure of a charismatic leader. The suicide of a patient following a range of interventions may leave particular personnel feeling responsible or deficient in some way. There may be anxiety about further deaths that can affect the degree of disquiet that the organisation can bear within its day-to-day functioning (see Clinical Example below of Mr D – note, this is a different patient and team to Ms A and the substance use team).

Clinical Example A crisis team struggling with anxiety in relation to Mr D

A crisis team sought consultation with regard to their current work with Mr D, a man who had made a serious suicide attempt two months previously. The team were finding it hard to allow Mr D much freedom despite his mood appearing to be steadily improving. They were aware that without any 'positive risk taking' Mr D's recovery might be stifled.

The team felt anxious working with Mr D, but at the start of the consultation it was unclear to what extent this anxiety was accurately tuning into something to do with Mr D, and what was more to do with the team's own functioning.

On exploration of the team's history, it transpired that six months previously, a long-standing patient of theirs, Mrs M, had killed herself. The consultation session then took an unexpected turn, as it allowed members of the team to express their feelings to do with Mrs M, the patient who had died, including feelings associated with various stages of grieving. Mrs M's suicide had been thoroughly investigated and the conclusions were that the care she had received had been more than adequate. The consultation allowed open discussion of the limitations of the service and of how not every death can be prevented.

After exploring this, the team were able to more accurately reflect on Mr D's current risk towards himself and what it felt like working with him. One team member summed it up by saying that one had to tolerate some risk of Mr D coming to harm in order for him to have a chance to get better. This felt disappointing to some members but also relieving, as this realisation freed them from the impossible and omnipotent task that they had unconsciously set themselves of never allowing any patient under their care to come to harm again.

Relationships with the Patient

A main focus of the consultation will be on the relationships between the clinicians and the patient and on developing a picture of the referred problem.

Patient's Relationship History with the Service

Typically, a safe starting point for this is to ask some basic questions around the context and history of the relationship with the patient: how long it has been going on for, and how frequent is the contact? What happens when there is contact with the patient, and what is the contact for? How has the relationship developed over time? If there have been changes in the therapeutic relationship, is there a sense of what brought these about?

Relational History of the Patient Prior to Arriving at the Service

This discussion will usually evolve into the staff saying something of what they know of the patient's history, in terms of what has been recounted to them by the patient. It should be borne in mind that this is a story about a story, rather than an objective truth about the person's history and experience. It is information that can be useful in terms of getting a general idea as to the relational history of the patient and what experiences of care they have had prior to arriving at the particular service they are now working with (see Clinical Example, the substance use team and Ms A – Part 3).

Substance use team and Ms A – Part 3 Ms A's relational history

As the discussion unfolded, it seemed clear that, whilst a part of Ms A wanted help, her expectation of care was that it would be delivered in a coercive and frightening way. This appeared to be associated with experiences of being forced into doing things by caregivers during her early adolescence (including being forced to eat), and then repeated in experiences in secure settings in her later teenage years where her disturbing behaviour resulted in her being restrained several times and receiving intra-muscular injections.

Staff Members' Current Experiences of What It Is Like Working with the Patient

This key aspect of the consultation is about providing a space for those seeking the consultation to reflect on how they are currently experiencing the relationship with the patient. The material that emerges here is of central concern and will form the root of any understandings arrived at.

We enquire closely about what sorts of feelings, thoughts, and behaviours are being evoked through being in relation to the patient. Linked to this, how do staff imagine the patient feels about them? What are the range and descriptions of those feelings? What behaviours, perhaps in terms of treatment provision/treatment restriction, have been evoked by these feelings? (See the substance use team and Ms A – Part 4.)

Substance use team and Ms A – Part 4 Clinicians' experience of the relationship with Ms A

The psychotherapist invited the group to talk about what it was like working with Ms A. Ms A had been involved with the substance use team for three years. Staff members experienced her as vulnerable and fragile, and in relation to this they spoke about feeling desperate and lost about what to 'do'. As the consultation went on, the staff articulated a need to 'get her better' which entailed her reducing use of intravenous opiates. One staff member said, 'Ms A needs to accept "proper" treatment soon before she deteriorates.'

It appeared that the team were trying harder and harder to help Ms A, offering her an increasing number of appointments each week with encouragement to start medical and psychological treatment. But the more appointments that were offered, the more they were disrupted – either through Ms not turning up or by arriving intoxicated.

This process needs to take careful and considerate enquiry, as staff may be unused to discussing openly how they feel about the people they treat, particularly if some of those feelings are what are traditionally referred to as 'negative' feelings and emotions. For example, in a service that has been established on the provision of care, prides itself on that provision, and is staffed with people who find it important to care, discussing feelings of dislike or of 'not-caring for' a patient can sometimes be anxiety-provoking to acknowledge.

Some therapists and the teams requesting consultation may find a structured approach useful in formulating patient and staff interactions. Reiss and Kirtchuk break this process down into four perspectives that link together in a cycle.[4] This is a way to capture, frame by frame, the dynamics of re-enactment, that is, how a patient's inner templates of relationships can inadvertently become played out in his relationships with others.

- Starting with the patient

  - How does the patient typically experience the staff (perspective A)?
  - How does the patient typically react to this (perspective B)?

- Then considering the staff
  - How do the treating clinicians typically experience the patient (perspective C)?
  - How do the clinicians react to this (perspective D)?[4]

(See Chapter 14 for a related but different structured way of formulating and working with staff-patient dynamics, which is tailored for patients with marked narcissistic difficulties.) Reiss and Kirtchuk have also produced a list of common relational experiences (based on the Operationalised Psychodynamic Diagnostic system[5]). This may be useful in reassuring clinicians that a range of experiences are expected and normal for patients and staff alike. This list can be used either as a 'menu' for clinicians to choose from or as a starting point that encourages people to find their own words (Box 19.5).

It is essential to try and develop a full picture of the various ways the patient may interact with different parts of the service. The therapist therefore encourages all staff to describe their day-to-day experiences in relation to the patient. There will be similarities as well as contrasts between how members of staff experience being with a patient. For example, a general practitioner found a patient deeply frustrating and defeating, whilst the receptionist enjoyed lengthy and enjoyable conversation with him. The therapist tries to assemble multiple perspectives of staff members to piece together a fuller picture.

Box 19.5 List of common relational experiences – this pertains to staff and patients alike (Reiss and Kirtchuk, 2009[4])

Allowing too much independence	Defying and opposing
Accepting and admiring	Insisting on their position
Attending to and caring	Revealing and exposing
Treating him/herself as special	Pouring out concerns and anxieties
Over-estimating and idealising	Relying on
Instructing and patronising	Clinging
Domineering and overwhelming	Giving up in despair
Demanding and imposing	Appeasing and complying
Accusing	Indignant and self-justifying
Putting down and humiliating	Hurt and touchy
Intimidating and attacking	Running away
Rejecting	Showing disgust
Abandoning	Cutting of contact
Ignoring	Keeping up a barrier

Reproduced from Reiss and Kirtchuk, 2009[4] (under STM permissions guidance)

The key point here is to try and make sense of not just what goes on between the patient and the staff, but to develop a detailed account of how these interactions leave people feeling, and how these feelings come to operate on the ongoing relationship between the two. Perhaps staff feel neglected or let down. Maybe they feel disappointed or maybe relieved. Maybe they feel a combination of some or all of these reactions. How do staff imagine the patient feels? All of these responses may provide valuable insights into what might be being communicated in the relationship. The aim of the session is then to go further by trying to tease out how these feelings might be saying something about the patient's experience and history, as well as trying to determine how the feelings are currently affecting the quality and nature of the care relationship. Figure 19.1 depicts a structured approach to describing the interpersonal dynamics between Ms A and the substance use team.

Drawing the Various Strands Together

As the consultation process goes on, the psychotherapist and the team try to reflect on how all these dynamics – that is, systemic factors as well as staff-patient dynamics – shed light on the situation that had become problematic to the point of requesting a consultation. This 'pulling together' is something that is grappled with and approached several times through the consultation and is refined and modified as the consultation progresses (see Clinical Example, the substance use team and Ms A – Part 5).

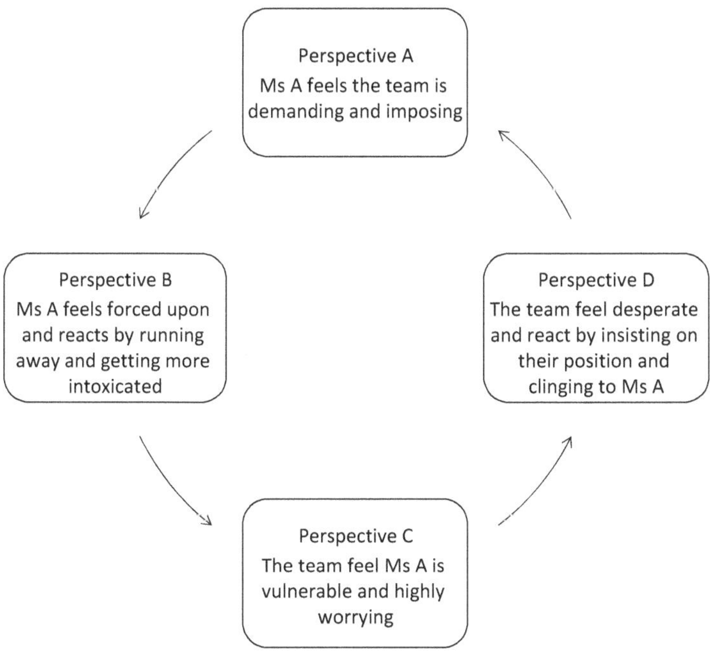

Figure 19.1 Applying the structured interpersonal dynamics approach (Reiss and Kirtchuk)[4] to the clinical example involving Ms A and the substance use team.

Substance use team and Ms A – Part 5 Towards the end of the first session – beginning to draw things together

An understanding of the nature and origins of Ms A's ambivalence about care was helpful for the team in making sense of Ms A's requests for help (with the desperation behind this), and her backing off when this was offered. This could be seen to be due to her fear of expected coercion in caring figures. Neither Ms A's inner desperation nor her fear about caring figures was expressed directly, but these were pieced together in the consultation process through analysis and synthesis of the history, staff countertransference, and staff actions.

The issues and feelings raised by working with Ms A also tapped into wider service sensitivities, in particular the ethos of insisting on abstinence from drugs, and the potential to project onto the patient what had worked for the staff.

This particular combination of existing service dynamics with the relational dynamic surrounding Ms A had led to desperation in the staff who tried harder and harder . . . yet ultimately ended up acting in a way that echoed disturbing elements in Ms A's internal world.

Reflections on Future Functioning

Once the consultation has considered relevant areas, the facilitator can invite the group to step back and reflect on what they wish to keep about their current approach to the patient, and what ideas they have about seeing/doing things differently. This is illustrated in the final part of the Clinical Example of the substance use team and Ms A.

Substance use team and Ms A – Part 6 Second session, one week later

The team reflected that well-meaning but overzealous attempts to insist Ms A accepted help were making things worse and felt like force-feeding to the patient. The team reframed their task as not to make Ms A 'take treatment', but instead to tolerate feeling desperate and not useful as carers, whilst continuing to be there for the Ms A, without either giving up or forcing care on her.

Postscript: Over time, the above understanding and approach improved the situation. Through the team taking a more measured approach (as opposed to insisting that Ms A must take treatment as per perspective D in Figure 19.1), Ms A felt less imposed on by the team and became less defensive. Ms A did, in fact, gradually begin contemplating accepting care from the team. The team continued to have countertransference feelings of 'not being useful' in relation to the slow pace of change, but now had more of a systemic understanding of these responses, and were less troubled by them.

Concluding Remarks

Consultation is usually requested at a point where the care relationship is perceived to be breaking down. This point represents a potentially serious threat to both the patient's health and also the well-being and functioning of the treating team. However, it is also a time where important underlying dynamics may have become visible and accessible.

This illustrative case example is quite 'neat' because it is fictionalised. Whilst in reality it may sometimes unfold in this way, the consultation may leave an incomplete or provisional understanding. In these latter circumstances, it is important and containing for all parties to talk about these limits and acknowledge what remains confusing or unclear. Furthermore, there may be team splits, and there will certainly be multiple different perspectives within a team – these have been simplified in the clinical example of Ms A and the substance use team for demonstration of the overall arc of a consultation process. The topic of team splitting has been covered in Chapter 15.

The psychodynamic consultation process has, at its heart, the aim of developing and maintaining existing caring relationships that carry with them the potential for health and life-giving psychological dynamics. Although a team typically presents for consultation with a focus on the patient they are struggling with, taking an interest in the wider system can generate a clearer understanding of the presenting problem.

References

1. Hinshelwood B, Chiesa M. Organisations, Anxiety and Defence. 1st edition. London: Wiley; 2001.
2. Lyth IM. Containing Anxiety in Institutions: Selected Essays, Vol. 1. Oxford, UK: Free Association Books; 1988.
3. Moore E. Personality disorder: its impact on staff and the role of supervision. Advances in Psychiatric Treatment 2012;18(1):44–55.
4. Reiss D, Kirtchuk G. Interpersonal dynamics and multidisciplinary teamwork. Advances in Psychiatric Treatment 2009;15 (6):462–9.
5. OPD Task Force, Kernberg OF, Clarkin JF, Cierpka M et al. Operationalized Psychodynamic Diagnostics (OPD), Foundations and Practical Handbook. Seattle: Hogrefe & Huber; 2000.

Chapter 20

A Psychodynamic Approach to Working with People Experiencing Multiple Exclusion Homelessness

Table of Contents

Introduction 291
Symptoms of a Multiply Excluded Homeless Group 292
A Developmental Perspective on Multiple Exclusion Homelessness 292
School and Teenage Experience 293
Inner and Interpersonal Dynamics 294
A Psychologically Informed Approach for Staff Working in the Homeless Sector 294
Housing First 297
Psychodynamic Practitioners Working in the Homeless Sector 297
Concluding Remarks 298

Introduction

James is a man who has slept rough for two decades. He approaches strangers on the street and starts up conversations asking for help with various things. They are drawn to him, but then he talks continuously in a way that pushes them away. It seems that an internal battle is going on in James and, for the external observer, it can be confusing to be in relation to someone who seems to both want and not want what is being offered, seemingly with equal strength, and sometimes within minutes of each other. There is a deep internal conflict between parts of him that are in need of care, and other parts that have developed through early experiences of neglect in caring relationships and feel that to seek care is the most dangerous thing he could ever do.

Long-term homelessness – sometimes referred to as 'multiple exclusion homelessness' – is a late emerging symptom of underlying difficulties in someone's relationships with care. In this chapter I aim to provide an introduction to the relational dynamics underlying multiple exclusion homelessness, and an approach to working in this area. What is written below is a synthesis of some of the themes that have emerged during my experience of working as a psychologist in the area of homelessness for fifteen years, both directly and through supporting staff in the field.

The term 'multiple exclusion homelessness' has been used to describe people 'adversely affected by a combination of factors such as family conflict, worklessness, poverty, mental ill health, substance misuse, physical impairments, and personal traumas, plus episodes of homelessness [. . .] They may be living chaotic lives and can experience serious difficulty in achieving settled accommodation or sustaining a tenancy.'[1] It is worth clarifying that this group of people represent a subgroup of all people experiencing episodes of homelessness; a multiple excluded homeless subgroup have particularly marked complications in their relationships with care, regularly lack supportive close or familial relationships, and experience deep social exclusion.[2]

Adults experiencing multiple exclusion homelessness have often, during their developmental years, experienced multiple care homes, disrupted attachments, un-forecasted separations, multiple and short-lived figures of support, to and fro from foster care to family of origin – these are all experiences that can lead a person to develop an understandable anxiety about the risks of trusting anyone to remain stable and present in their life. These dynamics may inadvertently be recreated in the person's adult life through the impermanency of different organisations they are involved with. Whilst this pattern may be familiar to the person seeking help, and while each contact may temporarily address the issue of the moment, the overall relational experience offered may serve to reinforce the underpinning dynamics. The people described in this chapter have the experience of being excluded from many different places, services, and environments either directly or by virtue of some of the access issues described in Chapters 15 (section on 'The Inverse Care Law') and 17.

Symptoms of a Multiply Excluded Homeless Group

The health consequences of lifelong difficulties in forming and maintaining relationships can lead to a whole range of difficulties. It is not unusual that the person may have a wide range of mental health problems including difficulties with eating, chronic anxiety and depression, self-harm and other forms of self-abuse, post-traumatic symptoms, dissociation, hearing voices, and may well have developed a relationship with substances as a way of managing inner distress. There may be a range of physical health problems, with some related to having a nervous system that is in a chronic state of high alert. Traumatic relationships may have left scars both visible and invisible, and the central nervous system may be subject to long-term damage through substance use and from assaults and accidents. There might be dental needs, podiatry needs, physiotherapy needs, dermatology needs, all of which may be dealt with in different services.

A Developmental Perspective on Multiple Exclusion Homelessness

Every single story is unique and personal to the individual concerned, but there are themes that are common across the life stories of many people who end up experiencing multiple exclusion homelessness. These themes paint a broad picture of some of the social, developmental, and interpersonal challenges that many of this group may have experienced long before the symptom of homelessness emerged. It is of course not exclusively the case that the circumstances and situations described below are ubiquitous either for those experiencing high levels of childhood adversity or for those who experience multiple exclusion homelessness. But clinical experience and studies looking at the early experiences of those who find themselves long-term homeless show that by the time the adult is experiencing multiple exclusion homelessness, it is typically very far from the first time they have felt separated from the world around them.[3]

Stories of early years often describe a chronic lack of safety manifest in experiences such as violence in the home, the presence of drugs and alcohol, expressed mental distress, physical and sexual mistreatment and abuse, neglect of physical and psychological care, and perhaps most pervasively, an atmosphere of fear and deep uncertainty. It can sometimes be difficult for service providers to understand why somebody would seemingly prefer to sleep on the streets rather than take up a hostel place or an offer of their own tenancy, but a hearing of what that person's experience of being 'housed' in their early life was like can often make some sense of this preference.

It is striking just how often accounts of early life describe an aloneness of experience. These experiences range from being left completely alone through to actions that display a disregard for the mind of the child. The experience of feeling excluded from the thoughts and concerns of primary caregivers is an often unspoken but clear theme in the detail. It can feel as if from some of the most formative years, the person has needed to develop a position of self-reliance and detachment as a way of staying safe and excluded from the distressing experiences around them (see also Chapter 14 for an in-depth discussion of the psychodynamics of narcissistic difficulties).

If we are to accept that it is through being housed in the minds of others in a safe and containing way that allows us to develop a sense of self, security, and confidence to explore the world, then we can start to see how a sense of early exclusion from others' minds can have serious long-term consequences. If there has been physical, psychological, or sexual mistreatment within caring relationships, it can be understood that to be housed in another's mind might come to be felt as dangerous and to be avoided at all costs.

School and Teenage Experience

The dynamics described above, which are first felt in the person's early years, may begin to get played out in school life. Many multiply excluded homeless people give descriptions of how their behaviour was challenging, of how they were experienced by others as a problem or unmanageable in some way, and of how they felt unwanted and excluded by school life for the ways in which they related to it.

For many, their schooling was disrupted both in terms of their attendance and of their capacity for learning when they were in attendance. The accounts talk of distress being shown in ways that evoked little sympathy as the person's actions and defences often gave rise to responses from others that resembled the adverse experiences that the person was originally struggling with. Reflections on these experiences by many leads to a description where even at an early stage in life *a feeling of safe familiarity is experienced at the point of exclusion*, even if that safety is accompanied by unhappiness. Conversely, the experience of being attended to is deeply unfamiliar and evokes an anxiety about being in someone's mind and a fear of being vulnerable.

Through early teens, relationships with substances might come to be seen as the only relationships that can be fully trusted and relied upon to give comfort, security, or sometimes a form of escape. This is an important topic that cannot be fully discussed here – suffice to say that the direct and indirect effects of substances often end up accentuating a person's unmet needs, the price paid for something to rely on.

Inner and Interpersonal Dynamics

Those early experiences of not being safely housed in another's mind can lead to an inner world where aspects of the individual – such as their vulnerabilities or their innate needs to connect, create, play, explore, and communicate – are excluded from being acknowledged or expressed through the development of internal defensive relationships that mirror the outside early experiences (see also 'Attributive Narcissism' in Chapter 14). Better to shut yourself up than to endure the pain of having someone else shut you up. Better to abuse yourself than to risk showing those parts of yourself to the world that were previously abused. It is a neat and devastating short cut that serves to maintain a position of familiar safety even if that means a person employs their distressing experiences against themself.[4]

These extreme difficulties in making use of relational opportunities can, over time, leave someone in a position of exclusion from some of the most fundamental aspects of human life. Developing a strong social group might prove hard, as might securing regular employment or any sort of long-term stability. This can lead to a wide range of additional social difficulties that can serve to compound one another.

As these adverse experiences build up, they can give rise to escalating need that can feel impossible to address within a service landscape organised around discrete symptoms. Furthermore, many services require an unwritten and unquantified relational capital to access that some people with these developmental difficulties simply may not have (see Chapter 17, section on 'Beginnings'). Exclusion can happen through a person being banned, removed, or suspended from a service or community for behaving (or relating) in ways that those places, or more specifically the people who occupy, organise, and own those places, experience as intolerable. Examples of this range from exclusion from a supermarket for appearing suspicious, to being barred from a health service for behaving aggressively or missing arranged appointments.

It could be understood that it is at least in part through these many micro interactions played out over time, that the typically *late emerging symptom of homelessness* can appear. By this stage the homelessness is often just the latest iteration of long-standing relational dynamics to do with feeling unhoused and excluded both from oneself and from the surrounding world.

A Psychologically Informed Approach for Staff Working in the Homeless Sector

Due to the relational dynamics described above, it can be very difficult for this group of people to access effective care from mainstream services as they are traditionally configured. The staff-service user relationship, while often viewed as important within mainstream service provision, is commonly seen as a vehicle through which treatments and tasks can be completed rather than as the treatment itself. By contrast, a psychologically informed service for people experiencing multiple exclusion homelessness understands that the reverse is often a more accurate description – *that the tasks and activities are really just the vehicle through which a relationship can develop* that carries the possibility of developing a sense of safety, trust, and continuity.

In the area of multiple exclusion homelessness, the vast majority of mental health work is not done by mental health specialists but rather occurs in the relationships with, typically non-statutory, support workers, hostel staff, and outreach workers. This staff group are often in contact with those they support for considerable lengths of time and intensity. They often live in the same accommodation, accompany people to appointments and meetings, and offer support with managing finances and other activities of daily living. Despite sometimes being viewed as lesser in status or importance than more formally qualified staff, they are typically an incredibly highly skilled, committed, and compassionate group of people, who provide an invaluable service. Principles of a psychologically informed approach for staff working in the homeless sector draw on much that is discussed in Chapter 17, and include:

- recognising the deep ambivalence that a person with this sort of relational history might have about seeking help and care (see Clinical Example 1)
- not giving up on someone just because they do not attend several arranged appointments
- understanding that falling into the traps of initial over-provision followed by provision removal once offered care is dismissed is unlikely to bring about meaningful change
- providing a low threshold for access
- a high commitment to the maintenance of and interest in the caring relationship

Clinical Example 1 Ambivalence about seeking care and the timescale required to form a connection

I can remember seeing someone in the waiting room who said they wanted to meet to talk about their childhood, and we arranged to meet the next day. He didn't turn up, and for several years we would bump into each other in the waiting room, street, or the hostel he was staying at, and each time we would have a little bit more conversation and arrange to meet sometime in the next few days. These *arranged* appointments would not be attended, but the discussion between us around making them that occurred in *unarranged* ways grew longer and more comfortable. Eventually we had been meeting in this way for three years or so when, seemingly out of the blue, he turned up for one of our arranged appointments. He came and we spoke for ten minutes or so before he left. Over the next couple of years, we would still meet in unarranged ways, but he began to attend the arranged meetings slightly more frequently. Some five years after first meeting, we ended up doing some useful work together through a six-month period of relatively well-attended pre-planned appointments. However, it felt like the key work – creating the basis for a non-excluding relationship – happened in those first five years of meeting. In terms of what was discussed latterly, it became clear why those first five years were so necessary.

This approach recognises that in attempting to provide care to people whose earlier experiences of care have been epitomised by neglect, abuse, and other mistreatment, developing a sense of psychological safety, connection, and trust in the present day requires many relational experiences and actions – this involves hard work on both sides and a long timescale. Without this understanding it can be all too easy to re-enact something of the impermanence, unreliability, and neglect that may have played a large part in giving rise to the unmet needs of those experiencing multiple exclusion homelessness (see Box 20.1).

Box 20.1 Traditional service approaches

In traditional homelessness service approaches, it is not unusual for a person seeking help with multiple exclusion homelessness to be allocated many different support workers over many years. Each of these workers may be tasked with sorting out a problem relating to being unhoused, and each of these contacts will typically end once the identified problem has been addressed.

Commonly, other needs emerge once the support has ended, necessitating another referral, often to another support agency. This can mean that over a ten-year period an individual may potentially have had ten different support workers, entailing ten different attachments and ten endings that the person had little or no say or control over.

Despite the deceptively simple description of 'sticking by someone', to try and do so can bring the staff member into contact with dynamics of neglect, abuse, and mistreatment. At times the worker will be unconsciously 'invited' to stop caring and become disinterested and detached in a way that the person seeking help may find more familiar and comfortable.[5] At other times, the roles may reverse, and the staff member may themselves feel neglected, abused, and mistreated by the service user they are working with (see Clinical Example 2). These experiences and attacks on care are not necessarily personal to the staff member and may be powerful communications of the relational dynamics governing the person's life, and the very thing that is limiting their health and well-being.

Clinical Example 2 Tolerating projected experiences and being prepared to carefully adapt the frame

I met a young woman who, after a similar appointment 'dance' as in Clinical Example 1, turned up to a first arranged appointment to sit and tell me that there was absolutely no point in us meeting because she had 'died years ago', and that nothing was ever going to change that. The feelings of being useless, defeated, and hopeless that I felt over the following years, combined with erratic attendance, seemed to offer some explanation as to why previous attempts at provision of mental health care had not come to anything. But the fact that she had ever come along at all suggested that there was a part of her somewhere that still had some hope of a connection.

It also became clear over time that the room setting (closed door, no windows) was not helping in terms of developing a sense of safety, and the time limitation was proving prohibitive in terms of her feeling too much regulation to allow a dialogue to develop. Meeting outside, either sitting in a quiet place where we could both look into the distance, or walking, freed things up and, again, over the following years, the material discussed made it clear why meeting at all, let alone in a room with a shut door might have felt extremely frightening.

One of the primary approaches in the face of these unconscious invitations into repeating distressing relationship patterns is to develop a process which offers the potential of becoming aware of these patterns and through this awareness minimise re-enacting them. Reflective practice and other forums for discussing the psychological aspects of the work have been previously described (Chapter 18). Through practices like these, a service may be able to offer a new position that carries the potential to break the cycle of exclusion and offer new relational experiences. While this sounds simple and straightforward on paper, in practice it requires a high degree of tolerance and commitment. When offering a caring relationship to those for whom care has never been straightforward, there is always a risk that the current relationship will come to reflect that familiarity of earlier relationships. Furthermore, there may be times when a person's (unconscious) defensive need to have familiarity outweighs the capacity of services to offer something different.

Housing First

There have been some specific models that seek to formalise the necessity for committed and open-ended relational care as a first line approach. For example, Housing First was developed by Sam Tsemberis as part of his work with Pathways to Housing in New York in the early 1990s,[6] and has since been adopted more widely and subjected to evaluation.[7] Originally developed to help those with mental health problems who were homeless and sleeping rough, the model was developed as a basic approach with anyone who was experiencing, or was at risk of, long-term homelessness, such as those leaving long-term psychiatric care or prison. It was developed as an alternative to more traditional approaches that typically had some sort of conditional element to the provision of housing, such as the person getting sober, or a demonstration in some other way that they were 'ready' to be housed. These 'staircase' approaches often led to people becoming stuck at one of the prerequisite stages and so never becoming housed, whereas the Housing First approach sidestepped all the traditional hurdles, housed a person based on need, and offered mobile, high-availability, and long-term support to the person in their own home once housed.

As well as helping someone to maintain a house and the stability and security that might go with that, the Housing First approach might also provide a sense of being psychologically housed within a reliable, non-abusive, and consistent relationship. Hence, a more accurate description of what is found useful might be 'relationship first'. With time this might allow the person seeking help to use this new relational experience as a secure base that allows them to make use of many of the services that they might benefit from accessing. But more than that, it may provide a relationship where parts of the person excluded for many years can begin to become alive again.

Psychodynamic Practitioners Working in the Homeless Sector

Traditional psychodynamic approaches of seeing individuals for therapy either in a one-to-one or group setting may not always be possible to initiate with people who might find it difficult to access the places where these interventions usually occur. Furthermore, given the specific demands, process, and potentially unsettling nature of psychodynamic psychotherapy, it may be considered that even if those experiencing multiple exclusion homelessness and associated symptoms could access the setting, then such a treatment may not always be indicated or appropriate.

Having a psychodynamically orientated practitioner working on-site in homelessness services can help counterbalance some of the difficulties people with multiple exclusion homelessness experience in accessing mental health services, whilst also offering support and reflective spaces to staff working in these services.

The person offering psychodynamically informed direct work in a homelessness service may need to allow a certain amount of careful flexibility around the external setting, including factors such as time, location, and frequency. For some people, the closed doors of small clinic rooms can evoke strong feelings of claustrophobia and anxiety (which may be linked to childhood abusive experiences) that interfere with broader thinking. With careful consideration to maintaining appropriate professional boundaries, meeting people within their accommodation or wherever feels most comfortable for the person can be helpful. If the practitioner can hold a psychodynamic frame within their own mind, then meeting in places that feel relatively familiar to the person seeking help, and for durations that might allow some thought to develop, can allow people who may otherwise find it impossible to access therapy to make some use of the therapeutic value of a psychodynamic approach.

The psychodynamically informed practitioner, with their interest and knowledge of human relations, can be of value in helping bring an understanding and informed approach to how systems and services operate in the homeless sector (see also Chapter 17). Areas in the homeless sector that might particularly benefit from analysis include policies about suspension and exclusion, duration of contact, and parameters of what is deemed to be relevant work.

A psychodynamic understanding may also be helpful in shaping appropriate commissioning to try and develop more psychologically informed service planning in wider services and in how services work together. A psychodynamic framework, if articulated in a clear and digestible way to commissioners and those in government, can shine a light on how experiences such as extreme poverty, social injustice, and inequality can impact upon human relations and subsequent life experiences.

Concluding Remarks

Bridging the relational gap across the levels of disconnection described in this chapter can be a long and difficult process. This chapter is not aimed at being a comprehensive account of this work, for there is much more to say on it, but the hope is to introduce some ideas about effective ways of working in an area of such need and importance.

The provision of the sort of relational consistency, reliability, and continuity that approaches such as Housing First and other high-commitment work contain may seem so obvious a solution as to be hiding in plain sight, but that does not mean it is straightforward work. This kind of work requires a psychologically informed approach to how the service is run, including a reflective space for the staff to process the psychological demands of the work. Feedback from those experiencing multiple exclusion homelessness is that it is the commitment and presence of someone who sticks with them past the point where others typically leave that has made the most difference to their life.[2] I suppose many of us would say the same thing about our own lives if asked.

References

1. Brown P, Morris G, Scullion L et al. Losing and finding a home: homelessness, multiple exclusion and everyday lives [Internet]. Manchester: University of Salford; 2012. http://usir.salford.ac.uk/id/eprint/35876/
2. Bowpitt G, Dwyer P, Sundin E et al. The support priorities of multiply excluded homeless people and their compatibility with support agency agendas – new research into multiple exclusion homelessness. Housing, Care and Support 2011;14 (1):31–2.
3. Fitzpatrick S, Bramley G, Johnsen S. Pathways into multiple exclusion homelessness in seven UK cities. Urban Studies 2013;50(1):148–68.

4. Fairbairn WRD. Psychoanalytic Studies of the Personality. London: Routledge & Kegan Paul; 1952.

5. Theodorou N, Johnsen S, Watts B, Burley A. Improving multiple exclusion homelessness (MEH) services: frontline worker responses to insecure attachment styles. The Journal of Mental Health Training, Education and Practice 2021;16(6):421–32.

6. Tsemberis SJ. Housing First: The Pathways Model to End Homelessness for People with Mental Illness and Addiction. Minnesota: Hazeldean Publishing; 2010.

7. Johnsen S, Blenkinsopp J, Rayment M. Scotland's Housing First Pathfinder Evaluation: First Interim Report (full report). 2021; https://doi.org/10.17861/c5n3-0h95

Chapter 21

Psychodynamic Psychotherapy Online and by Phone

Table of Contents

Introduction 300
Adaptations to the Therapeutic Frame 301
Technical and Practical Considerations 303
Technology and Equipment 303
Other Practical Considerations 303
Clinical Considerations regarding Therapy Online or by Phone 304
Clinical Encounters at the Interface of In-Person and Virtual Working 305
Finding a Tolerable Distance – Online Working as a Way In to Therapeutic Process 305
Hiding and Being Seen 307
Slipping into an Avatar World and Trying to Recover 308
Concluding Remarks 308

Introduction

How to be with self and others – this is a phrase that captures the essence of psychodynamic psychotherapy.[1] And as has already been discussed, one of the central aspects of psychodynamic psychotherapy is the relationship between patient and therapist. It is through this relationship that the patient may become more aware of patterns which impact on their relating to self and others.

Over the past decade there has been increasing literature written on what this therapeutic relationship can look like in a technological age in which we communicate more and more through smart phones, social media, and via platforms such as Skype and Zoom. However, despite the increasing literature that speaks to how this way of undertaking therapy can have its benefits in certain circumstances, meeting in person with the patient had remained the default position.[2]

That is, until the arrival of Covid-19. The pandemic (2020 onwards) necessitated a rapid shift in the way we conducted and maintained relationships. We learned to be with others in different ways – walking outdoors together, colleagues meeting communally over video calls, quizzes with friends over Zoom, more frequent FaceTime calls with family, whether living down the street or on the other side of the world. There is no doubt that these adapted forms of relating felt better than having no way of relating at all, but they did not negate the profound sense of loss – a loss of being tangibly with others and a longing for when this might again be possible.

This of course had an impact on the practice of psychodynamic psychotherapy and all other therapies. In an unsettling, frightening situation that brought a reduction to in-person social interactions and supports, it was understandable that fears about illness/health and experiences of distance and loss could intensify, and that some patients might need the containing relationship of therapy more than ever. As such, the need to provide ongoing therapies for patients led to a shift in the way psychodynamic therapy was practised, with a significant proportion of therapies being offered via telephone or online.[3]

Scharff notes that therapy 'is the encounter with an understanding mind in whatever setting that may occur',[4] which is a helpful and comforting thought when met with disruption to the familiar therapeutic setting. However, the disruption gives us cause to stop and consider what has changed, what might be gained, and what might be lost.

The following might sound obvious, yet it is important to say: psychodynamic psychotherapy with patients online or by phone is different to working psychodynamically in person. They are not like for like; one does not transfer directly on to the other. With this in mind, what happens then when the patient can no longer physically be with the therapist? When they can no longer experience the walk to the therapist's office, see that familiar piece of art on the wall, feel the texture of the rug underfoot, hear the predictable ticking of the clock, smell the particular scent that room alone holds? And perhaps most importantly, when they can no longer feel the presence of the therapist sitting with them, attending to what they are bringing?[5] This chapter will consider some of these differences and how they might offer opportunities and also challenges.

Adaptations to the Therapeutic Frame

Chapter 5 has looked at the frame in psychodynamic therapy and outlined the importance of a secure therapeutic frame in facilitating a holding environment in which the patient (and also the therapist) is able to explore and encounter the patient's inner world in a contained way.[6]

Working via telephone or video call constitutes a very definite change to the frame and therefore has the potential to feel unsettling in a number of ways, whilst also potentially providing the therapist with certain insights into the patient's world. One aspect of the frame is to provide a consistent and safe physical environment for sessions. The therapist usually is in control of this, ensuring a space which is comfortable and free from intrusions. However, working at a distance means that this now also becomes a task for the patient.[7] We are accustomed to imagining the patient's external environment through their narrative, but in this change to the frame we are invited into their home (or perhaps workplace). If working via video call, we can observe a patient's surroundings and how they position themselves (and us) within their environment. All of this can provide us with a further layer of understanding about someone.

Interruptions are more frequent in this way of working. I have experienced patients receiving various parcels and deliveries, unexpected visits from friends/family, pets that need attending to, cups of coffee being made, work emails pinging through, phones ringing or vibrating. With the disruption to the setting, I too have found it easier to feel pulled elsewhere. Other authors have noted this phenomenon – Russell has commented that colleagues had noticed changes in their behaviour from sipping cups of tea during sessions to secretly checking emails.[8] Lemma reminds us, 'It is not only the patient who benefits from the consistency of the setting. The therapist too benefits from being anchored in reality by it.'[1]

Some of these interruptions might be avoidable or at least mitigated when establishing a frame with the patient – a reminder to both patient and therapist to close down any other open tabs on computers and silence mobiles/other phones. In this way of working, it is likely that interruptions will become part of the fabric of the session, to be thought about, and explored where possible. However, if we find that the patient is consistently not able to establish a secure-enough frame for themselves, or if intrusions and interruptions lead to a lack of containment in the therapy, we may need to provide this for the patient through converting to in-person sessions (where this is possible).

As with in-person work, it is important to think analytically about how the patient is using the frame in terms of their predominant object relationships and habitual defences, and I give some examples of this later in the chapter.

A central and consistent element of the frame is the therapist, in terms of their 'analytic attitude', but also their physical presence.[9] Lemma speaks of the importance of the embodied experience and what is lost when the other is not physically present:

> The quality of the embodied experience with the caregiver and, we might add, between patient and therapist is vital. During such nonverbal exchanges, in which both parents and infants express their minds and respond to the other's mind mainly without awareness and often through the body, the parent's ability to make sense of the infant's non-verbally expressed internal world is key to laying the foundations for developing the capacity to mentalise experience.[1]

In online and telephone psychotherapy we lack some of the nonverbal signals that we would otherwise pick up on. Screen pixilation, delay in sound or visuals, image freezing, inability to engage in direct eye contact, all contribute to this. With telephone therapy there is a loss of all visual contact. Our brains work harder to process what we are receiving; we reposition, strain our eyes, speak slower or louder or more than normal, all of which challenge our attitude of 'evenly suspended attention'.[10] Again, it is important to acknowledge these are differences and so may require the therapist to modify their approach – to take breaks away from screens between patients, plan with the patient what will happen if the mode of communication becomes problematic, and to check understanding more frequently.[11]

The example below highlights another phenomenon, one that might be overlooked but speaks to the importance of transition and moving into a space that allows something different to occur.[12]

Clinical Example 1 The absence of a transition

Mr B had recently resumed face-to-face therapy sessions following a period of video call sessions during the Covid-19 pandemic. He had been keen to return to face-to-face sessions, feeling that, although the video sessions had allowed his therapy to continue, he had longed to return to being in the room for therapy where he found 'real connection'.

After several weeks of being back, Mr B spoke of something else he realised he had missed – his journey to and from his therapy sessions. To get to his appointments, he took a train, followed by a short walk. He noted how the journey to therapy allowed him to step away from what he was doing and emotionally ready himself for his session. He noted that the period after the session was an especially important transition. He spoke of often taking time to sit on a bench in a public garden near his therapist's office and continuing to reflect on what the session had brought up before using the journey home to start preparing himself for what would be happening when he arrived back at home/work.

He reflected that with video sessions, despite knowing that he should take some time to reflect and transition, this often didn't happen due to the immediacy of work or home life pressures waiting for him. He wondered if, as a result of this, 'something had gotten lost'.

Technical and Practical Considerations

Prior to consideration of working with a patient online or by phone, it is important for any therapist to consider technical and practical issues related to these modes of working.

Technology and Equipment

Both patient and therapist will need access to a reliable and high-speed broadband connection if using an online platform. It can be useful to try a video call with a colleague beforehand to check how well this is working from the therapist's end. The therapist will need a high-quality camera and may wish to use a headset in order to cut out echo and background noise, and to allow the therapist to speak in a more natural, conversational, tone. In addition, the use of a headset can reassure the patient that their narrative cannot be overheard. It may seem obvious, but the therapist needs to check what is behind them in their camera shot to ensure it is not too personal, and also check their lighting as too much shadow or darkness can be off-putting if the patient cannot see the therapist's face. It is important to use an appropriate online platform that operates with a high level of security (the therapist's affiliated organisation or regulatory body should have guidelines on accepted secure platforms and the procedures around using them).[13]

If undertaking phone sessions, it may be more dependable for both therapist and patient to use a landline, if possible, to minimise loss of reception and cutting out.

Other Practical Considerations

Before committing to online or phone sessions, the therapist may want to consider if the patient has been given enough information to understand that what they are consenting to undertake is different to in-person therapy, so that they can make an informed decision about how (or indeed if) they wish to undertake the sessions. This would be in conjunction with what the therapist may recommend based on clinical opinion of what might be well-suited for the patient and their needs, whilst also taking into account possible constraints on the capacity to offer in-person appointments.[13]

As already discussed, the therapist should encourage the patient to find somewhere that is comfortable, feels private, and where there is little risk of being interrupted. The same is essential for the therapist. As would apply in a 'standard' session, it is helpful for the therapist's surroundings to remain neutral and consistent in order to offer both patient and therapist a sense of containment.

At the beginning of therapy, it may be important to consider what might happen if a patient gets into a crisis. When we are physically present with a patient it can be more straightforward to put crisis plans into action, but with the added distance that online/telephone working brings, this can be more complex. It can be important to establish an emergency contact for the patient and to discuss with them how to manage a crisis should one arise during an online/phone session. This may be especially important to consider if we are working with a patient not in our local area.[11,13,14]

Clinical Considerations regarding Therapy Online or by Phone

Therapy that is carried out online or by phone can offer the opportunity to work with patients who might not otherwise be able to have therapy. This may be relevant for patients who do not have local access to psychodynamic psychotherapy or who travel frequently, or when travel is restricted (such as related to the Covid pandemic). Therapy online or by phone potentially offers access to therapy when travel to a department or office could be practically difficult or impossible, as is demonstrated in Clinical Example 2.

Clinical Example 2 Finding a space to play

Cleo was a HR manager in a very busy company and her working day often was filled with back-to-back video call meetings. She had started therapy online due to living over two hours away from the nearest provider of psychodynamic psychotherapy and not feeling able to miss work. She had come to therapy due to a long-standing belief that she was a failure. Her experience of her mother was of never quite being able to please her, that her mother didn't have enough space for her. She remembered desperately wanting her mother to 'play' with her, but it seemed there were always 'jobs' or 'work' to be done. She felt that she had spent her childhood trying to do something that would finally mean that her mother might find time to play with her or be proud of her.

Her therapist began to notice a few months into sessions that Cleo would seem tense and distracted. She spoke about being overwhelmed with work meetings and feeling like her boss was not happy with her. She began to cancel sessions at short notice.

The therapist noticed feeling frustrated that the patient seemed to not have time for the sessions, and the therapist herself felt more and more squeezed out. The therapist thought she was being given an experience (through projective identification) of what it felt like for this patient to be in relation to others, including growing up with her mother.

The therapist suggested to Cleo that perhaps the sessions might be starting to feel like just another work meeting, where she felt demands were being made of her. Cleo agreed with this, saying that she felt she couldn't quite 'be' in the sessions because of thinking about her next work meeting. She felt she was failing her therapist and sometimes couldn't face coming to the sessions because of this feeling.

Her therapist was able to interpret the patient's worry that the therapist would be as she had experienced her mother, disappointed in her, and not able to hear or understand her needs or difficulties. The patient seemed to feel relieved by this and they went on to explore this familiar position where she expected disappointment from others and would typically then withdraw from relationships. This enabled Cleo to speak with her boss and negotiate a time at the end of the day where she felt more freed up to have her online session.

Whilst working online or by phone can be beneficial and offer a more flexible way of working when this is needed, it will not be appropriate for every patient or every circumstance. As mentioned above, the patient now has to take part in providing a secure setting for themselves. For those for whom boundary issues are difficult, such as in borderline states of mind, this may be a challenge.[14] A colleague in peer supervision discussed a patient she had seen online for psychodynamic consultation. She had asked the patient if they had

Box 21.1 Questions to consider when reviewing the need for teleworking

- Is there still an ongoing need to work in this way?
- Is there any evidence that a way of working, which had initially allowed therapy to begin or continue, is now becoming a way to maintain distance unhelpfully, or is becoming a repetition or enactment of something from early experiences?
- Is there any suggestion that the patient is becoming more unstable? Are there new or increased episodes of self-harm or suicidal thinking? Is the patient becoming more withdrawn?

a private space in which to conduct the session and they said they had. Halfway through the session the therapist could hear someone else talking in the room. The patient said it was her boyfriend on the phone but that she didn't mind him being there. In the patient's background was a history of relationships where boundaries weren't respected or acknowledged; in this situation, it was helpful for the patient to come in for in-person sessions so that the therapist could create a safe and boundaried frame.

The impact on the therapeutic alliance of working virtually needs to be considered carefully before starting. Martin provides us with a helpful maxim: 'A general rule to remember is that patients who are more high risk in traditional settings are also likely to be high risk in telemental health care too.'[14] For patients who have difficulties with eating or those who have a problematic relationship with alcohol or drugs, it may be helpful to be physically present as working at a distance may perpetuate the hidden nature of the interpersonal dynamics associated with these presentations (as shown in Clinical Example 4 later in the chapter).

Telephone and online therapy may be helpful or even necessary at times, but as they diverge quite significantly from the standard frame, it can be helpful to review the decision to work in this way from time to time with the patient, and also in the therapist's own supervision (see Box 21.1).

Clinical Encounters at the Interface of In-Person and Virtual Working

The following section demonstrates some of my experiences of this way of working at the interface of in-person and online/phone work, both beneficial and detrimental. We particularly look at clinical scenarios where the work has moved from in-person to working online/phone (and sometimes back again to in-person), considering what effect these changes in setting may have on the patient-therapy dynamics. It is not intended to be exhaustive, but to illustrate the kinds of situations that may be encountered, particularly when external circumstances (e.g. the Covid-19 pandemic) influence the kind of work that is possible at a given point in time.

Finding a Tolerable Distance – Online Working as a Way In to Therapeutic Process

Clinical Example 3 describes a patient who experienced anxiety in the presence of others. She initially met with her therapist in person for weekly sessions before moving to online working, which was necessitated by the pandemic. This move to online working reduced the transference response to a more manageable one, enabling exploration and some resolution of the anxiety.

Clinical Example 3 Finding a tolerable distance

Astrid struggled to make connections with others, shutting herself off from intimacy in her relationships. She had sought out therapy to understand why this was the case in the hope that she might be able to let others in. When in the room with her therapist, Astrid would feel incredibly anxious, noting palpitations and dizziness at times. A pattern emerged in which she would begin to open up and become vulnerable in a session, but following this she would withdraw and miss several sessions.

Due to the pandemic, the therapy switched from face-to-face to online sessions. Following this change, Astrid found her anxiety during sessions to be less and found being in her own environment more comfortable. Her partner would look after their three-year-old daughter whilst she had her sessions. During one session, her therapist noticed a calling sound coming from the other side of the patient's living room door, which became louder in intensity. Astrid appeared not to notice. Finding it difficult to ignore, her therapist said, 'can you hear something?', to which Astrid replied that it was probably her daughter sitting at the door. The therapist reflected that perhaps her daughter wanted to see her. At this observation, Astrid arose and asked her daughter quite sternly to go to her dad.

The therapist showed interest in what was happening, and Astrid responded saying she thought that it would just be 'bothersome' if she had let her in. Her therapist said to Astrid that he wondered if perhaps at times she felt she had to leave the needy part of herself outside the sessions, and that she might worry that if she did not, she too would be bothersome. Astrid responded saying that this reminded her of how her mother had responded to her when she asserted her needs or looked for comfort as a small girl. She experienced her mother as being irritated with her for asking for 'too much'.

The therapist brought this session to supervision with a colleague who was curious about the therapist's comment 'perhaps your daughter wants to see you'. The therapist reflected that in that moment he had felt a sense of loss and a hope for reconnection. This projective identification helped the therapist consider that perhaps there was also an unconscious communication from the patient about wanting to be back in the room together, and that this also 'hooked' on to something he was feeling too.

Astrid started to enquire whether the department her therapist worked in was receiving patients in person again. She wondered if perhaps her therapist might already be seeing some of his 'sicker' patients. Her therapist reflected that perhaps she worried that she too was 'sick', but that for her to ask him about whether she might come back would be seen by him as asking for 'too much'. This seemed to bring some relief as she expressed to her own surprise that she had been hoping to return to in-person sessions.

For Astrid to talk about her desire for intimacy in the room with her therapist initially felt too overwhelming, but paradoxically the distance of working virtually made the exploration of her feelings more possible.

For Astrid, the initial change in setting from in-person to online was, in a way, fortuitous and brought about by the circumstances of the pandemic. On reflection though, it does raise questions about the conscious choice of the setting and whether, in particular circumstances, working online for a period might have therapeutic benefits. However, as Clinical Example 4 illustrates, by no means does this apply for all people.

Hiding and Being Seen

Clinical Example 4 illustrates how a move to telephone sessions initially seemed beneficial, but ultimately became a vehicle for the patient's tendency to hide their feelings and difficulties.

Clinical Example 4 Hiding on the phone and coming out of hiding

Jane was a woman in her 40s who moved to telephone therapy after two sessions. She was offered the option of online video sessions but declined this as the thought of letting the therapist see into her house felt too intrusive. She spoke of worrying about the therapist seeing 'the mess' of her house and what they would think about that; but there was also a more general sense of feeling that she needed to keep her space private, that there was something terrifying about letting someone in.

Jane had sought therapy due to long-standing anxiety. She worked as an archivist, enjoying the methodical and solitary nature of her work. She was an only child and spoke of a childhood marked with violent physical and emotional outbursts towards her by both parents, which left her wanting to hide away and retreat into a reclusive world.

She found relationships difficult, she was concerned that people did not like her, and she avoided social situations. However, she lived with her best friend and found this relationship to be a good support. Nevertheless, as therapy progressed, she spoke of jealousy that her flatmate was in a romantic relationship and her jealousy seemed to lead to tensions between them.

Initially, it felt like the move to phone sessions gave her more freedom to express herself without feeling the therapist's gaze (which she imagined might be disapproving or disgusted). However, following this tentative progress, the patient's relationship with her flatmate broke down when she became engaged and moved out to live with her fiancé. Jane felt this as a rejection which seemed to fit with her view of herself – that others would ultimately discard her. Following the breakdown of the friendship, she returned to a long-standing problematic relationship with cannabis. At this point, the therapist wondered with Jane about coming back in for in-person sessions, but Jane felt her anxiety was such that she could not do this. The therapist felt that she was not seeing or feeling things clearly with the patient. The therapist left the sessions feeling that, without being in the room with Jane or even having a visual link to her, it was impossible to know for certain what was happening.

The therapist spoke with Jane about her history of having to hide from others, even at times hiding her feelings from herself. This interpretation freed Jane up to talk about her cannabis use, letting the therapist know that it was becoming a problem which she felt was interfering with her ability to make use of therapy. They reflected together that her cannabis use was also a way of defending against feelings. Jane spoke of the anger she hid within herself, fearing that she was somehow responsible for driving people away.

Jane felt relief at being able to talk about this and to be met with containment, not violence or dismissal. She resumed face-to-face sessions, was able to cut down her cannabis use significantly, and remained in therapy for the duration of her treatment.

In this example, it initially appeared that telephone working seemed to facilitate a freedom in the therapy. However, the shift in setting unwittingly colluded in a repetition of the presenting interpersonal problem, which was to hide away from a persecutory object. The therapist made an interpretation which facilitated discussion of this central dynamic, and which then allowed them to meet face-to-face again. Although the patient may have been more anxious when back in the room, the potentially persecutory object was faced and eventually found not to have acted as expected. The patient expected the therapist to discharge her after finding out about her increased cannabis use but instead was able to discover that relationships could be about wanting to understand rather than cruelly dismiss.

Slipping into an Avatar World and Trying to Recover

Clinical Example 5 Patrick

Patrick had never met his therapist in person. He had a consultation via video link which then led to commencing online therapy. He presented with difficulties sustaining relationships, a fractured sense of self, and anger about his early experiences. He grew up with parents whose intense volatile involvement with each other led, in his experience, to the neglect of him and his two younger sisters. By Patrick's account, he and his siblings were often left alone whilst his parents were out socialising. He was aware of a deep wish to have intimate and lasting relationships with others, yet at the same time, he had an inability to do this.

Patrick spent much of his time online. He worked as an IT technician, was keen on gaming, and spent a lot of time on social media. He often used these platforms as a way of comparing himself to others and of regulating how others would see him. He made friendships with fellow online gamers, finding this a less anxiety-provoking way of meeting people.

He had been keen to start therapy and initially responded well to the frame surrounding the online therapy. However, as the therapeutic relationship became more established, he began logging on later and later to sessions. His therapist at times noticed that he appeared to be looking at other screens on his computer whilst talking to her, on occasion he would take a work call, muting the therapist for a short time until he had rescheduled the call.

Increasingly during sessions, his therapist would have the sense that she was being used as an avatar of a psychotherapist and not a real person – something that could be paused, muted, logged on to, controlled. She raised this with him, reflecting that perhaps in this virtual world, relationships were less threatening because he could control them. He could see that this rang true and began to talk about his fear of 'real' relationships, whilst acknowledging that he was finding his online interactions increasingly hollow. He reflected that his relationship with the therapist was starting to feel 'real' and that scared him and at times made him want to switch her off.

For patients where there is a need to control their objects, especially threatening and potentially dangerous objects, working at a distance may lead to acting out.[15] In the above case, the patient responded to an interpretation about the acting out and the work continued. However, this might not always be the case. A colleague shared their experience of an initial online psychodynamic consultation in which the patient invited him to view the implements she used to cut herself, describing with some pleasure how she might use them at a later date. He felt trapped and helpless, which linked to the patient's past experiences of abuse. He appropriately suggested that the follow-up consultation would be in an in-person setting where it was easier to provide boundaries and a secure setting. In cases such as these, supervision is essential, as is good communication with the patient's referrer and primary care doctor.

Concluding Remarks

Working online and by phone can be useful in certain circumstances. It is important to be mindful that psychodynamic therapy online or by phone requires a shift in frame, boundaries, and setting. In order for the therapy to remain helpful and containing, both therapist and patient should be clear on the framework and be able to review and consider in-person sessions if needed.

References

1. Lemma A. Digital Age on the Couch: Psychoanalytic Practice and New Media. London: Routledge; 2017.
2. Békés V, Aafjes-van Doorn K, Luo X et al. Psychotherapists' challenges with online therapy during COVID-19: concerns about connectedness predict therapists' negative view of online therapy and its perceived efficacy over time. Frontiers in Psychology. 2021;12.
3. Abraham A, Jithesh A, Doraiswamy S et al. Telemental health use in the COVID-19 pandemic: a scoping review and evidence gap mapping. Frontiers in Psychiatry. 2021;12.
4. Savege Scharff J. Telephone analysis. The International Journal of Psychoanalysis. 2010;91(4):989–992.
5. Lemma A, Caparrotta L. Psychoanalysis in the Technoculture Era. London: Routledge; 2014.
6. Winnicott D, Winnicott C, Shepherd R et al. Home Is Where We Start From: Essays by a Psychoanalyst. New York: Norton; 1984.
7. Savege Scharff J. Clinical issues in analysis over the telephone and the internet. In Savege Scharff J, ed. Psychoanalysis Online: Mental Health, Teletherapy and Training. London: Karnac Books Ltd; 2013.
8. Russell G. Screen Relations: The Limits of Computer-Mediated Psychoanalysis and Psychotherapy. 1st ed. London: Routledge; 2015.
9. Schafer R. The Analytic Attitude. 1st ed. London: Routledge; 1983.
10. Freud S, Strachey J, Freud A et al. The Standard Edition of the Complete Psychological Works of Sigmund Freud. *Vol. 12, The Case of Schreber; Papers on Technique; and Other Works*: (1911–1913). London: The Hogarth Press and the Institute of psycho-analysis; 2001.
11. Saju P, Konstantinidou H, O'Reilly J et al. Faculty of Medical Psychotherapy. Remote Therapy Guidelines [Internet]. London: Royal College of Psychiatrists; 2020 [cited 27 April 2022]. www.rcpsych.ac.uk/docs/default-source/members/faculties/medical-psychotherapy/rcpsych-remote-therapy-guidelines.pdf?sfvrsn=c0b0b2c_4
12. Tao L. Teleanalysis: problems, limitations, and opportunities. In Savege Scharff J, ed. Psychoanalysis Online 2. London: Routledge; 2015. pp. 105–23.
13. Guidance on online and telephone clinical work [Internet]. British Psychoanalytic Council; 2020 [cited 27 April 2022]. www.bpc.org.uk/download/1174/BPC-Guidelines-2.pdf
14. Martin A. Legal, Clinical and ethical issues in teletherapy. In Savege Scharff J, ed. Psychoanalysis Online. London: Karnac Books Ltd; 2013.
15. Roesler C. Tele-analysis: the use of media technology in psychotherapy and its impact on the therapeutic relationship. Journal of Analytical Psychology. 2017;62(3):372–94.

Chapter 22

Group Analysis and its Applications

'Group Analysis is a form of psychotherapy by the group, of the group, including the group therapist/conductor. It aims to achieve a healthier integration within the individual and in their network of relationships.'[1]

Table of Contents

Introduction 310
An Overview of Group Analytic History and Approach 311
The Primary Task 312
The Role of the Group Analytic Conductor 312
The Conductor as Administrator 313
The Conductor as Therapist 313
Membership 314
Context 316
Setting and Form 316
Group Analytic Endings 317
Group Phenomena 318
Concluding Remarks 319

Introduction

In this chapter our lens will be bifocal, looking at the analytic group that is set up to provide a particular kind of psychotherapy, and touching on ways in which this approach and understanding of group phenomena can be applied in wider group settings such as reflective practice groups. Brief vignettes will be woven into the chapter to illuminate a theoretical or psychotherapeutic aspect – within the scope of this chapter, these can offer only a glimpse of a group at work.

Christine Thornton says that 'the individual develops a sense of self through interaction with others, and all our learning, from the earliest moments of life, occurs in a relational context'.[2] Group analysis rests upon a range of ideas concerning 'the relationships of persons towards each other'.[3] Foulkes notes that group analytic theory shares common ground with psychoanalysis in theoretical and clinical orientation.[4] However, group analysis directs its attention to a fundamental understanding of man as a social being. Malcolm Pines reflects that the group analytical psychotherapist has to integrate:

> ... the psychoanalytical model of mind, together with sociological and anthropological perspectives on the human condition. The group analyst has to have a working knowledge

> of psychoanalytic theory but to also accept fully the social structure of the human being who is, as Foulkes put it 'permeated through and through by the colossal forces of society' so that even the most basic forces that drive us are developed and take shape and form within the human context.[5]

The emotional problems leading people into therapy (including trauma in its various guises) invariably arise out of family and social group history. This makes interpersonal relationships difficult at best or avoided at worst. It often seems odd to patients that a suggested 'cure' is the very medium, or a transferential representation of it, that has created the psychological pain in the first place. Isolation and shame are often in the service of mental illnesses, such as depression, which ensures disconnectedness. It is undoubtedly a risk to sit in a circle of strangers and for some it proves too hard. For those who can, it can be truly life-changing.

Group analysis is a treatment for psychological problems, a vehicle for deeper personal awareness, for characterological change, and a greater capacity for social connectedness. Group analysis cannot guarantee this outcome any more than any other psychological treatment can. What it offers is an opportunity for a different kind of discourse. It is a complex business being human, and group analysis creates a space for human beings to explore this complexity together.

An Overview of Group Analytic History and Approach

Group analysis, as a defined therapeutic approach, is young. Siegmund Heinrich Fuchs, a German, Jewish psychoanalyst, came to Britain in 1933. During his assimilation into British life, he became S. H. Foulkes. During the war he worked, alongside Tom Main and Harold Bridger, at The Northfield Military Neurosis Centre in Birmingham where they established and studied therapeutic groups.

He was one of the founding fathers of The Group Analytic Society in 1952 and was its first president. This is known today as The Group Analytic Society International (GASI). The Institute of Group Analysis (a UK-wide training organisation) was founded in 1971. Foulkes and James Anthony collaborated and published *Group Psychotherapy – The Psychoanalytic Approach* in 1957, revealing initial thoughts of group psychotherapy along 'psycho analytical lines'.[6] However, Foulkes developed a new group analytic approach. In its infancy, group analysis was influenced by such diverse sources as psychoanalysis, psychology, neurology, Marxism, and sociology. Another noteworthy influence is gestalt psychology. Max Wertheimer's 1912 publication *Experimental Studies of the Perception of Movement* marked the founding of the gestalt school, and gestalt theory posits that the whole of anything is greater than its constituent parts.[7] This approach challenged those theoretical orientations that separated experience into specific, separate, and unrelated components. In reading Foulkes, one can see how this shaped his approach to understanding the processes and phenomena in group analysis.

'Group analysis', a term first coined by Trigant Burrow, who was interested in 'social neurosis', continues to be shaped by the social contexts in which it is practised.[8] It embraces developments as diverse as neurobiology and attachment theory and is responsive to movements such as Black Lives Matter. Presently within the Institute of Group Analysis there is a growing awareness of how:

> ... intersecting power relations influence social relations across diverse societies as well as individual experiences in everyday life. As an analytic tool, intersectionality

> views categories of race, class, gender, sexuality, nation, ability, ethnicity, and age – among others – as interrelated and mutually shaping one another. Intersectionality is a way of understanding and explaining complexity in the world, in people, and in human experience.[9]

Morris Nitsun, in the foreword to Nick Barwick and Martin Weegmann's book *Group Therapy – A Group Analytic-Approach*, says:

> One of the hallmarks of group analysis, and essentially a strength, although sometimes a source of confusion, is its inter-disciplinary origins and orientation . . . [Group Analysis] is formed by divergent input from different fields, offering a complex discipline marked by a high degree of theoretical openness that may be frustrating in some respects but offers the potential for creative development.[10]

While it has its origins in a dyadic approach, it moves, as John Schlapobersky's book title says, 'from the couch to the circle'.[11] The Freudian concept of free association becomes a communicative process that encourages what Foulkes termed '"free floating" or spontaneous discussion'.[3] This is the process of 'building on what is said with something associated but different that deepens communication and understanding'.[12]

Put simply, group analysis is psychotherapy delivered in a group setting and format, in a group with no set agenda, in which anything can be talked about. The processes and phenomena that arise can seem complex. These mutually influencing phenomena function to maintain and nurture a therapeutic group experience. However, we have to acknowledge that counter therapeutic phenomena can threaten the helpfulness or very existence of a therapeutic group. A little will be said on this later.

Before addressing processes and phenomena it will be useful to consider the essential parts of creating the frame, boundaries, and culture that influence whether any group flourishes or flounders. Each area could command a separate chapter – only an introduction is intended here. Vignettes will be used to aid understanding.

The Primary Task

Foulkes stresses three, 'essential preconditions for *group psychotherapy* . . . :

(a) That the group relies on verbal communication.

(b) That the individual member is the object of treatment.

(c) That the group itself is the main therapeutic agency.'[13]

It is important to grasp here that the group harnesses and utilises its own 'power for therapeutic purposes and is therefore group treatment', emphasising that 'the group is treated for the sake of its individual members, and for no other reason. All psychotherapy is, in the last resort, treatment of the individual.'[13]

The aims of a therapy group are different to other groups and Foulkes notes that therapeutic groups tend to be 'composed of members who are particularly disturbed in their relationship to other people'.[14]

The Role of the Group Analytic Conductor

In group analysis the therapist is referred to as the group conductor. Barwick notes that Foulkes favoured the term conductor over that of leader. The term contains two aspects of the role for the group analyst. These encompass the tasks and responsibilities 'as "administrator" (the person responsible for establishing and maintaining the structure of therapy) ... [and] as "therapist" (the person facilitating process and interpreting content) ... [and] shaping the therapeutic culture of the group'.[15]

The Conductor as Administrator

The management of boundaries, administrative tasks, introducing new members, and managing the location of the group is the conductor's responsibility under what is called the 'dynamic administration' of the group.[16] Groups typically meet weekly or twice weekly. The time at which the group begins and ends is fixed by the conductor.

The Conductor as Therapist

Once established, the conductor's role is to help the group to grow a group analytic culture which '... results in the group becoming more and more a self-propelling instrument of therapy, taking their problems in their own hands' and is led only when it is really required by the therapist.[17] In the following quote, from their early work of 1957, Foulkes and Anthony say:

> [Group Analysis] lays stress on under-emphasis and sees merit in the minimum. It recognises the importance of the conductor's role, but it prevails on him to function as much as possible 'behind the scenes' in the background. He is there to be of service to the group. His attitude and behaviour are among the principal determinants of the situation, but his control of the group remains subtle and unobtrusive. He is a living example of Lao-Tze's great paradoxical statement that the greatest leader is he who seems to follow.[8]

In a mature group, the conductor may be able to assume an outwardly less active role than the conductor of a newly formed group, though the conductor's minimally interventive position will be evident from the start. The group members' task is to turn up each time the group meets, observe the group boundaries, and share whatever comes to mind. They are given no list of topics or instructions as to what to talk about or how to pass the time. Of course, this stimulates anxiety, but many arrive in their first group in the hope of sharing with others and this can lead to early identifications and support. The early needs of groups vary. Often new groups look to the conductor for direction. This wish is frustrated by the conductor's non-directive stance and so the group faces its first problem: how do they work together to manage this anxiety? The conductor will not leave the group to struggle if this creates overwhelming anxiety or risk of early dropouts. The conductor, alert to the group's capacities and observing whether they construct solutions that are in the direction of growth or destruction, will judiciously decide when it is essential to intervene, when this can be delayed giving the group time to experiment, and when no intervention is required.

The conductor is likely to intervene more in the initial stages of a new group. Malcolm Pines echoes the idea of servitude when he notes that the group conductor is:

> ... the first servant of the group, for a basic element of group analytic technique is our trust in the developmental capacities of the group, a belief that there is a maturational capacity, a potential, in the group for widening and deepening each person's knowledge of him-or herself and of others. [5]

In order for any group to develop, it needs its assembled members to come back and keep coming back. Creating a containing, safe-enough space is important. Group analysts vary in how much to provide in respect of this and groups have a way of letting the group conductor know if they feel that they are being under or over supported. Much of the conductor's continuous activity is unspoken as they allow the group to find their way.

Coming into therapy is a help-seeking endeavour that activates early attachment history. Group members vary in respect of ego-strength and affect regulation. Some people will be quiet, managing anxiety by deferring to others. Others will be more confident and able to risk opening up. Sometimes someone talks at length in a sort of monologue that shuts down reciprocity. Both the very withdrawn member and the monopolistic member present the conductor and the group with a dilemma. The conductor will assess whether the group needs an intervention to address the anxious silences or the over-talkative dominance to encourage the creation of shared discourse. The image of a ball of string being passed from one to another comes to mind but not in an ever-thickening string halo, more as an intricate web.

Membership

When starting a new group there is a need to generate referrals – or review waiting lists for who may be suitable. The traditional analytic group is a heterogeneous group of up to eight people who are strangers to each other. Groups can begin with fewer than this. It is often easier to recruit for an established group than build a new group so some group analysts will start with this in mind.

Group members invariably experience psychological difficulties that are commonly associated with their earliest experiences in groups (families, schools, peer groups). These difficulties (often called symptoms or problems) manifest in their personal relationships and in groups. This includes social groups, work groups, teams, and wider communities. This psychological distress is often called depression, anxiety, or personality traits. Strategies to cope with distress that a person has developed themselves may lead to becoming group avoidant, socially anxious, isolated, and lonely. Conversely they can lead to an over-involvement in the lives of others often characterised by a desperate need for attachment, approbation, or care. Humans are complex and the ways in which psychological problems manifest is both unique and universal. It is this universality that often provides early experiences of identification and support in the group.

Dorothy Stock Whitaker makes the important point that:

> One cannot assume that a group experience of some kind will be good for everyone under all circumstances. Certainly, persons are unlikely to profit from a group if they are unable to listen to and interact with others, or at the very least derive some comfort from being in physical proximity with others.[18]

Some people welcome group therapy if the dyadic transference (i.e. what it was like working one-to-one with a therapist) has felt too persecutory. Many people have seen depictions of therapy groups in films or plays – these dramatisations tend to emphasise angry aspects of groups. While exploring anger and conflict can be a helpful aspect of any exploratory therapy group, it is usually balanced by compassion and mutuality.

The clinical vignettes that follow offer a snapshot of different stages of a group (preparation, engaging, and leaving).

Clinical Example 1 Pre-group (preparation)

John, 34, experienced adverse childhood experiences including severe neglect, maternal depression, and paternal violence. He feels depressed, anxious, and avoids his friends. Unemployment has intensified long-held feelings of unworthiness and shame. Despite self-imposed isolation, he feels abandoned and resentful. He wants to be looked after but mistrusts others. His GP suggested psychotherapy.

Assessment has been completed and he is shocked when the therapist recommends group analysis to him. He is offered preparation sessions to think about this. Crucially, he has asked:

'Why would anyone want to join a group? No... I'm too private... You want me to talk to other people? To open up to strangers? I don't see the benefit of baring everything. You know I'm scared of angry people being up in each other's face... How could they possibly help me?... ***I certainly have nothing to offer them.****'*

These commonplace reactions to the offer of group therapy reflect aspects of John's personal history. Unconsciously he may be experiencing the therapist becoming emotionally unavailable to him like his mother. He is fearful of encountering someone like his angry father. He has friends but is cut off from the benefits of talking with them. His childhood poverty and trauma has been internalised, captured in having 'nothing to offer'. Preparation sessions enable an understanding of why this is the recommended therapy, and he agrees to join. The conductor approaches the first group holding John in mind as an individual, but also as part of a newly forming group matrix.

People who have experienced trauma are often hypersensitive to the presence of others and can experience a level of fear of repeat traumatisation that needs to be carefully considered before placing them in a therapy group. They may cope with a support group or something similar – a support group often includes persons who are linked by a shared characteristic or position, where the membership is aware of the shared experiences that connect them. Conversely, such an 'open secret' can feel too exposing. Despite careful assessment and selection by the therapist, a member may experience an analytic group – or indeed any kind of group – as intolerable, such is the force of their anxiety.

Clinical Example 2 In group (engaging)

The new group begins with the sharing of first names only. Most of the group then tentatively share anxieties at being there. Some previous experiences of therapy are shared. John and another member say nothing, and their bowed postures provide a visible mirroring resonance. The conductor waits to see how this will unfold but is prepared to intervene if they remain uninvolved.

Eric anxiously asks John: *Do I know you from another group?*

John: (looking flustered) *I don't know you or anyone.* (He looks down at the floor)

A group member (Mary) talks anxiously, joking, and filling the silence and Eric looks flattened. The warmth and curiosity in early exchanges is replaced by a quiet tension. As this group is in its infancy the conductor intervenes:

I can hear relief and anxiety but wonder if we are concerned with what being known in this group might mean or come to mean? I wonder if there are concerns about safety?

A discussion about confidentiality ensues and they begin to think about how they will stay safe. John says nothing. The talk turns to struggles with mood and anxiety, sharing what one member calls *'safe feelings'.*

The group then has a brief reflective silence. The conductor decides to trust the group to find its way. The talk begins to focus on 'getting it right or wrong', of not wishing to hurt each other. Most members join in, but John does not.

The conductor intervenes to offer that *'It seems that we are already seeing that we can't know what might be touched upon when we just meet and see what happens. When we just say what is on our minds.'*

Eric, looking at John, and seeming to catch his eye, says: *'You're a man of few words. I'm sorry for before. I don't want to know anyone . . . if you know what I mean.'*

JOHN: *No, I'm sorry . . . I think I know exactly what you mean . . . I don't really trust people anymore . . . I'm a bit scared to be honest.*

The conductor reflects that John has now joined the group. The group takes up the theme of trust and they share a little to do with situations when trust has been broken. It is maintained at a safe level but has emotional impact, which the conductor allows to develop without too much needed from her. She intervenes minimally to offer containing responses and early interpretations of their coming together.

Over the months, her interventions and the group's exchanges deepen in complexity and meaning. The initial dependency on the conductor is replaced with need for and investment in each other. Several members, including John, work through grief for their experience of blighted childhoods and lost relationships. Not all of John's problems are solved and he remains cautious around new members, sometimes withdrawing into silence. However, unlike his sense of his early years, he is neither ignored nor punished. He is allowed to slowly emerge into a less frightening reality.

Context

Some groups are offered in psychotherapy services while others are in inner city mental health hospitals. Applied groups can be in varied organisational settings, charities, or universities. The group analyst is mindful of the significance of the wider socio- economic context which houses or surrounds the group. This can manifest in the content or dynamic administration of the group. A group in a tranquil, rural setting is different to that in a prison-based therapeutic community. Group analysis carefully considers the capacity of the wider context to contain or threaten a group's existence.

Setting and Form

Group analysts run groups in settings over which they have varying degrees of control of the group room and its context. Consistent attention to relationships within the host organisation can mitigate certain intrusive elements, but these can still happen even in an environment that purports to be supportive.

Nowadays most analytic groups are weekly for one and a half hours per session. The fundamental requirement is a room that can be private and confidential. Chairs should be the same and the group should sit in a circle. A small central table can support a box of tissues but also can operate as a symbol of a core and circularly reflective space. This is not a social group, so normal conventions such as drinking or eating are discouraged.

Every member can see every other member, including the conductor, whose presence in the therapeutic circle positions them as a member of the group, while their role as conductor creates some separation as they have set the operational boundaries of the group. These boundaries include the day and times, no social contact between members, using only first names, and confidentiality. Boundary incidents such as meeting outside or coming late are considered to have psychodynamic significance. This is often taken up by the group conductor in a newly formed group, but in established groups it is often addressed by group members.

Contact with the conductor outside of the group is avoided. Of course, this can be necessary (e.g. a member experiences a mental health crisis) to provide essential support and help the patient to remain a member of the group. The patient is encouraged to bring this contact back to the group as, at some level, all communications are group-based communications.

Group analytic groups are slow-open groups meaning that the duration is not time-limited, and new members are added when spaces are available. The conductor will consider whether the current group needs time to process the changes. Knowing if and when to bring a new person into a group has administrative and therapeutic significance. Groups that are turbulent or processing feelings of loss may not be best placed to welcome a new member. Behr and Hearst point out that 'Groups which are specifically constituted for therapeutic purposes have to provide enough time and space to allow for the emergence and repair of longstanding relationships through the process of communication and analysis.'[19]

Time-limited closed groups, informed by group analytic principles, may also be offered in various settings. In these groups, the duration is fixed at the outset (often one and a half to two years) and all members join at the beginning with no new members added subsequently.

Group Analytic Endings

Barnes, Ernst, and Hyde observe that when a group member:

' . . . has moved through the stage of joining, to valuing the group where he can honestly explore feelings and relationships, to finding such relationships in his outside life, he is ready to leave. The group will have become less important: until the date for leaving is fixed.'[20]

Clinical Example 3 Leaving

KELLY: *So, this is your second last week John. You're brave* (she laughs) . : . *I'm never leaving*

Everyone laughs, except John who looks down, crying quietly. The group falls into a resonant, reflective silence. The conductor scans the group and sees that most have noticed John's tears. The conductor says nothing, hoping that group members will help John to process what he is feeling. The group is three years old, and several group members have developed an enquiring and analytical capacity. The conductor is aware that group members have differing levels of attachment to John. Some may be pleased for him while others may feel envy, anger, or ambivalence.

Mary says: *It is good to know that people can leave but I wish you weren't. Are you sure you'll be alright?*

Wiping his eyes, John says: *I'm not sure. I didn't go out with my friend yesterday. I said I was ill. I haven't done that in ages. Maybe I'm rushing things?*

KELLY: *Seems right that you might not be sure because this is a new step. I imagine leaving can take you back internally to how it all began . . . to that avoidant anxiety.*

A discussion about joining and leaving and John's particular journey follows. Those who are indifferent say little. Kevin remembers how John felt when he left home at 16 and suggests that John knows when he needs to get away from something. John feels recognised by Kevin remembering this but stresses that he had been fleeing violence at 16 and now was leaving *'the hand that feeds me, so to speak'* . The group analyst ponders as to drawing this out and its positive transferential elements. As she is thinking inwardly, John expresses his incredulity about struggling to leave, given how he had reacted to the offer of group therapy several years ago. He is grateful for the group and will miss their presence in his life. The conductor notes (inwardly), with pleasure, the central importance of the group as the therapeutic instrument. John adds that he will miss the conductor who, unlike his mother, has not needed him to look after her. Even though over the years he has tried hard to deny his attachment to the group or her, he feels it in his struggle to leave. He knows it is by having had the relationship with the group that he can say, *'It's my time to go.'*

Group Phenomena

The vignettes included key **group phenomena** that are part of the dynamic group matrix, and these concepts can be useful in considering all groups:

'The **Matrix** is the hypothetical web of communications and relationships in a given group. It is the common shared ground which ultimately determines the meaning and significance of all events and upon which all communications verbal and non-verbal rest.'[21]

Communication can be both verbal and nonverbal with the group analytic approach always encouraging verbal articulation of feelings and experience. Foulkes 'stressed the process of translation, which is the raising of communication from the inarticulate and autistic expression by the symptom to the recognition of underlying conflict and problems which can be conveyed, shared and discussed in everyday language'.[17] For more on this complex area, please refer to Foulkes. Fundamentally Foulkes emphasised the 'process of communication'[22] that is of particular importance and that, in addition to what is being said, the group analyst considers that 'everything happening is considered in its communicational aspect'.[17]

Mirroring is where 'the patient sees himself, or part of himself, in particular a repressed part of himself in the other members'.[17] This can enable a person to see a fellow group member reacting or emoting in a way that is personally familiar in some way or in a way that is connected to his own dilemma but expressed in an alternative way. This is linked to the experience of **resonance** where a 'certain tone or chord struck a specific resonance in the other receptive individual'.[21] This can be a very visceral resonance that leads, through the processes of communication, to profound recognition.

In all groups, **subgroups** can form. Sometimes two people will unconsciously form a couple to create a rescuing pair who will 'parent' the group.

A **condenser phenomenon** may be observed when there is a pooling of associated affects and cognitions,[23] where a group feeling, or group preoccupation builds to a point of shared emotional or verbal release.

Schlapobersky talks of three dimensions which are **'relational'**, **'reflective'**, and **'reparative'**.[24] Schlapobersky notes that 'relational moments are more than benign or affirmative. Many of the most profound relational moments arising in therapeutic groups involve conflict . . . [or] hostile opposition'.[24]

Scapegoating could be considered as a manifestation of a group's shared disturbance (fear reactions or prejudices that are as yet unarticulated) that gets located in an individual. This **location of disturbance**[25] needs to be addressed. When a conductor becomes alerted to this phenomenon, they may ask the group as a whole to consider what the individual may be holding or expressing on its behalf. It is also useful to consider any personal valency for roles such as carer, peacekeeper, latecomer, and designated 'group patient'.

Clinical Example 4 Reflective practice group

In a reflective group for managers, Mary is often late. When presenting her work, she becomes inarticulate especially when asked questions. The facilitator notices this pattern while knowing that she is considered a highly competent manager. The facilitator notices that the other group members encourage her to take an early turn in presenting, ask harder questions than others receive, or conversely take very little interest. The facilitator has much to consider in forming any interventions here. The intervention has to address the individual and the group. This is a delicate situation. These are not therapy group members. Nonetheless, the facilitator considers these interpersonal dynamics as having significance for the late individual and the whole group. The facilitator empathically encourages Mary to think about why it is hard to come for the start of the group, while not arousing too much shame which is easily activated. Additionally, the group is invited to consider the function of her being asked to present first and their responses.

Reactions range from bewilderment to a tentative recognition of annoyance, then envy. Responses are thought about in the context of their roles and organisational structures as opposed to their personal histories. Nonetheless, personal resonances are expressed that lead in turn to professional identifications and support. Mary acknowledges professional burnout and difficulty in committing to the group that resonates with the other managers. This leads to a realisation that 'the latecomer' is carrying the ambivalence for everyone, allowing them to unconsciously locate their care needs or anger in her. Exploration and analysis of these dynamics in the group leads to insights on a personal and professional level and they can then focus on generating strategies.

Concluding Remarks

Group analysis emphasises the centrality of a defined and specific *group analytic* approach, which posits the group, above all else, including its conductor, as simultaneously the fundament and the vital force of the analytic group. The dynamic processes are contained and enabled by the boundary that the group analyst puts around the group. This boundary needs to be constructed to fit with both the context and purpose of any therapy group. In group analysis the group conductor functions as both the therapist and dynamic administrator, which includes managing and analysing boundary incidents.

It is the group matrix and its dynamism that holds the potential to effect meaningful therapeutic growth and change. This is often considered to be one of Foulkes's most significant and lasting group analytic concepts.

The clinical vignettes show a conductor at work and some interventions that a group analyst may make while conducting an analytic group. Group analysis does not lose sight of the individual; however, it is crucial to emphasise that this is not individual therapy in a group setting, this is group analytic therapy.

This group has boundaries regarding space, time, and membership. This consistently recurring structure can enable a therapeutic process to be activated and maintained. Communication, both conscious and verbal or unconscious and enacted, is explored. The aim is for communication and, ultimately, understanding to become ever more articulate and available for analytic reflection.

There are many ways in which a group analytic understanding and approach can be usefully applied to non-therapy groups, a little of which we have seen.

References

1. Institute of Group Analysis. What Is Group Analysis? [Internet]. 2021 [cited 2021 Nov 10]. www.groupanalysis.org/about
2. Thornton C. Group analytic praxis in teams and organizations. In Thornton C. The Art and Science of Working Together: Practising Group Analysis in Teams and Organizations. Oxon: Routledge; 2019. pp. 22–30.
3. Foulkes SH. Group psychotherapy in the light of psycho-analysis. In Therapeutic Group Analysis. London: H. Karnac Books Ltd.; 2002. pp. 87–92.
4. Foulkes SH. Part II – introduction. In Therapeutic Group Analysis. London: H. Karnac Books Ltd.; 2002. pp. 85–6.
5. Pines M. Group analysis and healing. In Circular Reflections: Selected Papers on Group Analysis and Psychoanalysis. London: Jessica Kingsley Publishers Ltd.; 1998. pp. 77–87.
6. Foulkes SH, Anthony EJ. Preface. In Group Psychotherapy: The Psycho-Analytic Approach. London: Penguin; 1957. pp. 9–10.
7. Bauer P. Gestalt psychology [Internet]. 2020 [cited 2021 Nov 9]. www.britannica.com/science/Gestalt-psychology
8. Foulkes SH, Anthony EJ. Introductory survey. In Group Psychotherapy: The Psycho-Analytic Approach. London: Penguin; 1957. pp. 13–47.
9. Hill Collins P, Bilge S. What is intersectionality? In Intersectionality. 2nd ed. Cambridge: Polity Press, 2020. pp. 1–36.
10. Nitsun M. Foreword. In Barwick N, Weegmann M, eds. Group Therapy: A Group-Analytic Approach. Oxon: Routledge; 2018. pp. xi-xvii.
11. Schlapobersky, JR. From the Couch to the Circle: Group-Analytic Psychotherapy in Practice. Oxon: Routledge; 2016.
12. Barnes B, Ernst S, Hyde K. Working in the group – Part 2: interventions and interpretations; therapeutic activity. In Frosh S, ed. An Introduction to Groupwork: A Group-Analytic Perspective. London: Macmillan Press; 1999. pp. 101–23.
13. Foulkes SH, Anthony EJ. Significant features of the group-analytic group in relation to other types of human groups. In Group Psychotherapy: The Psycho-Analytic Approach. London: Penguin; 1957. pp. 51–63.
14. Foulkes SH. Concerning leadership in group-analytic psychotherapy. In Therapeutic Group Analysis. London: H. Karnac Books Ltd.; 2002. pp. 54–65.
15. Barwick N, Weegmann M. Core concepts: what does the conductor do? (part one). In Group Therapy: A Group-Analytic Approach. Oxon: Routledge; 2018. pp. 51–69.
16. Behr H, Hearst L. Dynamic administration. In Group-Analytic Psychotherapy: A Meeting of Minds. London: Whurr Publishers; 2005. pp. 42–54.
17. Foulkes SH. Outline and development of group analysis. In Therapeutic Group

Analysis. London: H. Karnac Books Ltd.; 2002. pp. 66–82.

18. Stock Whitaker, D. Necessary decisions and tasks when planning and conducting groups. In Pines M, Hopper E, eds. Using Groups to Help People. London: Routledge; 1989. pp. 3–31.
19. Behr H, Hearst L. The social and cultural basis of group analysis. In Group-Analytic Psychotherapy: A Meeting of Minds. London: Whurr Publishers; 2005. pp. 1–11.
20. Barnes B, Ernst S, Hyde K. Working in the group – part 1: negotiating the boundaries. In Frosh S, ed. An Introduction to Groupwork: A Group-Analytic Perspective. London: Macmillan Press; 1999. pp. 82–99.
21. Foulkes SH. A brief guide to group analytic theory and practice. In Therapeutic Group Analysis. London: H. Karnac Books Ltd.; 2002. pp. 281–98.
22. Foulkes SH. Psychodynamic processes in the light of psycho-analysis and group analysis. In Therapeutic Group Analysis. London: H. Karnac Books Ltd.; 2002. pp. 108–19.
23. Foulkes SH. Group analysis: a study in the treatment of groups on psycho-analytic lines. In Therapeutic Group Analysis. London: H. Karnac Books Ltd.; 2002. pp. 20–37.
24. Schlapobersky JR. Psychotherapy's three dimensions. In From the Couch to the Circle: Group-Analytic Psychotherapy in Practice. Oxon: Routledge; 2016. pp. 59–83.
25. Foulkes SH. Group therapy: survey, orientation, classification. In Therapeutic Group Analysis. London: H. Karnac Books Ltd.; 2002. pp. 47–53.

Glossary of Terms

Analytic attitude 'A particular way of listening: the therapist empathises with the client's subjective experience while at the same time being curious about its unconscious meaning, rather than trying to solve problems or give advice.'[1]

Acting out 'Expressing an unconscious wish or fantasy through impulsive action as a way of avoiding experiencing painful affects.'[2]

Ambivalence The existence of contradictory feelings or impulses about something or someone. For example, both really wanting care and also being terrified of care. One aspect or the other may be repressed. Ambivalence is contrasted with a state of having 'mixed feelings' which are 'based on a more realistic assessment of the imperfect nature' of the object.[3] (see also entry for 'object')

Archaic process A mental process (such as a defence mechanism) first arising in the early years of a person's life, when the mind has less well-developed capacities. Sometimes referred to as a 'primitive' developmental process.

'Borderline' developmental level of psychological functioning Referring to when someone has a 'stable instability on the border between the neurotic and psychotic ranges, characterised by a lack of identity integration and reliance on primitive defences without overall loss of reality testing'. (McWilliams[4] drawing on Kernberg 1975[5])

Containment A key relational process to do with how we recognise and manage our feelings. Containment starts when an individual projects (communicates) distressing or overwhelming feeling(s) to a trusted person (the 'container'). In a process of containment, the other person notices what is being communicated, experiences the feelings themself to a degree, and 'processes and contains the projected contents', that is, the recipient of the projections manages to make sense of and tolerate the distressing feelings using their inner resources, as opposed to becoming overwhelmed themself. Finally, the other person 're-projects back into the [individual] a modified form of the projection', perhaps by talking about the individual's feelings in a relatively calm and steady way.[6] This leaves the individual feeling more 'contained' – in other words, with more perspective about their original feelings which now feel more bearable.

Countertransference 'Feelings and emotional reactions of the therapist towards the patient resulting from both unresolved conflicts in the therapist and the projections of the patient.'[2]

Countertransference enactment When the therapist acts on their countertransference feelings as opposed to processing them. To a degree, partial countertransference enactments are inevitable in clinical work and, if reflected on by the therapist, can be put to therapeutic use. By contrast, larger countertransference enactments are unhelpful or harmful to the patient.

Defence mechanism A mental process that serves to avoid or manage distressing, difficult, or overwhelming feelings or experiences.

Depressive position A state of mind capable of integrating various dimensions of experience (the term 'depressive position' does not refer to a state of depression). In this state, others are experienced as having both 'good' and 'bad' parts, and, correspondingly, the individual experiences mixed feelings.[7] This integrated position is more complicated and reality-orientated than the 'paranoid-schizoid position', and comes with feelings of concern for others and the individual's impact on them.

Ego A term for the aspect of experience felt as 'I' [17] ('Ego' is a translation into Latin of the German word 'Ich' meaning 'I'.) In Freud's 'structural model' the ego is to do with (mostly) conscious thought and action and operates with rational, reality-based thinking; the ego serves a mediating or compromise function between the demands of the external world and aspects of inner life.

Fantasy/phantasy In psychodynamic terminology as applied in this book, 'phantasy' refers to an unconscious activity, whereas 'fantasy' refers to imaginative activity which is conscious or potentially accessible to consciousness, such as daydreaming, reverie, or mental images of scenarios we fear or desire. Conscious fantasy will, of course, be influenced by elements of unconscious phantasy. (We note, some writers do use 'fantasy' for both meanings, and specify whether they are referring to conscious or unconscious activity.)

'Good-enough' Term commonly used in psychodynamic writing, associated particularly with the work of Winnicott, originally with his notion of the 'good-enough mother'. The term 'good-enough' captures the ordinary and inevitable imperfectness of humans and our relationships. It recognises the potential opportunity for an individual's psychological development when the other in a relationship sometimes makes mistakes.

Internal conflict This refers to when two (or more) aspects of someone's life are in tension with each other or feel incompatible.

Interpretation When the therapist brings something to a patient's awareness that they were previously unaware of. An interpretation is a hypothesis, it is not intended to be an absolute truth and should be couched in a tentative manner.[8]

Introjection 'The process of internalising the qualities of an object. Introjection is essential to normal early development, but can also be a primitive defence mechanism in which the distinction between subject and object is blurred.'[2]

Mentalization 'A focus on mental states in oneself and others, recognising desires, needs, feelings, beliefs and reasons, especially in explanations of behaviour. Normal mentalization develops in the first few years of life in the context of safe and secure attachment relationships.'[2]

Mourning The process of coming to terms with the loss of someone or something significant. Mourning involves accepting and experiencing the reality of the loss and facing painful, sad, and often conflicted feelings.

Object 'Significant person in a person's world, the first significant object usually being the mother.'[2]

Object relationship 'The individual's mode of relation to the world, determined by the child's experience, perceptions and fantasies about their relationships with significant caregivers becoming incorporated in the mind at an early stage of development to become prototypical mental constructs which influence the individual's mode of relating to others in adulthood.'[2]

Paranoid-schizoid position A state of mind characterised by polarised extremes of perception and experience. Others and the self are experienced as either all good or all bad (i.e. 'paranoid'). This division into good and bad is called splitting ('schizoid' means involving splits).

Phantasy See entry on 'fantasy/phantasy'.

Psychodynamic frame The steady and reflective setting created by the therapist. This 'frames' a containing space that is conducive to the patient being able to undertake therapy. The psychodynamic frame allows a reference point for the patient's interpersonal patterns to become observable to both patient and therapist.

Psychologically informed service Where the design, practice, and principles of a service are informed by the best understandings of the psychological and emotional needs of people who the service is intended for, paying particular attention to those people with more complicated relationships with care and who may struggle to make use of the service.

Procedural memory An unconscious, non-verbal, memory system that encodes information about 'how-to-do' things. This is one of the main memory systems involved in 'how to be in a relationship'. Procedural memories 'cannot be directly translated into conscious memory and then into words: they can only be known by inference',[8] that is, by observation of interpersonal behaviour, including as this emerges in the therapy relationship.

Projection A universal defence mechanism whereby an individual unconsciously attributes experiences such as impulses, feelings, or desires to another person, by virtue of these experiences being intense, unacceptable, or particularly distressing to the individual. See also entry for 'projective identification.'

Projective identification 'Projection (as above), but a more powerful unconscious defence in which the person who has been invested with the individual's unwanted aspects may unconsciously identify with what has been projected into them and may feel unconsciously pressurised to act in some way.'[2] In other words, the projection gets 'under the skin' of the person on the receiving end. In some circumstances, projective identification may be regarded not as a defensive process but as an unconscious way of communicating to others (see also entry for 'containment').

Reflective practice group A group facilitated by a psychotherapist which brings a whole clinical team together, with the primary task being to reflect on and process staff-patient, team, and organisational dynamics, in order to sustain caring relationships with patients and to reduce the stresses of the work for staff.

Repression Key psychological defence, referring to the pushing out of awareness of distressing, painful, or conflictual internal experiences. Repression takes place unconsciously.

Self- and object-representations Paired representations of self and other within the mind that influence how one relates to oneself and others (see also 'object relationship').

Resistance Phenomenon during therapy when a patient's defence mechanisms are activated. Resistance in therapy is not something to be pushed against by the therapist (this is likely to increase resistance) but rather empathised with and explored.

Splitting 'Primitive defence mechanism in which incompatible and polarised experiences of self and other are kept apart to prevent conflict.'[2]

Superego 'Structure in the mind formed by the child's internalisation of parental standards and goals to establish the individual's moral conscience.'[2]

Therapeutic alliance The trusting, collaborative, and secure aspects of the relationship between patient and therapist 'that endures in spite of the strong and often negative emotions that may surface during treatment'[4] and which allows the patient and therapist to work together to effect beneficial change in the patient.

Transference A phenomenon whereby an individual experiences someone else not wholly as they 'really' are, but partially according to the individual's inner template of what relationships are like (the individual's internal object relations). Transference occurs not only in relation to an individual's therapist, but to a degree in all relationships.

Working through This refers to the process within therapy of repeatedly attending to a key issue or dynamic, in order to help facilitate change. The phrase conveys an appreciation of the time, repetition, and hard work needed for someone to hold less tightly on to old and familiar ways of being and to risk trying out new modes of operating in the world.

References

We thank Jessica Yakeley and Cambridge University Press for their permission to reproduce a number of definitions from a previously published work[2].

1. Lemma A, Roth A, Pilling S. The Competences Required to Deliver Effective Psychoanalytic/Psychodynamic Therapy. Research Department of Clinical, Educational and Health Psychology, UCL; 2008.
2. Yakeley J. Psychodynamic approaches to violence. BJPsych Advances 2018;24 (2):83–92.
3. Rycroft C. A Critical Dictionary of Psychoanalysis. Harmondsworth, London: Penguin; 1968.
4. McWilliams N. Psychoanalytic Diagnosis: Understanding Personality Structure in the Clinical Process. 2nd edition. New York: The Guilford Press; 2011.
5. Kernberg OF. Borderline Conditions and Pathological Narcissism. New York: J. Aronson; 1975.
6. Hinshelwood RD. A Dictionary of Kleinian Thought. Oxford, UK: Free Association Books; 1989.
7. Spillius B, Milton J, Garvey P et al. The New Dictionary of Kleinian Thought. London: Routledge; 2011.
8. Lemma A. Introduction to the Practice of Psychoanalytic Psychotherapy, 2nd ed. Chichester: Wiley Blackwell; 2016.

Index

acquisitive projective identification, 218–20
aggression dynamics. *see also* violence dynamics
  anxiety and, 174
  communication attempts, 252
  defined, 244–5
  releasing feelings, 251
  shame and humiliation, 250–1
  staff countertransference and boundaries, 252–4
anaclitic pattern (depression)
  acquisitive projective identification, 193–6
  expression of, 188–90
analytic attitude
  defined, 99–100
  free association, 100
analytic attitude, aspects
  neutrality, 100–1
  relative anonymity, 101–3
  restraint, 103–4
anger dynamics
  as basic emotional response, 245
  borderline states of mind, 246
  in combination with other feelings, 246
  due to communication problems, 247–9
  expression to others, 246
  in relationships, 245
  response to loss, 245
anxiety, psychodynamic approaches
  aggression and, 174
  archaic anxieties, 174–6
  containment importance, 173
  critical internal object, 179–80
  developmental hierarchy, 173
  internal conflict signal, 178–9
  overview, 171–3
  separation anxiety, 176–7
  therapist experience of, 180–2
archaic defence mechanisms, 28–9
assessment, psychodynamic psychotherapy
  consultation background, 151–4
  defence mechanisms, 155–6
  early childhood experiences, 154–5
  formulation, 159–60
  internal world organisation, 157–8
  object relations patterns, 158
attachment theory, 12, 25
attributive projective identification, 220–2

Balint, Michael, 11
Balint groups, 11
Bion, W.R., 21
borderline internal world organisation, 157
borderline states of mind
  anger dynamics, 246
  dynamics overview, 200
  ending therapy, 208
  initial therapy encounter, 201
  internal world organisation, 157
  in late phase of therapy, 147–8
  versus narcissism, 212
  relations to self and others, 206–8
  self-harm, 202–6
  technique adaptations, 209
Bowlby, John, 11–12, 25

change mechanisms, psychodynamic psychotherapy
  exploration of past memories, 71
  memory, 72–4
  narrative healing power, 71
  therapeutic alliance between patient and therapist, 72
  working through the transference, 72
child analysis. *see also* early development, psychodynamic psychotherapy theory
  Anna Freud, 9
  depression and, 186
  Donald Winnicott, 12–13
  early experiences in assessment, 151–4
  homelessness, 292–3
  Ian Suttie, 10
  John Bowlby, 11–12
  Melanie Klein, 9–10
  Ronald Fairbairn, 10–11
  Second World War effects on, 13
communication (group), 318
complementary responses, 41
concordant responses, 41
condenser phenomenon, 318
containment process
  anxiety and, 173
  defined, 21
  narcissism, 216–17
  projective identification, 37–9
countertransference dynamics
  anger and violence, 252–4
  complementary responses, 41
  concordant responses, 41
  contemporary therapy approach, 42–3
  empirical studies, 59
  late therapy phase, 145
  narcissism, 217–18
  psychodynamic consultation, 281
  role-responsiveness, 41–2
  self-harm (client), 205
  Sigmund Freud, 41

defence mechanisms (psychodynamic psychotherapy)
archaic defences, 28–9
assessment, 151–4
mature defences, 29
narcissistic, 214–15
neurotic defences, 29
reasons for, 27–8
resistance as, 122
Sigmund Freud, 27
unconscious nature of, 28
depression, psychodynamic approaches
adverse childhood experiences, 186
anaclitic pattern, 188–90, 193–6
as basic emotional response, 187–8
general therapy principles, 192–3
introjective pattern, 190–1, 196–8
overview, 184–5
theory behind, 185–92
dream interpretation, 4, 105

early development, psychodynamic psychotherapy theory. *see also* child analysis
communication, 20
family life, 20
importance, 19
individual constitution, 19
innate emotional needs, 20
object relations development, 21–5
parent-infant attunement, 21
reflective functioning/ mentalizing, 20
W.R. Bion, 21
early phase (psychodynamic therapy)
in clinical practice, 135–6
close listening, 133–4
formulation unfolding, 134–5
therapeutic alliance between patient and therapist, 131–2
therapist manner, 133
Ego (psychoanalysis), 4

Fairbairn, Ronald, 10–11, 22
formulation
acquisitive projective identification, 220
from assessment, 159–60
attributive projective identification, 222
narcissism, 218
Relational Affective Formulation (RAF), 226–7
free association
in analytic attitude, 100, 105
psychoanalysis, 4
relationship with therapist, 47
Freud, Anna, 9
Freud, Sigmund
background, 3–4
case histories, 5
clinical practice, 5
countertransference dynamics, 41
divided opinion on, 3
dream interpretation, 105
legacy, 5–7
object relations theory, 22
psychoanalysis, 4
structural model, 27

goals, psychodynamic psychotherapy
complications, 95–6
final stage, 92–3
initial phase, 90
life adjustment, 94
middle phase, 91–2
neuroscience perspective, 95
procedural, 95
structural personality change, 94
summary, 66
symptom relief, 93–4
tension between, 89–90
group analysis
background, 310–11
context, 316
endings, 317–18
group phenomena, 318–19
history, 311–12
membership, 314–16
primary task, 312
setting, 316–17
group analysis, conductor role
administrator, 313
reflective practice group, 319
therapist as, 312–14

holding environment, 80
hypnotism
history, 3
psycho-therapeutics, 3

Id (psychoanalysis), 4
innate emotional needs, 20
internal conflict, 27
internal object relations
anxiety and, 179–80
development, 22–3
internal world organisation
borderline, 157
neurotic, 157
psychotic, 157
introjective pattern (depression)
expression of, 187–8
therapy dynamics, 196–8
inverse care law, 239
invisible relationships (emotional), 234–5

Janet, Pierre, 3

Klein, Melanie, 9–10

late phase (psychodynamic psychotherapy)
basic principles, 144
borderline states, 147–8
patient detachment, 145
patient gratitude, 146
perspectives, 144
post-termination, 148–9
productivity of, 143–4
separation, 143
transference/ countertransference, 145
verbalization, 144
when therapy has not been helpful, 147
location of disturbance, 319

matrix, 318
medications, 76–7
memory classification
sensory memory, 72
summary table, 73
working memory, 72
memory classification, declarative/explicit
defined, 72
episodic memory, 72
semantic memory, 72

memory classification, non-declarative/implicit
- associative memory, 74
- emotional memory, 74
- procedural memory, 74

mesmerism, 3
Middle Group (psychotherapy), 11–13
middle phase (psychodynamic therapy)
- action formulation, 139
- change through therapeutic relationship, 139
- gap between insight and change, 136
- mourning process, 142
- resistance, 136–7
- working through, 140–1

mirroring, 318
moral treatment (psychological), 2–3
multiple exclusion homelessness
- background, 291–2
- developmental perspective, 292–3
- Housing First priority, 297
- inner and interpersonal dynamics, 294
- practitioners, 297–8
- psychologically informed services, 294–7
- symptoms of, 292

narcissism, dynamics
- versus borderline states of mind, 212
- complexity, 213
- developmental theories, 45–6
- hospital admission consequences, 213–14
- versus neurotic difficulties, 215
- object relations patterns, 46
- overview, 211–12
- polarities, 44
- severity, 212–13

narcissism, psychodynamic therapy
- acquisition and attribution, 222–3
- acquisitive projective identification, 218–20
- attributive projective identification, 220–2
- containment process, 216–17
- defences and resistance, 214–15
- definition perspectives, 211
- formulation, 218, 220
- length of therapy time, 47
- projective identification, 215–16
- Relational Affective Formulation (RAF), 223
- self boundaries, 222
- therapeutic frame, 47
- therapist relatinship, 47
- transference and countertransference, 217–18

Narcissus myth, 45
neurotic defence mechanisms
- internal world organisation, 157
- versus narcissism, 215
- repression, 29

object relations development
- assessment of patterns, 158
- internal object relations, 22–3
- narcissistic, 46
- problem solving dynamics, 26
- psychodynamic early development, 21–5
- response patterns, 25
- world accommodation, 25

object relations theory
- defined, 9–10
- language of, 22
- Ronald Fairbairn, 22
- Sigmund Freud, 22

Oedipus complex, 4
online/phone psychodynamic psychotherapy
- background, 300–1
- clinical considerations, 304–5
- practical consideration, 303–4
- technology/equipment, 303
- therapeutic frame adaptations, 301–3

online/phone psychodynamic psychotherapy interface considerations
- avatar world, 308
- hiding and being seen, 307–8
- tolerable distance in, 306

parenting
- John Bowlby, 11–12
- parent-infant attunement, 21

play, 20
pleasure principle (psychoanalysis), 4–5
projection (psychodynamic psychotherapy)
- consequence of, 34
- defined, 33
- degrees of, 33–4
- target, 34
- types of, 34

projective identification
- containment, 37–9
- defined, 34–5
- forms of, 35–6
- narcissism, 215–16
- two-step process, 35
- unconscious nature of, 35
- without containment, 36–7

psychoanalysis
- dream interpretation, 4
- free association, 4
- Freud's legacy, 5–7
- Oedipus complex, 4
- pleasure principle versus reality principle, 4–5
- structural model, 4
- topographical model of mind, 4

psychodynamic consultation, clinical team
- common staff patient relational experiences, 286
- future functioning, 288
- goal of, 281
- information synthesis, 287–8
- initial discussions, 280–1
- interest level, 282–3
- past history, 283–4
- patient relationships, 284–7
- reasons for, 278
- reflective practice group overlap, 279
- staff relationships, 283
- therapist countertransference, 281

psychodynamic psychotherapy
- brief versus long-term, 75
- countertransference, 109–11
- countertransference dynamics, 59
- defined, 65
- dimensions, 106–8
- empirical basis, 51–2

psychodynamic (cont.)
  empirical evidence base, 59–60
  open-ended versus closed, 75–6
  processes and techniques, 53–5
  psychotropic medications and, 76–7
  range of schools/slants, 68–9
  transference dynamics, 59
psychodynamic psychotherapy, clinical trials
  beneficial results, 52–3
  post-termination efficacy studies, 53
  therapy duration, 53
psychodynamic psychotherapy, features
  affect and emotional expression, 67
  defences and resistance, 67
  interpersonal relations, 68
  past experiences, 68
  pattern identification, 67
  therapy relationship, 68
  wishes and fantasies, 68
psychodynamic psychotherapy, spectrum of technique
  clarification, 115
  confrontation, 115–16
  empathic validation, 114
  exploration and elaboration, 115
  information giving, 114–15
  interpretation, 116–19
  support/affirmation, 113–14
psychodynamic psychotherapy, structure
  early phase, 130–6
  late phase, 143–9
  middle phase, 142
  overview, 128–30
psychodynamic psychotherapy, techniques
  analytic attitude, 99–104
  Relational Affective Formulation (RAF), 223
  rupture and repair, 111–12
  transference, 106–11
  working through, 121
  working with resistance, 121–5
psychodynamic psychotherapy theory, core concepts
  defence mechanisms, 27–9
  depressive position, 31
  empathy to resistance and defence mechanisms, 30
  integration position, 31
  internal conflict, 27
  life transitions, 32
  paranoid-schizoid position, 31
  resistance, 29–30
  splitting position, 31–2
psychodynamic psychotherapy theory, early development
  communication, 20
  family life, 20
  importance, 19
  individual constitution, 19
  innate emotional needs, 20
  object relations development, 21–5
  parent-infant attunement, 21
  reflective functioning/mentalizing, 20
  W.R. Bion, 21
psychodynamic psychotherapy theory, relational dynamics
  countertransference, 41–4
  projection, 33–4
  projective identification, 34–5
  supervision for, 43
  transference, 39–41
psychodynamic psychotherapy, therapist influences
  general therapy competence, 56
  multi-cultural competence, 56–7
  reflective capacity, 55–6
  therapeutic alliance between patient and therapist, 57–9
psychodynamic psychotherapy, wider applications
  background, 231–4
  clinical team splitting, 239–40
  engagement, 237
  inverse care law, 239
  invisible relationships, 234–5
  relational health, 238–9
  slow pace of change toleration, 237–8
  staff responses to, 235–7
  system dynamics, 241
  therapeutic change potential complications, 239
psychologically informed environment, 259
psychologically informed planned environment, 259
psychologically informed services
  background, 258–9
  beginnings, 261–2
  endings, 266–7
  homelessness, 294–7
  language control importance, 260–1
  needs enquiry, 259–60
  professionals' ambivalence, 263–4
  reasons for, 258
  time requirements, 262–3
  treatment, 265–6
psychosis
  history of psychotherapy treatment, 13–14
  internal world organisation, 157
psycho-therapeutics
  history, 3
  Pierre Janet and, 3
psychotherapy, history
  early twentieth century developments, 8–10
  First World War and shellshock, 7–8
  lending authority to modern, 2
  Middle Group, 11–13
  opposing opinions on, 1–2
  origin of modern, 2–3
  psychosis, 13–14
  Scottish contribution, 10–11
  Second World War effects on, 13
  Sigmund Freud, 3–7
  unconscious nature of mental functioning, 24

randomised control trial (RCT), 263
reality principle (psychoanalysis), 4–5
reflective practice group
  defined, 270

facilitation, 274–6
framing, 272–3
in group analysis, 319
key activities, 270
overlap with psychodynamic consultation, 279
overview, 269–70
set up, 273–4
Relational Affective Formulation (RAF)
mutative factors table, 225
overview, 223
states of mind table, 223
system wide approach, 223–4
therapy adaptations, 224–5
Relational Affective Formulation (RAF), assessment
early attachment history and object relations, 226
formulation, 226–7
overview, 225–6
professional relations, 226
symptoms, 226
repression defence mechanism, 29
resistance (therapy)
acting out, 125
attention to, 122
as defence mechanism, 122
defined, 121
flight into health, 123
in middle phase, 136–7
missed sessions, 124
silence, 123
strategy summary, 122–3
terminal phase, 125
time-keeping, 124
resonance experience, 318

self-harm (client)
challenge in therapy, 202
countertransference enactments, 205
early experiences in assessment, 202–3
meaning and dynamics of, 204–5
splitting of self, 205–6
unbearable feeling expression, 203
shellshock, 7–8
space framing. *see also* therapeutic frame
early encounters, 81–2
encounter unfolding, 84
session edges, 85
and therapeutic framing, 79–81
space framing, analytic
consistency, 83
ending session, 83–4
note taking, 82
reliability, 83
room arrangement, 82
splitting of self
clinical team, 239–40
as core concept, 31–2
self-harm and, 205–6
suicide and, 205–6
still-face experiment, 247
suicide, 205–6
Super-ego (psychoanalysis), 4
supervisory process
discovery in, 162–3
emergent understanding, 163
idealisation of, 164
not giving interpretations, 162
note taking, 163
overview, 43
principal aim of, 164–5
supervisee relations, 165–7
transference awareness, 163–4
Suttie, Ian, 10

Tavistock Institute of Human Relations, 8–9
therapeutic alliance between patient and therapist
and change effect, 72
in early therapy phase, 131–2
empirical studies, 57–8
as goal of psychodynamic psychotherapy, 91
periodic ruptures in, 58–9
therapeutic frame. *see also* space framing
boundary violations, 86–7
limits of, 85–6
in narcissistic object relations, 47
online/phone adaptations, 301–3
therapy relationship, 80
in therapy space, 80
third position, 102
topographical model of mind, 4
transference
empirical studies, 59
late therapy phase, 145
narcissism, 217–18
negative, 108–9
psychodynamic psychotherapy empirical research, 54–5
transference (psychoanalysis), 5
transference dynamics, 39–41

violence dynamics. *see also* aggression dynamics
communication attempts, 252
early childhood and, 250
releasing feelings, 251
self-preservation violence, 251–2
shame and humiliation, 250–1
societal response to, 254–5
staff countertransference boundaries, 252–4

Winnicott, Donald, 12–13

For EU product safety concerns, contact us at Calle de José Abascal, 56–1°,
28003 Madrid, Spain or eugpsr@cambridge.org.

www.ingramcontent.com/pod-product-compliance
Lightning Source LLC
LaVergne TN
LVHW010352040626
840462LV00024B/276
* 9 7 8 1 0 0 9 1 0 8 5 0 8 *